Microsoft®

Office 2007

Essential Concepts and Techniques

Gary B. Shelly

Thomas J. Cashman

Misty E. Vermaat

Contributing Authors

Steven G. Forsythe

Mary Z. Last

Philip J. Pratt

Jeffrey J. Quasney

Susan L. Sebok

COURSE TECHNOLOGY
CENGAGE Learning™

Australia • Brazil • Japan • Korea • Mexico • Singapore • Spain • United Kingdom • United States

COURSE TECHNOLOGY
CENGAGE Learning™

Microsoft Office 2007:
Essential Concepts and Techniques
Gary B. Shelly
Thomas J. Cashman
Misty E. Vermaat

Executive Editor: Alexandra Arnold

Senior Product Managers: Reed Curry, Mali Jones

Product Manager: Heather Hawkins

Associate Product Manager: Klenda Martinez

Editorial Assistant: Jon Farnham

Senior Marketing Manager: Joy Stark-Vancs

Marketing Coordinator: Julie Schuster

Print Buyer: Julio Esperas

Director of Production: Patty Stephan

Lead Production Editor: Matthew Hutchinson

Production Editors: Cathie DiMassa, Jill Klaffky,
    Phillipa Lehar

Developmental Editors: Jill Batistick, Amanda
    Brodkin, Laurie Brown, Lyn Markowicz

Proofreaders: John Bosco, Kim Kosmatka

Indexer: Rich Carlson

QA Manuscript Reviewers: John Freitas,
    Serge Palladino, Chris Scriver, Danielle Shaw,
    Marianne Snow, Teresa Storch

Art Director: Bruce Bond

Cover and Text Design: Joel Sadagursky

Cover Photo: Jon Chomitz

Compositor: GEX Publishing Services

For product information and technology assistance, contact us at
Cengage Learning Customer & Sales Support, 1-800-354-9706
For permission to use material from this text or product, submit all
requests online at **cengage.com/permissions**
Further permissions questions can be emailed to
permissionrequest@cengage.com

ISBN-13: 978-1-4188-4374-8

ISBN-10: 1-4188-4374-1

Course Technology
25 Thomson Place
Boston, Massachusetts 02210
USA

Cengage Learning is a leading provider of customized learning solutions with office locations around the globe, including Singapore, the United Kingdom, Australia, Mexico, Brazil, and Japan. Locate your local office at:
international.cengage.com/region

Cengage Learning products are represented in Canada by Nelson Education, Ltd.

For your lifelong learning solutions, visit **course.cengage.com**

Purchase any of our products at your local college store or at our preferred online store **www.ichapters.com**

Printed in the United States of America
3 4 5 6 7 8 9 10 09 08

Microsoft® Office 2007
Essential Concepts and Techniques

Contents

Microsoft Office **Word 2007**

CHAPTER ONE
Creating and Editing a Word Document

Microsoft Office **Excel 2007**

CHAPTER ONE
Creating a Worksheet and an Embedded Chart

Microsoft Office **Access 2007**

CHAPTER ONE
Creating and Using a Database

Microsoft Office **PowerPoint 2007**

CHAPTER ONE
Creating and Editing a Presentation

Appendices

Preface

The Shelly Cashman Series® offers the finest textbooks in computer education. We are proud of the fact that our series of Microsoft Office 4.3, Microsoft Office 95, Microsoft Office 97, Microsoft Office 2000, Microsoft Office XP, and Microsoft Office 2003 textbooks have been the most widely used books in education. With each new edition of our Office books, we have made significant improvements based on the software and comments made by instructors and students.

Microsoft Office 2007 contains more changes in the user interface and feature set than all other previous versions combined. Recognizing that the new features and functionality of Microsoft Office 2007 would impact the way that students are taught skills, the Shelly Cashman Series development team carefully reviewed our pedagogy and analyzed its effectiveness in teaching today's Office student. An extensive customer survey produced results confirming what the series is best known for: its step-by-step, screen-by-screen instructions, its project-oriented approach, and the quality of its content.

We learned, though, that students entering computer courses today are different than students taking these classes just a few years ago. Students today read less, but need to retain more. They need not only to be able to perform skills, but to retain those skills and know how to apply them to different settings. Today's students need to be continually engaged and challenged to retain what they're learning.

As a result, we've renewed our commitment to focusing on the user and how they learn best. This commitment is reflected in every change we've made to our Office 2007 books.

Objectives of This Textbook

Microsoft Office 2007: Essential Concepts and Techniques is intended for a course that includes an essential introduction to Office 2007. No experience with a computer is assumed, and no mathematics beyond the high school freshman level is required. The objectives of this book are:

- To teach the fundamentals of Microsoft Office Word 2007, Microsoft Office Excel 2007, Microsoft Office Access 2007, Microsoft Office PowerPoint 2007, and Microsoft Windows Vista
- To expose students to practical examples of the computer as a useful tool
- To acquaint students with the proper procedures to create documents, worksheets, databases, and presentations suitable for coursework, professional purposes, and personal use
- To help students discover the underlying functionality of Office 2007 so they can become more productive
- To develop an exercise-oriented approach that allows learning by doing

The Shelly Cashman Approach

Features of the Shelly Cashman Series Microsoft Office 2007 books include:

- **Project Orientation** Each chapter in the book presents a project with a practical problem and complete solution in an easy-to-understand approach.

- **Plan Ahead Boxes** The project orientation is enhanced by the inclusion of Plan Ahead boxes. These new features prepare students to create successful projects by encouraging them to think strategically about what they are trying to accomplish before they begin working.

- **Step-by-Step, Screen-by-Screen Instructions** Each of the tasks required to complete a project is clearly identified throughout the chapter. Now, the step-by-step instructions provide a context beyond point-and-click. Each step explains why students are performing a task, or the result of performing a certain action. Found on the screens accompanying each step, call-outs give students the information they need to know when they need to know it. Now, we've used color to distinguish the content in the call-outs. The Explanatory call-outs (in black) summarize what is happening on the screen and the Navigational call-outs (in red) show students where to click.

- **Q&A** Found within many of the step-by-step sequences, Q&As raise the kinds of questions students may ask when working through a step sequence and provide answers about what they are doing, why they are doing it, and how that task might be approached differently.

- **Experimental Steps** These new steps, within our step-by-step instructions, encourage students to explore, experiment, and take advantage of the features of the Office 2007 new user interface. These steps are not necessary to complete the projects, but are designed to increase the confidence with the software and build problem-solving skills.

- **Thoroughly Tested Projects** Unparalleled quality is ensured because every screen in the book is produced by the author only after performing a step, and then each project must pass Course Technology's Quality Assurance program.

- **Other Ways Boxes and Quick Reference Summary** The Other Ways boxes displayed at the end of most of the step-by-step sequences specify the other ways to do the task completed in the steps. Thus, the steps and the Other Ways box make a comprehensive reference unit. A Quick Reference Summary at the end of the book contains all of the tasks presented in the chapters, and all ways identified of accomplishing the tasks.

- **BTW** These marginal annotations provide background information, tips, and answers to common questions that complement the topics covered, adding depth and perspective to the learning process.

- **Integration of the World Wide Web** The World Wide Web is integrated into the Office 2007 learning experience by (1) BTW annotations that send students to Web sites for up-to-date information and alternative approaches to tasks; (2) a Microsoft Business Certification Program Web page so students can prepare for the certification examinations; (3) a Quick Reference Summary Web page that summarizes the ways to complete tasks (mouse, Ribbon, shortcut menu, and keyboard); and (4) the Learn It Online section at the end of each chapter, which has chapter reinforcement exercises, learning games, and other types of student activities.

- **End-of-Chapter Student Activities** Extensive student activities at the end of each chapter provide the student with plenty of opportunities to reinforce the materials learned in the chapter through hands-on assignments. Several new types of activities have been added that challenge the student in new ways to expand their knowledge, and to apply their new skills to a project with personal relevance.

Q&A

What is a maximized window?

A maximized window fills the entire screen. When you maximize a window, the Maximize button changes to a Restore Down button.

Other Ways

1. Click Italic button on Mini toolbar
2. Right-click selected text, click Font on shortcut menu, click Font tab, click Italic in Font style list, click OK button
3. Click Font Dialog Box Launcher, click Font tab, click Italic in Font style list, click OK button
4. Press CTRL+I

BTW

Minimizing the Ribbon
If you want to minimize the Ribbon, right-click the Ribbon and then click Minimize the Ribbon on the shortcut menu, double-click the active tab, or press CTRL+F1. To restore a minimized Ribbon, right-click the Ribbon and then click Minimize the Ribbon on the shortcut menu, double-click any top-level tab, or press CTRL+F1. To use commands on a minimized Ribbon, click the top-level tab.

Organization of This Textbook

Microsoft Office 2007: Essential Concepts and Techniques consists of a chapter that introduces Microsoft Windows Vista, one chapter each on Microsoft Office Word 2007, Microsoft Office Excel 2007, and Microsoft Office Access 2007, and PowerPoint 2007, seven appendices and a Quick Reference Summary.

End-of-Chapter Student Activities

A notable strength of the Shelly Cashman Series Microsoft Office 2007 books is the extensive student activities at the end of each chapter. Well-structured student activities can make the difference between students merely participating in a class and students retaining the information they learn. The activities in the Shelly Cashman Series Office books include the following.

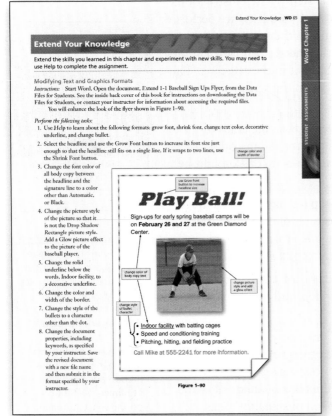

Figure 1–90

CHAPTER SUMMARY A concluding paragraph, followed by a listing of the tasks completed within a chapter together with the pages on which the step-by-step, screen-by-screen explanations appear.

LEARN IT ONLINE Every chapter features a Learn It Online section that is comprised of six exercises. These exercises include True/False, Multiple Choice, Short Answer, Flash Cards, Practice Test, and Learning Games.

APPLY YOUR KNOWLEDGE This exercise usually requires students to open and manipulate a file from the Data Files that parallels the activities learned in the chapter. To obtain a copy of the Data Files for Students, follow the instructions on the inside back cover of this text.

EXTEND YOUR KNOWLEDGE This exercise allows students to extend and expand on the skills learned within the chapter.

MAKE IT RIGHT This exercise requires students to analyze a document, identify errors and issues, and correct those errors and issues using skills learned in the chapter.

IN THE LAB Three all new in-depth assignments per chapter require students to utilize the chapter concepts and techniques to solve problems on a computer.

CASES AND PLACES Five unique real-world case-study situations, including Make It Personal, an open-ended project that relates to student's personal lives, and one small-group activity.

Instructor Resources CD-ROM

The Shelly Cashman Series is dedicated to providing you with all of the tools you need to make your class a success. Information about all supplementary materials is available through your Course Technology representative or by calling one of the following telephone numbers: Colleges, Universities, and Continuing Ed departments, 1-800-648-7450; High Schools, 1-800-824-5179; and Career Colleges, Business, Government, Library and Resellers, 1-800-477-3692.

The Instructor Resources CD-ROM for this textbook include both teaching and testing aids. The contents of each item on the Instructor Resources CD-ROM (ISBN 1-4239-1226-8) are described on the following pages.

INSTRUCTOR'S MANUAL The Instructor's Manual consists of Microsoft Word files, which include chapter objectives, lecture notes, teaching tips, classroom activities, lab activities, quick quizzes, figures and boxed elements summarized in the chapters, and a glossary page. The new format of the Instructor's Manual will allow you to map through every chapter easily.

LECTURE SUCCESS SYSTEM The Lecture Success System consists of intermediate files that correspond to certain figures in the book, allowing you to step through the creation of a project in a chapter during a lecture without entering large amounts of data.

SYLLABUS Sample syllabi, which can be customized easily to a course, are included. The syllabi cover policies, class and lab assignments and exams, and procedural information.

FIGURE FILES Illustrations for every figure in the textbook are available in electronic form. Use this ancillary to present a slide show in lecture or to print transparencies for use in lecture with an overhead projector. If you have a personal computer and LCD device, this ancillary can be an effective tool for presenting lectures.

POWERPOINT PRESENTATIONS PowerPoint Presentations is a multimedia lecture presentation system that provides slides for each chapter. Presentations are based on chapter objectives. Use this presentation system to present well-organized lectures that are both interesting and knowledge based. PowerPoint Presentations provides consistent coverage at schools that use multiple lecturers.

SOLUTIONS TO EXERCISES Solutions are included for the end-of-chapter exercises, as well as the Chapter Reinforcement exercises. Rubrics and annotated solution files, as described below, are also included.

RUBRICS AND ANNOTATED SOLUTION FILES The grading rubrics provide a customizable framework for assigning point values to the laboratory exercises. Annotated solution files that correspond to the grading rubrics make it easy for you to compare students' results with the correct solutions whether you receive their homework as hard copy or via e-mail.

TEST BANK & TEST ENGINE In the ExamView test bank, you will find our standard question types (40 multiple-choice, 25 true/false, 20 completion) and new objective-based question types (5 modified multiple-choice, 5 modified true/false and 10 matching). Critical Thinking questions are also included (3 essays and 2 cases with 2 questions each) totaling the test bank to 112 questions for every chapter with page number references, and when appropriate, figure references. A version of the test bank you can print also is included. The test bank comes with a copy of the test engine, ExamView, the ultimate tool for your objective-based testing needs. ExamView is a state-of-the-art test builder that is easy to use. ExamView enables you to create paper-, LAN-, or Web-based tests from test banks designed specifically for your Course Technology textbook. Utilize the ultra-efficient QuickTest Wizard to create tests in less than five minutes by taking advantage of Course Technology's question banks, or customize your own exams from scratch.

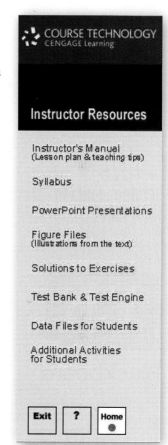

LAB TESTS/TEST OUT The Lab Tests/Test Out exercises parallel the In the Lab assignments and are supplied for the purpose of testing students in the laboratory on the material covered in the chapter or testing students out of the course.

DATA FILES FOR STUDENTS All the files that are required by students to complete the exercises are included. You can distribute the files on the Instructor Resources CD-ROM to your students over a network, or you can have them follow the instructions on the inside back cover of this book to obtain a copy of the Data Files for Students.

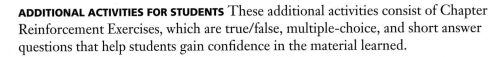

ADDITIONAL ACTIVITIES FOR STUDENTS These additional activities consist of Chapter Reinforcement Exercises, which are true/false, multiple-choice, and short answer questions that help students gain confidence in the material learned.

Assessment & Training Solutions
SAM 2007

SAM 2007 helps bridge the gap between the classroom and the real world by allowing students to train and test on important computer skills in an active, hands-on environment.

SAM 2007's easy-to-use system includes powerful interactive exams, training or projects on critical applications such as Word, Excel, Access, PowerPoint, Outlook, Windows, the Internet, and much more. SAM simulates the application environment, allowing students to demonstrate their knowledge and think through the skills by performing real-world tasks.

Designed to be used with the Shelly Cashman series, SAM 2007 includes built-in page references so students can print helpful study guides that match the Shelly Cashman series textbooks used in class. Powerful administrative options allow instructors to schedule exams and assignments, secure tests, and run reports with almost limitless flexibility.

Student Edition Labs

Our Web-based interactive labs help students master hundreds of computer concepts, including input and output devices, file management and desktop applications, computer ethics, virus protection, and much more. Featuring up-to-the-minute content, eye-popping graphics, and rich animation, the highly interactive Student Edition Labs offer students an alternative way to learn through dynamic observation, step-by-step practice, and challenging review questions.

Online Content

Blackboard is the leading distance learning solution provider and class-management platform today. Course Technology has partnered with Blackboard to bring you premium online content. Instructors: Content for use with *Microsoft Office 2007: Essential Concepts and Techniques* is available in a Blackboard Course Cartridge and may include topic reviews, case projects, review questions, test banks, practice tests, custom syllabi, and more.

Course Technology also has solutions for several other learning management systems. Please visit course.com today to see what's available for this title.

Workbook for Microsoft Office 2007: Introductory Concepts and Techniques

This highly popular supplement (ISBN 1-4188-4335-0) includes a variety of activities that help students recall, review, and master the concepts presented. The Workbook complements the end-of-chapter material with an outline; a self-test consisting of true/false, multiple-choice, short answer, and matching questions; and activities calculated to help students develop a deeper understanding of the information presented.

CourseCasts Learning on the Go. Always Available...Always Relevant.

Want to keep up with the latest technology trends relevant to you? Visit our site to find a library of podcasts, CourseCasts, featuring a "CourseCast of the Week," and download them to your portable media player at http://coursecasts.course.com.

Our fast-paced world is driven by technology. You know because you are an active participant — always on the go, always keeping up with technological trends, and always learning new ways to embrace technology to power your life.

Ken Baldauf, a faculty member of the Florida State University (FSU) Computer Science Department, is responsible for teaching technology classes to thousands of FSU students each year. He knows what you know; he knows what you want to learn. He is also an expert in the latest technology and will sort through and aggregate the most pertinent news and information so you can spend your time enjoying technology, rather than trying to figure it out.

Visit us at http://coursecasts.course.com to learn on the go!

CourseNotes

Course Technology's CourseNotes are six-panel quick reference cards that reinforce the most important and widely used features of a software application in a visual and user-friendly format. CourseNotes will serve as a great reference tool during and after the student completes the course. CourseNotes for Microsoft Office 2007, Word 2007, Excel 2007, Access 2007, PowerPoint 2007, Microsoft Windows Vista, and more are available now!

About Our New Cover Look

Learning styles of students have changed, but the Shelly Cashman Series' dedication to their success has remained steadfast for over 30 years. We are committed to continually updating our approach and content to reflect the way today's students learn and experience new technology.

This focus on the user is reflected in our bold new cover design, which features photographs of real students using the Shelly Cashman Series in their courses. Each book features a different user, reflecting the many ages, experiences, and backgrounds of all of the students learning with our books. When you use the Shelly Cashman Series, you can be assured that you are learning computer skills using the most effective courseware available.

We would like to thank the administration and faculty at the participating schools for their help in making our vision a reality. Most of all, we'd like to thank the wonderful students from all over the world who learn from our texts and now appear on our covers.

Microsoft Office 2007

1 Introduction to Windows Vista

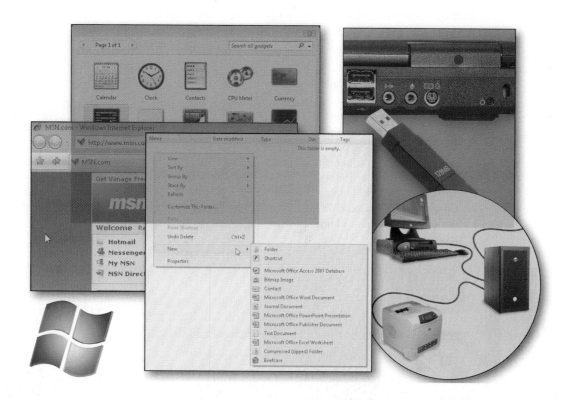

Objectives

You will have mastered the material in this chapter when you can:

- Start Windows Vista, log on to the computer, and identify the objects on the desktop

- Customize the Windows Sidebar with Gadgets

- Perform basic mouse operations

- Display the Start menu and start an application program

- Open, minimize, maximize, restore, move, size, scroll, and close a window

- Display drive and folder contents

- Create a folder in Folder Windows and WordPad

- Browse the Web using Windows Internet Explorer 7.0, a URL, and tabbed browsing

- Download folders from scsite.com

- Copy, move, rename, and delete files

- Search for files using a word or phrase in the file or by name

- Use Windows Help and Support

- Log off from the computer and turn it off

1 | Introduction to Windows Vista

What Is an Operating System?

An **operating system** is the set of computer instructions, called a computer program, that controls the allocation of computer hardware such as memory, disk devices, printers, and CD and DVD drives, and provides the capability for you to communicate with the computer. The most popular and widely used operating systems is **Microsoft Windows**. **Microsoft Windows Vista** is the newest version of Microsoft Windows. Windows Vista allows you to communicate with and control the computer.

Project Planning Guidelines

> Working with an operating system requires a basic knowledge of how to start the operating system, log on and log off the computer, and identify the objects on the Windows Vista desktop. As a starting point, you must be familiar with the Start menu and its commands, and be able to start an application. You should be able to personalize the operating system to allow you to work more efficiently. You will want to know how to manipulate windows as well as create a folder, display folder contents, recognize a disk drive, and download information from the Internet. You should be able to copy, move, rename, delete, and search for files. If you encounter a problem, Windows Help and Support is available to answer any questions you may have.

Overview

As you read through this chapter, you will learn how to use the Windows Vista operating system by performing these general tasks:

- Start the Windows Vista operating system.
- Log on to the computer.
- Perform basic mouse operations.
- Add and Remove a gadget to the Windows Sidebar.
- Open the Start menu and start an application program.
- Add and delete icons on the desktop.
- Open, minimize, maximize, restore, move, size, scroll, and close a window.
- Display drive and folder contents.
- Create folders and download folders from the Internet.
- Copy, move, rename, delete, and search for files.
- Use Help and Support.
- Log off and turn off the computer.

What Is a User Interface?

A **user interface** is the combination of hardware and software that you use to communicate with and control the computer. Through the user interface, you are able to make selections on the computer, request information from the computer, and respond to messages displayed by the computer.

Hardware and software together form the user interface. Among the hardware devices associated with a user interface are the monitor, keyboard, and mouse (Figure 1–1). The **monitor** displays messages and provides information. You respond by entering data in the form of a command or other response using an input device such as a **keyboard** or **mouse**.

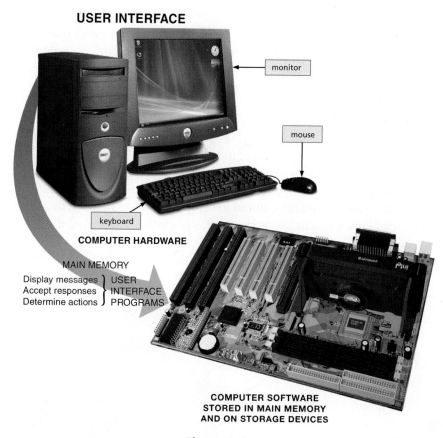

USER INTERFACE

monitor

mouse

keyboard

COMPUTER HARDWARE

MAIN MEMORY

Display messages ⎫ USER
Accept responses ⎬ INTERFACE
Determine actions ⎭ PROGRAMS

COMPUTER SOFTWARE
STORED IN MAIN MEMORY
AND ON STORAGE DEVICES

Figure 1–1

The computer software associated with the user interface consists of the programs that engage you in dialogue. The computer software determines the messages you receive, the manner in which you should respond, and the actions that occur based on your responses.

The goal of an effective user interface is to be **user-friendly**, which means the software can be used easily by individuals with limited training. A **graphical user interface**, or **GUI** (pronounced gooey), is a user interface that displays graphics in addition to text when it communicates with the user.

To communicate with the operating system, you can use a mouse. A **mouse** is a pointing device used with Windows Vista that may be attached to the computer by a cable or may be wireless.

Many common tasks, such as logging on to the computer or logging off, are performed by pointing to an item and then clicking the item. **Point** means you move the mouse across a flat surface until the mouse pointer on the monitor rests on the item of choice. As you move the mouse across a flat surface, the optical sensor on the underside of the mouse senses the movement of the mouse, and the mouse pointer moves across the computer desktop in the same direction. In Office 2007, you can point to buttons on the Ribbon in a window and observe a live preview of the effect of selecting that button.

Click means you press and release the primary mouse button, which in most cases is the left mouse button. In most cases, you must point to an item before you click it.

Windows Vista

The Windows Vista operating system simplifies the process of working with documents and applications by transferring data between documents, organizing the manner in which you interact with the computer, and using the computer to access information on the Internet or an intranet. Windows Vista is used to run **application programs**, which are programs that perform a specific function such as word processing.

In business, Windows Vista is commonly used on standalone computers, client computers, and portable computers. A standalone computer is not part of a computer network, and has access only to software that is installed on it, and hardware directly connected to it. A **client** is a computer connected to a server. A **server** is a computer that controls access to the hardware and software on a network and provides a centralized storage area for programs, data, and information. Portable computers, often referred to as laptop computers, can be used either as standalone computers or clients. Figure 1–2 illustrates a simple computer network consisting of a server, three client computers, and a laser printer connected to the server.

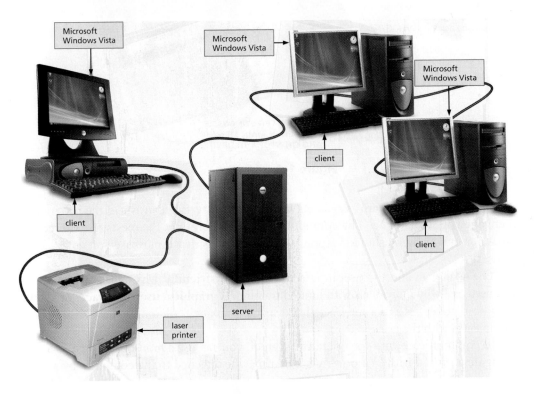

Figure 1–2

Windows Vista Operating System Editions

The Windows Vista operating systems is available in five editions: Windows Vista Home Basic, Windows Vista Home Premium, Windows Vista Business, Windows Vista Ultimate, and Windows Vista Enterprise. Windows Vista Ultimate (called **Windows Vista** for the rest of the chapter) is an operating system that performs every function necessary for you to communicate with and use the computer. The five editions of Windows Vista are described in Table 1–1.

Table 1–1 Windows Vista Editions

Edition	Description
Windows Vista Home Basic	This edition is easy to set up and maintain, provides security and parental controls, allows access to e-mail, simplifies searching for pictures and music, and allows the creation of simple documents.
Windows Vista Home Premium Edition	This edition is designed for individuals who have a home desktop or mobile PC. The built-in Windows Media Center allows you to watch and record television, play video games, listen to music, and burn and play CDs and DVDs.
Windows Vista Business Edition	This edition is the first operating system designed specifically for the needs of small and mid-sized businesses. Features include keeping PCs up-to-date and running smoothly, as well as powerful ways to find, organize, and share information on the road or in the office. Additional features include Windows Tablet PC capability, PC-to-PC synchronization, Domain Join, Group Policy support, and Encrypting File System.
Windows Vista Ultimate Edition	This edition, the most complete edition of the five, contains the most advanced capabilities, and is the choice of individuals who want the power, security, and mobility needed for work and the entertainment features desired for fun. The edition includes support for Windows Tablet and Touch Technology, Windows SideShow, Windows Mobility Center, Windows DreamScene, and Windows BitLocker Secure Online Key storage.
Windows Vista Enterprise	This edition was designed to help global organizations and enterprises with complex IT infrastructures to lower IT costs, reduce risk, and stay connected. This edition is only available to Volume License customers who have PCs covered by Microsoft Software Assurance. Windows BitLocker Drive Encryption is used to help prevent sensitive data and intellectual property from being lost or stolen.

Windows Vista Basic Interface and Windows Aero

Windows Vista offers two different GUIs, depending on your hardware configuration. Computers with up to 1 GB of RAM work with the Windows Vista Basic interface (Figure 1–3a). Computers with more than 1 GB of RAM can work also with the Windows Aero interface (Figure 1–3b), which provides an enhanced visual experience designed for Windows Vista, including additional navigation options, and animation. Windows Aero features a transparent glass design with subtle window animations and new window colors. The Windows Vista Business, Windows Vista Enterprise, Windows Vista Home Premium, and Windows Vista Ultimate editions have the ability to use Windows Aero. In this chapter, all figures were created on a computer using the Windows Vista Basic interface.

Figure 1–3

Starting Windows Vista

It is not an unusual occurrence for multiple people to use the same computer in a work, educational, recreational, or home setting. Windows Vista uses User Accounts to organize the resources that are made available to a person when they use the computer. A **user account** identifies to Windows Vista which resources a person can use when using the computer. Associated with a user account is a **user name**, which identifies the person to Windows Vista, and a **password**, a string of letters, numbers, and special characters, which is used to restrict access to a user account's resources to only those who know the password. In Windows Vista, you can choose a picture to associated with your user name as well.

In a work or school environment your user name and password may be set up for you automatically. Usually, you are given the option to reset the password to something that only you know. A good password is important for ensuring the security and privacy of your work. When you turn on the computer, an introductory black screen consisting of a progress bar and copyright message (© Microsoft Corporation) are displayed. After a short time, the Windows Vista logo and Welcome screen are displayed on the desktop (Figure 1–4).

Plan Ahead

Determine a user name and password.

Before logging on to the computer, you must have a unique user name and password.

1. Choose a user name that is unique and non-offensive. Your user name may be automatically set for you in a work or educational setting.

2. Choose a password that no one could guess. Do not use any part of your first or last name, your spouse's or child's name, telephone number, street address, license plate number, Social Security number, and so on.

3. Be sure your password is at least six characters long, mixed with letters and numbers.

4. Protect your password. Change your password frequently and do not disclose it to anyone or write it on a slip of paper kept near the computer. E-mail and telemarketing scams often ask you to disclose a password, so be wary, if you did not initiate the inquiry or telephone call.

Figure 1–4

The **Welcome screen** shows the user names of every computer user on the computer. Clicking the user name or picture begins the process of logging on to the computer. The list of user names on your computer will be different.

At the bottom of the Welcome screen is the Ease of access button, Windows Vista logo, and a Shut down button. Clicking the **Ease of access button** displays the Ease of Access Center. The Ease of Access Center provides access to tools you can use to optimize your computer to accomodate the needs of the mobility, hearing and vision impaired. To the right of the Ease of access button is the Windows Vista logo. Located in the lower corner of the Welcome screen is the **Shut down button**. Clicking this button shuts down Windows Vista and the computer. To the right of the Shut down button is the **Shut down options arrow**, which provides access to a menu containing 3 commands, Restart, Sleep, and Shut Down.

The **Restart command** closes open programs, shuts down Windows Vista, and then restarts Windows Vista, and displays the Welcome screen. The **Sleep command** waits for Windows Vista to save your work and then turns off the fans and hard disk. To wake the computer from the Sleep state, press the Power button or lift the laptop cover, and log on to the computer. The **Shut Down command** shuts down and turns off the computer.

Logging On to the Computer

After starting Windows Vista, you must log on to the computer. **Logging on** to the computer opens your user account and makes the computer available for use.

If you are using a computer to step through the project in this chapter and you want your screen to match the figures in this book, you should change your screen's resolution to 1024 × 768. For information about how to change a computer's resolution, read Appendix E.

To Log On to the Computer

The following steps illustrate how to log on to the computer. In this chapter, the user name SC Series is used in the figures.

1

- Click your user name on the Welcome screen to display the password text box.

Q&A   What is a text box?

A text box is a rectangular area in which you can enter text.

- Type your password in the password text box as shown in Figure 1–5.

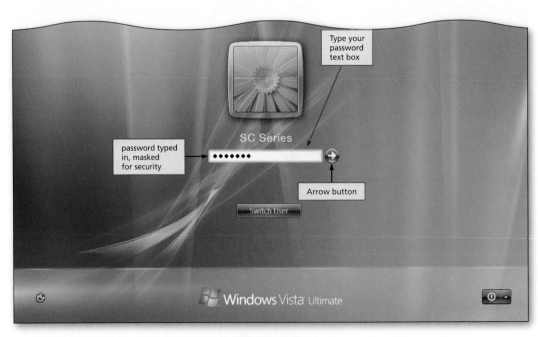

Figure 1–5

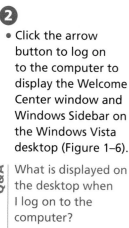

2

- Click the arrow button to log on to the computer to display the Welcome Center window and Windows Sidebar on the Windows Vista desktop (Figure 1–6).

Q&A What is displayed on the desktop when I log on to the computer?

The Recycle Bin icon, Welcome Center, Windows Sidebar, and taskbar are displayed on the desktop.

Q&A What if the Computer displays a different desktop design?

Windows Vista offers many standard desktop backgrounds, so any background is fine. The background design shown in Figure 1–6 is called img24.

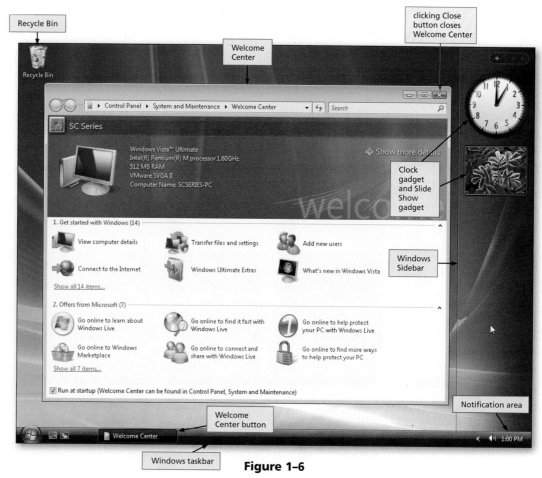

Figure 1–6

The Windows Vista Desktop

The Windows Vista desktop is similar to a real physical desktop. It is the main work area when you are logged into Windows Vista. When you open a program, it appears on the desktop. Some items are on the desktop by default. For instance, the **Recycle Bin**, the location of files that have been deleted, sits on the desktop by default. You can customize your desktop so that programs and files you use often are out on your desktop and easily accessible.

Also on the Windows Vista desktop is the Windows Sidebar. The **Windows Sidebar** is a long, vertical strip on the right edge of the desktop that holds mini-programs called gadgets (Figure 1–6). A **gadget** is a mini-program that provides continuously updated information, such as current weather information, news updates, traffic information, and Internet radio streams. You can customize your Sidebar to hold gadgets that you choose.

Across the bottom of the Windows Vista desktop is the Windows Taskbar (Figure 1–6). The Windows Taskbar contains the Start button, which you use to access programs, files, folders, and settings on your computer. It also shows you which programs are currently running on your computer, by displaying a button per program.

In addition, the Windows Vista desktop may contain the Welcome Center Window. The **Welcome Center** is displayed when the computer is used for the first time and allows you to complete a set of tasks to optimize the computer. The tasks may include adding user accounts, transferring files and settings from another computer, and connecting to the Internet.

To Close the Welcome Center Window

The Welcome Center window is displayed when you launch Windows Vista for the first time, and subsequently unless you turn it off. If the Welcome Center window is displayed, you can close it prior to beginning any other operations using Windows Vista. This provides you with a clear desktop with which to work. The following step illustrates how to close the Welcome Center window.

- Click the Close button in the top right corner of the Welcome Center window to close the Welcome Center window (Figure 1–7).

Q&A

Are there other ways to access the Welcome Center if it doesn't appear at startup?

Yes. The Welcome Center features are available in the Control Panel under System and Maintenance.

Figure 1–7

To Add a Gadget to the Windows Sidebar

When you start Windows Vista, some gadgets are attached to the Windows Sidebar. There are many additional gadgets that can be added according to personal preference. Gadgets can be found in the **Gadget Gallery**, which is a collection of gadgets. To use gadgets, they must be added to the Windows Sidebar. One method to add a gadget to the Windows Sidebar is to double-click the gadget in the Gadget Gallery. **Double-click** means you quickly press and release the left mouse button twice without moving the mouse. The steps on the following page illustrate how to open the Gadget Gallery and add a gadget to the Windows Sidebar.

1

• Click the Add Gadgets button to open the Gadget Gallery on the desktop. (Figure 1–8).

Q&A Where can I find additional gadgets?

You can find more gadgets on the www.microsoft.com website by searching for "sidebar gadgets".

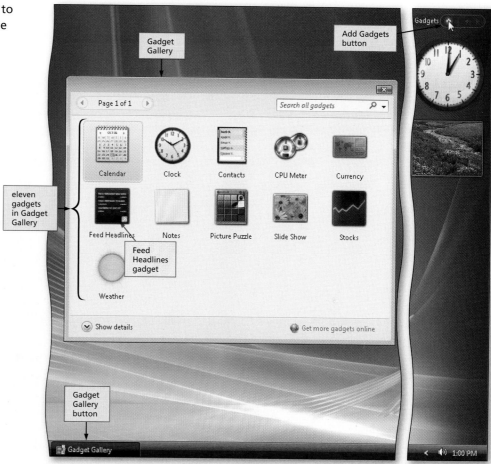

Figure 1–8

2

• Double-click the Feed Headlines gadget in the Gadget Gallery to add the gadget to the top of the Windows Sidebar and display frequently updated headlines (Figure 1–9).

3

• Click the Close button to close the Gadget Gallery.

Q&A Can I customize the Windows Sidebar?

Yes. You can select which gadgets you want to add or remove, add multiple instances of a particular gadget, and detach one or more gadgets from the Sidebar and place them on the desktop

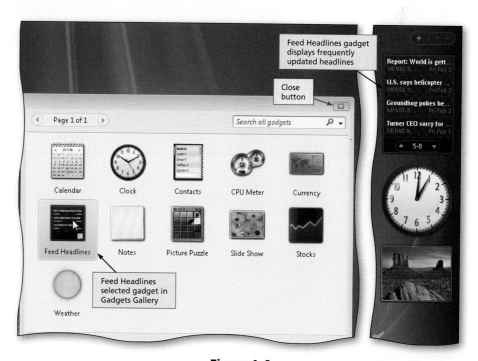

Figure 1–9

To Remove a Gadget from the Windows Sidebar

In addition to adding gadgets to the Windows Sidebar, you may want to customize the desktop by removing one or more gadgets from the sidebar. The following step illustrates how to remove a gadget from the Windows Sidebar.

1

- Point to the Feed Headlines gadget to make the Close button visible. (Figure 1–10).

2

- Click the Close button to remove the Feed Headlines gadget from the Windows Sidebar.

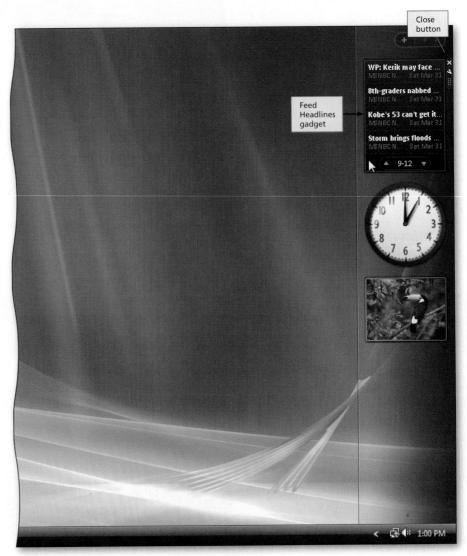

Figure 1–10

Other Ways
1. Right-click gadget, click Close Gadget

To Open the Start Menu

A **menu** is a list of related items, including folders, programs, and commands. Each **command** on a menu performs a specific action, such as searching for files or obtaining Help. The **Start menu** allows you to access programs and files on the computer and contains commands that allow you to connect to and browse the Internet, start an e-mail program, start application programs, store and search for documents, customize the computer, and obtain Help on thousands of topics. The Start menu contains the All Programs command, Search box, and right pane. The following steps open the Start menu, display the All Programs list, and then display the Accessories list.

1

- Click the Start button on the Windows Vista taskbar to open the Start menu (Figure 1–11).

Q&A

What are the various sections on the Start menu?

The left pane contains the pinned items list, frequently used programs list, All Programs command, and the Search box. The right pane contains the computer user name and illustration, list links, Power button, Lock this computer button, and Lock menu arrow.

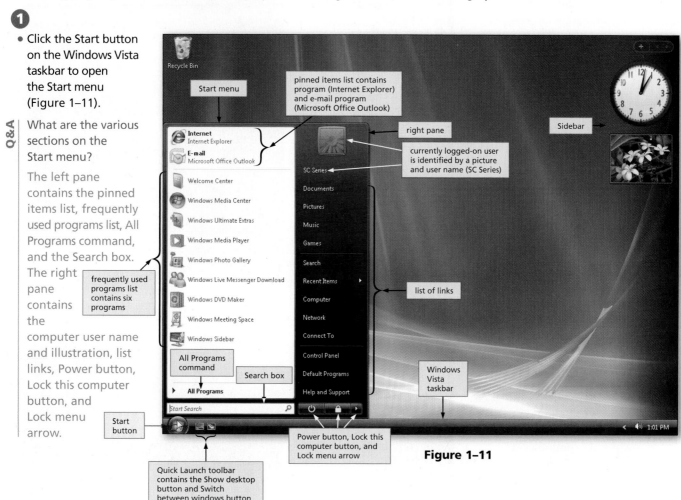

Figure 1–11

2

- Point to All Programs at the bottom of the left pane on the Start menu to display the All Programs list (Figure 1–12).

Q&A

What happens when you point to All Programs on the Start menu?

The All Programs list is displayed and the word Back is displayed at the bottom of the All Programs list.

Figure 1–12

3

- Click Accessories to expand the list of programs and folders in the Accessories folder (Figure 1–13).

Q&A

What are Accessories?

Accessories are application programs that accomplish a variety of tasks commonly required on a computer. For example, the Accessories programs include Calculator, Notepad, Paint, etc.

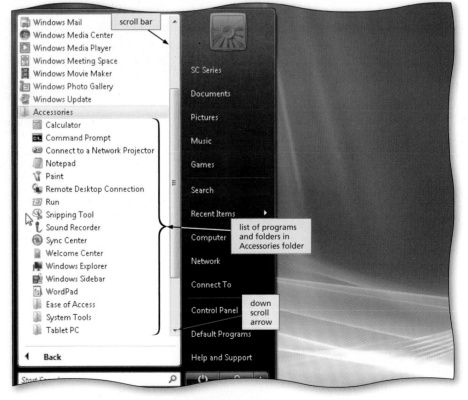

Figure 1–13

To Scroll Using Scroll Arrows, the Scroll Bar, and the Scroll Box

A **scroll bar** is a bar that displays when the contents of an area may not be completely visible. A vertical scroll bar contains an **up scroll arrow**, a **down scroll arrow**, and a **scroll box** that enables you to view areas that currently are not visible. In Figure 1–14, a vertical scroll bar displays along the right side of the All Programs list. Scrolling can be accomplished in three ways: (1) click the scroll arrows; (2) click the scroll bar; and (3) drag the scroll box. **Drag** means you point to an item, hold down the left mouse button, move the item to the desired location, and then release the left mouse button. The following steps scroll the items in the All Programs list.

1

- Click the down scroll arrow on the vertical scroll bar to display additional folders at the bottom of the All Programs list (Figure 1–14). You may need to click more than once to get to the bottom of the All Programs list.

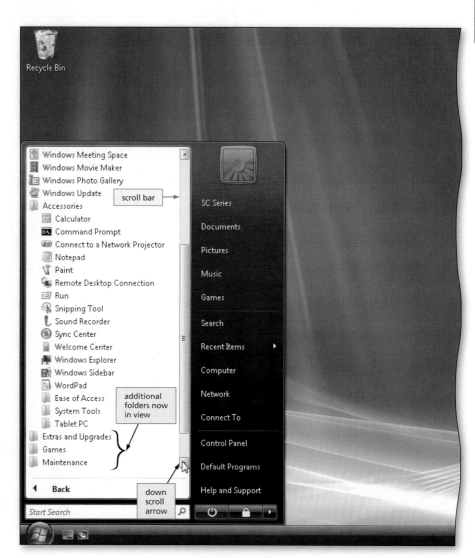

Figure 1–14

- Click the scroll bar above the scroll box to move the scroll box to the top of the scroll bar and display the top of the All Programs list (Figure 1–15).

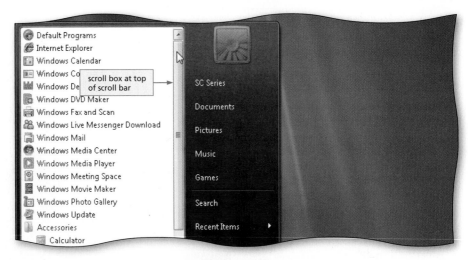

Figure 1–15

- Drag the scroll box down the scroll bar until the scroll box is about halfway down the scroll bar (Figure 1–16).

- Click an open area on the desktop to close the Start menu.

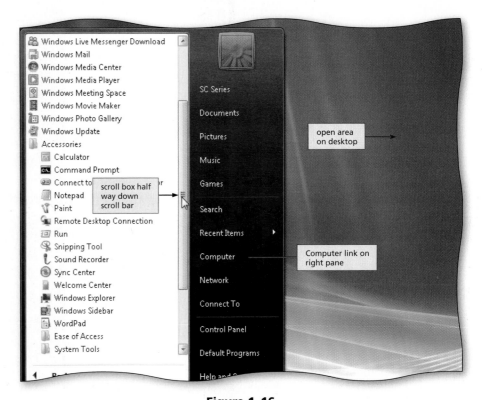

Figure 1–16

To Add an Icon to the Desktop

In addition to gadgets, you may want to add icons to the desktop. An **icon** is a picture that represents a file, folder, object, or program. For example, you may want to add the Computer icon to the desktop so you can view the contents of the computer folder without having to use the Start menu. The steps on the following page add the Computer icon to the desktop.

- Click the Start button to open the Start menu.

- Right-click Computer on the right pane to select the Computer link and display a shortcut menu (Figure 1–17).

Q&A What is a shortcut menu?

A shortcut menu appears when you right-click an object and includes commands specifically for use with the object clicked.

Figure 1–17

- Click Show on Desktop to close the shortcut menu and display the Computer icon on the desktop (Figure 1–18).

Q&A Why should I use a shortcut menu?

A shortcut menu speeds up your work and adds flexibility to your interaction with the computer by making often used items available in multiple locations.

- Click an open area on the desktop to close the Start menu.

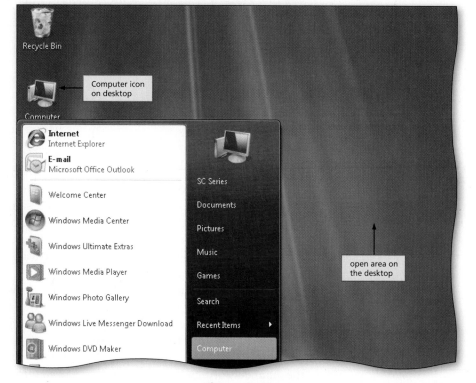

Figure 1–18

To Open a Window Using a Desktop Icon

When an icon, like the Computer icon, is displayed on the desktop, you can use the icon to open the application or window it represents. One method for opening a window with a desktop icon is to double-click the icon. The following step opens the Computer window on the desktop by double-clicking the Computer icon on the desktop.

1

- Double-click the Computer icon on the desktop to open the Computer window (Figure 1–19).

Q&A

What does the Computer window allow me to do?

The Computer window allows you to view the contents of the computer.

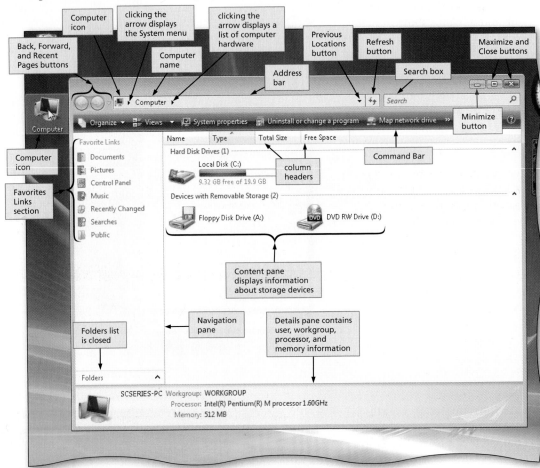

Figure 1–19

Other Ways

1. Right-click desktop icon, click Open on shortcut menu
2. Press WINDOWS+E

Folder Windows

Folder windows are the key tools for finding, viewing, and managing information on the computer. Folder Windows have common design elements, illustrated in Figure 1–19. The three buttons to the left of the **Address bar** allow you to navigate the contents of the left pane and view recent pages. On the right of the title bar are the Minimize button, Maximize button, and Close button that can be used to specify the size of the window or close the window.

The two right arrows in the Address bar allow you to visit different locations on the computer and display a list of computer hardware. The **Previous Locations button** saves the locations you have visited and displays the locations using computer path names.

The **Refresh button** at the end of the Address bar refreshes the contents of the right pane of the Computer window. The **Search box** to the right of the Address bar contains the dimmed word, Search. You can type a term into the Search box for a list of files, folders, shortcuts, and such containing that term within the location you are searching.

The **Command Bar** contains five buttons used to accomplish various tasks on the computer related to organizing and managing the contents of the open window. The area below the Command Bar contains the Navigation pane and four column headers (Name, Type, Total Size, and Free Space) on the right. The **Navigation pane** on the left contains the Favorite Links section and the Folders list. The **Favorite Links list** contains your documents, pictures, music files, and more.

Four **column headers** displayed in the right pane allow you to sort and group the entries below the column header.

To Minimize and Redisplay a Window

Two buttons on the title bar, the Minimize button and the Maximize button, allow you to control the way a window is displayed on the desktop. The following steps minimize and then redisplay the Computer window.

1

- Click the Minimize button on the title bar of the Computer window to minimize the Computer window (Figure 1–20).

Q&A What happens to the Computer window when I click the Minimize button?

The Computer window is still available, but it is no longer the active window. It collapses down to a non-recessed, light gray and black button on the task bar.

Figure 1–20

2

- Click the Computer button on the taskbar to display the Computer window (Figure 1–21).

Q&A Why does the Computer button on the taskbar change?

The button changes to reflect the status of the Computer window. A recessed button indicates that the Computer window is active on the screen. A non-recessed button indicates that the Computer window is not active, but is open.

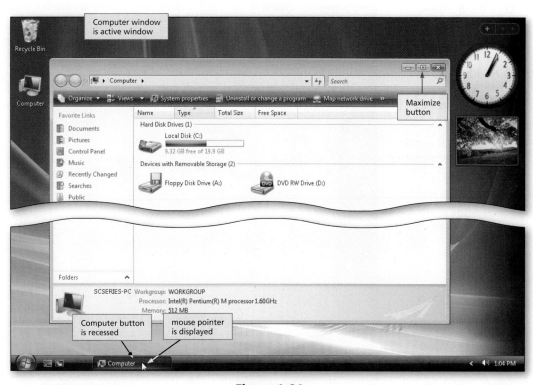

Figure 1–21

Other Ways

1. Right-click title bar, click Minimize, on taskbar click taskbar button
2. Press WINDOWS+M, press WINDOWS+SHIFT+M

To Maximize and Restore a Window

Sometimes information shown in a window is not completely visible. One method of displaying more contents in a window is to enlarge the window using the **Maximize button**, so the window fills the entire screen. If a window is filling the entire screen and you want to see part of the desktop, you can use the **Restore** button to return the window to its previous state. The following steps maximize and restore the Computer window.

1

• Click the Maximize button on the title bar of the Computer window to maximize the Computer window (Figure 1–22).

Q&A

When a window is maximized, can you also minimize it?

Yes. Click the Minimize button to minimize the window.

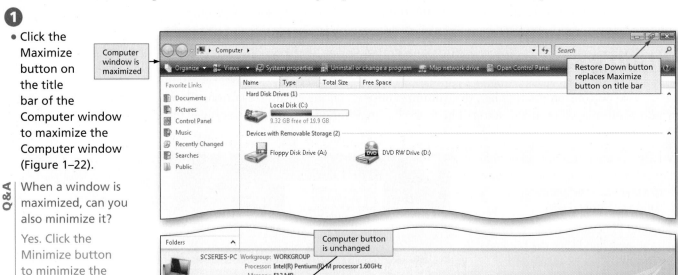

Figure 1–22

2

• Click the Restore Down button on the title bar of the Computer window to return the Computer window to its previous size (Figure 1–23).

Q&A

What happens to the Restore Down button when I click it?

The Maximize button replaces the Restore Down button on the title bar.

Other Ways

1. Right-click title bar, click Maximize, right-click title bar, click Restore
2. Double-click title bar, double-click title bar

Figure 1–23

To Close a Window

You can click the **Close button** on the title bar of a window to close the window and remove the taskbar button from the Windows taskbar. The following step closes the Computer window.

- Click the Close button on the title bar of the Computer window to close the Computer window (Figure 1–24).

Q&A What happens to the Computer window when I click the Close button?

The Computer window closes and the Computer button no longer is displayed in the taskbar button area.

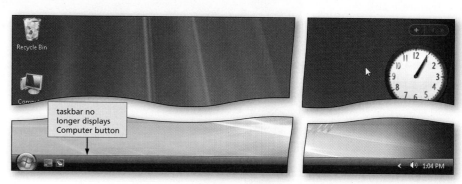

Figure 1–24

Other Ways

1. Right-click title bar, click Close
2. Press ALT+F4

To Open a Window Using the Start Menu

Previously, you opened the Computer window by double-clicking the Computer icon on the desktop. Another method of opening a window and viewing the contents of the window is to click a link on the Start menu. The **Pictures folder** is a convenient location to store your digital pictures, view and share your pictures, and edit pictures. The following steps open the Pictures window using the Pictures link on the Start menu.

- Open the Start menu (Figure 1–25).

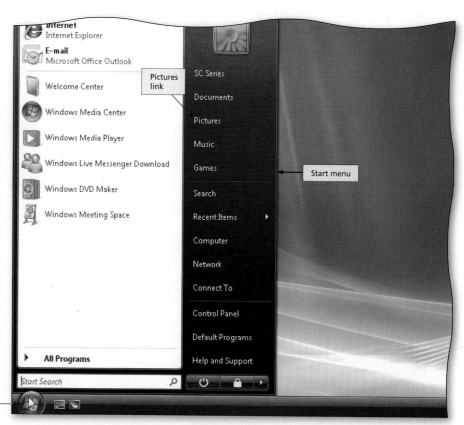

Figure 1–25

2

• Click Pictures on the Start menu to open the Pictures window (Figure 1–26).

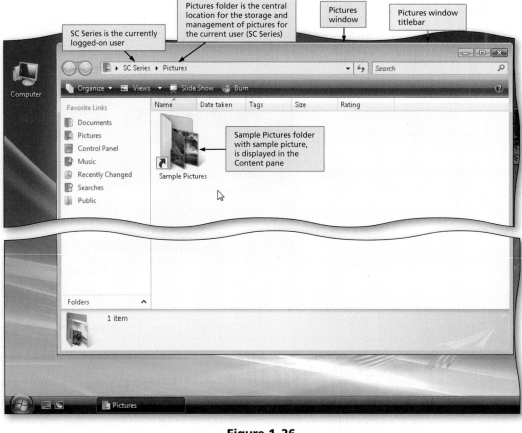

Figure 1–26

Other Ways

1. Click Start button, right-click Pictures, click Open

To Move a Window by Dragging

You can move any open window to another location on the desktop by pointing to the title bar of the window and then dragging the window. The following step drags the Pictures window to the top of the desktop.

1

• Drag the Pictures window title bar so the window moves to the top of the desktop as shown in Figure 1–27.

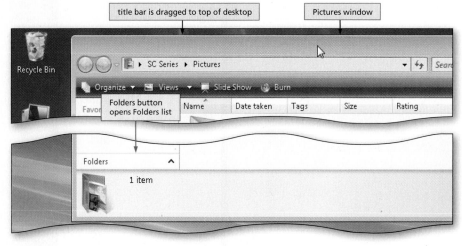

Figure 1–27

Other Ways

1. Right-click title bar, click Move, drag window

To Expand the Folders List

The Folders list in the Pictures window is collapsed and an up arrow appears to the right of the Folders name (see Figure 1–27 on the previous page). Clicking the up arrow or the Folders button expands the Folders list and reveals the contents of the Folders list. The following step expands the Folders list in the Pictures window.

1

- Click the Folders button to expand the Folders list in the Navigation pane of the Pictures window (Figure 1–28).

Q&A

What is shown in the Folders list?

The Folders list displays a hierarchical structure of files, folders, and drives on the computer.

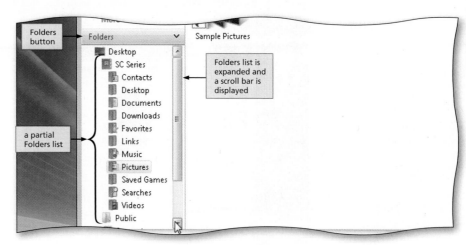

Figure 1–28

To Size a Window by Dragging

You can resize any open window to a more desirable size by pointing to one of the outside borders of the window and then dragging the window in or out. The following steps drag the bottom border of the Pictures window downward to enlarge the window until the contents of the Folders list is visible.

1

- Point to the bottom border of the Pictures window until the mouse pointer changes to a two-headed arrow.

- Drag the bottom border downward until the entire contents of the Folders list are visible and the scroll bar no longer appears (Figure 1–29).

Q&A

Can I drag anything else to enlarge or shrink the window?

You can drag the left, right, and top borders and any window corner.

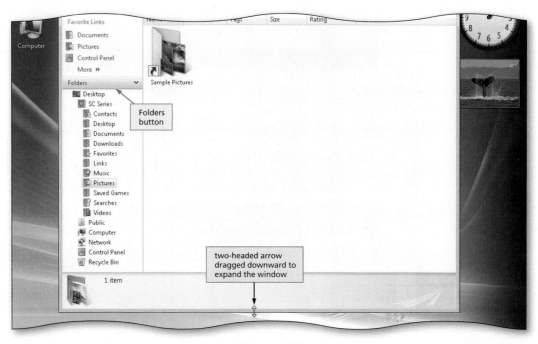

Figure 1–29

To Collapse the Folders List

When the Folders list is expanded, a down arrow is displayed. In the following step, you will collapse the list by clicking the Folders button.

- Click the Folders button to collapse the Folders list (Figure 1–30).

Q&A Is there another way to collapse the Folders list?

Yes. You can click the down arrow to collapse the Folders list.

Q&A Should I keep the Folders list expanded or collapsed?

If you need to use the contents within the Folders list, it is handy to keep the Folders list expanded. You can collapse the Folders list when the information is not needed.

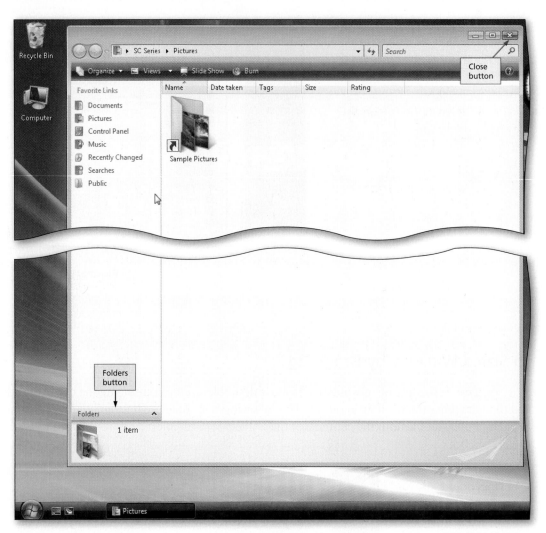

Figure 1–30

To Close a Window

After you have completed work in a window, normally you will close the window. The following step closes the Pictures window.

1 Click the Close button on the title bar in the Pictures window to close the Pictures window.

To Delete a Desktop Icon by Right-Dragging

Sometimes, you will want to remove an icon from the desktop. One method of deleting an icon from the desktop is to right-drag the icon to the Recycle Bin icon on the desktop. **Right-drag** means you point to an item, hold down the right mouse button, move the item to the desired location, and then release the right mouse button. When you right-drag an object, a shortcut menu is displayed. The shortcut menu contains commands specifically for use with the object being dragged. The following steps delete the Computer icon by right-dragging the icon to the Recycle Bin icon. A **dialog box** is displayed whenever Windows Vista needs to supply information to you or wants you to enter information or select among several options. The Confirm Delete dialog box is used in the following steps.

- Point to the Computer icon on the desktop, hold down the right mouse button, drag the Computer icon over the Recycle Bin icon, and then release the right mouse button to display a shortcut menu (Figure 1–31).

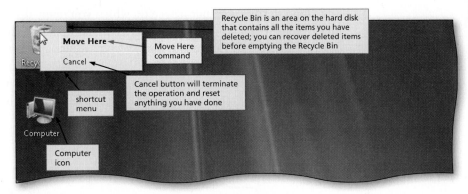

Figure 1–31

- Click Move Here on the shortcut menu to close the shortcut menu and display the Confirm Delete dialog box (Figure 1–32).

Q&A

Why should I right-drag instead of simply dragging?

Although you can move icons by dragging with the primary (left) mouse button and by right-dragging with the secondary (right) mouse button, it is strongly suggested you right-drag because a shortcut menu appears and, in most cases, you can specify the exact operation you want to occur. When you drag using the left mouse button, a default operation takes place and that operation may not be the operation you intended to perform.

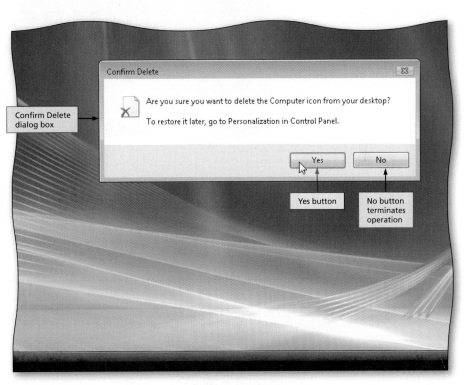

Figure 1–32

③

- Click the Yes button to delete the Computer icon and close the Confirm Delete dialog box.

Other Ways

1. Drag icon to Recycle Bin, click Yes button
2. Right-click icon, click Delete, click Yes button

Summary of Mouse and Windows Operations

You have seen how to use the mouse to point, click, right-click, double-click, drag, and right-drag in order to accomplish certain tasks on the desktop. The use of a mouse is an important skill when using Windows Vista. In addition, you have learned how to move around and use windows on the Windows Vista desktop.

The Keyboard and Keyboard Shortcuts

The **keyboard** is an input device on which you manually key in, or type, data. Figure 1–33 illustrates the rechargeable Wireless Entertainment Desktop 8000 keyboard designed for use with Microsoft Office and the Internet. Keyboards can be basic input devices, or in the case of the keyboard illustrated, can serve other purposes, such as providing USB ports for plugging in hardware, and specialized buttons such as the Windows Gadget button, which allow access to certain Windows Vista features at the touch of a button.

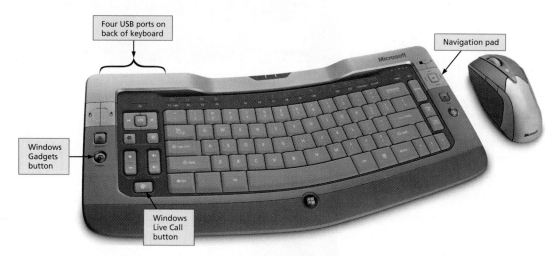

Figure 1–33

Many tasks you accomplish with a mouse can also be accomplished using a keyboard. To perform tasks using the keyboard, you must understand the notation used to identify which keys to press. This notation is used throughout Windows Vista to identify a **keyboard shortcut**.

Keyboard shortcuts consist of (1) pressing a single key (such as press the F1 key); or (2) pressing and holding down one key and pressing a second key, as shown by two key names separated by a plus sign (such as press CTRL+ESC). For example, to obtain help about Windows Vista, you can press the F1 key and to open the Start menu, hold down the CTRL key and then press the ESC key (press CRTL+ESC).

Starting an Application Program

One of the basic tasks you can perform using Windows Vista is starting an application program. A **program** is a set of computer instructions that carries out a task on the computer. An **application program** is a set of specific computer instructions that is designed to allow you to accomplish a particular task. For example, a **word processing program** is an application program that allows you to create written documents; a **presentation graphics program** is an application program that allows you to create graphic presentations for display on a computer; and a **Web browser program** is an application program that allows you to search for and display **Web pages**, documents designed to be viewed using a Web browser.

The **default Web browser program** (Internet Explorer) appears in the pinned items list on the Start menu shown in Figure 1–34. Because the default **Web browser** is selected during the installation of the Windows Vista operating system, the default Web browser on your computer may be different. In addition, you can easily select another Web browser as the default Web browser. Another frequently used Web browser program is **Mozilla Firefox**.

What Is Internet Explorer?

Internet Explorer is a **Web browsing program** that allows you to search for and view Web pages, save pages you find for use in the future, maintain a list of the pages you visit, send and receive e-mail messages, and edit Web pages. The Internet Explorer application program is included with the Windows Vista operating system software and Microsoft Office software, or you can download it from the Internet.

To Start an Application Using the Start Menu

A common activity performed on a computer is starting an application program to accomplish specific tasks. You can start an application program by using the Start menu. To illustrate the use of the Start menu to start an application program, the following steps start Internet Explorer using the Internet command on the Start menu.

- Open the Start menu (Figure 1–34).

Q&A

Is Internet Explorer included in the All Programs list?

Yes. All application programs stored on the computer are listed on the All Programs list. Internet Explorer also is on the pinned items list because it is used often, but you can start Internet Explorer from the All Programs list as well.

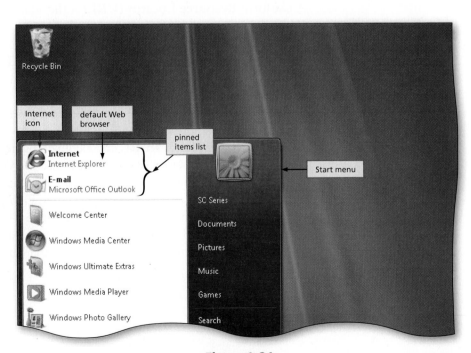

Figure 1–34

2

- Click the Internet icon in the pinned items list on the Start menu to start Windows Internet Explorer (Figure 1–35).

Q&A

What is displayed in the Windows Internet Explorer window?

A title bar, Address bar, Standard toolbar, Instant Search box, scroll bar, status bar, and display area where pages from the World Wide Web display.

Each Web page has a unique address, called a Web address or URL which distinguishes it from all other pages on the Internet

Figure 1–35

Other Ways

1. Click Start button, point to All Programs, click Internet Explorer

Uniform Resource Locator (URL)

A **Uniform Resource Locator (URL)** is the address on the World Wide Web where a Web page is located. It often is composed of three parts (Figure 1–36 on page WIN 29). The first part is the **protocol**. A protocol is a set of rules. Most Web pages use the Hypertext Transfer Protocol. **Hypertext Transfer Protocol (HTTP)** describes the rules used to transmit Web pages electronically over the Internet. You enter the protocol in lowercase as http followed by a colon and two forward slashes (http://). If you do not begin a URL with a protocol, Internet Explorer will assume it is http, and automatically will append http:// to the front of the URL.

The second part of a URL is the domain name. The **domain name** is the Internet address of the computer on the Internet where the Web page is located. The domain name in the URL in Figure 1–36 on the next page is www.scsite.com.

The last part of the domain name (com in Figure 1–36 on the next page) indicates the type of organization that owns the Web site. Table 1–2 shows some types of organizations and their extensions. In addition to the 14 domain name extensions listed in the table, there are country specific extensions, such as .uk for the United Kingdom and .dk for Denmark.

http://www.scsite.com/GreatOutdoors

colon, forward slashes, and periods are required punctuation

protocol used to transfer page from Web site to your computer

domain name of Web site

file specification or path of Web page at Web site

Figure 1–36

Table 1–2 Organizations and their Domain Name Extensions			
Organization	**Extension**	**Organization**	**Extension**
Commercial	.com	aviation	.aero
Educational	.edu	businesses	.biz
Government	.gov	co-operatives	.coop
Military	.mil	general	.info
Major network support	.net	museums	.museum
Organizations not covered above	.org	individuals	.name
International	.int	professionals	.pro

The optional third part of a URL is the file specification of the Web page. The **file specification** includes the file name and possibly a directory or folder name. This information is called the **path**. If no file specification of a Web page is specified in the URL, a default Web page is displayed.

Browsing the World Wide Web

One method to browse the World Wide Web is to find URLs that identify interesting Web sites in magazines or newspapers, on television, from friends, or even from just browsing the Web. URLs of well-known companies and organizations usually contain the company's name and institution's name. For example, ibm.com is the IBM Corporation URL, and umich.edu is the URL for the University of Michigan.

When you find a URL of a Web page you want to visit, enter the URL into the Address bar. The following steps show how to view a Web site provided by Thomson Course Technology and visit the Web page titled SC Site – Shelly Cashman Series Student Resources Web site, which contains student resources for use with Shelly Cashman Series textbooks. The URL for the SC Site – Shelly Cashman Series Student Resources Web site is:

www.scsite.com

You are not required to provide the leading http:// protocol when initially typing the URL in the Address bar. Internet Explorer will insert http:// and assume the www automatically, if you do not supply it.

To Browse the Web by Entering a URL

The SC Site — Shelly Cashman Series Student Resources Web site contains student resources for use with Shelly Cashman Series textbooks. The URL for this Web page is www.scsite.com.

When you find the URL of a Web page you want to visit, enter the URL into the Address bar. The following steps show how to display the Web page from the Shelly Cashman Series.

- Click the Address bar to select the URL in the Address bar (Figure 1–37).

Q&A

What happens when I click the Address bar?

Internet Explorer selects the URL in the Address bar and the mouse pointer changes to an I-beam.

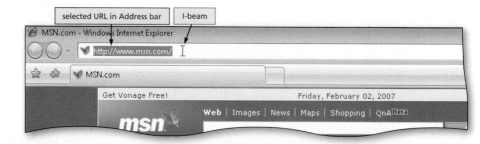

Figure 1–37

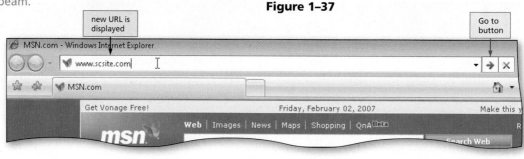

Figure 1–38

- Type
www.scsite.com in the Address bar to display the new URL in the Address bar (Figure 1–38).

Q&A

Must I type www. in the URL?

No. If you type scsite.com, Internet Explorer automatically will add www.

- Click the Go to button to display the SC Site –Shelly Cashman Series Student Resources Web site (Figure 1–39).

Q&A

The Go to button changes after I click it. Why?

When you type the URL, the button changes to the Go to button. After the page is displayed, the button changes to the Refresh button. When you click the Refresh button, the Web page is downloaded again from the Web server, resulting in the most up-to-date version of the page being displayed.

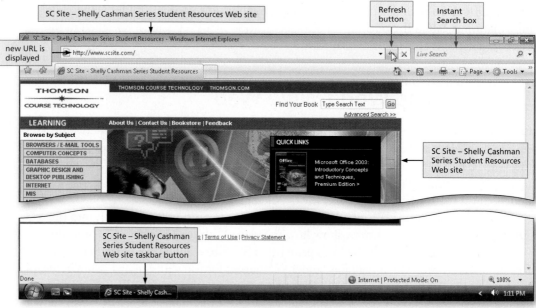

Figure 1–39

To Open a Link in a New Tab

You can view multiple Web pages in a single window using tabbed pages. A **tabbed page** consists of a tab in the Internet Explorer window and the associated Web page. When you start Internet Explorer only one tab is displayed, but you can open as many tabbed pages as you want. The following steps use the Instant Search box and the Course Technology – Shelly Cashman Series link to open a Web page on a new tabbed page.

- Click the Instant Search box and type `Shelly Cashman Series` in the Instant Search box (Figure 1–40).

Q&A

What is an Instant Search box?

It is a text box in which you can type a term which then can be searched for by a Search engine. Internet Explorer provides an Instant Search box in the upper right corner of the window.

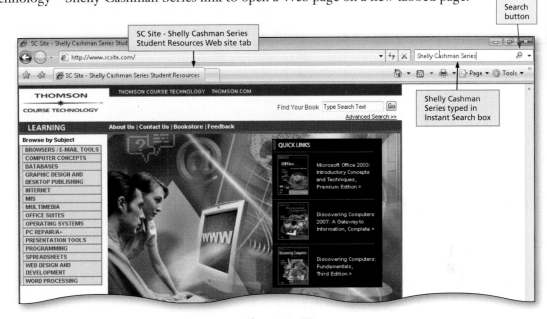

Figure 1–40

- Click the Search button to the right of the Instant Search box to display the results of the Web search (Figure 1–41).

Figure 1–41

• If necessary, scroll to view the Course Technology –Shelly Cashman Series link.

• Right-click the Course Technology –Shelly Cashman Series link to display a shortcut menu (Figure 1–42).

Q&A

What happens when I just click a link?

The Web page will open on the same tabbed page as the search results and will replace the search results page.

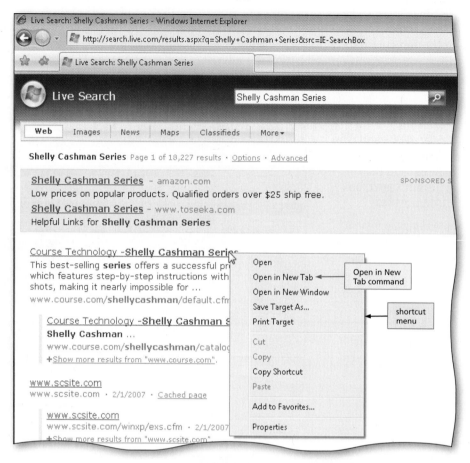

Figure 1–42

• Click the Open in New Tab command on the shortcut menu to close the shortcut menu and display the Course Technology –Shelly Cashman Series tab (Figure 1–43).

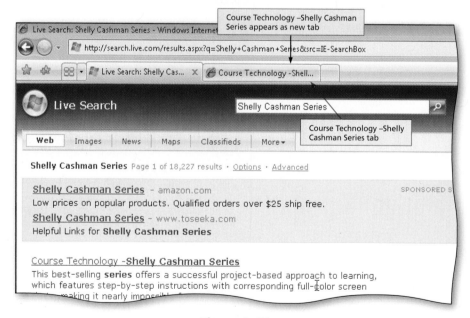

Figure 1–43

Other Ways

1. While holding down CTRL, click link

To Switch Between Tabs

You can display the contents of any tabbed page by clicking the tab, as shown in the following step which activates the Course Technology –Shelly Cashman Series tab.

- Click the Course Technology –Shelly Cashman Series tab to activate the tab and display The Shelly Cashman Series® Web page in the display area (Figure 1–44).

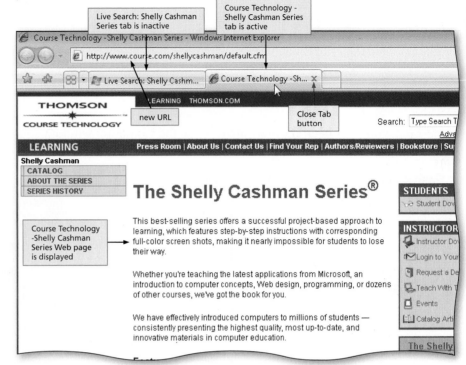

Figure 1–44

Other Ways	
1. Press CTRL+TAB, press CTRL+TAB	2. Press CTRL+2, press CTRL+1

To Close a Tab

You can keep as many tabbed pages open as necessary. If you no longer have a need for the tabbed page to be open, you can close the tab using the following steps.

- Click the Close Tab button in the Course Technology –Shelly Cashman Series tab to close the Course Technology –Shelly Cashman Series tab (Figure 1–45).

- Click the Close button on the title bar to close the Live Search: Shelly Cashman Series - Windows Internet Explorer window.

Figure 1–45

Working with Folders

The steps below allow you to view the contents of the computer, the hierarchy of drives and folders on the computer, and the files and folders in each folder. In this section, you will expand and collapse drives and folders, display drive and folder contents, create a new folder, copy a file between folders, and rename and then delete a file. These are common operations that you should understand how to perform.

To Work with Folders

First, you must open the Start menu, open the Computer window, and then maximize the window.

1
- Open the Start menu (Figure 1–46).

Figure 1–46

2
- Click Computer on the Start menu to display the Computer window (Figure 1–47).

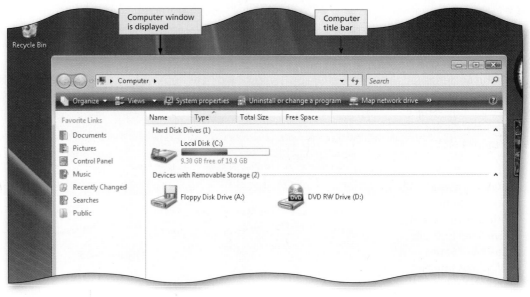

Figure 1–47

3

- If necessary, double-click the Computer title bar to maximize the Computer window.

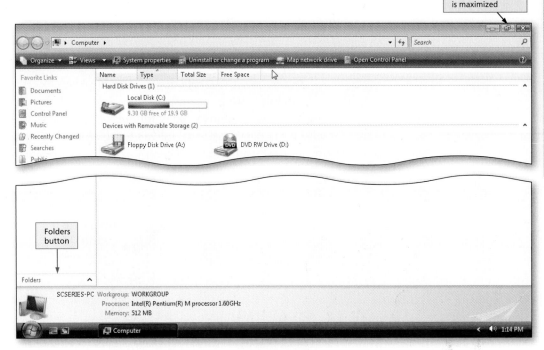

Figure 1–48

4

- If necessary, click the Folders button to display the Folders list (Figure 1–49).

Q&A

Is it possible to display my folders and drives in the right pane differently than what is shown in Figure 1–49?

You can display files and folders in the right pane in several different views. Currently, the drives and folders in the right pane are displayed in Tiles view.

 Experiment

- Click a black arrow in the Folders list and observe the changes in the window. Then click the resulting white arrow to return the window to its previous state. Do the same for another black arrow and resulting white arrow.

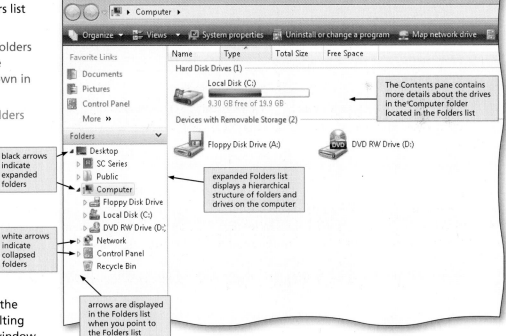

Figure 1–49

Other Ways

1. Click Start button, right-click Computer, click Explore on shortcut menu
2. Press WINDOWS+E

Using a Hierarchical Format to Organize Files and Folders

Besides navigating drives and folder, you also need to be able to create and organize the files and folders on the computer. A file may contain a spreadsheet assignment given by the computer teacher, a research paper assigned by the English teacher, an electronic quiz given by the Business teacher, or a study sheet designed by the Math teacher. You should organize and store these files in folders to avoid misplacing a file and to help you quickly find a file.

Assume you are a freshman taking four classes (Business, Computer, English, and Math). You want to design a series of folders for the four classes you are taking in the first semester of your freshman year. To accomplish this, you arrange the folders in a **hierarchical format**. The hierarchical structure of folders for the Freshman year is shown in Figure 1–50.

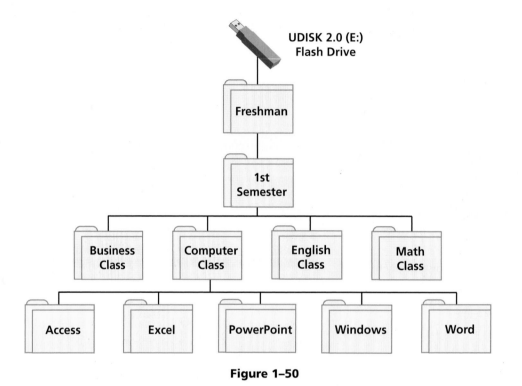

Figure 1–50

The hierarchy contains five levels. The first level contains the storage device, in this case a flash drive. Windows Vista identifies the storage device with a letter, and, in some cases, a name. In Figure 1–50, the flash drive is identified as UDISK 2.0 (E:). The second level contains the Freshman folder, the third level contains the 1st Semester folder, the fourth level contains four folders (Business Class, Computer Class, English Class, and Math Class), and the fifth level contains five folders (Access, Excel, PowerPoint, Windows, and Word).

The vertical and horizontal lines in the hierarchy chart form a pathway that allows you to navigate to a drive or folder. Each pathway is a means of navigation to a specific location on a computer or network. A **path** consists of a drive letter (preceded by a drive name when necessary) and colon, to identify the storage device, and one or more folder names. Each drive or folder in the hierarchy chart has a corresponding path. When you click a drive or folder icon in the Folders list, the corresponding path appears in the Address bar. Table 1–3 contains examples of paths and their corresponding drives and folders. These paths are referred to as **breadcrumb trails**, showing you where the current page or folder is in the hierarchy.

When the hierarchy in Figure 1–50 is created, the UDISK 2.0 (E:) drive is said "to contain" the Freshman folder, the Freshman folder is said "to contain" the 1st Semester folder, and so on. In addition, this hierarchy can easily be expanded to include folders from the Sophomore, Junior, and Senior years and any additional semesters.

Table 1–3 Paths and Corresponding Drives and Folders

Path	Drive and Folder
Computer ► UDISK 2.0 (E:)	Drive E (UDISK 2.0 (E:))
Computer ► UDISK 2.0 (E:) ► Freshman	Freshman folder on drive E
Computer ► UDISK 2.0 (E:) ► Freshman ► 1st Semester	1st Semester folder in Freshman folder on drive E
Computer ► UDISK 2.0 (E:) ► Freshman ► 1st Semester ► Computer Class ► Word	Word folder in Computer Class folder in 1st Semester folder in Freshman folder on drive E

Removable Media and Network Drives

Types of removable media such as USB flash drives are ideal for storing files and folders on a computer. A **USB flash drive**, sometimes called a **keychain drive**, is a flash memory storage device that plugs into a USB port on a computer. A **USB port**, short for universal serial bus port, can be found on most computers. USB flash drives, like the one shown in Figure 1–51, are convenient for mobile users because they are small and lightweight enough to be transported on a keychain or in a pocket.

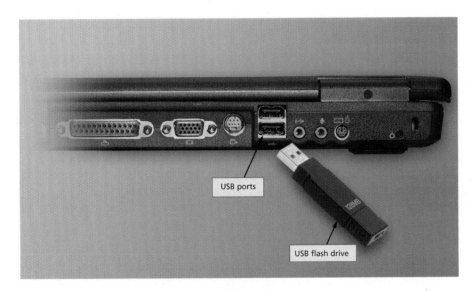

USB ports

USB flash drive

Figure 1–51

Instead of a USB drive, you might use files stored on a network drive. A **network** is a collection of computers and devices connected together for the purpose of sharing information between computer users. In some cases, students might be required to store their files on a network drive found on the school's computer network. A **network drive** is a storage device that is connected to the server on the computer network. A **server** controls access to the hardware, software, and other resources on the network and provides a centralized storage area for programs, data, and information. If student files reside on the network drive on the school's network, files may be accessed from a school computer, or from a personal computer with permission from the school. Ask your teacher if the school requires you to use a network drive.

To Plug a USB Flash Drive into a USB Port

Although other removable media may be used for storage, the USB flash drive is one of the more popular drives. To store files and folders on the USB flash drive, you must plug the USB flash drive into a USB port on the computer. After you do, the flash drive window is displayed on the desktop. The removable media drive name on your computer may be different. The following step plugs a USB flash drive into a USB port.

1

- Plug the USB flash drive into a USB port on the computer to display the UDISK 2.0 (E:) window (Figure 1–52).

Q&A

What does UDISK 2.0 (E:) mean?

UDISK 2.0 is the name of a particular type of USB drive. (E:) is the drive letter assigned by Windows Vista to your remov-able drive. The name and drive letter of your USB drive might be different.

2

- Close the UDISK 2.0 (E:) window.

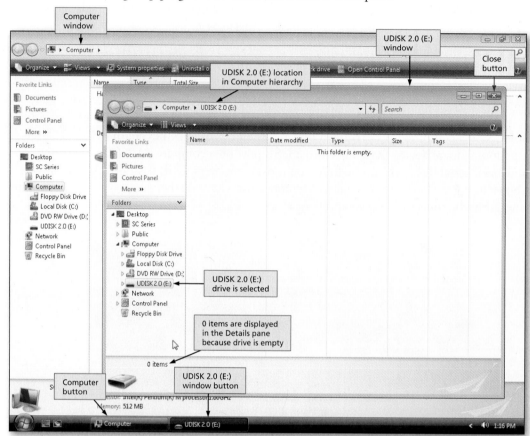

Figure 1–52

Naming a Folder

When you create a folder, such as the Freshman folder in Figure 1–50 on page 36, you must name the folder. A folder name should describe the folder and its contents. A folder name can contain up to 255 characters, including spaces. Any uppercase or lower-case character is valid when creating a folder name, except a backslash (\), slash (/), colon (:), asterisk (*), question mark (?), quotation marks ("), less than symbol (<), greater than symbol (>), or vertical bar (|). Folder names cannot be CON, AUX, COM1, COM2, COM3, COM4, LPT1, LPT2, LPT3, PRN, or NUL. The same rules for naming folders also apply to naming files.

To Create a Folder on a Removable Drive

To create a folder on a removable drive, you must open the UDISK 2.0 (E:) drive and then create the folder in the right pane. The following steps create the Freshman folder on the UDISK 2.0 (E:) drive.

1

- Double-click the UDISK 2.0 (E:) icon in the Folders list to open it.

- Right-click an open area of the right pane to display a shortcut menu.

- Point to New on the shortcut menu to display the New submenu (Figure 1–53).

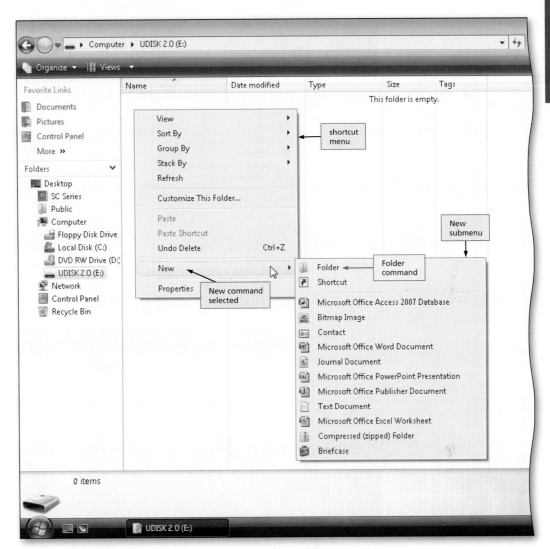

Figure 1–53

2

- Click Folder on the New submenu to display the new Folder icon.

- Type Freshman in the text box to name the folder.

- Press the ENTER key to create the Freshman folder on the UDISK 2.0 (E:) drive (Figure 1–54).

Q&A What happens when I press the ENTER key?

The Freshman folder is displayed in the File list, which contains the folder name, date modified, and file folder type.

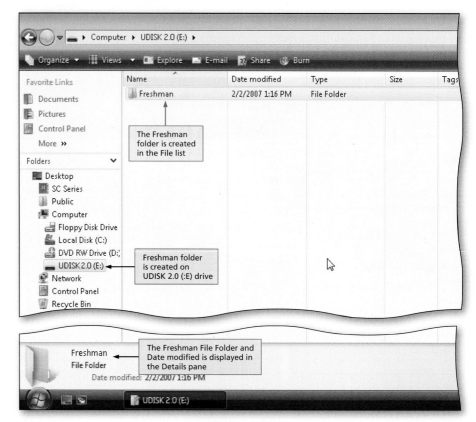

Figure 1–54

Downloading a Hierarchy of Folders into the Freshman Folder

After creating the Freshman folder on the UDISK 2.0 (E:) drive, the remaining folders in the hierarchical structure (see Figure 1–50), starting with the 1st Semester folder, should be downloaded to the Freshman folder. **Downloading** is the process of a computer receiving information, such as a set of files or folders from a Web site, from a server on the Internet. To make the task of creating the folders easier, the folders have been created and stored in a hierarchical structure on the SC Site - Shelly Cashman Series Student Resources Web site.

To Download a Hierarchy of Folders into the Freshman Folder

The following steps download the folders in the hierarchical structure into the Freshman folder.

1 Start Internet Explorer by clicking the Start button on the taskbar and then clicking Internet on the Start menu.

2 Click the Address box on the Address bar, type scsite.com in the Address box, and then click the Go button.

3 When the SC Site - Shelly Cashman Series Student Resources Web site is displayed, use the Browse by Subject navigation bar, click Office Suites, and then click Microsoft Office 2007.

4 In the center of the screen, locate your textbook and click the title (for example, Microsoft Office 2007: Introductory Concepts and Techniques, Windows Vista Edition).

5 Scroll down to display the Data Files for Students (Windows) area and then click the Windows Vista Chapter 1 Data Files link.

6 When the File Download – Security Warning dialog box is displayed, click the Run button.

7 When the Internet Explorer – Security Warning dialog box is displayed, click the Run button.

8 When the WinZip Self-Extractor dialog box is displayed, type the removable media drive letter of your removable media drive followed by a colon, backslash, and folder name (Freshman) (for example, E:\Freshman).

9 Click the Unzip button.

10 When Windows displays the WinZip Self-Extractor dialog box, click the OK button.

11 Click the Close button in the WinZip Self-Extractor dialog box.

12 Click the Close button in the SC Site – Shelly Cashman Series Student Resources Web site window (Figure 1–55).

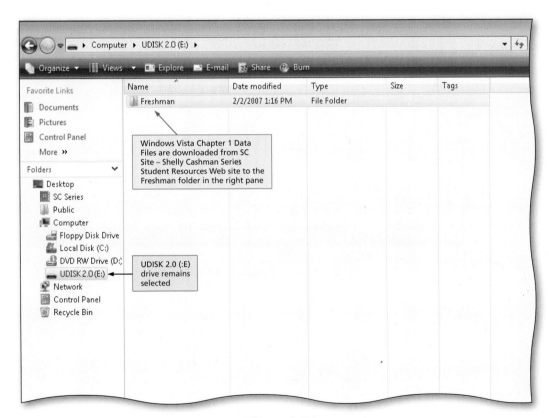

Figure 1–55

To Expand a Drive

Folder Windows display the hierarchy of items in the Folders list and the contents of drives and folders in the right pane. You might want to expand a drive to view its contents in the Folders list. The following step expands a drive.

- Point to any item in the Folders list to display arrows, and then click the white arrow to the left of the UDISK 2.0 (E:) icon in the Folders list to display the Freshman folder.

Q&A

Why are there black arrows and white arrows in the Folders list?

The black arrows represent folders and drives that contain other folders that have been expanded to show their contents. The white arrows represent folders and drives that contain other folders that have not been expanded.

- Click the white arrow next to the Freshman folder, and then click the white arrow next to the 1st Semester folder to display its contents (Figure 1–56).

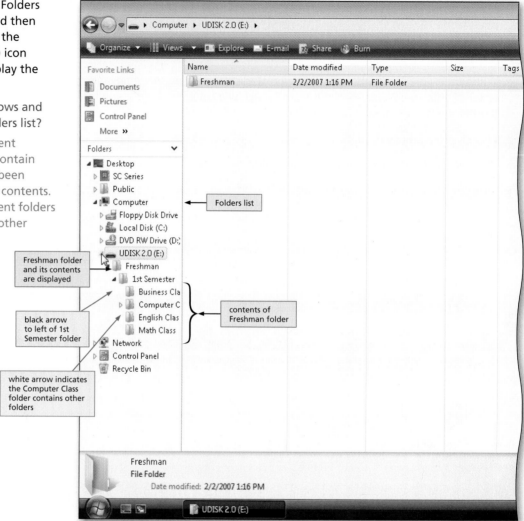

Figure 1–56

Other Ways

1. Double-click drive icon in Folders list
2. Select drive to expand using ARROW keys, press RIGHT ARROW on keyboard
3. Select drive to expand, press RIGHT ARROW

To Collapse a Folder

When a black arrow is displayed to the left of a folder icon in the Folders list, the folder is expanded and shows all the folders it contains. The following step collapses the 1st Semester folder.

1

- Click the black arrow to the left of the 1st Semester folder icon in the Folders list to collapse the 1st Semester folder (Figure 1–57).

Q&A Why is the 1st Semester folder indented below the Freshman folder in the Folders list?

The folder is indented below the Freshman icon to show that the folder is contained within the Freshman folder.

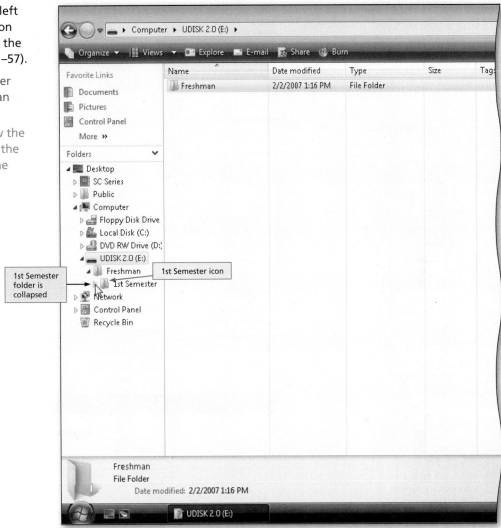

Figure 1–57

Other Ways

1. Double-click folder icon in Folders list
2. Select folder to collapse using ARROW keys, press LEFT ARROW on keyboard
3. Select folder to collapse, press LEFT ARROW

To Display the Contents of a Folder

Clicking a folder icon in the Folders list displays the contents of the drive or folder in the File list and displays the path in the Address bar. The following step displays the contents of the 1st Semester folder.

1

• Click the 1st Semester icon in the Folders list to display the contents of the 1st Semester folder in the File list (Figure 1–58).

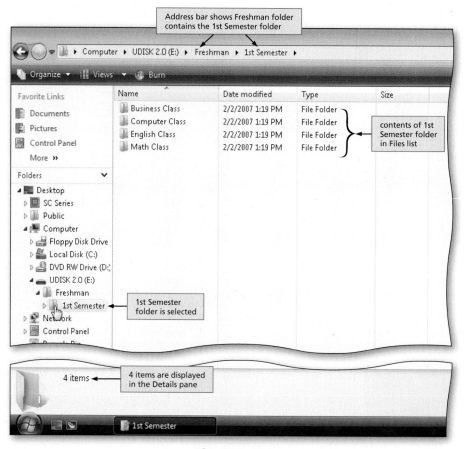

Figure 1–58

Other Ways

1. Right-click 1st Semester icon, click Explore on shortcut menu

Creating a Document and Folder Using WordPad

The Freshman folder was created in the UDISK 2.0 (E:) drive when you downloaded the files. You also can create a folder anytime you save a file in a Windows application. For example, you can use WordPad to create a document and then save the new document in a folder. **WordPad** is a word processing program included with Windows Vista that allows you to create a limited variety of personal and business documents.

As one of the programs in the Accessories list, one method to start the WordPad application is to display the Start menu, click All Programs, click Accessories, and click WordPad in the Accessories list.

An easier method to start WordPad is to use the Start Search box on the Start menu. The **Start Search** box allows you to find a specific application, file, e-mail, or Internet favorite by typing the first few letters in the Start Search box at the bottom of the Start menu.

To Start WordPad Using the Start Search Box

Assume you want to create a WordPad document that lists your homework for Friday, April 11. The first step is to start the WordPad application using the Start Search box. The following steps find and then start WordPad based on using the Start Search box at the bottom of the Start menu.

1

- Open the Start menu.

- Type w (the first letter in the WordPad name) in the Start Search box on the Start menu to display a list of programs, favorites, and history (Figure 1–59).

Q&A

What is displayed on the Start menu when I type the letter w?

A list of programs, favorites, and history. The WordPad program does not appear yet. As you type the entire program name, fewer selections remain in the list until you find your selection or no items match your search term.

Figure 1–59

• Type the letter o (the second letter in the WordPad name) in the Start Search box on the Start menu to display a list of programs, favorites, history, and files (Figure 1–60).

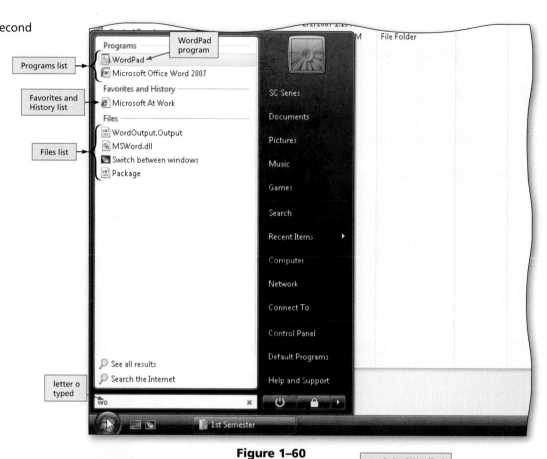

Figure 1–60

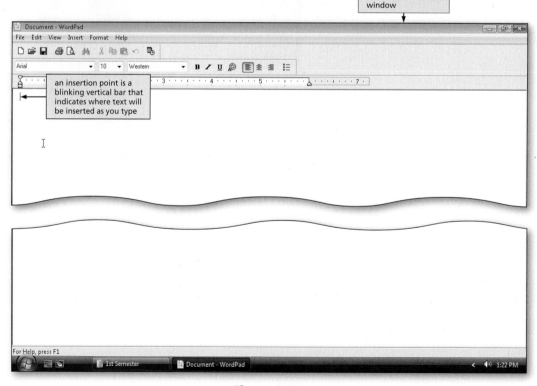

• Click WordPad in the Programs list to start the WordPad application and display a new blank document in the WordPad window (Figure 1–61).

• If the WordPad window is not maximized, click the Maximize button on the title bar to maximize the window.

Q&A

Could I continue typing the remainder of the letters in the WordPad name?

Yes. To start the program you still need to click WordPad in the Programs list to start the WordPad application.

Figure 1–61

To Type Text

After starting WordPad, you can enter the text for a new document. To enter text in the document, you type on the keyboard. The following steps enter text in the new WordPad document.

- Type `Friday, April 11` and then press the ENTER key twice.

- Type `Finish - The Bike Delivers Data Base` and then press the ENTER key.

- Type `Read - Next Project` and then press the ENTER key (Figure 1–62).

Q&A What if I make an error while typing?

You can press the BACKSPACE key to delete the error and then retype the text correctly.

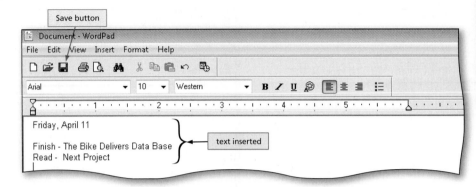

Figure 1–62

To Save a WordPad Document in a New Folder

After typing the text of a WordPad document, you can create a folder in which to save the document, and then save the document in the created folder. The following steps save the new document in a created folder named Homework, with a name of Friday, April 11. The Homework folder is created within the Computer Class folder (see the hierarchy in Figure 1–50 on page 36).

- Click the Save button on the Standard toolbar to display the Save As dialog box.

- If necessary, double-click the Save As dialog box title bar to maximize the Save As dialog box (Figure 1–63).

Q&A Why is the Document file name selected in the File name text box?

It is selected in the File name text box as the default file name.
You can change the default file name by immediately typing the new name.

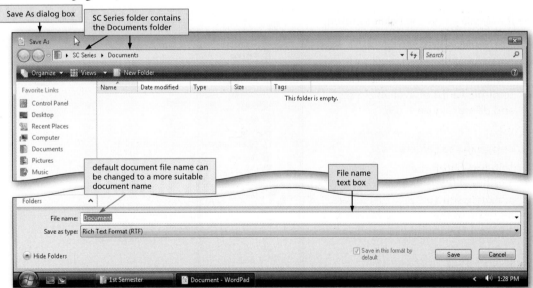

Figure 1–63

2

- Type Friday, April 11 in the File name text box. Do not press the ENTER key after typing the file name (Figure 1–64).

Q&A What happens if I press the ENTER key after typing the file name?

If you press the ENTER key, the Save As dialog box closes and the file is saved in the Documents folder. If you want to save the file in a folder other than the Documents folder, you must select the desired folder.

Q&A What if the Navigation pane does not appear in the Save As dialog box?

Click the Browse Folders button.

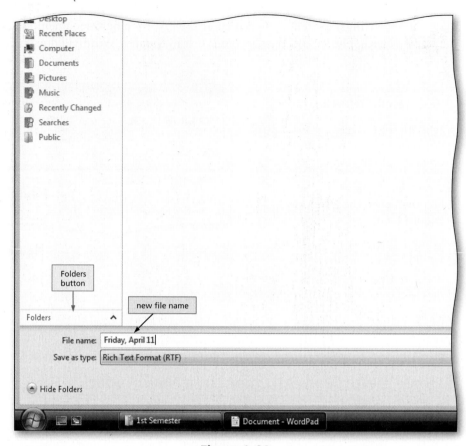

Figure 1–64

3

- If necessary, click the Folders button to expand the Folders list.

- Click the white arrow next to the Computer icon in the Folders list to display a list of available disks and drives (Figure 1–65).

Q&A What if I don't see the white arrows in the Folders list?

To display both the white and black arrows, point to any item in the Folders list.

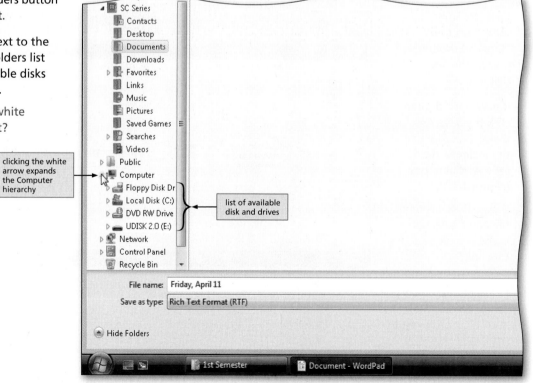

Figure 1–65

- Click UDISK 2.0 (E:) in the Folders list to display the contents of the UDISK 2.0 (E:) folder in the File list (Figure 1–66).

Q&A Is it OK if my list of drives and folders is different from the one in Figure 1–66?

Yes. Folders and drives can be unique for each computer.

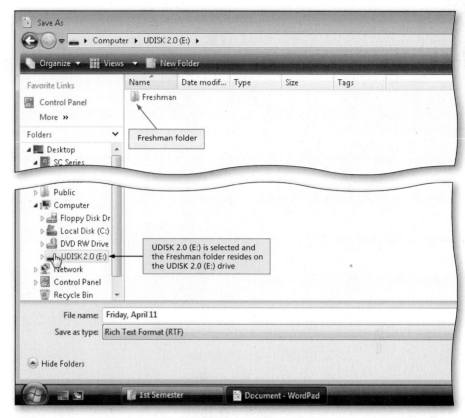

Figure 1–66

- Double-click the Freshman folder in the File list of the Save As dialog box to display the 1st Semester folder in the File list (Figure 1–67).

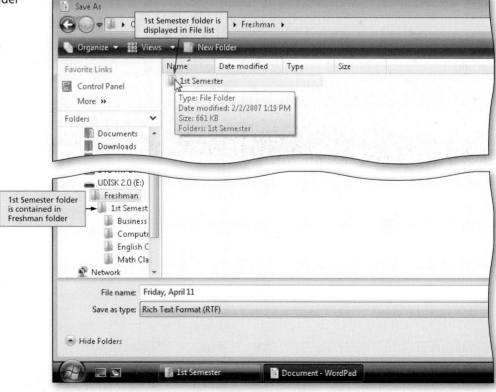

Figure 1–67

● Double-click the 1st Semester folder in the File list of the Save As dialog box to display the contents of the 1st Semester folder (Figure 1–68)

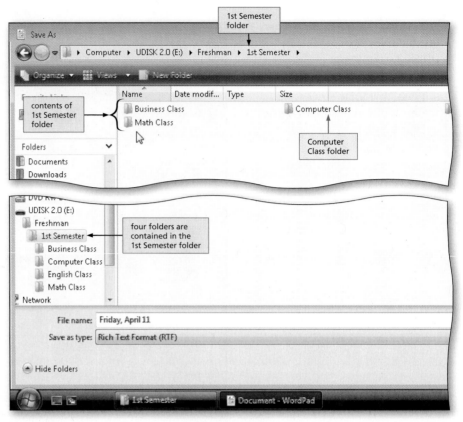

Figure 1–68

● Double-click the Computer Class folder in the File list of the Save As dialog box to display the contents of the Computer Class folder (Figure 1–69).

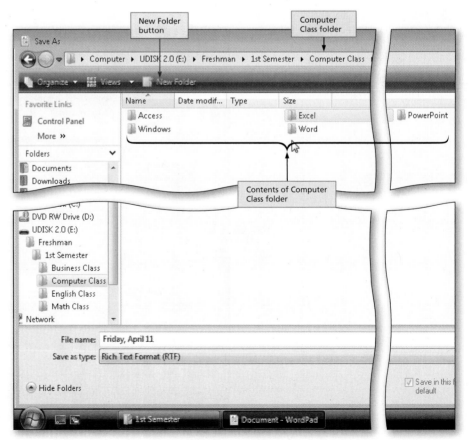

Figure 1–69

8

- Click the New Folder button on the Save As dialog toolbar to create a new folder within the Computer Class folder.

- Type Homework as the name of the folder and then press the ENTER key (Figure 1–70).

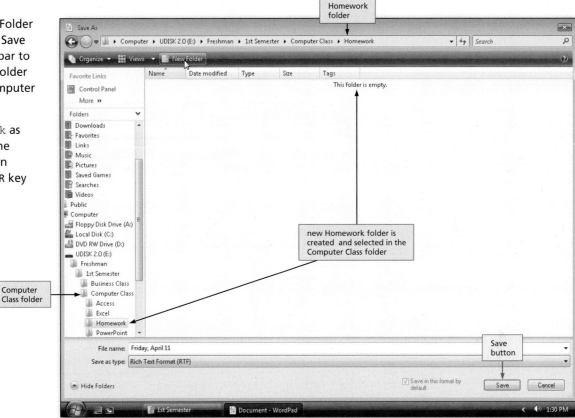

Figure 1–70

9

- Click the Save button in the Save As dialog box to save the Friday, April 11 document to its new location in the Homework folder (Figure 1–71).

- Click the Close button in the Friday, April 11 - WordPad window to close the window.

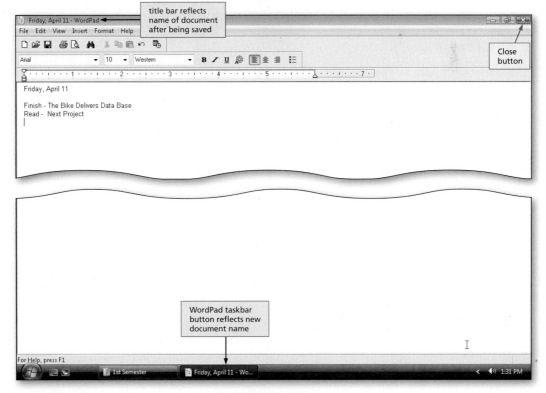

Figure 1–71

To Verify the Contents of a Folder

After saving the Friday, April 11 document in the Homework folder, you can verify that the document was correctly saved in the Homework folder. The following step verifies the Homework folder contains the Friday, April 11 document.

- Click the white arrow next to the 1st Semester icon in the Folders list to display the folders within the 1st Semester folder.

- Click the white arrow next to the Computer Class icon in the Folders list to display the folders within the Computer Class folder.

- Click the Homework icon in the Folders list to select the Homework folder and display the contents of the Homework folder in the right pane (Figure 1–72).

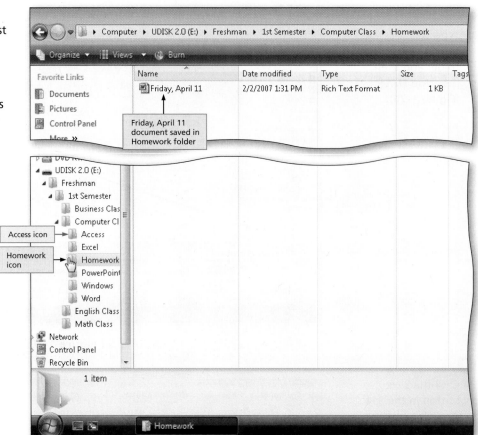

Figure 1–72

File Management

Being able to manage the files on the computer is one of the most important computer skills you can have. **File management** includes copying, moving, renaming, and deleting files and folders on the computer.

To Copy a File by Right-Dragging

When copying files, the drive and folder containing the files to be copied are called the **source drive** and **source folder**, respectively. The drive and folder to which the files are copied are called the **destination drive** and **destination folder**, respectively. The Access folder contains two Access database files (SciFi Scene and The Bike Delivers).

The following steps on the next page show one method of copying files - right-drag a file icon from the right pane to a folder or drive icon in the Folders list. The following steps on the next page copy the The Bike Delivers file from the Access folder (source folder) to the Homework (destination folder). The UDISK 2.0 (E:) drive is both the source drive and the destination drive.

1

- Click the Access folder in the Folders list to select the Access folder and display its contents in the right pane (Figure 1–73).

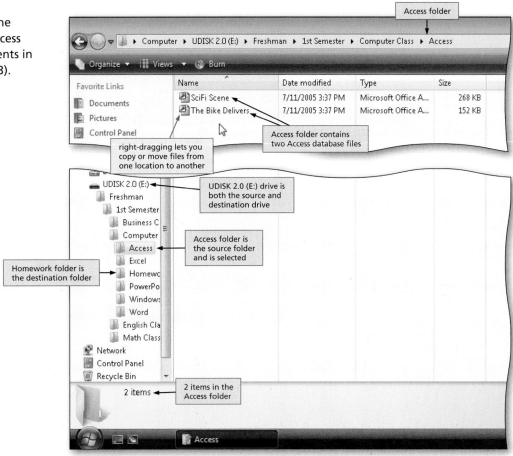

Figure 1–73

2

- Right-drag the The Bike Delivers icon from the right pane onto the Homework folder icon in the Folders list to open the shortcut menu (Figure 1–74).

Q&A

What should I do if I right-drag a file to the wrong folder?

Click Cancel on the shortcut menu, and then right-drag the file to the correct folder.

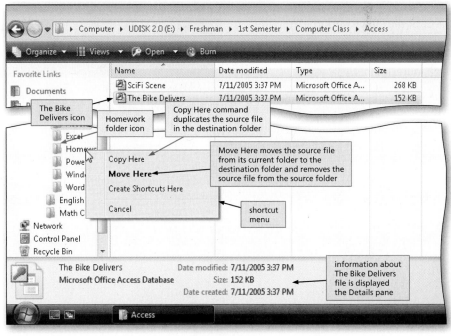

Figure 1–74

- Click Copy Here on the shortcut menu to copy The Bike Delivers file to the Homework folder.

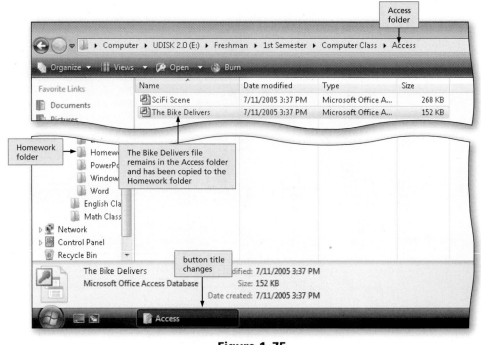

Figure 1–75

Other Ways

1. Right-click file to copy, click Copy on the shortcut menu, right-click Homework folder, click Paste on the shortcut menu

2. Select file to copy, press CTRL+C, select Homework folder, press CTRL+V

To Display the Contents of a Folder

After copying a file, you might want to examine the folder or drive where the file was copied to ensure it was copied properly. The following step displays the contents of the Homework folder.

- Click the Homework folder in the Folders list to display the contents of the Homework folder (Figure 1–76).

Q&A

Can I copy or move more than one file at a time?

Yes. To copy or move multiple files, select each file to be copied or moved by clicking the file icon while holding down the CTRL key. Then, right-drag the selected files to the destination folder using the same technique as right-dragging a single file.

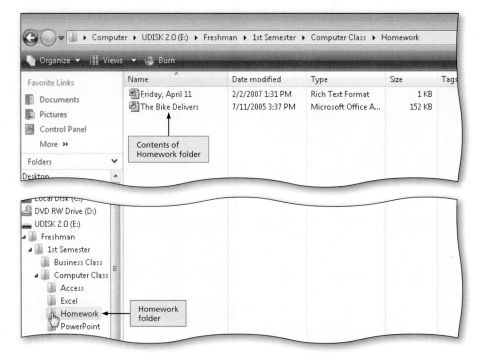

Figure 1–76

To Rename a File

In some circumstances, you may want to rename a file or a folder. This could occur when you want to distinguish a file in one folder or drive from a copy, or if you decide you need a better name to identify a file. The Word folder in Figure 1–77 contains the three Word documents (Barn and Silo, Fall Harvest, and Lake at Sunset). In this case, you decide to change the Fall Harvest name to Great Fall Harvest. The following steps change the name of the Fall Harvest file in the Word folder to Great Fall Harvest.

1

- Click the Word folder in the left pane to display the three files it contains in the right pane.

- Right-click the Fall Harvest icon in the right pane to select the Fall Harvest icon and display a shortcut menu (Figure 1–77).

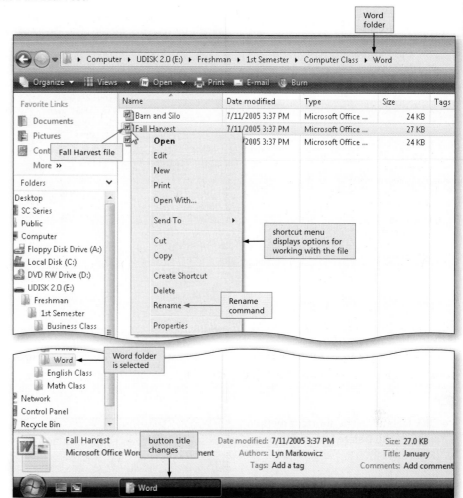

Figure 1–77

2

- Click Rename on the shortcut menu to select the file name for renaming.

- Type `Great Fall Harvest` and then press the ENTER key (Figure 1–78).

Q&A

Are there any risks to renaming files that are located on the hard disk?

If you inadvertently rename a file that is associated with certain programs, the programs may not be able to find the file and, therefore, may not execute properly. Always use caution when renaming files.

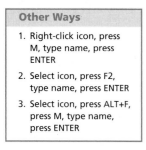

Other Ways

1. Right-click icon, press M, type name, press ENTER

2. Select icon, press F2, type name, press ENTER

3. Select icon, press ALT+F, press M, type name, press ENTER

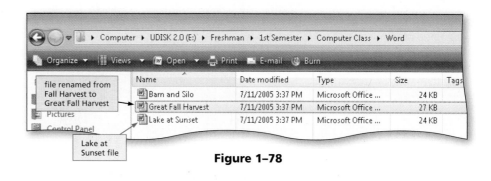

Figure 1–78

To Delete a File by Right-Clicking

A final task you may want to perform is to delete a file. Exercise extreme caution when deleting a file or files. When you delete a file from a hard drive, the deleted file is stored in the Recycle Bin where you can recover it until you empty the Recycle Bin. If you delete a file from removable media, the file is gone permanently once you delete it. The following steps delete the Lake at Sunset file.

- Right-click the Lake at Sunset icon in the right pane to select the icon and open a shortcut menu (Figure 1–79).

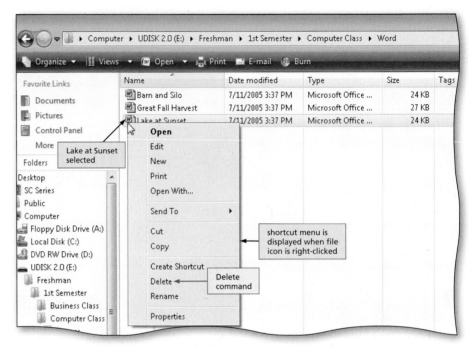

Figure 1–79

- Click Delete on the shortcut menu to open the Delete File dialog box (Figure 1–80).

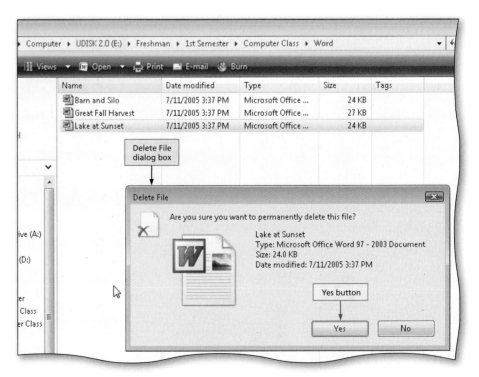

Figure 1–80

3

- Click the Yes button in the Delete File dialog box to remove the Lake at Sunset file (Figure 1–81).

Q&A Can I use this same technique to delete a folder?

Yes. Right-click the folder and then click Delete on the shortcut menu. When you delete a folder, all the files and folders contained in the folder you are deleting, together with any files and folders on lower hierarchical levels, are deleted as well.

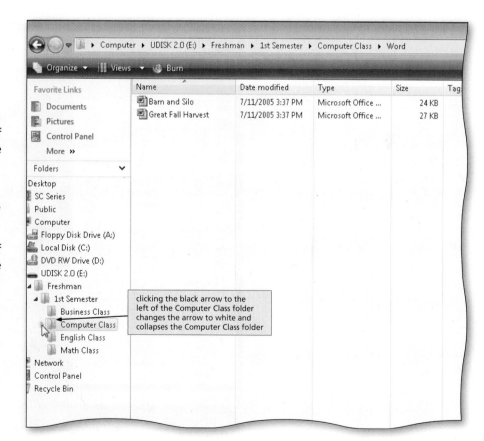

Figure 1–81

Other Ways

1. Select icon, press ALT+F, press D, press Y

To Close Expanded Folders

Sometimes, after you have completed work with expanded folders, you will want to close the expanded folders while still leaving the Word window open. The following steps close the Computer Class folder, 1st Semester folder, Freshman folder, and UDISK 2.0 (E:) drive.

1

- Click the black arrow to the left of the Computer Class folder in the Folders list to collapse the Computer Class folder (Figure 1–82).

2

- Click the black arrow to the left of the 1st Semester folder to collapse the folder.

- Click the black arrow to the left of the Freshman folder to collapse the folder.

- Click the black arrow to the left of the UDISK 2.0 (E:) drive to collapse the drive.

Figure 1–82

Other Ways

1. Click expanded folder icon, press LEFT ARROW

To Close the Computer Window

When you have finished working, you can close the Folders list and close the Computer window. The following steps close the Computer window.

1 Click the Close button on the Computer window title bar to close the Computer window.

2 Remove the USB flash drive from the USB port.

Using Help and Support

One of the more powerful Windows Vista features is Windows Help and Support. **Windows Help and Support** is available when using Windows Vista, or when using any application program running under Windows Vista. It contains answers to many questions you may ask with respect to the Windows Vista operating system.

To Start Windows Help and Support

Before you can access the Windows Help and Support services, you must start Help and Support. One method of starting Help and Support uses the Start menu. The following steps start Help and Support.

1

- Open the Start menu (Figure 1–83).

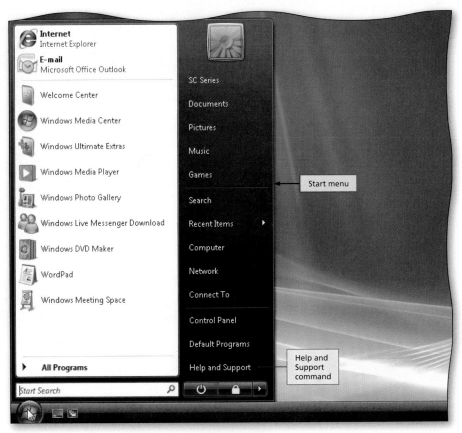

Figure 1–83

2

- Click Help and Support to display the Windows Help and Support window.

- If necessary, click the Maximize button on the Windows Help and Support title bar to maximize the Windows Help and Support window (Figure 1–84).

Q&A What does Windows Help and Support contain?

Windows Help and Support contains a title bar, navigation toolbar, Find an answer area, Ask someone area, and Information from Microsoft area

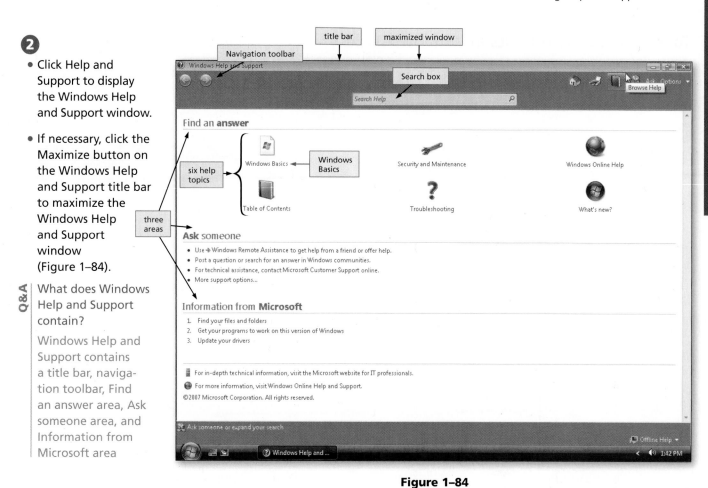

Figure 1–84

Table 1–4 shows the content areas in the Windows Help and Support Center.

Other Ways

1. Press CTRL+ESC, press RIGHT ARROW, press UP ARROW, Press ENTER
2. Press WINDOWS+F1

Table 1–4 Windows Help and Support Center Content Areas	
Area	**Function**
Find an answer	Area contains six Help topics: Windows Basics, Table of Contents, Security and Maintenance, Troubleshooting, Windows Online Help, and What's new? Clicking a category displays a list of subcategories and Help topics related to the category.
Ask someone	Area contains Windows Remote Assistance allowing you to get help from a friend or offer help, post a question or search for an answer in Windows communities, get technical assistance from Microsoft Customer Support online. Clicking the More support options link allows you to search the Knowledge Base, get in-depth technical information from Microsoft Website for IT professionals, and Windows Online Help and Support.
Information from Microsoft	Area contains links to Find your files and folders, Get your programs to work on this version of Windows, and Update your drives.

To Browse for Help Topics in Windows Basics

After starting Windows Help and Support, the next action is to find the Help topic in which you are interested. The following steps use the 'Find an answer' area in the Windows Help and Support Center to find a Help topic that describes how to use the Windows Help and Support Center.

• Click Windows Basics in the 'Find an answer' area to display the Windows Basics: all topics heading (Figure 1–85).

Figure 1–85

• Scroll down to view Getting help topic (Figure 1–86).

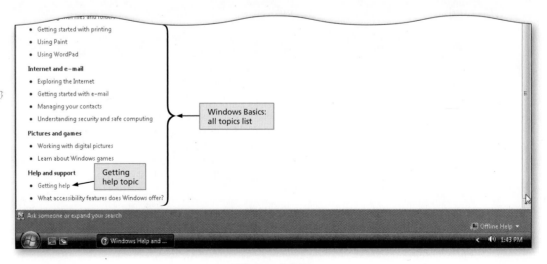

Figure 1–86

3

- Click the Getting help topic (Figure 1–87).

- Read the information in the Getting help topic.

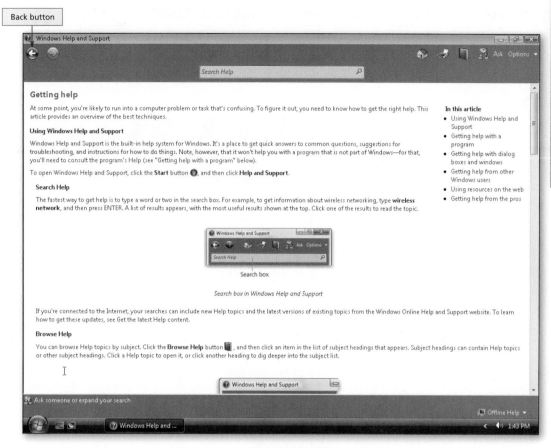

Figure 1–87

4

- Click the Back button on the Navigation toolbar two times to return to the Find an answer area (Figure 1–88).

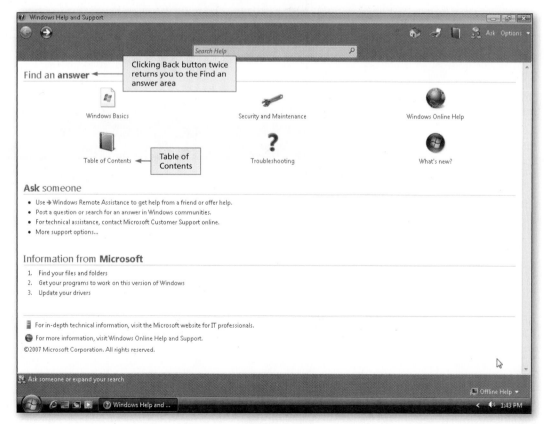

Figure 1–88

To Search for Help Topics Using the Table of Contents

A second method of finding answers to your questions about Windows Vista is to use the Table of Contents. The **Table of Contents** contains a list of entries, each of which references one or more Help topics. The following steps obtain help and information about what you need to set up a home network.

- Click the Table of Contents link in the Find an answer area to display the Table of Contents (Figure 1–89).

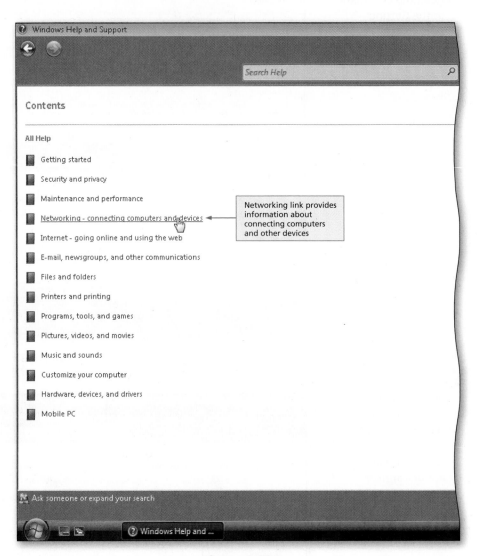

Figure 1–89

2

- Click the 'Networking – connecting computers and devices' link in the Contents area (Figure 1–90).

Q&A What happens if the topic I am interested in is not included in the table of contents?

Type the term into the Search Help text box in the Windows Help and Support window, and then press ENTER to find information about your topic.

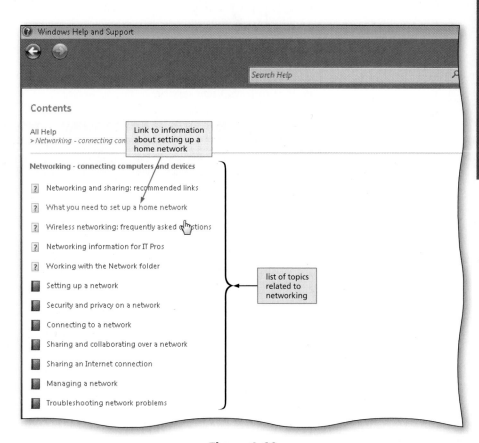

Figure 1–90

3

- Click the 'What you need to set up a home network' link (Figure 1–91).

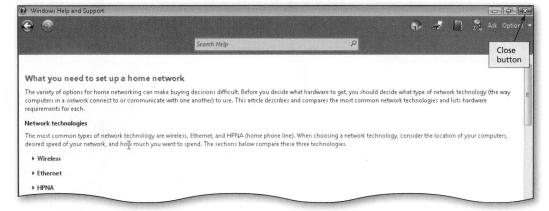

Figure 1–91

To Close Windows Help and Support

The following step shows how to close Windows Help and Support.

1 Click the Close button on the title bar of the Windows Help and Support window to close the Windows Help and Support window.

Logging Off and Turning Off the Computer

After completing your work with Windows Vista, you should close your user account by logging off the computer. In addition to logging off, there are several options available for ending your Windows Vista session. Table 1–5 illustrates the various options for ending your Windows Vista session.

Table 1–5 Options and Methods for Ending a Windows Vista Session	
Option	**Method**
Switch User	Click the Start button, point to the arrow next to the Lock button, and then click Switch User to keep your programs running in the background (but inaccessible until you log on again), which can allow another user to log on.
Log Off	Click the Start button, point to the arrow next to the Lock button, and then click Log Off to close all your programs but leave the computer running so that another user can log on.
Lock	Click the Start button, and then click the Lock button to deny anyone except those you have authorized access to log on to the computer.
Restart	Click the Start button, point to the arrow next to the Lock button, and then click Restart to shut down and then restart the computer.
Sleep	Click the Start button, click the Sleep button, wait for Windows to save your work, and then power down to a hibernating state.
Shut Down	Click the Start button, point to the arrow next to the Lock button, and then click Shut Down to close all your programs and turn off the computer.

To Log Off the Computer

Logging off the computer closes any open applications, allows you to save any unsaved documents, ends the Windows Vista session, and makes the computer available for other users. The following steps log off the computer.

- Open the Start menu (Figure 1–92).

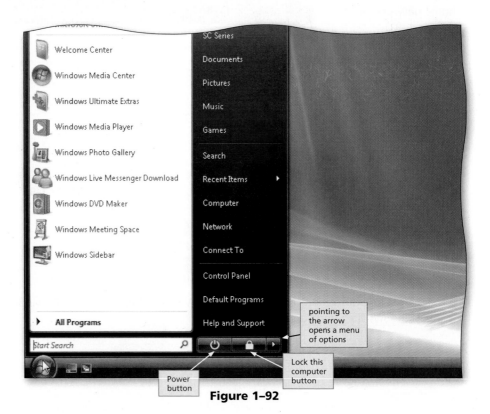

Figure 1–92

2

- Point to the arrow to the right of the 'Lock this computer' button to display a menu. (Figure 1–93).

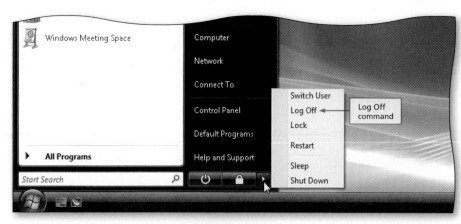

Figure 1–93

3

- Click the Log Off command, and then wait for Windows Vista to prompt you to save any unsaved and log off (Figure 1–94).

Q&A Why should I log off the computer?

It is important to log off the computer so you do not lose your work. Some users of Windows Vista have turned off their computers without following the log off procedure only to find data they thought they had stored on disk lost.

Figure 1–94

To Turn Off the Computer

After logging off, you also may want to shut down the computer using the Shut down button or the Shut down options arrow in the lower corner of the Welcome screen. Clicking the left button shuts down your computer, and clicking the right button displays a menu containing three commands (Restart, Sleep, and Shut Down) that can be used to restart the computer, put the computer into sleep mode, and shut down the computer). The following step turns off the computer. If you are not sure about turning off the computer, simply read the step.

- Click the Shut down button on the Welcome screen to shut down the computer.

Other Ways

1. Press ALT+F4, press the down arrow, select Shut Down, press OK

Chapter Summary

In this chapter you have learned about the Windows Vista graphical interface. You started Windows Vista, learned the components of the desktop and the six mouse operations. You opened, closed, moved, resized, minimized, maximized, and scrolled a window. You used Folder Windows to expand and collapse drives and folders, display drive and folder contents, create a folder, copy a file between folders, and rename and then delete a file. You used Internet Explorer to browse using a URL and tabs. You learned about the hierarchical format, removable media flash drives, and you used WordPad to type and save a document in a newly created folder. You searched for files using a word or phrase in the file or by name, you obtained help about using Windows Vista, and shut down Windows Vista.

1. Log On to the Computer (WIN 8)
2. Close the Welcome Center Window (WIN 10)
3. Add a Gadget to the Windows Sidebar (WIN 10)
4. Remove a Gadget from the Windows Sidebar (WIN 12)
5. Open the Start Menu (WIN 13)
6. Scroll Using Scroll Arrows, the Scroll Bar, and the Scroll Box (WIN 15)
7. Add an Icon to the Desktop (WIN 16)
8. Open a Window Using the Desktop Icon (WIN 18)
9. Minimize and Redisplay a Window (WIN 19)
10. Maximize and Restore a Window (WIN 20)
11. Close a Window (WIN 21, WIN 24)
12. Open a Window Using the Start Menu (WIN 21)
13. Move a Window by Dragging (WIN 22)
14. Expand the Folders List (WIN 23)
15. Size a Window by Dragging (WIN 23)
16. Collapse the Folders List (WIN 24)
17. Delete a Desktop Icon by Right-Dragging (WIN 25)
18. Start an Application Using the Start Menu (WIN 27)
19. Browse the Web by Entering a URL (WIN 30)
20. Open a Link in a New Tab (WIN 31)
21. Switch Between Tabs (WIN 33)
22. Close a Tab (WIN 33)
23. Work with Folders (WIN 34)
24. Plug a USB Flash Drive into a USB Port (WIN 38)
25. Create a Folder on a Removable Drive (WIN 39)
26. Download a Hierarchy of Folders (WIN 40)
27. Expand a Drive (WIN 42)
28. Collapse a Folder (WIN 43)
29. Display the Contents of a Folder (WIN 44)
30. Start WordPad Using the Start Search Box (WIN 45)
31. Type Text (WIN 47)
32. Save a WordPad Document in a New Folder (WIN 47)
33. Verify the Contents of a Folder (WIN 52)
34. Copy a File by Right-Dragging (WIN 52)
35. Display the Contents of a Folder (WIN 54)
36. Rename a File (WIN 55)
37. Delete a File by Right-Clicking (WIN 56)
38. Close Expanded Folders (WIN 57)
39. Start Windows Help and Support (WIN 58)

If you have a SAM user profile, you may have access to hands-on instruction, practice, and assessment. Log in to your SAM account (http://sam2007.course.com) to launch any assigned training activities or exams that relate to the skills covered in this chapter.

Learn It Online

Test your knowledge of chapter content and key terms.

Instructions: To complete the Learn It Online exercises, start your browser, click the Address bar, and then enter the Web address scsite.com/winvista2007/learn. When the Windows Learn It Online page is displayed, click the link for the exercise you want to complete and then read the instructions.

Chapter Reinforcement TF, MC, and SA
A series of true/false, multiple choice, and short answer questions that test your knowledge of the chapter content.

Flash Cards
An interactive learning environment where you identify chapter key terms associated with displayed definitions.

Practice Test
A series of multiple choice questions that test your knowledge of chapter content and key terms.

Who Wants To Be a Computer Genius?
An interactive game that challenges your knowledge of chapter content in the style of a television quiz show.

Wheel of Terms
An interactive game that challenges your knowledge of chapter key terms in the style of the television show *Wheel of Fortune.*

Crossword Puzzle Challenge
A crossword puzzle that challenges your knowledge of key terms presented in the chapter.

In the Lab

Using the guidelines, concepts, and skills presented in this chapter, complete the following Labs.

Lab 1: Windows Vista Demos

Instructions: Use a computer to perform the following tasks.

Part 1: Windows Vista Demos

1. If necessary, start Windows Vista and then log on to the computer.
2. Click the Start button and then click Help and Support on the Start menu.
3. If necessary, maximize the Windows Help and Support window.
4. Click What's new? in the 'Find an answer' area in the Windows Help and Support window.

Part 2: What's New in Windows Vista?

1. In the Searching and organizing area, click the 'Demo: Working with files and folders' link, and then click the 'Watch the demo' link. As you watch the demo, answer the questions below.

    a. The Start menu provides access to several folders. What are the three folders mentioned?

    _____

    b. How do you create a new folder?

    _____

    c. If you use a folder frequently, where should you put the folder?

    _____

2. Click the Back button below the Windows Help and Support title to return to the What's new in Windows Vista heading.

Part 3: What's New in Security?

1. In the Security area, click the green arrow to the left of the 'Click to open the Security Center' link. Answer the questions below.

    a. What are the four security essentials shown in the Windows Security Center.

    b. Close the Windows Security Center.

    c. In the Security area, click the 'Demo: Security basics' link and then click the Read the transcript' link.

    d. What's the quickest way to check your computer's security status and fix security problems.

    _____

    e. What does a firewall do?

    _____

    f. What does it mean when all the lights in the Security Center are green?

    _____

2. Click the Back button below the Windows Help and Support title to return to the 'What's new in Windows Vista Ultimate' page.

Part 4: What's New in Parental Controls?

1. Scroll down to view the Parental Controls area.

    a. In the Parental Controls area, click the 'What can I control with Parental Controls?' link.

    b. What can I do with Parental Controls?

    _____

    _____

    c. After setting up Parental Controls, how can a parent keep a record of a child's computer activity?

    _____

2. Click the Back button below the Windows Help and Support title to view the topics in the Windows and Help Support window.

Part 5: What's New in the Pictures Area?

1. Scroll down the Windows Help and Support window to view the Pictures area.

    a. In the Pictures area, click the 'Working with digital pictures' link.

    b. What are the two main ways to import pictures?

    _____

    _____

2. Click the Back button below the Windows Help and Support title to view the topics in the Windows Help and Support window.

Part 6: What's New in the Mobile PC Features Area?

1. If necessary, scroll to view the Mobile PC features area, click the Using Windows Mobility Center link. Answer the following question.

    a. How do you open the Mobility Center?

    _____

    _____

2. Click the Close button in the Windows Help and Support window.

In the Lab

Lab 2: Internet Explorer

Instructions: Use a computer to perform the following tasks.

1. Start Windows Vista and connect to the Internet.

2. Right-click the Start button on the taskbar, click Explore on the shortcut menu, and then maximize the Start Menu window.

3. If necessary, open the Folders list so the Start Menu and Programs icons are visible.

4. Click the Programs icon in the Start Menu folder.

5. Double-click the Internet Explorer shortcut icon in the Contents pane to start the Internet Explorer application. What is the URL of the Web page that appears in the Address bar in the Windows Internet Explorer window? _____

6. Click the URL in the Address bar in the Windows Internet Explorer window to select it. Type `scsite.com` and then press the ENTER key.

7. If necessary, scroll the Web page to display the Browse by Subject navigation bar containing the subject categories. Clicking a subject category displays the book titles in that category.

8. Click Operating Systems in the Browse by Subject navigation bar.

9. Click the Windows Vista link.

10. Right-click the first Windows Vista textbook cover image on the Web page, click Save Picture As on the shortcut menu, type `Windows Vista Cover` in the File name box, and then click the Save button in the Save Picture dialog box to save the image in the Pictures folder.

Continued >

In the Lab *continued*

11. Click the Close button in the Windows Internet Explorer window.

12. If necessary, scroll to the top of the Folders list to make the drive (C:) icon visible.

13. Click the black arrow to the left of the drive (C:) icon.

14. Click the Documents folder name in the Favorites Links list.

15. Click the Pictures folder name in the Folders list.

16. Right-click the Windows Vista Cover icon and then click Properties on the shortcut menu.

    a. What type of file is the Windows Vista Cover file? _____

    b. When was the file last modified? _____

    c. With what application does this file open? _____

17. Click the Cancel button in the Windows Vista Cover Properties dialog box.

18. If necessary, click the Close button in the Auto Play window.

19. Insert a USB flash drive into your computer.

19. Right-drag the Windows Vista Cover icon to the USB flash drive icon in the Folders list. Click Move Here on the shortcut menu. Click the USB flash drive icon in the Folders list.

    a. Is the Windows Vista Cover file stored on the USB flash drive? _____

20. Click the Close button in the USB flash drive window.

In the Lab

Lab 3: Getting Help

Instructions: Use a computer to perform the following tasks.

Part 1: Using Windows Basics to Get Help

1. If necessary, start Windows Vista and then log on to the computer.

2. Click the Start button and then click Help and Support on the Start menu.

3. If necessary, maximize the Windows Help and Support window.

4. Click Windows Basics icon in the 'Find an answer' area.

5. Click the 'Turning off your computer properly' link. Why are there two different looking Power buttons?

   _____

   _____

6. Click the Back button in the upper-left corner of the Windows Help and Support window.

Part 2: Using Desktop Fundamentals to Get Help

1. Look in the Desktop fundamentals area and identify the three parts of the desktop.

   _____

2. Click the 'Getting started with printing' link. List the three types of printers shown in the Getting started with printing area.

   _____

3. Click the Back button in the upper-left corner of the Windows Help and Support window.

4. If necessary, scroll to view the Getting help topic under the 'Help and support' heading. Click the Getting help link. List the eight ways to get help.

_____

_____

5. Click the Back button twice in the upper-left corner of the Windows Help and Support window.

Part 3: Using Table of Contents to Get Help

1. Click the Table of Contents icon in the 'Find an answer' area.

2. Click the 'E-mail, newsgroups, and other communications' link. List six communication options.

_____

_____

3. Click Newsgroups in the Contents list.

4. Click the 'What are newsgroups?' in the Contents list.

5. Describe what a newsgroup is.

_____

_____

6. Click the Back button four times in the upper-left corner of the Windows Help and Support window.

Part 4: Using Security and Maintenance to Get Help

1. Click the Security and Maintenance link in the 'Find an answer' area.

2. What does Windows Defender prevent?

_____

3. What's so important about Back up and Restore?

_____

_____

4. Click the Back button in the upper-left corner of the Windows Help and Support window.

Part 5: Using Troubleshooting to Get Help

1. Click the Troubleshooting icon in the 'Find an answer' area.

2. Click the Connect to the Internet link under the 'Using the web' heading.

3. Click the 'What do I need to connect to the Internet?' link.

4. What do you use to connect to the Internet?

_____

5. Click the Back button three times in the upper-left corner of the Windows Help and Support.

Part 6: Using Windows Online Help to Get Help

1. Click Windows the Online Help icon in the 'Find an answer' area to open Internet Explorer to the Windows Vista: Help and How-to window.

2. Click the 'Music and sounds' icon.

3. What can you do in the Music and sounds area in the Windows Help and How-to Web site?

_____

_____

4. Close the Windows Vista: Help Music window, and then close the Windows Help and Support window.

In the Lab

Lab 4: Downloading the Word 2007 Chapters 1–3 Data Files

Instructions: Use the SC Site—Shelly Cashman Series Student Resources Web site to download the Word 2007 Chapters 1–3 Data Files into the Word folder.

Part 1: Plug the USB Flash Drive into the USB Port

1. If necessary, launch Windows Vista and log on to the computer.

2. Plug the USB flash drive into the USB port on the computer. The UDISK 2.0 (E:) window should display on the desktop and should contain the Freshman folder.

3. If the Freshman folder does not display in the UDISK 2.0 (E:) window, follow the steps in Chapter One to create the hierarchy of folders shown in Figure 1–50 on page WIN 36.

Part 2: Download the Word 2007 Chapters 1-3 Data Files into the Word Folder

1. Start Internet Explorer by clicking the Start button on the taskbar and then clicking Internet on the Start menu.

2. Click the Address box on the Address bar, type `scsite.com` in the Address box, and then click the Go button.

3. When the SC Site — Shelly Cashman Series Student Resources Web site is displayed, use the Browse by Subject navigation bar, click Office Suites, and then click Microsoft Office 2007.

4. In the center of the screen, locate your textbook, and then click the title (for example, Microsoft Office 2007: Introductory Concepts and Techniques, Windows Vista Edition).

5. When the page for your textbook displays, click the Word Chapters 1–3 Data Files link (You may need to scroll down the page).

6. When the File Download – Security Warning dialog box is displayed, click the Run button.

7. When the Internet Explorer – Security Warning dialog box is displayed, click the Run button.

8. When the WinZip Self-Extractor dialog box displays, click the Browse button.

9. Click the plus sign to the left of the removable drive, click the plus sign to the left of the Freshman folder, click the plus sign to the left of the 1st Semester folder, click the plus sign to the left of the Computer Class folder, and then click the Word folder.

10. Click the OK button in the Browse for Folder dialog box.

11. Click the Unzip button in the WinZip Self-Extractor dialog box.

12. When a smaller WinZip Self-Extractor dialog box appears, click the OK button.

13. Click the Close button in the WinZip Self-Extractor dialog box.

14. Click the Close button in the SC Site — Shelly Cashman Series Student Resources Web site window.

15. Verify the Word 2007 Chapters 1–3 Data Files folder is contain in the Word folder.

16. Close the Word window. Unplug the USB flash drive from the USB port.

1 Creating and Editing a Word Document

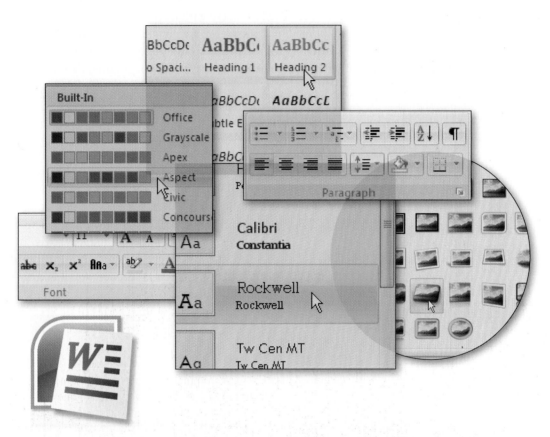

Objectives

You will have mastered the material in this chapter when you can:

- Start and quit Word
- Describe the Word window
- Enter text in a document
- Check spelling as you type
- Save a document
- Format text, paragraphs, and document elements
- Undo and redo commands or actions

- Insert a picture and format it
- Print a document
- Change document properties
- Open a document
- Correct errors in a document
- Use Word's Help

1 | Creating and Editing a Word Document

What Is Microsoft Office Word 2007?

Microsoft Office Word 2007 is a full-featured word processing program that allows you to create professional-looking documents and revise them easily. A document is a printed or electronic medium people use to communicate with others. With Word, you can develop many types of documents, including flyers, letters, memos, resumes, reports, fax cover sheets, mailing labels, and newsletters. Word also provides tools that enable you to create Web pages. From within Word, you can place these Web pages directly on a Web server.

Word has many features designed to simplify the production of documents and make documents look visually appealing. Using Word, you easily can change the shape, size, and color of text. You can include borders, shading, tables, images, pictures, charts, and Web addresses in documents.

While you are typing, Word performs many tasks automatically. For example, Word detects and corrects spelling and grammar errors in several languages. Word's thesaurus allows you to add variety and precision to your writing. Word also can format text, such as headings, lists, fractions, borders, and Web addresses, as you type.

This latest version of Word has many new features to make you more productive. For example, Word has many predefined text and graphical elements designed to assist you with preparing documents. Word also includes new charting and diagramming tools; uses themes so that you can coordinate colors, fonts, and graphics; and has a tool that enables you to convert a document to a PDF format.

To illustrate the features of Word, this book presents a series of projects that use Word to create documents similar to those you will encounter in academic and business environments.

Project Planning Guidelines

> The process of developing a document that communicates specific information requires careful analysis and planning. As a starting point, establish why the document is needed. Once the purpose is determined, analyze the intended readers of the document and their unique needs. Then, gather information about the topic and decide what to include in the document. Finally, determine the document design and style that will be most successful at delivering the message. Details of these guidelines are provided in Appendix A. In addition, each project in this book provides practical applications of these planning considerations.

Project — Document with a Picture

To advertise a sale, promote a business, publicize an event, or convey a message to the community, you may want to create a flyer and post it in a public location. Libraries, schools, churches, grocery stores, and other places often provide bulletin boards or windows for flyers. These flyers announce personal items for sale or rent (car, boat, apartment); garage or block sales; services being offered (animal care, housecleaning, lessons); membership, sponsorship, or donation requests (club, church, charity); and other messages. Flyers are an inexpensive means of reaching the community, yet many go unnoticed because they are designed poorly.

The project in this chapter follows general guidelines and uses Word to create the flyer shown in Figure 1–1. This colorful, eye-catching flyer advertises horseback riding lessons at Tri-Valley Stables. The picture of the horse and rider entices passersby to stop and look at the flyer. The headline on the flyer is large and colorful to draw attention into the text. The body copy below the headline briefly describes key points of the riding lessons, and the bulleted list below the picture concisely highlights important additional information. The signature line of the flyer calls attention to the stable name and telephone number. Finally, the graphical page border nicely frames and complements the contents of the flyer.

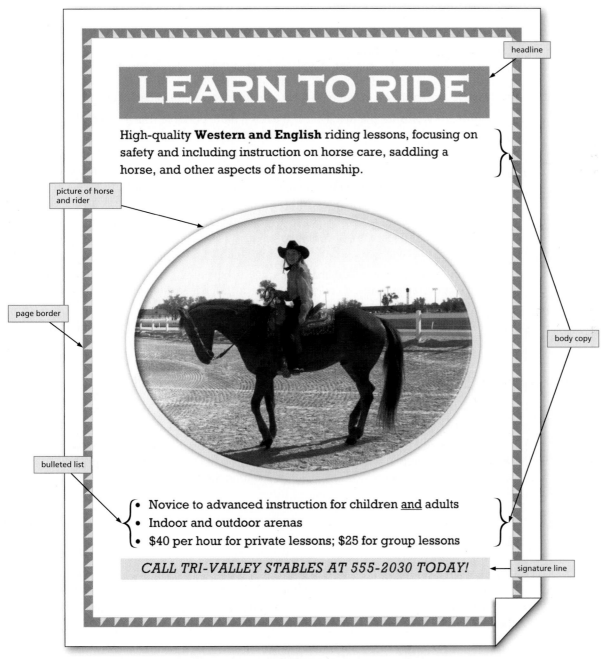

Figure 1–1

Overview

As you read this chapter, you will learn how to create the flyer shown in Figure 1–1 on the previous page by performing these general tasks:

- Enter text in the document.
- Save the document.
- Format the text in the document.
- Insert a picture in the document.
- Format the picture.
- Add a border to the page.
- Print the document.

Plan Ahead

> **General Project Guidelines**
>
> When creating a Word document, the actions you perform and decisions you make will affect the appearance and characteristics of the finished document. As you create a flyer, such as the project shown in Figure 1–1, you should follow these general guidelines:
>
> 1. **Choose the words for the text.** Follow the *less is more* principle. The less text, the more likely the flyer will be read. Use as few words as possible to make a point.
>
> 2. **Determine where to save the flyer.** You can store a document permanently, or **save** it, on a variety of storage media including a hard disk, USB flash drive, or CD. You also can indicate a specific location on the storage media for saving the document.
>
> 3. **Identify how to format various elements of the text.** The overall appearance of a document significantly affects its ability to communicate clearly. Examples of how you can modify the appearance, or **format**, of text include changing its shape, size, color, and position on the page.
>
> 4. **Find the appropriate graphical image.** An eye-catching graphical image should convey the flyer's overall message. It could show a product, service, result, or benefit, or visually convey a message that is not expressed easily with words.
>
> 5. **Establish where to position and how to format the graphical image.** The position and format of the graphical image should grab the attention of passersby and draw them into reading the flyer.
>
> 6. **Determine whether the flyer needs a page border, and if so, its style and format.** A graphical, color-coordinated page border can further draw attention to a flyer and nicely frame its contents. Be careful, however, that a page border does not make the flyer look too cluttered.
>
> When necessary, more specific details concerning the above guidelines are presented at appropriate points in the chapter. The chapter also will identify the actions performed and decisions made regarding these guidelines during the creation of the flyer shown in Figure 1–1.

Starting Word

BTW

The Word Window
The screen in Figure 1-3 shows how the Word window looks the first time you start Word after installation on most computers. Your screen may look different depending on your screen resolution and Word settings.

If you are using a computer to step through the project in this chapter and you want your screen to match the figures in this book, you should change your screen's resolution to 1024 × 768. For information about how to change a computer's resolution, read Appendix E.

Note: If you are using Windows XP, see Appendix F for alternate steps.

To Start Word

The following steps, which assume Windows Vista is running, start Word based on a typical installation. You may need to ask your instructor how to start Word for your computer.

1

- Click the Start button on the Windows Vista taskbar to display the Start menu.

- Click All Programs at the bottom of the left pane on the Start menu to display the All Programs list.

- Click Microsoft Office in the All Programs list to display the Microsoft Office list (Figure 1–2).

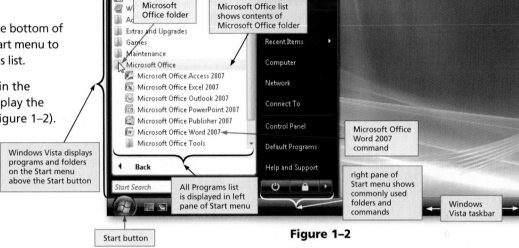

Figure 1–2

2

- Click Microsoft Office Word 2007 to start Word and display a new blank document in the Word window (Figure 1–3).

- If the Word window is not maximized, click the Maximize button next to the Close button on its title bar to maximize the window.

Q&A

What is a maximized window?

A maximized window fills the entire screen. When you maximize a window, the Maximize button changes to a Restore Down button.

3

- If the Print Layout button is not selected, click it so that your screen layout matches Figure 1–3.

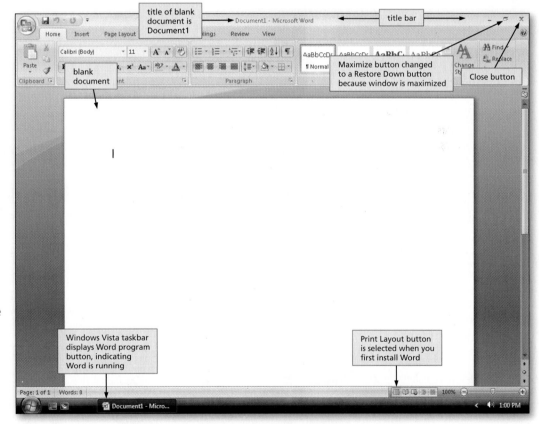

Figure 1–3

Other Ways

1. Double-click Word icon on desktop, if one is present
2. Click Microsoft Office Word 2007 on Start menu

The Word Window

The Word window consists of a variety of components to make your work more efficient and documents more professional. These include the document window, Ribbon, Mini toolbar and shortcut menus, Quick Access Toolbar, and Office Button. Some of these components are common to other Microsoft Office 2007 programs; others are unique to Word.

Document Window

You view a portion of a document on the screen through a **document window** (Figure 1–4). The default (preset) view is **Print Layout view**, which shows the document on a mock sheet of paper in the document window.

The Word document window in Figure 1–4 contains an insertion point, mouse pointer, scroll bar, and status bar. Other elements that may appear in the document window are discussed later in this and subsequent chapters.

Insertion Point The **insertion point** is a blinking vertical bar that indicates where text, graphics, and other items will be inserted. As you type, the insertion point moves to the right, and when you reach the end of a line, it moves downward to the beginning of the next line.

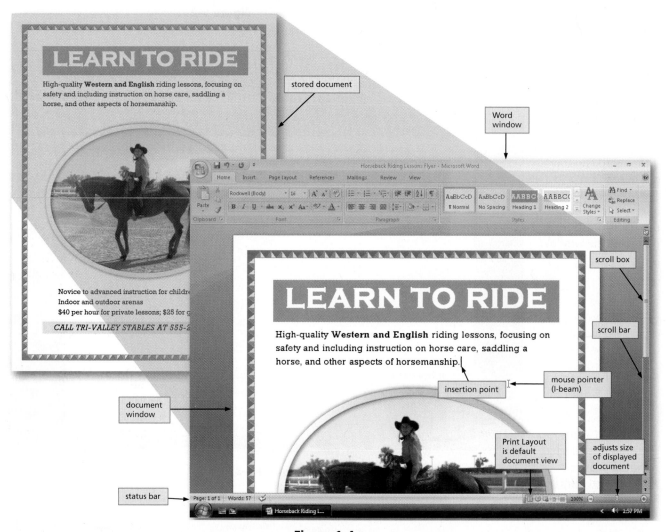

Figure 1–4

Mouse Pointer   The **mouse pointer** becomes different shapes depending on the task you are performing in Word and the pointer's location on the screen. The mouse pointer in Figure 1–4 is the shape of an I-beam.

Scroll Bar   You use a **scroll bar** to display different portions of a document in the document window. At the right edge of the document window is a vertical scroll bar. If a document is too wide to fit in the document window, a horizontal scroll bar also appears at the bottom of the document window. On a scroll bar, the position of the **scroll box** reflects the location of the portion of the document that is displayed in the document window. A **scroll arrow** is located at each end of a scroll bar. To scroll through, or display different portions of the document in the document window, you can click a scroll arrow or drag the scroll box.

Status Bar   The **status bar**, located at the bottom of the document window above the Windows Vista taskbar, presents information about the document, the progress of current tasks, and the status of certain commands and keys; it also provides controls for viewing the document. As you type text or perform certain commands, various indicators and buttons may appear on the status bar.

The left edge of the status bar in Figure 1–4 shows the current page followed by the total number of pages in the document, the number of words in the document, and a button to check spelling and grammar. Toward the right edge are buttons and controls you can use to change the view of a document and adjust the size of the displayed document.

Ribbon

The **Ribbon**, located near the top of the Word window, is the control center in Word (Figure 1–5a). The Ribbon provides easy, central access to the tasks you perform while creating a document. The Ribbon consists of tabs, groups, and commands. Each **tab** surrounds a collection of groups, and each group contains related commands.

When you start Word, the Ribbon displays seven top-level tabs: Home, Insert, Page Layout, References, Mailings, Review, and View. The **Home tab**, called the primary tab, contains the more frequently used commands. To display a different tab on the Ribbon, click the top-level tab. That is, to display the Insert tab, click Insert on the Ribbon. To return to the Home tab, click Home on the Ribbon. The tab currently displayed is called the **active tab**.

To display more of the document in the document window, some users prefer to minimize the Ribbon, which hides the groups on the Ribbon and displays only the top-level tabs (Figure 1–5b). To use commands on a minimized Ribbon, click the top-level tab.

BTW

Minimizing the Ribbon
If you want to minimize the Ribbon, right-click the Ribbon and then click Minimize the Ribbon on the shortcut menu, double-click the active tab, or press CTRL+F1. To restore a minimized Ribbon, right-click the Ribbon and then click Minimize the Ribbon on the shortcut menu, double-click any top-level tab, or press CTRL+F1. To use commands on a minimized Ribbon, click the top-level tab.

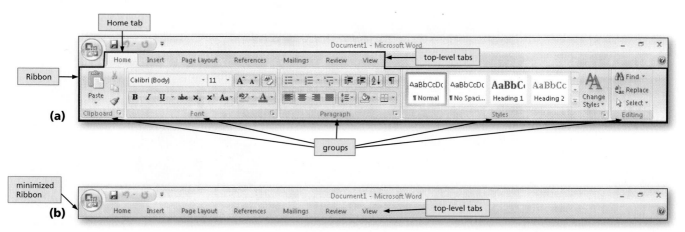

Figure 1–5

Each time you start Word, the Ribbon appears the same way it did the last time you used Word. The chapters in this book, however, begin with the Ribbon appearing as it did at the initial installation of the software. If you are stepping through this chapter on a computer and you want your Ribbon to match the figures in this book, read Appendix E.

In addition to the top-level tabs, Word displays other tabs, called **contextual tabs**, when you perform certain tasks or work with objects such as pictures or tables. If you insert a picture in the document, for example, the Picture Tools tab and its related subordinate Format tab appear (Figure 1–6). When you are finished working with the picture, the Picture Tools and Format tabs disappear from the Ribbon. Word determines when contextual tabs should appear and disappear based on tasks you perform. Some contextual tabs, such as the Table Tools tab, have more than one related subordinate tab.

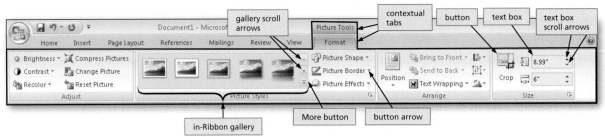

Figure 1–6

Commands on the Ribbon include buttons, boxes (text boxes, check boxes, etc.), and galleries (Figure 1–6). A **gallery** is a set of choices, often graphical, arranged in a grid or in a list. You can scroll through choices on an in-Ribbon gallery by clicking the gallery's scroll arrows. Or, you can click a gallery's More button to view more gallery options on the screen at a time. Some buttons and boxes have arrows that, when clicked, also display a gallery; others always cause a gallery to be displayed when clicked. Most galleries support **live preview**, which is a feature that allows you to point to a gallery choice and see its effect in the document — without actually selecting the choice (Figure 1–7).

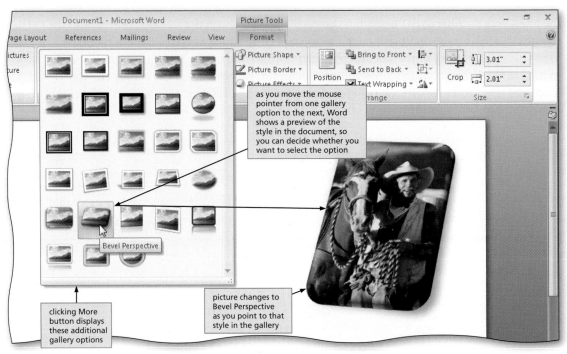

Figure 1–7

Some commands on the Ribbon display an image to help you remember their function. When you point to a command on the Ribbon, all or part of the command glows in shades of yellow and orange, and an Enhanced ScreenTip appears on the screen. An **Enhanced ScreenTip** is an on-screen note that provides the name of the command, available keyboard shortcut(s), a description of the command, and sometimes instructions for how to obtain help about the command (Figure 1–8). Enhanced ScreenTips are more detailed than a typical ScreenTip, which usually only displays the name of the command.

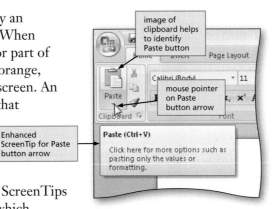

Figure 1–8

The lower-right corner of some groups on the Ribbon has a small arrow, called a **Dialog Box Launcher**, that when clicked, displays a dialog box or a task pane with additional options for the group (Figure 1–9). When presented with a dialog box, you make selections and must close the dialog box before returning to the document. A **task pane**, by contrast, is a window that can remain open and visible while you work in the document.

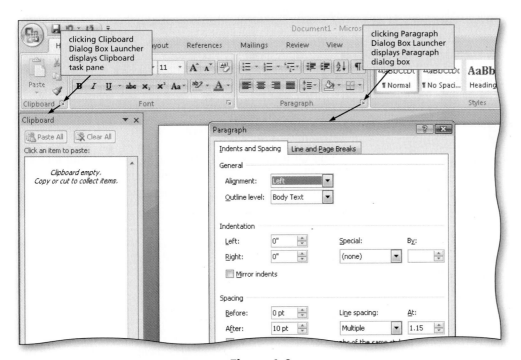

Figure 1–9

Mini Toolbar and Shortcut Menus

The **Mini toolbar**, which appears automatically based on tasks you perform, contains commands related to changing the appearance of text in a document. All commands on the Mini toolbar also exist on the Ribbon. The purpose of the Mini toolbar is to minimize mouse movement. For example, if you want to use a command that currently is not displayed on the active tab, you can use the command on the Mini toolbar — instead of switching to a different tab to use the command.

When the Mini toolbar appears, it initially is transparent (Figure 1–10a). If you do not use the transparent Mini toolbar, it disappears from the screen. To use the Mini toolbar, move the mouse pointer into the toolbar, which causes the Mini toolbar to change from a transparent to bright appearance (Figure 1–10b).

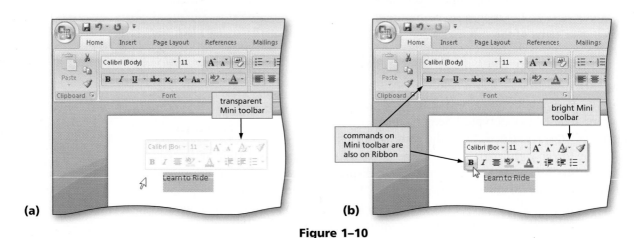

Figure 1–10

A **shortcut menu**, which appears when you right-click an object, is a list of frequently used commands that relate to the right-clicked object. When you right-click a scroll bar, for example, a shortcut menu appears with commands related to the scroll bar. If you right-click an item in the document window, Word displays both the Mini toolbar and a shortcut menu (Figure 1–11).

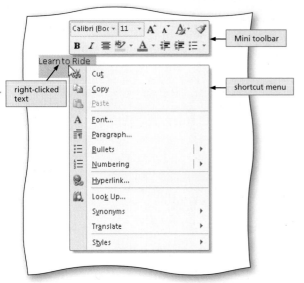

Figure 1–11

Quick Access Toolbar

The **Quick Access Toolbar**, located by default above the Ribbon, provides easy access to frequently used commands (Figure 1–12a). The commands on the Quick Access Toolbar always are available, regardless of the task you are performing. Initially, the Quick Access Toolbar contains the Save, Undo, and Redo commands. If you click the Customize Quick Access Toolbar button, Word provides a list of commands you quickly can add to and remove from the Quick Access Toolbar (Figure 1–12b).

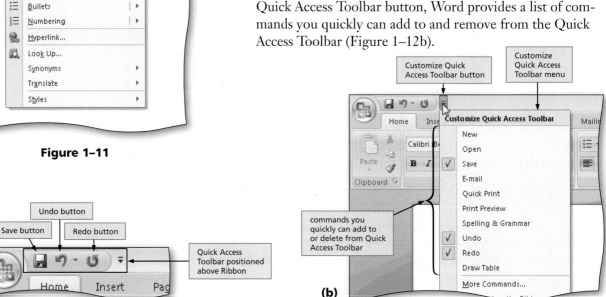

Figure 1–12

You also can add other commands to or delete commands from the Quick Access Toolbar so that it contains the commands you use most often. As you add commands to the Quick Access Toolbar, its commands may interfere with the document title on the title bar. For this reason, Word provides an option of displaying the Quick Access Toolbar below the Ribbon (Figure 1–13).

Figure 1–13

Each time you start Word, the Quick Access Toolbar appears the same way it did the last time you used Word. The chapters in this book, however, begin with the Quick Access Toolbar appearing as it did at the initial installation of the software. If you are stepping through this chapter on a computer and you want your Quick Access Toolbar to match the figures in this book, you should reset your Quick Access Toolbar. For more information about how to reset the Quick Access Toolbar, read Appendix E.

BTW

Quick Access Toolbar Commands
To add a Ribbon command to the Quick Access Toolbar, right-click the command on the Ribbon and then click Add to Quick Access Toolbar on the shortcut menu. To delete a command from the Quick Access Toolbar, right-click the command on the Quick Access Toolbar and then click Remove from Quick Access Toolbar on the shortcut menu. To display the Quick Access Toolbar below the Ribbon, right-click the Quick Access Toolbar and then click Show Quick Access Toolbar Below the Ribbon on the shortcut menu.

Office Button

While the Ribbon is a control center for creating documents, the **Office Button** is a central location for managing and sharing documents. When you click the Office Button, located in the upper-left corner of the window, Word displays the Office Button menu (Figure 1–14a). A **menu** contains a list of commands.

When you click the New, Open, Save As, and Print commands on the Office Button menu, Word displays a dialog box with additional options. The Save As, Print, Prepare, Send, and Publish commands have an arrow to their right. If you point to this arrow, Word displays a **submenu**, which is a list of additional commands associated with the selected command (Figure 1–14b). For the Prepare, Send, and Publish commands that do not display a dialog box when clicked, you can point either to the command or the arrow to display the submenu.

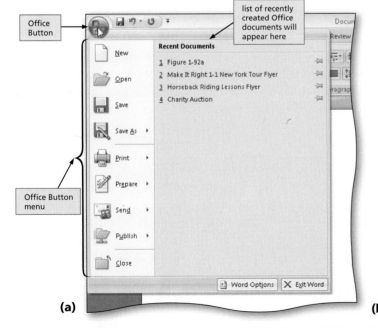

(a)

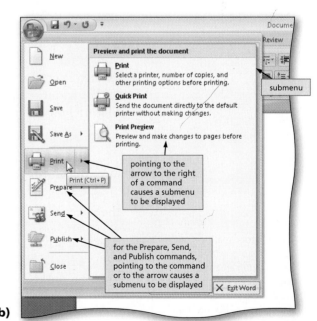

(b)

Figure 1–14

Key Tips

If you prefer using the keyboard instead of the mouse, you can press the ALT key on the keyboard to display a **Key Tip badge**, or keyboard code icon, for certain commands (Figure 1–15). To select a command using the keyboard, press its displayed code letter, or **Key Tip**. When you press a Key Tip, additional Key Tips related to the selected command may appear. For example, to select the New command on the Office Button menu, press the ALT key, then press the F key, and then press the N key.

To remove the Key Tip badges from the screen, press the ALT key or the ESC key until all Key Tip badges disappear, or click the mouse anywhere in the Word window.

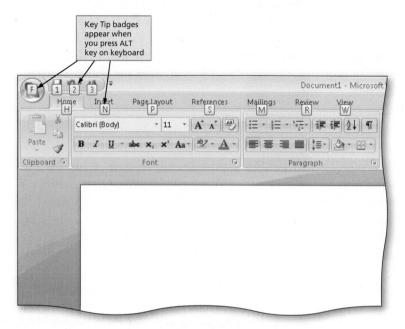

Figure 1–15

Entering Text

The first step in creating a document is to enter its text by typing on the keyboard. By default, Word positions text you type at the left margin. In a later section of this chapter, you will learn how to format, or change the appearance of, the entered text.

Plan Ahead

Choose the words for the text.
The text in a flyer is organized into three areas: headline, body copy, and signature line.

- The headline is the first line of text on the flyer. It conveys the product or service being offered, such as a car for sale or personal lessons, or the benefit that will be gained, such as a convenience, better performance, greater security, higher earnings, or more comfort.

- The body text consists of all text between the headline and the signature line. This text highlights the key points of the message in as few words as possible. It should be easy to read and follow. While emphasizing the positive, the body text must be realistic, truthful, and believable.

- The signature line, which is the last line of text on the flyer, contains contact information or identifies a call to action.

To Type Text

To begin creating the flyer in this chapter, you type the headline in the document window. The following steps type this first line of text in the document.

- Type Learn to Ride as the headline (Figure 1–16).

What if I make an error while typing?

You can press the **BACKSPACE** key until you have deleted the text in error and then retype the text correctly.

Why did the Spelling and Grammar Check icon appear on the status bar?

When you begin typing text, the **Spelling and Grammar Check icon** appears on the status bar with an animated pencil writing on paper that indicates Word is checking for spelling and grammar errors. When you stop typing, the pencil changes to a blue check mark (no errors) or a red X (potential errors found). Word flags potential errors in the document with a red or green wavy underline. Later, this chapter shows how to fix flagged errors.

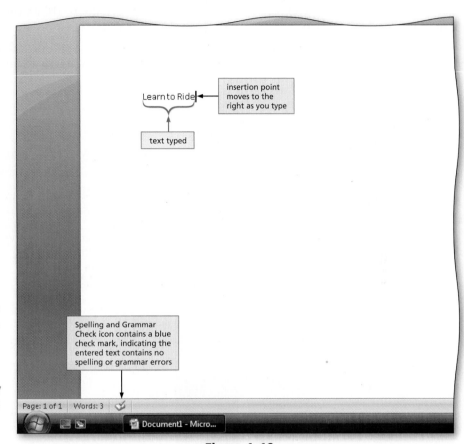

Figure 1–16

- Press the ENTER key to move the insertion point to the beginning of the next line (Figure 1–17).

Why did blank space appear between the headline and the insertion point?

Each time you press the ENTER key, Word creates a new paragraph and inserts blank space between the two paragraphs. Later in this chapter, you will learn how to adjust the spacing between paragraphs.

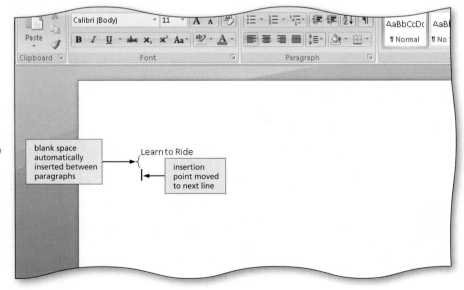

Figure 1–17

To Display Formatting Marks

To indicate where in a document you press the ENTER key or SPACEBAR, you may find it helpful to display formatting marks. A **formatting mark**, sometimes called a **nonprinting character**, is a character that Word displays on the screen but is not visible on a printed document. For example, the paragraph mark (¶) is a formatting mark that indicates where you pressed the ENTER key. A raised dot (·) shows where you pressed the SPACEBAR. Other formatting marks are discussed as they appear on the screen.

Depending on settings made during previous Word sessions, your Word screen already may display formatting marks (Figure 1–18). The following step displays formatting marks, if they do not show already on the screen.

1

- If necessary, click Home on the Ribbon to display the Home tab.

- If it is not selected already, click the Show/Hide ¶ button on the Home tab to display formatting marks on the screen (Figure 1–18).

Q&A

What if I do not want formatting marks to show on the screen?

If you feel the formatting marks clutter the screen, you can hide them by clicking the Show/Hide ¶ button again. It is recommended that you display formatting marks so that you visually can identify when you press the ENTER key, SPACEBAR, and other keys associated with nonprinting characters; therefore, the document windows presented in this book show the formatting marks.

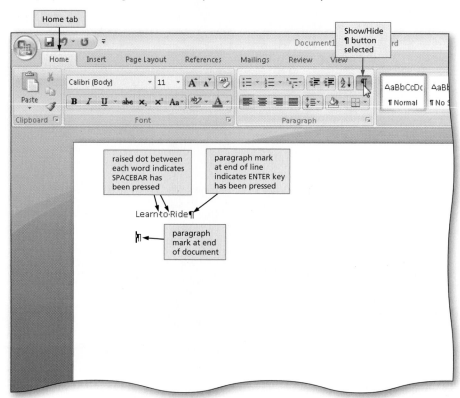

Figure 1–18

Other Ways

1. Press CTRL+SHIFT+*

BTW

Strange Formatting Marks
With some fonts, the formatting marks are not displayed on the screen properly. For example, the raised dot in each space may be displayed behind a character instead of in the space between two characters, causing the characters to look incorrect.

Wordwrap

Wordwrap allows you to type words in a paragraph continually without pressing the ENTER key at the end of each line. When the insertion point reaches the right margin, Word automatically positions the insertion point at the beginning of the next line. As you type, if a word extends beyond the right margin, Word also automatically positions that word on the next line along with the insertion point.

Word creates a new paragraph each time you press the ENTER key. Thus, as you type text in the document window, do not press the ENTER key when the insertion point reaches the right margin. Instead, press the ENTER key only in these circumstances:

1. To insert blank lines in a document

2. To begin a new paragraph

3. To terminate a short line of text and advance to the next line

4. To respond to questions or prompts in Word dialog boxes, task panes, and other on-screen objects

To Wordwrap Text as You Type

The next step in creating the flyer is to type the body copy. The following step wordwraps the text in the body copy.

- **Type** High-quality Western and English riding lessons, focusing on safety and including instruction on horse care, saddling a horse, and other aspects of horsemanship.

Why does my document wrap on different words?

Differences in wordwrap relate to the printer used by your computer. That is, the printer controls where wordwrap occurs for each line in your document. Thus, it is possible that the same document could wordwrap differently if printed on different printers.

- Press the ENTER key to position the insertion point on the next line in the document (Figure 1–19).

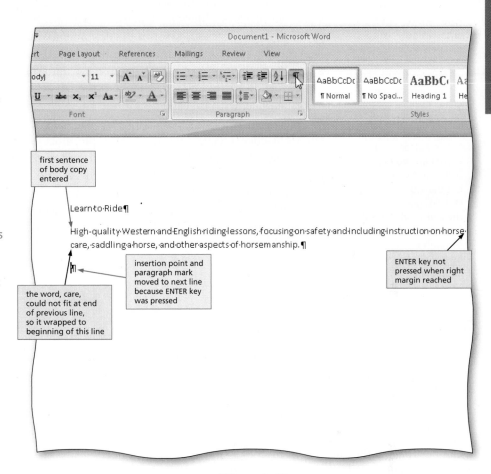

Figure 1–19

To Insert a Blank Line

In the flyer, the picture of the horse and rider should be positioned below the paragraph just entered. The picture will be inserted after all text is entered and formatted. Thus, you will leave a blank line in the document for the picture. To enter a blank line in a document, press the ENTER key without typing any text on the line. The following step inserts one blank line below the first paragraph of body copy.

- Press the ENTER key to insert a blank line in the document (Figure 1–20).

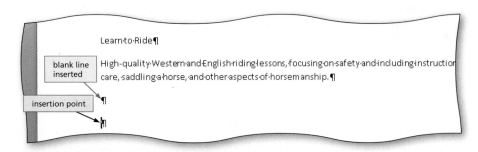

Figure 1–20

BTW

Automatic Spelling Correction

As you type, Word automatically corrects some misspelled words. For example, if you type recieve, Word automatically fixes the misspelling and displays the word, receive, when you press the SPACEBAR or type a punctuation mark. To see a complete list of automatically corrected words, click Office Button, click the Word Options button, click Proofing in the left pane of the Word Options dialog box, click the AutoCorrect Options button, and then scroll through the list of words near the bottom of the dialog box.

Spelling and Grammar Check

As you type text in a document, Word checks your typing for possible spelling and grammar errors. If all of the words you have typed are in Word's dictionary and your grammar is correct, as mentioned earlier, the Spelling and Grammar Check icon on the status bar displays a blue check mark. Otherwise, the icon shows a red X. In this case, Word flags the potential error in the document window with a red or green wavy underline. A red wavy underline means the flagged text is not in Word's dictionary (because it is a proper name or misspelled). A green wavy underline indicates the text may be incorrect grammatically. Although you can check the entire document for spelling and grammar errors at once, you also can check these flagged errors as they appear on the screen.

To display a list of corrections for flagged text, right-click the flagged text. When you right-click a flagged word, for example, a list of suggested spelling corrections appears on the screen. A flagged word, however, is not necessarily misspelled. For example, many names, abbreviations, and specialized terms are not in Word's main dictionary. In these cases, you tell Word to ignore the flagged word. As you type, Word also detects duplicate words while checking for spelling errors. For example, if your document contains the phrase, to the the store, Word places a red wavy underline below the second occurrence of the word, the.

To Check Spelling and Grammar as You Type

In the following steps, the word, instruction, has been misspelled intentionally as intrution to illustrate Word's check spelling as you type feature. If you are doing this project on a computer, your flyer may contain other misspelled words, depending on the accuracy of your typing.

1

- **Type** Novice to advanced intrution **and then press the** SPACEBAR (Figure 1–21).

Q&A What if Word does not flag my spelling and grammar errors with wavy underlines?

To verify that the check spelling and grammar as you type features are enabled, click the Office Button and then click the Word Options button. When the Word Options dialog box is displayed, click Proofing, and then ensure the 'Check spelling as you type' and 'Mark grammar errors as you type' check boxes have check marks. Also ensure the 'Hide spelling errors in this document only' and 'Hide grammar errors in this document only' check boxes do not have check marks. Click the OK button.

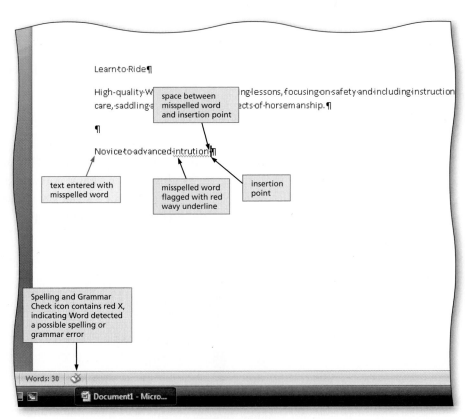

Figure 1–21

2

- Right-click the flagged word (intrution, in this case) to display a shortcut menu that includes a list of suggested spelling corrections for the flagged word (Figure 1–22).

Q&A

What if, when I right-click the misspelled word, my desired correction is not in the list on the shortcut menu?

You can click outside the shortcut menu to close the menu and then retype the correct word, or you can click Spelling on the shortcut menu to display the Spelling dialog box. Chapter 2 discusses the Spelling dialog box.

Q&A

What if a flagged word actually is, for example, a proper name and spelled correctly?

Right-click it and then click Ignore All on the shortcut menu to instruct Word not to flag future occurrences of the same word.

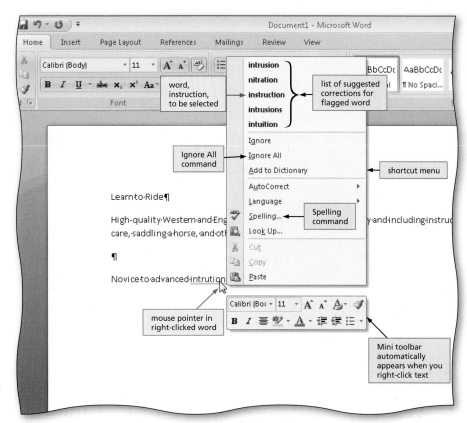

Figure 1–22

3

- Click instruction on the shortcut menu to replace the misspelled word in the document (intrution) with the word, instruction (Figure 1–23).

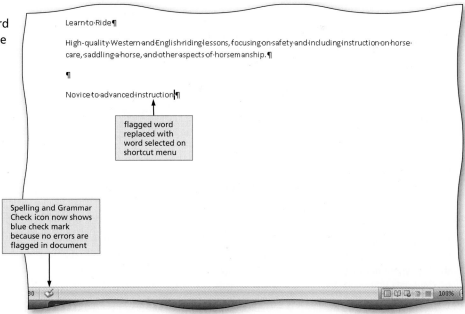

Figure 1–23

<table>
<tr><th colspan="1">Other Ways</th></tr>
<tr><td>1. Click Spelling and Grammar Check icon on status bar, click correct word on shortcut menu</td></tr>
</table>

To Enter More Text

In the flyer, the text yet to be entered includes the remainder of the body copy, which will be formatted as a bulleted list, and the signature line. The following steps enter the remainder of text in the flyer.

1 Press the END key to move the insertion point to the end of the current line.

2 Type `for children and adults` and then press the ENTER key.

3 Type `Indoor and outdoor arenas` and then press the ENTER key.

4 Type `$40 per hour for private lessons; $25 for group lessons` and then press the ENTER key.

5 To complete the text in the flyer, type `Call Tri-Valley Stables at 555-2030 today!` (Figure 1–24).

Learn·to·Ride¶

High-quality·Western·and·English·riding·lessons,·focusing·on·safety·and·including·instruction·on·horse-care,·saddling·a·horse,·and·other·aspects·of·horsemanship.¶

¶

Novice·to·advanced·instruction·for·children·and·adults¶

Indoor·and·outdoor·arenas¶

$40·per·hour·for·private·lessons;·$25·for·group·lessons¶

Call·Tri-Valley·Stables·at·555-2030·today!¶

three paragraphs of body copy that will be formatted as a bulleted list entered

signature line entered

Figure 1–24

BTW

Character Widths
Many word processing documents use variable character fonts, where some characters are wider than others; for example, the letter w takes up more space than the letter i.

Saving the Project

While you are creating a document, the computer stores it in memory. When you save a document, the computer places it on a storage medium such as a USB flash drive, CD, or hard disk. A saved document is referred to as a **file**. A **file name** is the name assigned to a file when it is saved.

It is important to save a document frequently for the following reasons:

- The document in memory will be lost if the computer is turned off or you lose electrical power while Word is open.
- If you run out of time before completing your project, you may finish your document at a future time without starting over.

BTW

File Type
Depending on your Windows Vista settings, the file type .docx may be displayed immediately to the right of the file name after you save the file. The file type .docx is a Word 2007 document. Previous versions of Word had a file type of .doc.

**Plan
Ahead**

Determine where to save the document.
When saving a document, you must decide which storage medium to use.

- If you always work on the same computer and have no need to transport your projects to a different location, then your computer's hard disk will suffice as a storage location. It is a good idea, however, to save a backup copy of your projects on a separate medium in case the file becomes corrupted or the computer's hard disk fails.

- If you plan to work on your projects in various locations or on multiple computers, then you should save your projects on a portable medium, such as a USB flash drive or CD. The projects in this book use a USB flash drive, which saves files quickly and reliably and can be reused. CDs are easily portable and serve as good backups for the final versions of projects because they generally can save files only one time.

To Save a Document

You have performed many tasks while creating this project and do not want to risk losing the work completed thus far. Accordingly, you should save the document. The following steps save a document on a USB flash drive using the file name, Horseback Riding Lessons Flyer.

Note: If you are using Windows XP, see Appendix F for alternate steps.

- With a USB flash drive connected to one of the computer's USB ports, click the Save button on the Quick Access Toolbar to display the Save As dialog box (Figure 1–25).

- If the Navigation pane is not displayed in the Save As dialog box, click the Browse Folders button to expand the dialog box.

- If a Folders list is displayed below the Folders button, click the Folders button to remove the Folders list.

Q&A

Do I have to save to a USB flash drive?

No. You can save to any device or folder. A **folder** is a specific location on a storage medium. You can save to the default folder or a different folder. You also can create your own folders, which is explained later in this book.

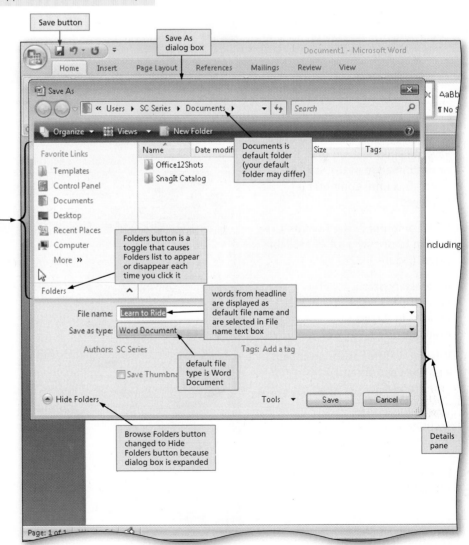

Figure 1–25

2

- **Type** Horseback Riding Lessons Flyer in the File name text box to change the file name. Do not press the ENTER key after typing the file name (Figure 1–26).

Q&A What characters can I use in a file name?

A file name can have a maximum of 260 characters, including spaces. The only invalid characters are the backslash (\), slash (/), colon (:), asterisk (*), question mark (?), quotation mark ("), less than symbol (<), greater than symbol (>), and vertical bar (|).

Q&A What are file properties and tags?

File properties contain information about a file such as the file name, author name, date the file was modified, and tags. A tag is a file property that contains a word or phrase about a file. You can organize and locate files based on their file properties.

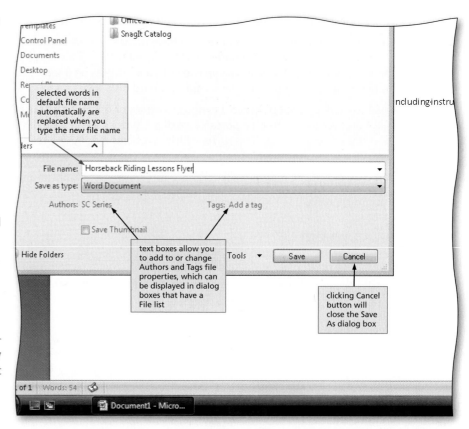

Figure 1–26

3

- If Computer is not displayed in the Favorite Links section, drag the top or bottom edge of the Save As dialog box until Computer is displayed.

- Click Computer in the Favorite Links section to display a list of available drives (Figure 1–27).

- If necessary, scroll until UDISK 2.0 (E:) appears in the list of available drives.

Q&A Why is my list of drives arranged and named differently?

The size of the Save As dialog box and your computer's configuration determine how the list is displayed and how the drives are named.

Q&A How do I save the file if I am not using a USB flash drive?

Use the same process, but select your desired save location in the Favorite Links section.

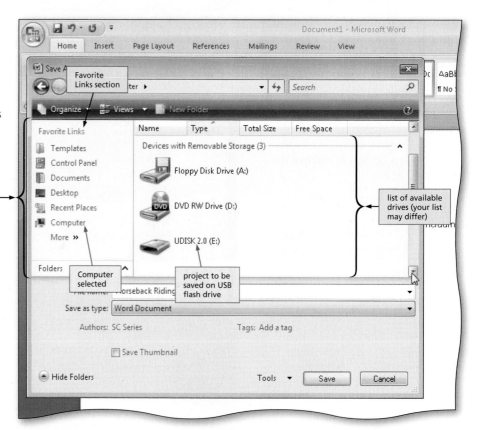

Figure 1–27

4

- Double-click UDISK 2.0
  (E:) in the Computer
  list to select the USB
  flash drive, Drive E
  in this case, as the
  new save location
  (Figure 1–28).

 Q&A

What if my USB flash
drive has a different
name or letter?

It is very likely that
your USB flash drive
will have a different
name and drive letter
and be connected to
a different port.
Verify the device in
your Computer list is
correct.

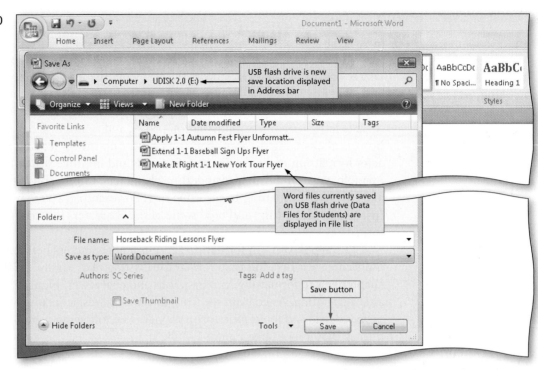

Figure 1–28

5

- Click the Save
  button in the Save As
  dialog box to save the
  document on the USB
  flash drive with the
  file name, Horseback
  Riding Lessons Flyer
  (Figure 1–29).

Q&A

How do I know
that the project
is saved?

While Word is saving
your file, it briefly
displays a message on
the status bar indicat-
ing the amount of the
file saved. In addi-
tion, your USB drive
may have a light that
flashes during the
save process.

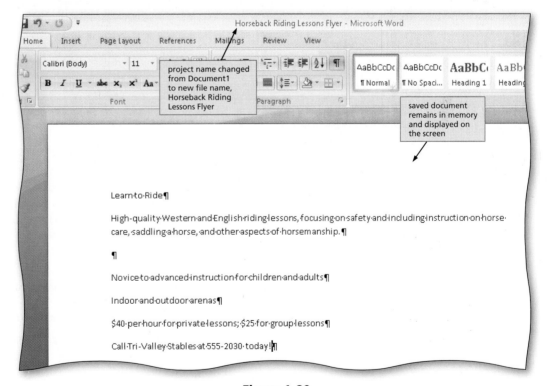

Figure 1–29

Other Ways
1. Click Office Button, click Save, type file name, click Computer, select drive or folder, click Save button   2. Press CTRL+S or press SHIFT+F12, type file name, click Computer, select drive or folder, click Save button

Formatting Paragraphs and Characters in a Document

With the text for the flyer entered, the next step is to format its paragraphs and characters. Paragraphs encompass the text from the first character in a paragraph up to and including a paragraph mark (¶). **Paragraph formatting** is the process of changing the appearance of a paragraph. For example, you can center or indent a paragraph. Characters include letters, numbers, punctuation marks, and symbols. **Character formatting** is the process of changing the way characters appear on the screen and in print. You use character formatting to emphasize certain words and improve readability of a document. For example, you can italicize or underline characters. Often, you apply both paragraph and character formatting to the same text. For example, you may center a paragraph (paragraph formatting) and bold some of the characters in a paragraph (character formatting).

Although you can format paragraphs and characters before you type, many Word users enter text first and then format the existing text. Figure 1–30a shows the flyer in this chapter before formatting its paragraphs and characters. Figure 1–30b shows the flyer after formatting. As you can see from the two figures, a document that is formatted is easier to read and looks more professional. The following pages discuss how to format the flyer so that it looks like Figure 1–30b.

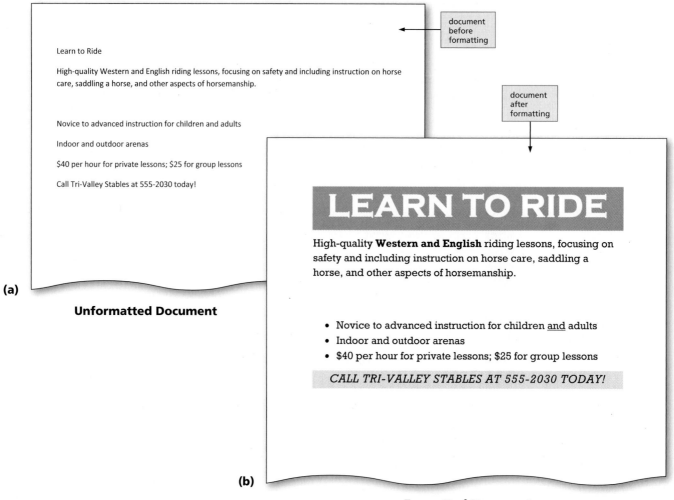

Figure 1–30

Fonts, Font Sizes, Styles, and Themes

Characters that appear on the screen are a specific shape and size. The **font**, or typeface, defines the appearance and shape of the letters, numbers, and special characters. In Word, the default font usually is Calibri (Figure 1–31 on the next page). You can leave characters in the default font or change them to a different font. **Font size** specifies the size of the characters and is determined by a measurement system called points. A single **point** is about 1/72 of one inch in height. The default font size in Word typically is 11 (Figure 1–31). A character with a font size of 11 is about 11/72 or a little less than 1/6 of one inch in height. You can increase or decrease the font size of characters in a document.

When you create a document, Word formats the text using a particular style. A **style** is a named group of formatting characteristics, including font and font size. The default style in Word is called the **Normal style**, which most likely uses 11-point Calibri font. If you do not specify a style for text you type, Word applies the Normal style to the text. In addition to the Normal style, Word has many other built-in, or predefined, styles that you can use to format text. You also can create your own styles. Styles make it easy to apply many formats at once to text. After you apply a style to text, you easily can modify the text to include additional formats. You also can modify the style.

To assist you with coordinating colors and fonts and other formats, Word uses document themes. A document **theme** is a set of unified formats for fonts, colors, and graphics. The default theme fonts are Cambria for headings and Calibri for body text (Figure 1–31). Word includes a variety of document themes. By changing the document theme, you quickly give your document a new look. You also can define your own document themes.

Plan Ahead

Identify how to format various elements of the text.
By formatting the characters and paragraphs in a document, you can improve its overall appearance. In a flyer, consider the following formatting suggestions.

- **Increase the font size of characters.** Flyers usually are posted on a bulletin board or in a window. Thus, the font size should be as large as possible so that passersby easily can read the flyer. To give the headline more impact, its font size should be larger than the font size of the text in the body copy. If possible, make the font size of the signature line larger than the body copy but smaller than the headline.

- **Change the font of characters**. Use fonts that are easy to read. Try to use only two different fonts in a flyer, for example, one for the headline and the other for all other text. Too many fonts can make the flyer visually confusing.

- **Change paragraph alignment.** The default alignment for paragraphs in a document is **left-aligned**, that is, flush at the left margin of the document with uneven right edges. Consider changing the alignment of some of the paragraphs to add interest and variety to the flyer.

- **Highlight key paragraphs with bullets.** A **bullet** is a dot or other symbol positioned at the beginning of a paragraph. Use bullets to highlight important paragraphs in a flyer.

- **Emphasize important words**. To call attention to certain words or lines, you can underline them, italicize them, or bold them. Use these formats sparingly, however, because overuse will minimize their effect and make the flyer look too busy.

- **Use color.** Use colors that complement each other and convey the meaning of the flyer. Vary colors in terms of hue and brightness. Headline colors, for example, can be bold and bright. Signature lines should stand out more than body copy but less than headlines. Keep in mind that too many colors can detract from the flyer and make it difficult to read.

To Apply Styles

In the flyer, you want the headline and the signature line to be emphasized more than the other text. Word provides heading styles designed to emphasize this type of text. The first step in formatting the flyer is to apply the Heading 1 style to the headline and the Heading 2 style to the signature line. The default Heading 1 style is a 14-point Cambria bold font. The default Heading 2 style is a 13-point Cambria bold font. The default theme color scheme uses shades of blue for headings.

To apply a style to a paragraph, you first position the insertion point in the paragraph and then apply the style. The following steps apply heading styles to paragraphs.

- Press CTRL+HOME (that is, press and hold down the CTRL key, press the HOME key, and then release both keys) to position the insertion point at the top of the document (Figure 1–31).

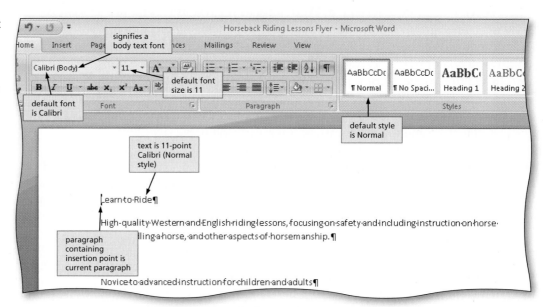

Figure 1–31

- Point to Heading 1 in the Styles gallery to display a live preview in the document of the Heading 1 style (Figure 1–32).

What happens if I move the mouse pointer?

If you move the mouse pointer away from the gallery, the text containing the insertion point returns to the Normal style.

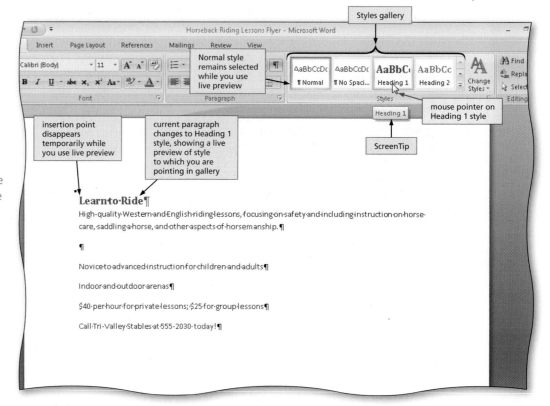

Figure 1–32

3

- Click Heading 1 in the Styles gallery to apply the Heading 1 style to the headline (Figure 1–33).

Q&A

Why did a square appear on the screen near the left edge of the headline?

The square is a nonprinting character, like the paragraph mark, that indicates text to its right has a special paragraph format applied to it.

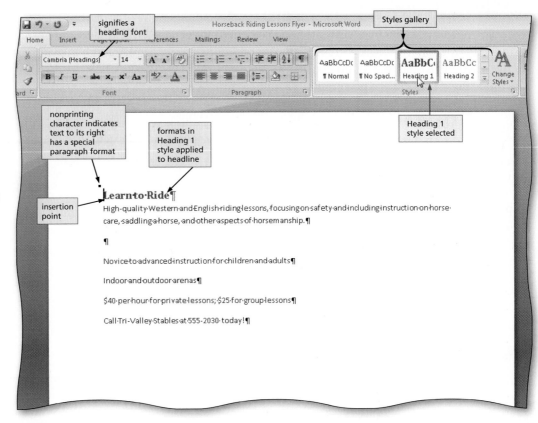

Figure 1–33

4

- Press CTRL+END (that is, press and hold down the CTRL key, press the END key, and then release both keys) to position the insertion point at the end of the document.

- Click Heading 2 in the Styles gallery to apply the Heading 2 style to the signature line (Figure 1–34).

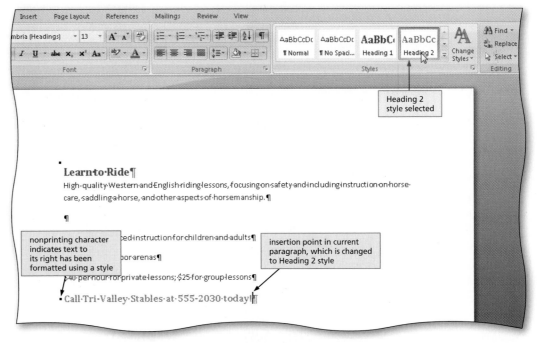

Figure 1–34

Other Ways

1. Click Styles Dialog Box Launcher, click desired style in Styles task pane

2. Press CTRL+SHIFT+S, click Style Name box arrow in Apply Styles task pane, click desired style in list

To Center a Paragraph

The headline in the flyer currently is left-aligned (Figure 1–35). You want the headline to be **centered**, that is, positioned horizontally between the left and right margins on the page. Thus, you will center the paragraph containing the headline. Recall that Word considers a single short line of text, such as the three-word headline, a paragraph. The following steps center a paragraph.

- Click somewhere in the paragraph to be centered (in this case, the headline) to position the insertion point in the paragraph to be formatted (Figure 1–35).

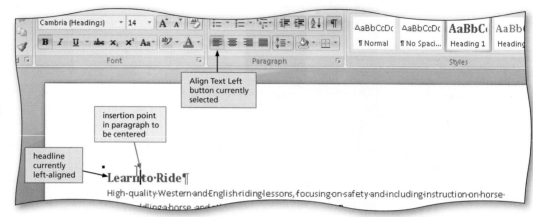

Figure 1–35

- Click the Center button on the Home tab to center the headline (Figure 1–36).

What if I want to return the paragraph to left-aligned?

Click the Align Text Left button on the Home tab.

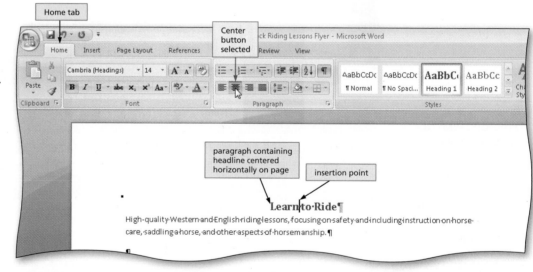

Figure 1–36

Other Ways		
1. Right-click paragraph, click Center button on Mini toolbar	2. Right-click paragraph, click Paragraph on shortcut menu, click Indents and Spacing tab, click Alignment box arrow, click Centered, click OK button	3. Click Paragraph Dialog Box Launcher, click Indents and Spacing tab, click Alignment box arrow, click Centered, click OK button 4. Press CTRL+E

Formatting Single Versus Multiple Paragraphs and Characters

As shown in the previous pages, to format a single paragraph, simply move the insertion point in the paragraph and then format the paragraph. Likewise, to format a single word, position the insertion point in the word and then format the word.

To format *multiple* paragraphs or words, however, you first must select the paragraphs or words you want to format and then format the selection. If your screen normally displays dark letters on a light background, which is the default setting in Word, then selected text displays light letters on a dark background.

To Select a Line

The font size of characters in the Heading 1 style, 14 point, is too small for passersby to read in the headline of the flyer. To increase the font size of the characters in the headline, you must first select the line of text containing the headline. The following steps select a line.

- Move the mouse pointer to the left of the line to be selected (in this case, the headline) until the mouse pointer changes to a right-pointing block arrow (Figure 1–37).

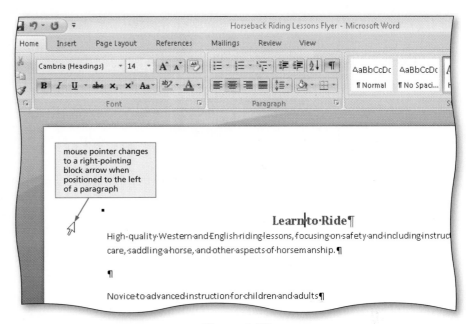

Figure 1–37

2

- While the mouse pointer is a right-pointing block arrow, click the mouse to select the entire line to the right of the mouse pointer (Figure 1–38).

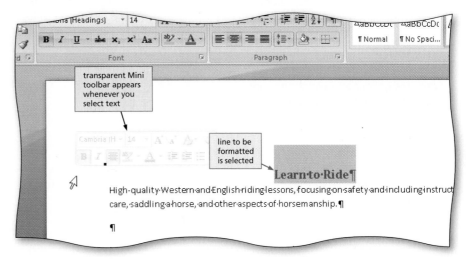

Figure 1–38

Other Ways	
1. Drag mouse through line	2. With insertion point at beginning of desired line, press SHIFT+DOWN ARROW

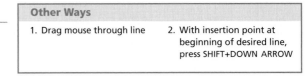

To Change the Font Size of Selected Text

The next step is to increase the font size of the characters in the selected headline. You would like the headline to be as large as possible and still fit on a single line, which in this case is 48 point. The following steps increase the font size of the headline from 14 to 48 point.

- With the text selected, click the Font Size box arrow on the Home tab to display the Font Size gallery (Figure 1–39).

Q&A

Why are the font sizes in my Font Size gallery different from those in Figure 1–39?

Font sizes may vary depending on the current font and your printer driver.

Q&A

What happened to the Mini toolbar?

The Mini toolbar disappears if you do not use it. These steps use the Font Size box arrow on the Home tab instead of the Font Size box arrow on the Mini toolbar. If a command exists both on the currently displayed tab and the Mini toolbar, this book uses the command on the tab. When the command is not on the currently displayed tab, the Mini toolbar is used.

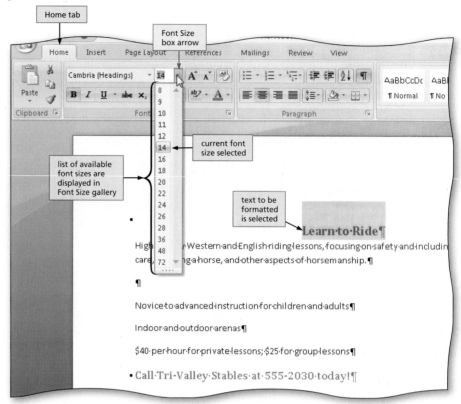

Figure 1–39

- Point to 48 in the Font Size gallery to display a live preview of the headline at 48 point (Figure 1–40).

 **Experiment**

- Point to various font sizes in the Font Size gallery and watch the font size of the headline change in the document window.

- Click 48 in the Font Size gallery to increase the font size of the selected text to 48.

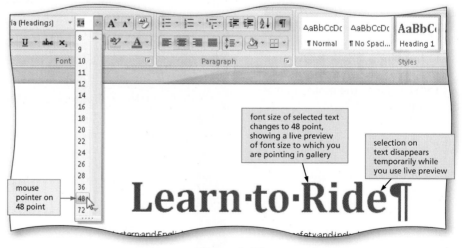

Figure 1–40

Other Ways		
1. Click Font Size box arrow on Mini toolbar, click desired font size in Font Size gallery 2. Right-click selected text, click Font on shortcut menu, click Font tab, select desired	font size in Size list, click OK button 3. Click Font Dialog Box Launcher, click Font tab, select desired font size in Size list, click OK button	4. Press CTRL+SHIFT+P, click Font tab, select desired font size in Size list, click OK button

To Change the Font of Selected Text

As mentioned earlier, the default Heading 1 style uses the font called Cambria. Word, however, provides many other fonts to add variety to your documents. To draw more attention to the headline, you change its font so it differs from the font of other text in the flyer. The following steps change the font from Cambria to Copperplate Gothic Bold.

1

• With the text selected, click the Font box arrow on the Home tab to display the Font gallery (Figure 1–41).

Will the fonts in my Font gallery be the same as those in Figure 1–41?

Your list of available fonts may differ, depending on the type of printer you are using.

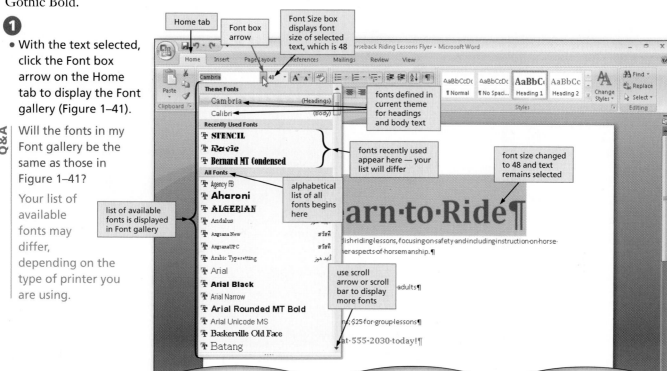

Figure 1–41

2

• Scroll through the Font gallery, if necessary, and then point to Copperplate Gothic Bold (or a similar font) to display a live preview of the headline in Copperplate Gothic Bold font (Figure 1–42).

 **Experiment**

• Point to various fonts in the Font gallery and watch the font of the headline change in the document window.

3

• Click Copperplate Gothic Bold (or a similar font) to change the font of the selected text to Copperplate Gothic Bold.

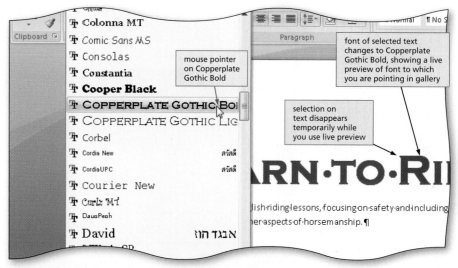

Figure 1–42

Other Ways

1. Click Font box arrow on Mini toolbar, click desired font in Font gallery

2. Right-click selected text, click Font on shortcut menu, click

Font tab, select desired font in Font list, click OK button

3. Click Font Dialog Box Launcher, click Font tab, select desired font in Font list, click OK button

4. Press CTRL+SHIFT+F, click Font tab, select desired font in the Font list, click OK button

To Select Multiple Paragraphs

The next formatting step in creating the flyer is to increase the font size of the characters between the headline and the signature line so that they are easier to read from a distance. To change the font size of the characters in multiple lines, you first must select all the lines to be formatted. The following steps select multiple lines.

- Move the mouse pointer to the left of the first paragraph to be selected until the mouse pointer changes to a right-pointing block arrow (Figure 1–43).

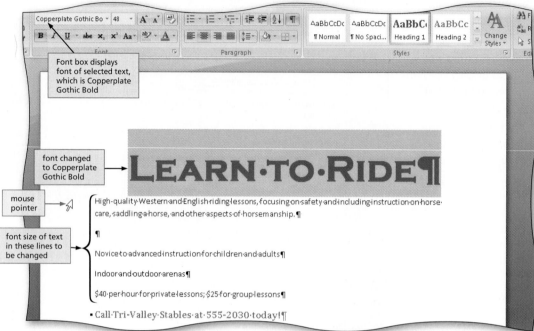

Figure 1–43

- Drag downward to select all lines that will be formatted (Figure 1–44).

 Q&A

How do I *drag* the mouse?

Dragging is the process of holding down the mouse button while moving the mouse and then releasing the mouse button.

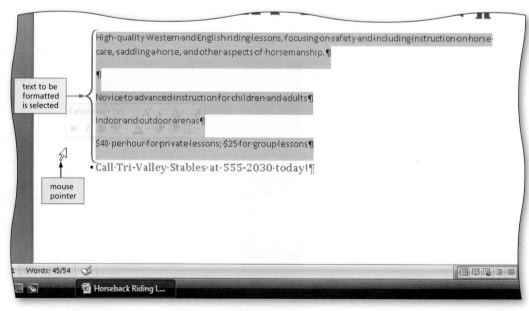

Figure 1–44

Other Ways

1. With insertion point at beginning of desired line, press SHIFT+DOWN ARROW repeatedly until all lines are selected

To Change the Font Size of Selected Text

The characters between the headline and the signature line in the flyer currently are 11 point. To make them easier to read from a distance, this flyer uses 16 point for these characters. The following steps change the font size of the selected text.

1 With the text selected, click the Font Size box arrow on the Home tab to display the Font Size gallery.

2 Click 16 in the Font Size gallery to increase the font size of the selected text to 16.

To Format a Line

In the flyer, the signature line is to be centered to match the paragraph alignment of the headline. Also, its text should have a font size larger than the rest of the body copy. The following steps center the line and increase its font size to 18.

1 Click somewhere in the paragraph to be centered (in this case, the signature line) to position the insertion point in the paragraph to be formatted.

2 Click the Center button on the Home tab to center the signature line.

3 Move the mouse pointer to the left of the line to be selected (in this case, the signature line) until the mouse pointer changes to a right-pointing block arrow and then click to select the line.

4 With the signature line selected, click the Font Size box arrow on the Home tab and then click 18 in the Font Size gallery to increase the font size of the selected text to 18 (Figure 1–45).

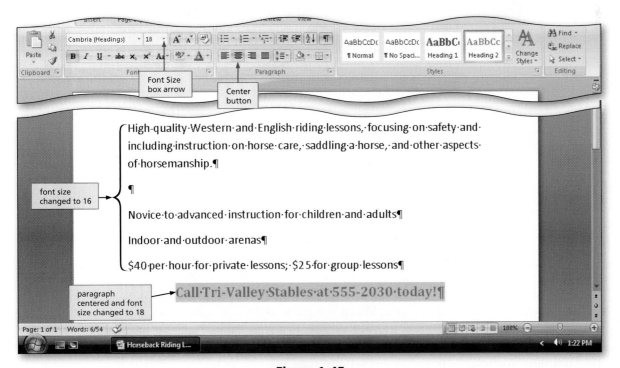

Figure 1–45

To Bullet a List of Paragraphs

The next step is to format the three important points above the signature line in the flyer as a bulleted list. A **bulleted list** is a series of paragraphs, each beginning with a bullet character. The three lines each end with a paragraph mark because you pressed the ENTER key at the end of each line. Thus, these three lines actually are three separate paragraphs.

To format a list of paragraphs with bullets, you first must select all the lines in the paragraphs. The following steps bullet a list of paragraphs.

1

- Move the mouse pointer to the left of the first paragraph to be selected until the mouse pointer changes to a right-pointing block arrow.

- Drag downward until all paragraphs (lines) that will be formatted with a bullet character are selected.

2

- Click the Bullets button on the Home tab to place a bullet character at the beginning of each selected paragraph (Figure 1–46).

Q&A

How do I remove bullets from a list or paragraph?

Select the list or paragraph and click the Bullets button again.

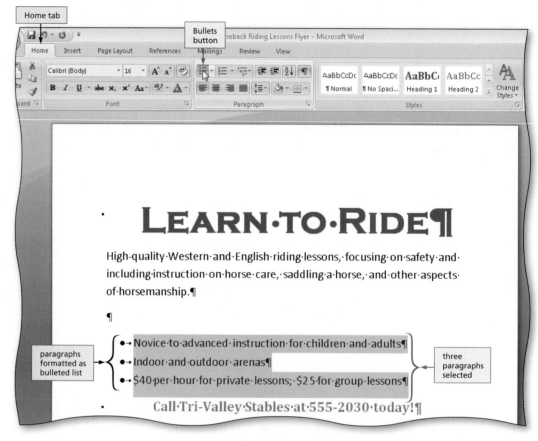

Figure 1–46

Other Ways

1. Right-click selected paragraphs, click Bullets button on Mini toolbar

2. Right-click selected paragraphs, point to Bullets on shortcut menu, click desired bullet style

To Undo and Redo an Action

Word provides a means of canceling your recent command(s) or action(s). For example, if you format text incorrectly, you can undo the format and try it again. When you point to the Undo button, Word displays the action you can undo as part of the ScreenTip.

If, after you undo an action, you decide you did not want to perform the undo, you can redo the undone action. Word does not allow you to undo or redo some actions, such as saving or printing a document. The next steps undo the bullet format just applied and then redo the bullet format.

1

- Click the Undo button on the Quick Access Toolbar to remove the bullets from the selected paragraphs (Figure 1–47).

2

- Click the Redo button on the Quick Access Toolbar to place a bullet character at the beginning of each selected paragraph again (shown in Figure 1–46).

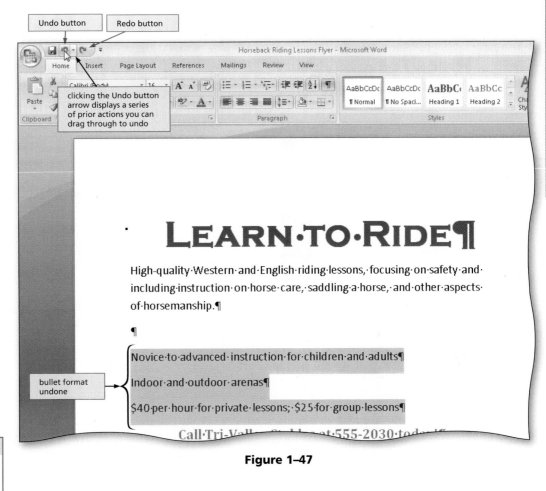

Figure 1–47

Other Ways

1. Press CTRL+Z; press CTRL+Y

To Select a Group of Words

To emphasize the types of riding lessons, Western and English, these words are bold in the flyer. To format a group of words, you first must select them. The following steps select a group of words.

1

- Position the mouse pointer immediately to the left of the first character of the text to be selected, in this case, the W in Western (Figure 1–48).

Q&A Why did the shape of the mouse pointer change?

The mouse pointer's shape is an I-beam when positioned in unselected text in the document window.

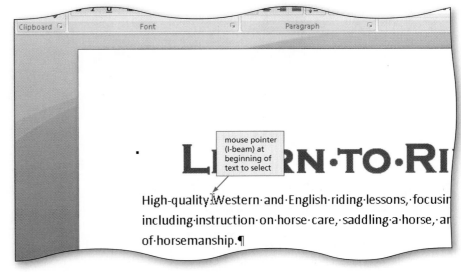

Figure 1–48

2

- Drag the mouse pointer through the last character of the text to be selected, in this case, the h in English (Figure 1–49).

Q&A Why did the mouse pointer shape change again?

When the mouse pointer is positioned in selected text, its shape is a left-pointing block arrow.

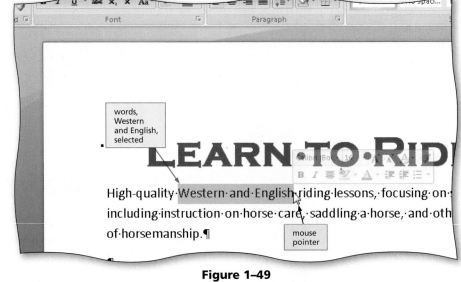

Figure 1–49

To Bold Text

Bold characters display somewhat thicker and darker than those that are not bold. The following step formats the selected words, Western and English, as bold.

1

- With the text selected, click the Bold button on the Home tab to format the selected text in bold (Figure 1–50).

Q&A How would I remove a bold format?

You would click the Bold button a second time, or you immediately could click the Undo button on the Quick Access Toolbar.

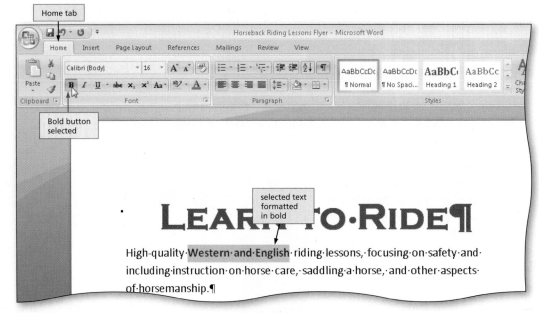

Figure 1–50

To Underline a Word

As with bold text, underlines are used to emphasize or draw attention to specific text. **Underlined** text prints with an underscore (_) below each character. In the flyer, the word, and, in the first bulleted paragraph is emphasized with an underline.

As with a single paragraph, if you want to format a single word, you do not need to select the word. Simply position the insertion point somewhere in the word and apply the desired format. The following step formats a word with an underline.

1

- Click somewhere in the word to be underlined (and, in this case).

- Click the Underline button on the Home tab to underline the word containing the insertion point (Figure 1–51).

Q&A How would I remove an underline?

You would click the Underline button a second time, or you immediately could click the Undo button on the Quick Access Toolbar.

Q&A Are other types of underlines available?

In addition to the basic solid underline shown in Figure 1–51, Word has many decorative underlines, such as double underlines, dotted underlines, and wavy underlines. You can access the decorative underlines and also change the color of an underline through the Underline gallery.

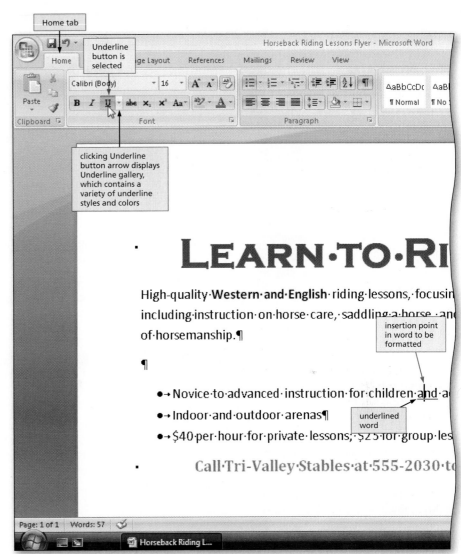

Figure 1–51

Other Ways

1. Right-click text, click Font on shortcut menu, click Font tab, click Underline style box arrow, click desired underline style, click OK button

2. Click Font Dialog Box Launcher, click Font tab, click Underline style box arrow, click desired underline style, click OK button

3. Press CTRL+U

To Italicize Text

To further emphasize the signature line, this line is italicized in the flyer. **Italicized** text has a slanted appearance. The following steps select the text and then italicize it.

- Point to the left of the line to be selected (in this case, the signature line) and click when the mouse pointer is a right-pointing block arrow.

- Click the Italic button on the Home tab to italicize the selected text.

- Click inside the selected text to remove the selection (Figure 1–52).

Q&A How would I remove an italic format?

You would click the Italic button a second time, or you immediately could click the Undo button on the Quick Access Toolbar.

Q&A How can I tell what formatting has been applied to text?

The selected buttons and boxes on the Home tab show formatting characteristics of the location of the insertion point. With the insertion point in the signature line, the Home tab shows these formats: 18-point Cambria bold italic font, centered paragraph, and Heading 2 style.

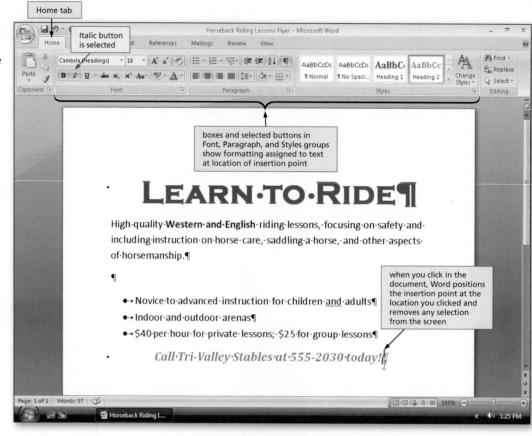

Figure 1–52

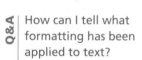

Other Ways

1. Click Italic button on Mini toolbar
2. Right-click selected text, click Font on shortcut menu, click Font tab, click Italic in Font style list, click OK button
3. Click Font Dialog Box Launcher, click Font tab, click Italic in Font style list, click OK button
4. Press CTRL+I

Document Formats

One advantage of using styles to format text is that you easily can change the formats of styles and themes in your document to give it a different or new look. Recall that a style is a named group of formatting characteristics and a theme is a set of unified formats for fonts, colors, and graphics. In Word, you can change the style set, theme colors, and theme fonts.

- The predefined styles in the Styles gallery, such as Heading 1 and Heading 2, each known as a **Quick Style**, are part of a style set. A **style set** consists of a group of frequently used styles formatted so they look pleasing when used together. When you change the style set, formats assigned to each Quick Style also change.

- Each **color scheme** in a theme identifies 12 complementary colors for text, background, accents, and links in a document. With more than 20 predefined color schemes, Word provides a simple way to select colors that work well together.
- Each theme has a **font set** that defines formats for two fonts: one for headings and another for body text. In Word, you can select from more than 20 predefined coordinated font sets to give the document's text a new look.

Use color.

When choosing color, associate the meaning of color to your message:

- Red expresses danger, power, or energy, and often is associated with sports or physical exertion.
- Brown represents simplicity, honesty, and dependability.
- Orange denotes success, victory, creativity, and enthusiasm.
- Yellow suggests sunshine, happiness, hope, liveliness, and intelligence.
- Green symbolizes growth, healthiness, harmony, blooming, and healing, and often is associated with safety or money.
- Blue indicates integrity, trust, importance, confidence, and stability.
- Purple represents wealth, power, comfort, extravagance, magic, mystery, and spirituality.
- White stands for purity, goodness, cleanliness, precision, and perfection.
- Black suggests authority, strength, elegance, power, and prestige.
- Gray conveys neutrality and thus often is found in backgrounds and other effects.

To Change the Style Set

To symbolize perfection and precision in the flyer, the characters in the headline are white. The style set, called Modern, formats Heading 1 characters in white. It also formats the Heading 1 and Heading 2 styles in all capital letters and places a background color around the paragraphs, which further emphasize the headline and signature line in the flyer. Thus, you will change the style set from Default to Modern. The following steps change a style set.

- Click the Change Styles button on the Home tab to display the Change Styles menu (Figure 1–53).

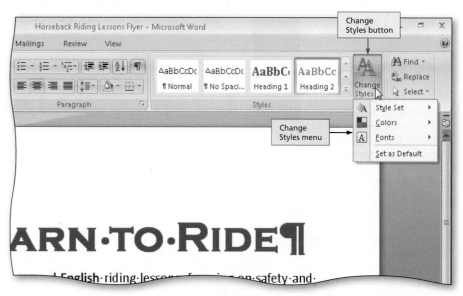

Figure 1–53

- Point to Style Set on the Change Styles menu to display the Style Set gallery.

- Point to Modern in the Style Set gallery to display a live pre-view of the formats associated with the Modern style set (Figure 1–54).

 Experiment

- Point to various style sets in the Style Set gallery and watch the formats of the styled text change in the document window.

- Click Modern in the Style Set gallery to change the document style set to Modern.

Q&A What if I want to return to the original style set?

You would click the Change Styles button, click Style Set on the Change Styles menu, and then click Default in the Style Set gallery, or you could click the Undo button on the Quick Access Toolbar.

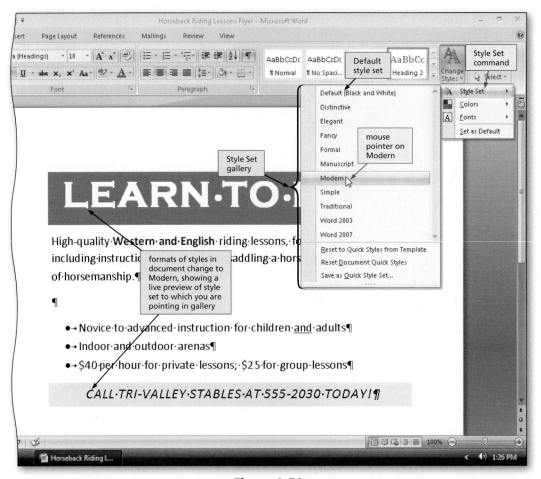

Figure 1–54

BTW

Style Formats

To see the formats assigned to a particular style in a document, click the Styles Dialog Box Launcher on the Home tab and then click the Style Inspector button in the Styles task pane. Position the insertion point in the style and then point to the Paragraph formatting or Text level formatting areas in the Style Inspector task pane to display an Enhanced ScreenTip describing formats assigned to the location of the insertion point. You also can click the Reveal Formatting button in the Style Inspector to display the Reveal Formatting task pane.

To Change Theme Colors

To suggest enthusiasm, success, and honesty, the background colors around the headline and signature line paragraphs in the flyer use shades of orange and brown. In Word, the color scheme called Aspect uses these colors. Thus, you will change the color scheme to Aspect. The following steps change theme colors.

1

- Click the Change Styles button on the Home tab to display the Change Styles menu.

- Point to Colors on the Change Styles menu to display the Colors gallery.

- Point to Aspect in the Colors gallery to display a live preview of the Aspect color scheme (Figure 1–55).

 Experiment

- Point to various color schemes in the Colors gallery and watch the paragraph background colors change in the document window.

2

- Click Aspect in the Colors gallery to change the document theme colors to Aspect.

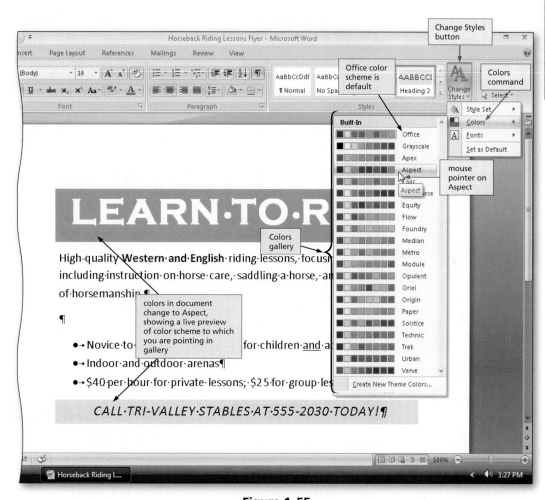

Figure 1–55

Q&A What if I want to return to the original color scheme?

You would click the Change Styles button, click Colors on the Change Styles menu, and then click Office in the Colors gallery.

Other Ways

1. Click Theme Colors button arrow on Page Layout tab, select desired color scheme

To Change Theme Fonts

Earlier in this chapter, you changed the font of the headline to Copperplate Gothic Bold. In this flyer, all text below the headline should be the Rockwell font, instead of the Calibri font, because it better matches the western tone of the flyer. Thus, the next step is to change the current font set, which is called Office, to a font set called Foundry, which uses the Rockwell font for headings and body text.

If you previously changed a font using buttons on the Ribbon or Mini toolbar, Word will not alter those when you change the font set because changes to the font set are not applied to fonts changed individually. This means the font headline in the flyer will stay as Copperplate Gothic Bold when you change the font set. The following steps change the font set to Foundry.

- Click the Change Styles button on the Home tab.

- Point to Fonts on the Change Styles menu to display the Fonts gallery.

- Scroll through the Fonts gallery until Foundry is displayed and then point to Foundry to display a live preview of the Foundry font set (Figure 1–56).

 **Experiment**

- Point to various font sets in the Fonts gallery and watch the fonts below the headline change in the document window.

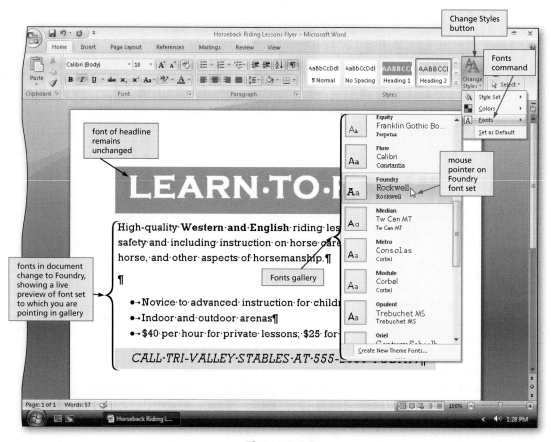

Figure 1–56

- Click Foundry in the Fonts gallery to change the document theme fonts to Foundry.

What if I want to return to the original font set?

You would click the Change Styles button, click Fonts on the Change Styles menu, and then click Office in the Fonts gallery.

Other Ways
1. Click Theme Fonts button arrow on Page Layout tab, select desired font set

Inserting and Formatting a Picture in a Word Document

With the text formatted in the flyer, the next step is to insert a picture in the flyer and format the picture. Flyers usually contain graphical images, such as a picture, to attract the attention of passersby.

Note: If you are using Windows XP, see Appendix F for alternate steps.

Find the appropriate graphical image.
To use graphical images, also called graphics, in a Word document, the image must be stored digitally in a file. Files containing graphical images are available from a variety of sources:

- Word includes a collection of predefined graphical images that you can insert in a document.

- Microsoft has free digital images on the Web for use in a document. Other Web sites also have images available, some of which are free, while others require a fee.

- You can take a picture with a digital camera and **download** it, which is the process of copying the digital picture from the camera to your computer.

- With a scanner, you can convert a printed picture, drawing, or diagram to a digital file.

If you receive a picture from a source other than yourself, do not use the file until you are certain it does not contain a virus. A **virus** is a computer program that can damage files and programs on your computer. Use an antivirus program to verify that any files you use are virus free.

Plan Ahead

Establish where to position and how to format the graphical image.
The content, size, shape, position, and format of a graphic should capture the interest of passersby, enticing them to stop and read the flyer. Often, the graphic is the center of attraction and visually the largest element on a flyer. If you use colors in the graphical image, be sure they are part of the document's color scheme.

Plan Ahead

To Insert a Picture

The next step in creating the flyer is to insert the picture of the horse and rider so that it is centered on the blank line above the bulleted list. The picture, which was taken with a digital camera, is available on the Data Files for Students. See the inside back cover of this book for instructions on downloading the Data Files for Students, or contact your instructor for information about accessing the required files. The following steps insert a centered picture, which, in this example, is located on the same USB flash drive that contains the saved flyer.

- To position the insertion point where you want the picture to be located, press CTRL+HOME and then press the DOWN ARROW key four times.

- Click the Center button on the Home tab to center the paragraph that will contain the picture.

- Click Insert on the Ribbon to display the Insert tab (Figure 1–57).

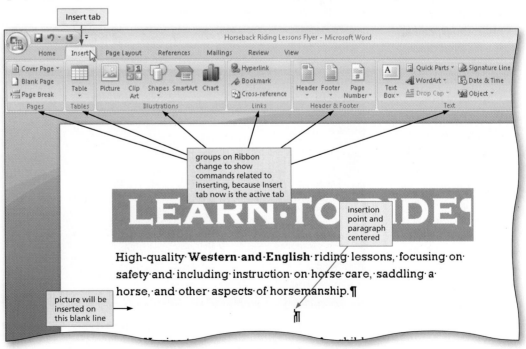

Figure 1–57

- With your USB flash drive connected to one of the computer's USB ports, click the Insert Picture from File button on the Insert tab to display the Insert Picture dialog box.

- If the Folders list is displayed below the Folders button, click the Folders button to remove the Folders list.

- If necessary, click Computer in the Favorite Links section and then scroll until UDISK 2.0 (E:) appears in the list of available drives.

- Double-click UDISK 2.0 (E:) to select the USB flash drive, Drive E in this case, as the device that contains the picture.

- Click Horse and Rider to select the file name (Figure 1–58).

Q&A What if the picture is not on a USB flash drive?

Use the same process, but select the device containing the picture in the Favorite Links section.

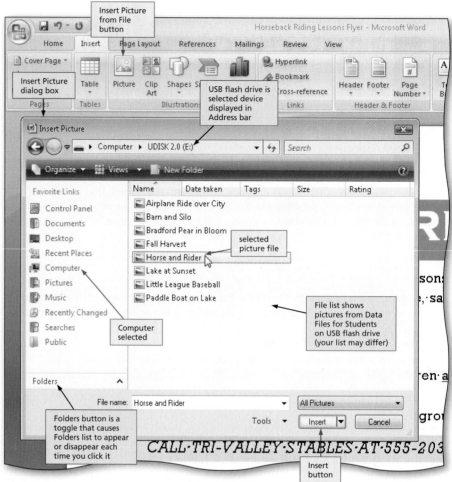

Figure 1–58

- Click the Insert button in the dialog box to insert the picture at the location of the insertion point in the document (Figure 1–59).

Q&A What are the symbols around the picture?

A selected graphic appears surrounded by a **selection rectangle**, which has small squares and circles, called **sizing handles**, at each corner and middle location.

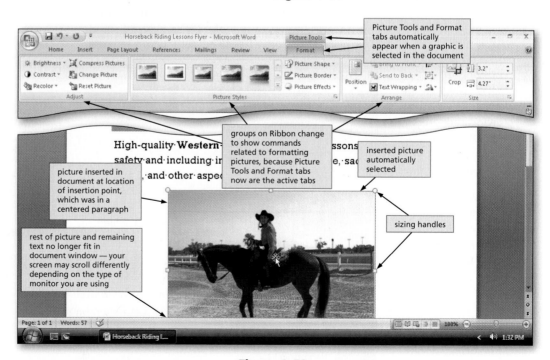

Figure 1–59

Scrolling

As mentioned at the beginning of this chapter, you view only a portion of a document on the screen through the document window. At some point when you type text or insert graphics, Word will **scroll** the top or bottom portion of the document off the screen. Although you cannot see the text and graphics once they scroll off the screen, they remain in the document.

As shown in Figure 1–59, when you insert the picture in the flyer, the text and graphics are too long to fit in the document window. Thus, to see the bottom of the flyer, you will need to scroll downward.

You may use either the mouse or the keyboard to scroll to a different location in a document. With the mouse, you can use the scroll arrows or the scroll box on the scroll bar to display a different portion of the document in the document window, and then click the mouse to move the insertion point to that location. Table 1–1 explains various techniques for using the scroll bar to scroll vertically with the mouse.

BTW

Minimize Wrist Injury
Computer users frequently switch between the keyboard and the mouse during a word processing session; such switching strains the wrist. To help prevent wrist injury, minimize switching. For instance, if your fingers already are on the keyboard, use keyboard keys to scroll. If your hand already is on the mouse, use the mouse to scroll.

Table 1–1 Using the Scroll Bar to Scroll with the Mouse	
SCROLL DIRECTION	**MOUSE ACTION**
Up	Drag the scroll box upward.
Down	Drag the scroll box downward.
Up one screen	Click anywhere above the scroll box on the vertical scroll bar.
Down one screen	Click anywhere below the scroll box on the vertical scroll bar.
Up one line	Click the scroll arrow at the top of the vertical scroll bar.
Down one line	Click the scroll arrow at the bottom of the vertical scroll bar.

When you use the keyboard to scroll, the insertion point automatically moves when you press the appropriate keys. Table 1–2 outlines various techniques to scroll through a document using the keyboard, some of which you have seen used in this chapter.

Table 1–2 Scrolling with the Keyboard	
SCROLL DIRECTION	**KEY(S) TO PRESS**
Left one character	LEFT ARROW
Right one character	RIGHT ARROW
Left one word	CTRL+LEFT ARROW
Right one word	CTRL+RIGHT ARROW
Up one line	UP ARROW
Down one line	DOWN ARROW
To end of line	END
To beginning of line	HOME
Up one paragraph	CTRL+UP ARROW
Down one paragraph	CTRL+DOWN ARROW
Up one screen	PAGE UP
Down one screen	PAGE DOWN
To top of document window	ALT+CTRL+PAGE UP
To bottom of document window	ALT+CTRL+PAGE DOWN
To beginning of document	CTRL+HOME
To end of document	CTRL+END

To Apply a Picture Style

Earlier in this chapter, you applied the heading styles to the headline and signature line in the flyer. Word also provides styles for pictures, allowing you easily to change the basic rectangle format to a more visually appealing style. Word provides a gallery of more than 25 picture styles, which include a variety of shapes, angles, borders, and reflections. The flyer in this chapter uses an oval picture style that has a border around its edges. The following steps apply a picture style to the picture in the flyer.

1

- Click the down scroll arrow on the vertical scroll bar as many times as necessary until the entire picture is displayed in the document window (Figure 1–60).

Q&A What if the Picture Tools and Format tabs no longer are displayed on my Ribbon?

Double-click the picture to display the Picture Tools and Format tabs.

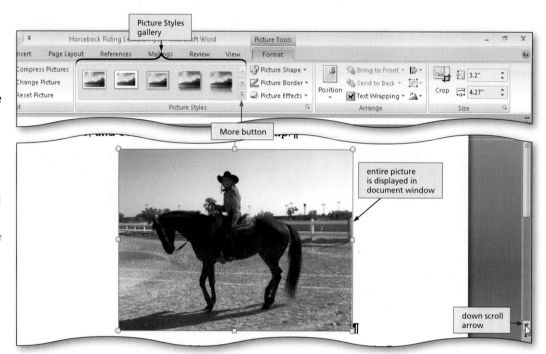

Figure 1–60

2

- Click the More button in the Picture Styles gallery, which shows more gallery options.

- Point to Metal Oval in the Picture Styles gallery to display a live preview of that style applied to the picture in the document (Figure 1–61).

Experiment

- Point to various picture styles in the Picture Styles gallery and watch the format of the picture change in the document window.

3

- Click Metal Oval in the Picture Styles gallery to apply the selected style to the picture.

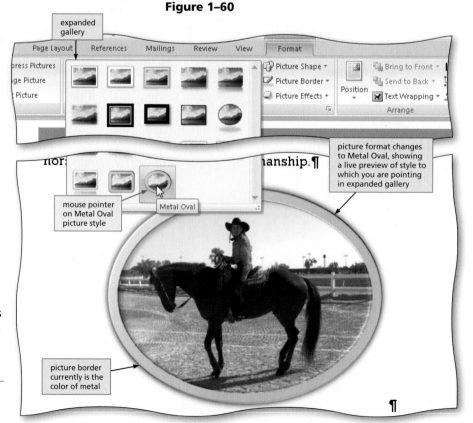

Figure 1–61

To Change a Picture Border Color

The flyer in this chapter has a tan border around the picture. Earlier in this chapter, you changed the color scheme to Aspect. To coordinate the border color with the other colors in the document, you will use a shade of tan in Aspect color scheme for the picture border. Any color galleries you display show colors defined in this current color scheme. The following steps change the picture border color.

1

- Click the Picture Border button arrow on the Format tab to display the Picture Border gallery.

Q&A What if the Picture Tools and Format tabs no longer are displayed on my Ribbon?

Double-click the picture to display the Picture Tools and Format tabs.

- Point to Tan, Background 2 (third theme color from left in the first row) in the Picture Border gallery to display a live preview of that border color on the picture (Figure 1–62).

Experiment

- Point to various colors in the Picture Border gallery and watch the border color on the picture change in the document window.

2

- Click Tan, Background 2 in the Picture Styles gallery to change the picture border color.

Figure 1–62

To Zoom the Document

The next step in formatting the picture is to resize it. Specifically, you will increase the size of the picture. You do not want it so large, however, that it causes the flyer text to flow to a second page. You can change the zoom so that you can see the entire document on the screen at once. Seeing the entire document at once helps you determine the appropriate size of the picture. The steps on the next page zoom the document.

Experiment

- Repeatedly click the Zoom Out and Zoom In buttons on the status bar and watch the size of the document change in the document window.

- Click the Zoom Out or Zoom In button as many times as necessary until the Zoom level button displays 50% on its face (Figure 1–63).

Q&A | If I change the zoom percentage, will the document print differently?

Changing the zoom has no effect on the printed document.

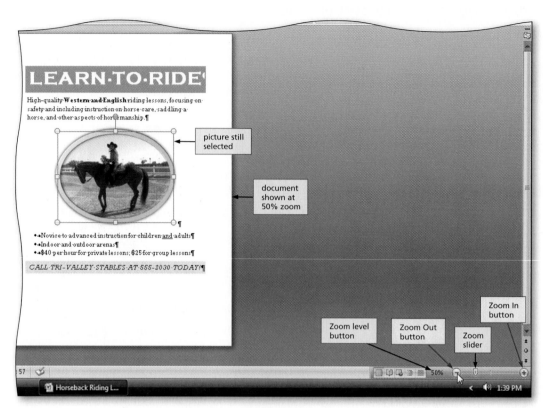

Figure 1–63

Other Ways

1. Drag Zoom slider on status bar	2. Click Zoom level button on status bar, select desired zoom percent or type, click OK button	3. Click Zoom button on View tab, select desired zoom percent or type, click OK button

To Resize a Graphic

The next step is to resize the picture. **Resizing** includes both enlarging and reducing the size of a graphic. The picture in the flyer should be as large as possible, without causing any flyer text to flow to a second page.

With the entire document displaying in the document window, you will be able to see how the resized graphic will look on the entire page. The following steps resize a selected graphic.

- With the graphic still selected, point to the upper-right corner sizing handle on the picture so that the mouse pointer shape changes to a two-headed arrow (Figure 1–64).

Q&A | What if my graphic (picture) is not selected?

To select a graphic, click it.

Figure 1–64

2

- Drag the sizing handle diagonally outward until the crosshair mouse pointer is positioned approximately as shown in Figure 1–65.

3

- Release the mouse button to resize the graphic.

Q&A What if the graphic is the wrong size?

Repeat Steps 1, 2, and 3.

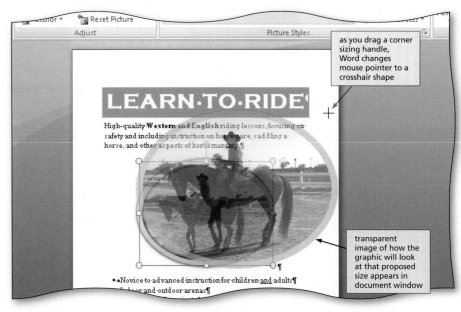

Figure 1–65

4

- Click outside the graphic to deselect it (Figure 1–66).

Q&A What happened to the Picture Tools and Format tabs?

When you click outside of a graphic or press a key to scroll through a document, Word deselects the graphic and removes the Picture Tools and Format tabs from the screen.

Q&A What if I want to return a graphic to its original size and start again?

With the graphic selected, click the Size Dialog Box Launcher on the Format tab to display the Size dialog box, click the Size tab, click the Reset button, and then click the Close button.

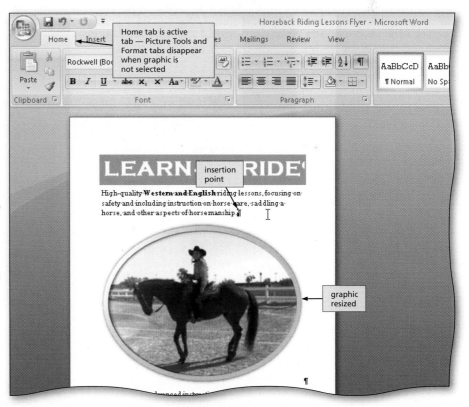

Figure 1–66

Other Ways	
1. Enter graphic height and width in Shape Height and Shape Width text boxes in Size group on Format tab in Picture Tools tab	2. Click Size Dialog Box Launcher on Format tab in Picture Tools tab, click Size tab, enter desired height and width values in text boxes, click Close button

Enhancing the Page

With the text and graphics entered and formatted, the next step is to look at the page as a whole and determine if it looks finished in its current state. As you review the page, answer these questions:

- Does it need a page border to frame its contents, or would a page border make it look too busy?
- Is the spacing between paragraphs and graphics on the page adequate? Do any sections of text or graphics look as if they are positioned too closely to the items above or below them?

You determine that a graphical, color-coordinated border would enhance the flyer. You also notice that the flyer would look more proportionate if it had a little more space below the headline and above the graphic. The following pages make these enhancements to the flyer.

To Add a Page Border

In Word, you can add a border around the perimeter of an entire page. In this flyer, you add a graphical border that uses a shade of brown from the Aspect color scheme. The following steps add a graphical page border.

- Click Page Layout on the Ribbon to display the Page Layout tab.

- Click the Page Borders button on the Page Layout tab to display the Borders and Shading dialog box (Figure 1–67).

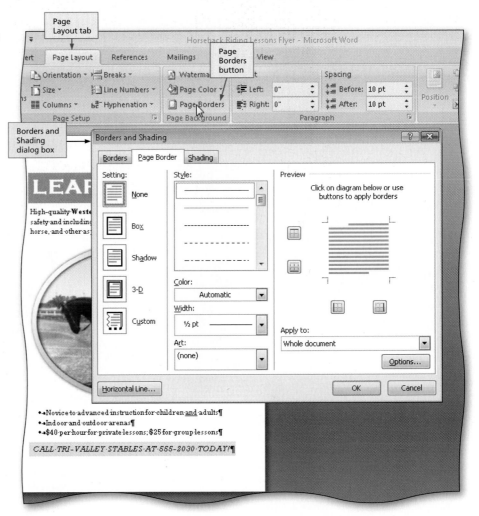

Figure 1–67

2

- Click the Art box arrow to display the Art gallery.

- Click the down scroll arrow in the Art gallery until the art border shown in Figure 1–68 appears.

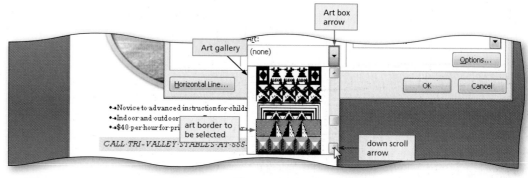

Figure 1–68

3

- Click the art border shown in Figure 1–68 to display a preview of the selection in the Preview area of the dialog box.

- Click the Color box arrow to display a Color gallery (Figure 1–69).

 Q&A Do I have to use an art border?

No. You can select a solid or decorative line in the Style list.

Q&A Can I add color to every border type?

You can color all of the line styles and many of the art borders.

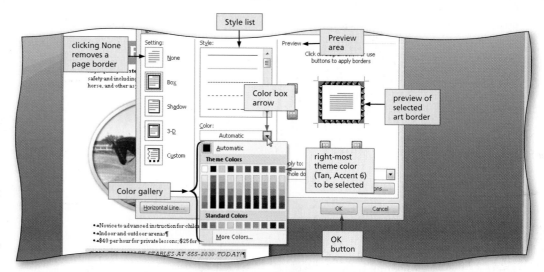

Figure 1–69

4

- Click the right-most theme color (Tan, Accent 6) in the Color gallery to display a preview of the selection in the Preview area.

- Click the OK button to add the border to the page (Figure 1–70).

 Q&A What if I wanted to remove the border?

Click None in the Setting list in the Borders and Shading dialog box.

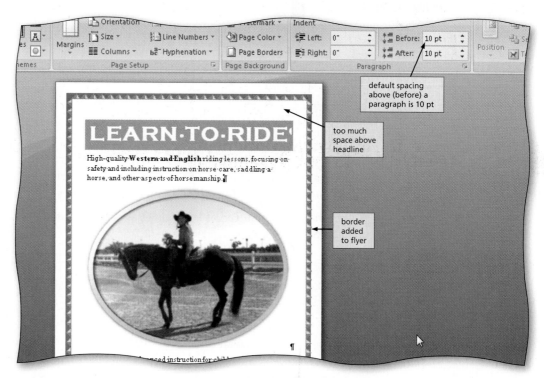

Figure 1–70

To Change Spacing Above and Below Paragraphs

The default spacing above a heading paragraph in Word is 10 points. In the flyer, you want to remove this spacing so the headline is closer to the page border. The default spacing below (after) a body text paragraph is 0 points. Below the first paragraph of body copy in the flyer, you want to increase this space. The following steps change the spacing above and below paragraphs.

1

- Position the insertion point in the paragraph to be adjusted, in this case, the headline.

- Click the Spacing Before box down arrow on the Page Layout tab as many times as necessary until 0 pt is displayed in the Spacing Before text box (Figure 1–71).

Q&A

Why is a blank space still between the border and the headline?

The space is a result of Word's preset left, right, top, and bottom margins and other settings.

2

- Position the insertion point in the paragraph below the headline.

- Click the Spacing After box up arrow on the Page Layout tab as many times as necessary until 24 pt is displayed in the Spacing After text box, shown in Figure 1–72. (If the text flows to two pages, resize the picture so that it is smaller.)

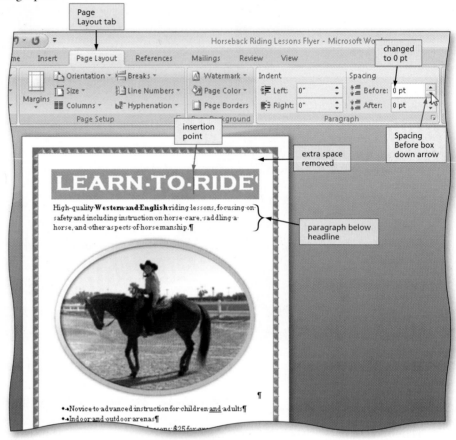

Figure 1–71

BTW

Centering Page Contents Vertically
You can center page contents vertically between the top and bottom margins. To do this, click the Page Setup Dialog Box Launcher on the Page Layout tab, click the Layout tab in the dialog box, click the Vertical alignment box arrow, click Center in the list, and then click the OK button.

To Zoom the Document

You are finished enhancing the page and no longer need to view the entire page in the document window. Thus, the following step changes the zoom back to 100 percent.

1 Click the Zoom In button as many times as necessary until the Zoom level button displays 100% on its face, shown in Figure 1–72.

Changing Document Properties and Saving Again

Word helps you organize and identify your files by using **document properties**, which are the details about a file. Document properties, also known as **metadata**, can include such information as the project author, title, or subject. **Keywords** are words or phrases that further describe the document. For example, a class name or document topic can describe the file's purpose or content.

Document properties are valuable for a variety of reasons:

- Users can save time locating a particular file because they can view a document's properties without opening the document.

- By creating consistent properties for files having similar content, users can better organize their documents.

- Some organizations require Word users to add document properties so that other employees can view details about these files.

Five different types of document properties exist, but the more common ones used in this book are standard and automatically updated properties. **Standard properties** are associated with all Microsoft Office documents and include author, title, and subject. **Automatically updated properties** include file system properties, such as the date you create or change a file, and statistics, such as the file size.

BTW

Printing Document Properties
To print document properties, click the Office Button to display the Office Button menu, point to Print on the Office Button menu to display the Print submenu, click Print on the Print submenu to display the Print dialog box, click the Print what box arrow, click Document properties to instruct Word to print the document properties instead of the document, and then click the OK button.

To Change Document Properties

The **Document Information Panel** contains areas where you can view and enter document properties. You can view and change information in this panel at any time while you are creating a document. Before saving the flyer again, you want to add your name and course information as document properties. The following steps use the Document Information Panel to change document properties.

1

- Click the Office Button to display the Office Button menu.

- Point to Prepare on the Office Button menu to display the Prepare submenu (Figure 1–72).

Q&A

What other types of actions besides changing properties can you take to prepare a document for distribution?

The Prepare submenu provides commands related to sharing a document with others, such as allowing or restricting people to view and modify your document, checking to see if your document will open in earlier versions of Word, and searching for hidden personal information.

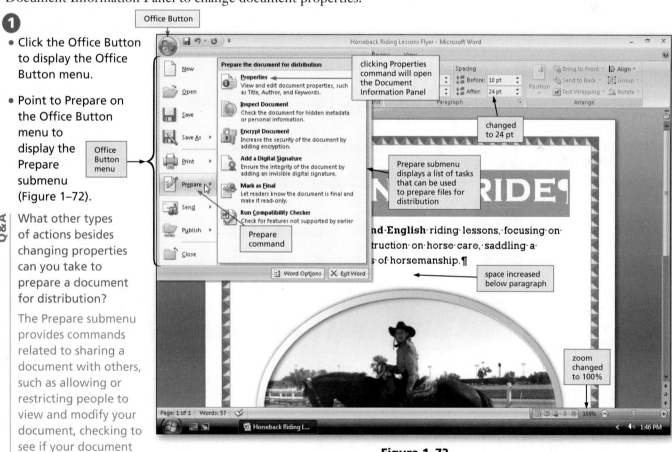

Figure 1–72

2

- Click Properties on the Prepare submenu to display the Document Information Panel (Figure 1–73).

Q&A

Why are some of the document properties in my Document Information Panel already filled in?

The person who installed Microsoft Office 2007 on your computer or network may have set or customized the properties.

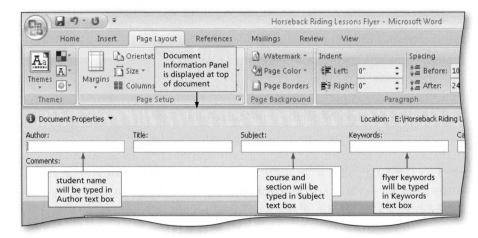

Figure 1–73

3

- Click the Author text box, if necessary, and then type your name as the Author property. If a name already is displayed in the Author text box, delete it before typing your name.

- Click the Subject text box, if necessary delete any existing text, and then type your course and section as the Subject property.

- If an AutoComplete dialog box appears, click its Yes button.

- Click the Keywords text box, if necessary delete any existing text, and then type Tri-Valley Stables as the Keywords property (Figure 1–74).

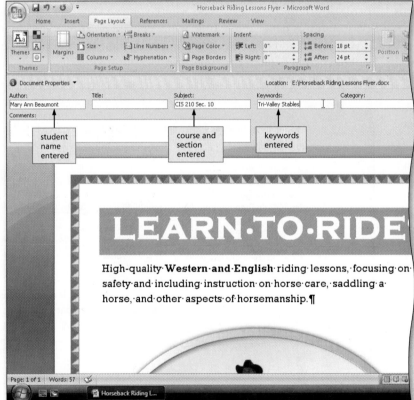
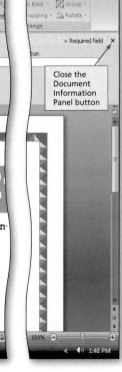

Figure 1–74

Q&A

What types of document properties does Word collect automatically?

Word records such details as how long you worked at creating your project, how many times you revised the document, and what fonts and themes are used.

4

- Click the Close the Document Information Panel button so that the Document Information Panel no longer is displayed.

To Save an Existing Document with the Same File Name

Saving frequently cannot be overemphasized. You have made several modifications to the document since you saved it earlier in the chapter. When you first saved the document, you clicked the Save button on the Quick Access Toolbar, the Save As dialog box appeared, and you entered the file name, Horseback Riding Lessons Flyer. If you want to use the same file name to save the changes made to the document, you again click the Save button on the Quick Access Toolbar. The following step saves the document again.

1

- Click the Save button on the Quick Access Toolbar to overwrite the previous Horseback Riding Lessons Flyer file on the USB flash drive (Figure 1–75).

Q&A Why did the Save As dialog box not appear?

Word overwrites the document using the settings specified the first time you saved the document. To save the file with a different file name or on different media, display the Save As dialog box by clicking the Office Button and then clicking Save As on the Office Button menu. Then, fill in the Save As dialog box as described in Steps 2 through 5 on pages WD 20 and WD 21.

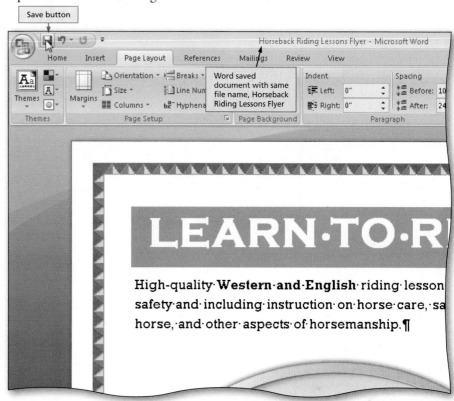

Figure 1–75

Other Ways

1. Press CTRL+S or press SHIFT+F12

Printing a Document

After you create a document, you often want to print it. A printed version of the document is called a **hard copy** or **printout**.

Printed copies of your document can be useful for the following reasons:

- Many people prefer proofreading a hard copy of the document rather than viewing it on the screen to check for errors and readability.

- Hard copies can serve as reference material if your storage medium is lost or becomes corrupted and you need to re-create the document.

It is a good practice to save a document before printing it, in the event you experience difficulties with the printer.

BTW

Conserving Ink and Toner
You can instruct Word to print draft quality documents to conserve ink or toner by clicking the Office Button, clicking the Word Options button, clicking Advanced in the left pane of the Word Options dialog box, scrolling to the Print area, placing a check mark in the 'Use draft quality' check box, and then clicking the OK button. To print the document with these settings, click the Office Button, point to Print, and then click Quick Print.

To Print a Document

With the completed document saved, you may want to print it. The following steps print the contents of the saved Horseback Riding Lessons Flyer project.

- Click the Office Button to display the Office Button menu.

- Point to Print on the Office Button menu to display the Print submenu (Figure 1–76).

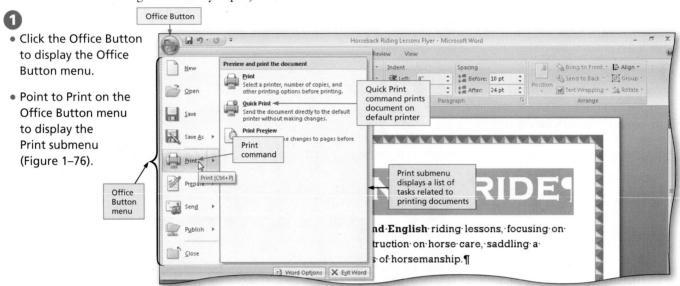

Figure 1–76

- Click Quick Print on the Print submenu to print the document.

- When the printer stops, retrieve the hard copy of the Horseback Riding Lessons Flyer (Figures 1–77).

Q&A How can I print multiple copies of my document other than issuing the Quick Print command twice?

Click the Office Button, point to Print on the Office Button menu, click Print on the Print submenu, increase the number in the Number of copies box, and then click the OK button.

Q&A Do I have to wait until my document is complete to print it?

No, you can follow these steps to print a document at any time while you are creating it.

BTW

Printed Borders

If one or more of your borders do not print, click the Page Borders button on the Page Layout tab, click the Options button in the dialog box, click the Measure from box arrow and click Text, change the four text boxes to 15 pt, and then click the OK button in each dialog box. Try printing the document again. If the borders still do not print, adjust the text boxes in the dialog box to a number smaller than 15 point.

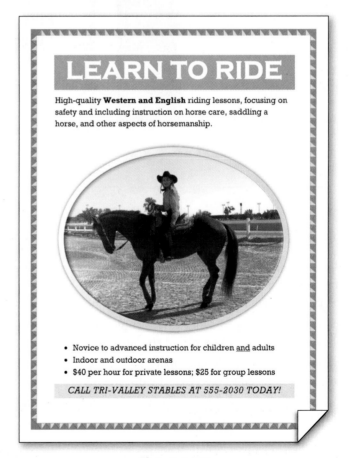

Figure 1–77

Other Ways

1. Press CTRL+P, press ENTER

Quitting Word

When you quit Word, if you have made changes to a document since the last time the file was saved, Word displays a dialog box asking if you want to save the changes you made to the file before it closes that window. The dialog box contains three buttons with these resulting actions: the Yes button saves the changes and then quits Word; the No button quits Word without saving changes; and the Cancel button closes the dialog box and redisplays the document without saving the changes.

If no changes have been made to an open document since the last time the file was saved, Word will close the window without displaying a dialog box.

To Quit Word with One Document Open

You saved the document prior to printing and did not make any changes to the project. The Horseback Riding Lessons Flyer project now is complete, and you are ready to quit Word. When one Word document is open, the following steps quit Word.

1
- Point to the Close button on the right side of the Word title bar (Figure 1–78).

2
- Click the Close button to quit Word.

Q&A What if I have more than one Word document open?

You would click the Close button for each open document. When you click the last open document's Close button, Word also quits. As an alternative, you could click the Office Button and then click the Exit Word button on the Office Button menu, which closes all open Word documents and then quits Word.

Figure 1–78

Starting Word and Opening a Document

Once you have created and saved a document, you may need to retrieve it from your storage medium. For example, you might want to revise the document or reprint it. Opening a document requires that Word is running on your computer.

To Start Word

The following steps, which assume Windows Vista is running, start Word.

1 Click the Start button on the Windows Vista taskbar to display the Start menu.

2 Click All Programs at the bottom of the left pane on the Start menu to display the All Programs list and then click Microsoft Office in the All Programs list to display the Microsoft Office list.

3 Click Microsoft Office Word 2007 in the Microsoft Office list to start Word and display a new blank document in the Word window.

4 If the Word window is not maximized, click the Maximize button on its title bar to maximize the window.

Other Ways

1. Double-click Office Button
2. With multiple documents open, click Office Button, click Exit Word on Office Button menu
3. Right-click Microsoft Word button on Windows Vista taskbar, click Close on shortcut menu
4. Press ALT+F4

Note: If you are using Windows XP, see Appendix F for alternate steps.

To Open a Document from Word

Earlier in this chapter you saved your project on a USB flash drive using the file name, Horseback Riding Lessons Flyer. The following steps open the Horseback Riding Lessons Flyer file from the USB flash drive.

1

• With your USB flash drive connected to one of the computer's USB ports, click the Office Button to display the Office Button menu (Figure 1–79).

Q&A

What files are shown in the Recent Documents list?

Word displays the most recently opened document file names in this list. If the name of the file you want to open appears in the Recent Documents list, you could click it to open the file.

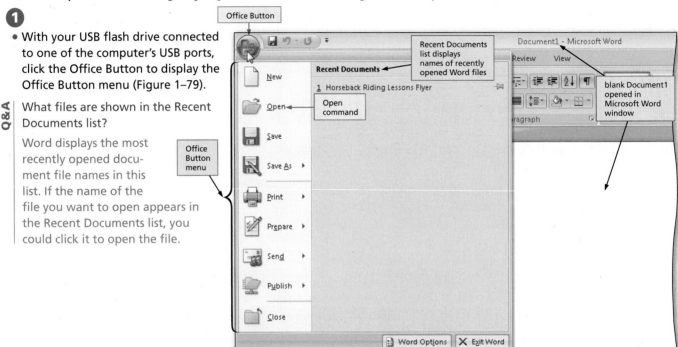

Figure 1–79

2

• Click Open on the Office Button menu to display the Open dialog box.

• If the Folders list is displayed below the Folders button, click the Folders button to remove the Folders list.

• If necessary, click Computer in the Favorite Links section and then scroll until UDISK 2.0 (E:) appears in the list of available drives.

• Double-click UDISK 2.0 (E:) to select the USB flash drive, Drive E in this case, as the new open location.

• Click Horseback Riding Lessons Flyer to select the file name (Figure 1–80).

Q&A

How do I open the file if I am not using a USB flash drive?

Use the same process, but be certain to select your device in the Computer list.

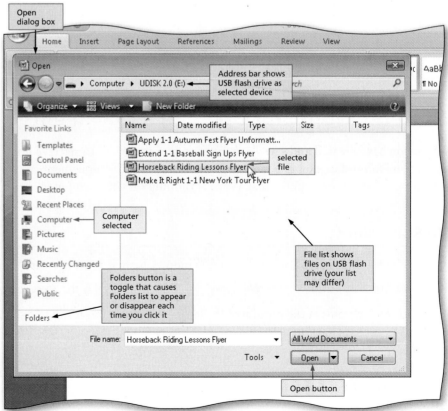

Figure 1–80

3

- Click the Open button to open the selected file and display the Horseback Riding Lessons Flyer document in the Word window (Figure 1–81).

Q&A

Why is the Word icon and document name on the Windows Vista taskbar?

When you open a Word file, a Word program button is displayed on the taskbar. The button in Figure 1–81 contains an ellipsis because some of its contents do not fit in the allotted button space. If you point to a program button, its entire contents appear in a ScreenTip, which in this case would be the file name followed by the program name.

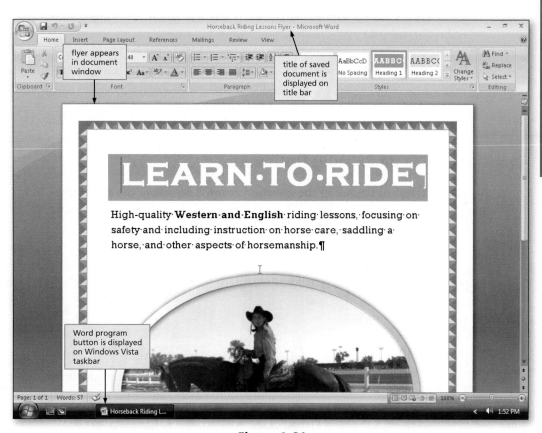

Figure 1–81

Other Ways

1. Click Office Button, click file name in Recent Documents list
2. Press CTRL+O, select file name, press ENTER

Correcting Errors

After creating a document, you often will find you must make changes to it. For example, the document may contain an error, or new circumstances may require you to add text to the document.

Types of Changes Made to Documents

The types of changes made to documents normally fall into one of the three following categories: additions, deletions, or modifications.

Additions Additional words, sentences, or paragraphs may be required in a document. Additions occur when you omit text from a document and want to insert it later. For example, additional types of riding lessons may be offered.

BTW

Print Preview
You can preview a document before printing it by clicking the Office Button, pointing to Print, and then clicking Print Preview. When finished previewing the document, click the Close Print Preview button.

Deletions   Sometimes, text in a document is incorrect or is no longer needed. For example, group lessons might not be offered. In this case, you would delete the words, $25 for group lessons, from the flyer.

Modifications   If an error is made in a document or changes take place that affect the document, you might have to revise a word(s) in the text. For example, the fee per hour may change from $40 to $50 for private lessons.

To Insert Text in an Existing Document

Word inserts text to the left of the insertion point. The text to the right of the insertion point moves to the right and downward to fit the new text. The following steps insert the word, various, to the left of the word, aspects, in the flyer.

- Scroll through the document and then click to the left of the location of text to be inserted (in this case, the a in aspects) to position the insertion point where text should be inserted (Figure 1–82).

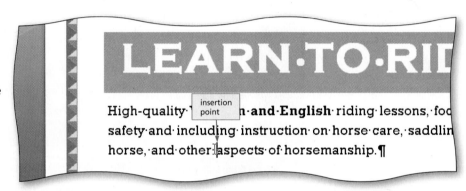

Figure 1–82

- Type various and then press the SPACEBAR to insert the word, various, to the left of the insertion point (Figure 1–83).

Why did the text move to the right as I typed?

In Word, the default typing mode is **insert mode**, which means as you type a character, Word moves all the characters to the right of the typed character one position to the right.

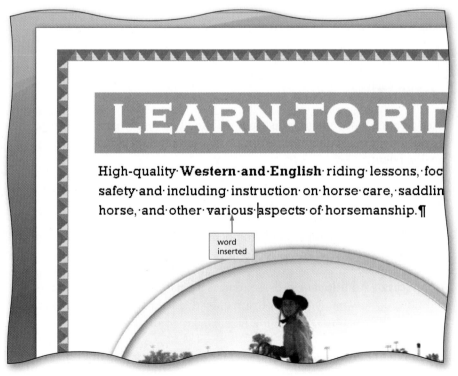

Figure 1–83

Deleting Text from an Existing Document

It is not unusual to type incorrect characters or words in a document. As discussed earlier in this chapter, you can click the Undo button on the Quick Access Toolbar to immediately undo a command or action — this includes typing. Word also provides other methods of correcting typing errors.

To delete an incorrect character in a document, simply click next to the incorrect character and then press the BACKSPACE key to erase to the left of the insertion point, or press the DELETE key to erase to the right of the insertion point.

To Select a Word and Delete It

To delete a word or phrase, you first must select the word or phrase. The following steps select the word, various, that was just added in the previous steps and then delete the selection.

- Position the mouse pointer somewhere in the word to be selected (in this case, various), as shown in Figure 1–84.

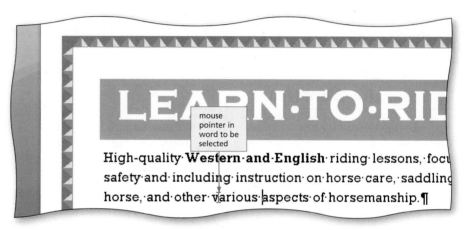

Figure 1–84

2
- Double-click the word to select it (Figure 1–85).

3
- With the text selected, press the DELETE key to delete the selected text (shown in Figure 1–82).

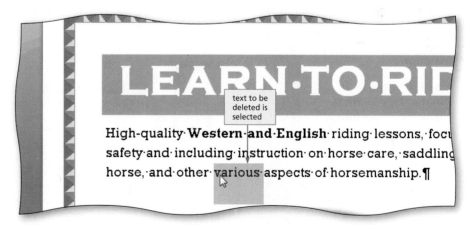

Figure 1–85

Closing the Entire Document

Sometimes, everything goes wrong. If this happens, you may want to close the document entirely and start over with a new document. You also may want to close a document when you are finished with it so you can begin your next document. If you wanted to close a document, you would use the steps on the next page.

To Close the Entire Document and Start Over

1. Click the Office Button and then click Close.
2. If Word displays a dialog box, click the No button to ignore the changes since the last time you saved the document.
3. Click the Office Button and then click New on the Office Button menu. When Word displays the New Document dialog box, click Blank document and then click the Create button.

BTW

Word Help
The best way to become familiar with Word Help is to use it. Appendix C includes detailed information about Word Help and exercises that will help you gain confidence in using it.

Word Help

At any time while using Word, you can find answers to questions and display information about various topics through **Word Help**. Used properly, this form of assistance can increase your productivity and reduce your frustrations by minimizing the time you spend learning how to use Word.

This section introduces you to Word Help. Additional information about using Word Help is available in Appendix C.

To Search for Word Help

Using Word Help, you can search for information based on phrases such as save a document or format text, or key terms such as copy, save, or format. Word Help responds with a list of search results displayed as links to a variety of resources. The following steps, which use Word Help to search for information about selecting text, assume you are connected to the Internet.

1

• Click the Microsoft Office Word Help button near the upper-right corner of the Word window to open the Word Help window.

• Type select text in the 'Type words to search for' text box at the top of the Word Help window (Figure 1–86).

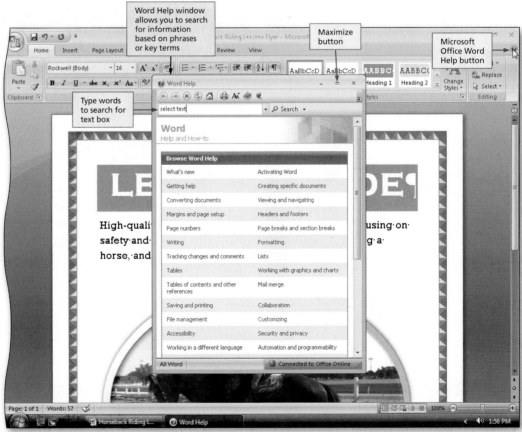

Figure 1–86

2

- Press the ENTER key to display the search results.

- Click the Maximize button on the Word Help window title bar to maximize the Help window (Figure 1–87).

Q&A Where is the Word window with the Horseback Riding Lessons Flyer document?

Word is open in the background, but the Word Help window is overlaid on top of the Word window. When the Word Help window is closed, the document will reappear.

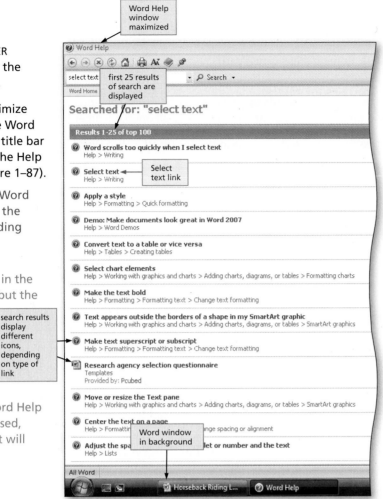

Figure 1–87

3

- Click the Select text link to display information about selecting text (Figure 1–88).

Q&A What is the purpose of the buttons at the top of the Word Help window?

Use the buttons in the upper-left corner of the Word Help window to navigate through Help, change the display, show the Word Help table of contents, and print the contents of the window.

4

- Click the Close button on the Word Help window title bar to close the Word Help window and redisplay the Word window.

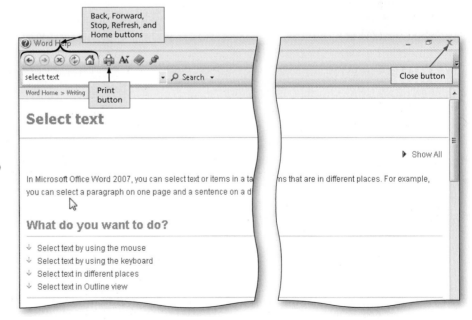

Figure 1–88

Other Ways
1. Press F1

BTW

Quick Reference
For a table that lists how to complete the tasks covered in this book using the mouse, Ribbon, shortcut menu, and keyboard, see the Quick Reference Summary at the back of this book, or visit the Word 2007 Quick Reference Web page (scsite.com/wd2007/qr).

To Quit Word

The following steps quit Word.

1 Click the Close button on the right side of the title bar to quit Word; or if you have multiple Word documents open, click the Office Button and then click the Exit Word button on the Office Button menu to close all open documents and quit Word.

2 If necessary, click the No button in the Microsoft Office Word dialog box so that any changes you have made are not saved.

Chapter Summary

In this chapter you have learned how to enter text in a document, format text, insert a picture, format a picture, add a page border, and print a document. The items listed below include all the new Word skills you have learned in this chapter.

1. Start Word (WD 5)
2. Type Text (WD 13)
3. Display Formatting Marks (WD 14)
4. Wordwrap Text as You Type (WD 15)
5. Insert a Blank Line (WD 15)
6. Check Spelling and Grammar as You Type (WD 16)
7. Save a Document (WD 19)
8. Apply Styles (WD 24)
9. Center a Paragraph (WD 26)
10. Select a Line (WD 27)
11. Change the Font Size of Selected Text (WD 28)
12. Change the Font of Selected Text (WD 29)
13. Select Multiple Paragraphs (WD 30)
14. Bullet a List of Paragraphs (WD 32)
15. Undo and Redo an Action (WD 32)
16. Select a Group of Words (WD 33)
17. Bold Text (WD 34)
18. Underline a Word (WD 35)
19. Italicize Text (WD 36)
20. Change the Style Set (WD 37)
21. Change Theme Colors (WD 39)
22. Change Theme Fonts (WD 39)
23. Insert a Picture (WD 41)
24. Apply a Picture Style (WD 44)
25. Change a Picture Border Color (WD 45)
26. Zoom the Document (WD 45)
27. Resize a Graphic (WD 46)
28. Add a Page Border (WD 48)
29. Change Spacing Above and Below Paragraphs (WD 50)
30. Change Document Properties (WD 51)
31. Save an Existing Document with the Same File Name (WD 53)
32. Print a Document (WD 54)
33. Quit Word with One Document Open (WD 55)
34. Open a Document from Word (WD 56)
35. Insert Text in an Existing Document (WD 58)
36. Select a Word and Delete It (WD 59)
37. Close the Entire Document and Start Over (WD 60)
38. Search for Word Help (WD 60)

 If you have a SAM user profile, you may have access to hands-on instruction, practice, and assessment. Log in to your SAM account (http://sam2007.course.com) to launch any assigned training activities or exams that relate to the skills covered in this chapter.

BTW

Certification
The Microsoft Certified Application Specialist (MCAS) program provides an opportunity for you to obtain a valuable industry credential – proof that you have the Word 2007 skills required by employers. For more information, see Appendix G or visit the Word 2007 Certification Web page (scsite.com/wd2007/cert).

Learn It Online

Test your knowledge of chapter content and key terms.

Instructions: To complete the Learn It Online exercises, start your browser, click the Address bar, and then enter the Web address `scsite.com/wd2007/learn`. When the Word 2007 Learn It Online page is displayed, click the link for the exercise you want to complete and then read the instructions.

Chapter Reinforcement TF, MC, and SA
A series of true/false, multiple choice, and short answer questions that test your knowledge of the chapter content.

Flash Cards
An interactive learning environment where you identify chapter key terms associated with displayed definitions.

Practice Test
A series of multiple choice questions that test your knowledge of chapter content and key terms.

Who Wants To Be a Computer Genius?
An interactive game that challenges your knowledge of chapter content in the style of a television quiz show.

Wheel of Terms
An interactive game that challenges your knowledge of chapter key terms in the style of the television show *Wheel of Fortune*.

Crossword Puzzle Challenge
A crossword puzzle that challenges your knowledge of key terms presented in the chapter.

Apply Your Knowledge

Reinforce the skills and apply the concepts you learned in this chapter.

Modifying Text and Formatting a Document
Instructions: Start Word. Open the document, Apply 1-1 Autumn Fest Flyer Unformatted, from the Data Files for Students. See the inside back cover of this book for instructions on downloading the Data Files for Students, or contact your instructor for information about accessing the required files.

The document you open is an unformatted flyer. You are to modify text, format paragraphs and characters, and insert a picture in the flyer.

Perform the following tasks:
1. Delete the word, entire, in the sentence of body copy below the headline.
2. Insert the word, Creek, between the text, Honey Farm, in the sentence of body copy below the headline. The sentence should end: ...Honey Creek Farm.
3. At the end of the signature line, change the period to an exclamation point. The sentence should end: ...This Year's Fest!
4. Apply the Heading 1 style to the headline. Apply the Heading 2 style to the signature line.
5. Center the headline and the signature line.
6. Change the font and font size of the headline to 48-point Cooper Black, or a similar font.
7. Change the font size of body copy between the headline and the signature line to 22 point.
8. Change the font size of the signature line to 28 point.
9. Bullet the three lines (paragraphs) of text above the signature line.
10. Bold the text, October 4 and 5.

Continued >

Apply Your Knowledge *continued*

11. Underline the word, and, in the first bulleted paragraph.

12. Italicize the text in the signature line.

13. Change the theme colors to the Civic color scheme.

14. Change the theme fonts to the Opulent font set.

15. Change the zoom to 50 percent so the entire page is visible in the document window.

16. Change the spacing before the headline paragraph to 0 point. Change the spacing after the headline paragraph to 12 point.

17. Insert the picture of the combine centered on the blank line above the bulleted list. The picture is called Fall Harvest and is available on the Data Files for Students. Apply the Snip Diagonal Corner, White picture style to the inserted picture. Change the color of the picture border to Orange, Accent 6.

18. The entire flyer now should fit on a single page. If it flows to two pages, resize the picture or decrease spacing before and after paragraphs until the entire flyer text fits on a single page.

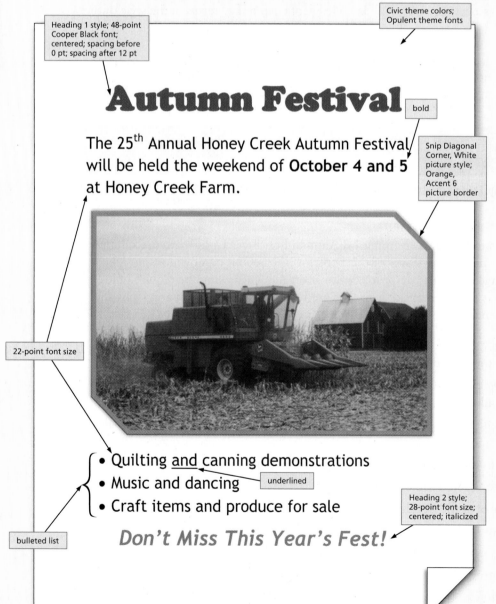

Heading 1 style; 48-point Cooper Black font; centered; spacing before 0 pt; spacing after 12 pt

Civic theme colors; Opulent theme fonts

Autumn Festival

bold

The 25th Annual Honey Creek Autumn Festival will be held the weekend of **October 4 and 5** at Honey Creek Farm.

Snip Diagonal Corner, White picture style; Orange, Accent 6 picture border

22-point font size

- Quilting <u>and</u> canning demonstrations
- Music and dancing
- Craft items and produce for sale

underlined

bulleted list

Don't Miss This Year's Fest!

Heading 2 style; 28-point font size; centered; italicized

19. Enter the text, Honey Creek, as the keywords. Change the other document properties, as specified by your instructor.

20. Click the Office Button and then click Save As. Save the document using the file name, Apply 1-1 Autumn Fest Flyer Formatted.

21. Position the Quick Access Toolbar below the Ribbon. Save the document again by clicking the Save button. Reposition the Quick Access Toolbar above the Ribbon.

22. Submit the revised document, shown in Figure 1–89, in the format specified by your instructor.

Figure 1–89

Extend Your Knowledge

Extend the skills you learned in this chapter and experiment with new skills. You may need to use Help to complete the assignment.

Modifying Text and Graphics Formats

Instructions: Start Word. Open the document, Extend 1-1 Baseball Sign Ups Flyer, from the Data Files for Students. See the inside back cover of this book for instructions on downloading the Data Files for Students, or contact your instructor for information about accessing the required files.

You will enhance the look of the flyer shown in Figure 1–90.

Perform the following tasks:

1. Use Help to learn about the following formats: grow font, shrink font, change text color, decorative underline, and change bullet.

2. Select the headline and use the Grow Font button to increase its font size just enough so that the headline still fits on a single line. If it wraps to two lines, use the Shrink Font button.

3. Change the font color of all body copy between the headline and the signature line to a color other than Automatic, or Black.

4. Change the picture style of the picture so that it is not the Drop Shadow Rectangle picture style. Add a Glow picture effect to the picture of the baseball player.

5. Change the solid underline below the words, Indoor facility, to a decorative underline.

6. Change the color and width of the border.

7. Change the style of the bullets to a character other than the dot.

8. Change the document properties, including keywords, as specified by your instructor. Save the revised document with a new file name and then submit it in the format specified by your instructor.

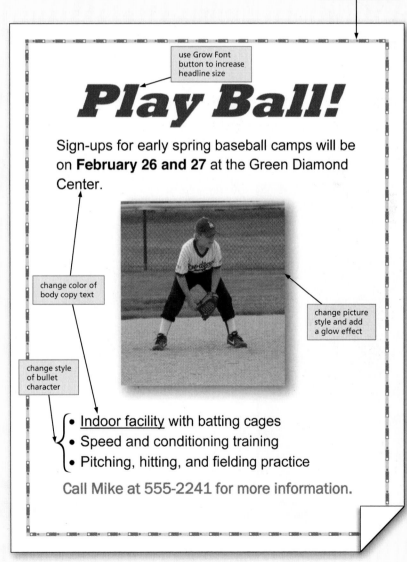

change color and width of border

use Grow Font button to increase headline size

change color of body copy text

change style of bullet character

change picture style and add a glow effect

Figure 1–90

Make It Right

Analyze a document and correct all errors and/or improve the design.

Correcting Spelling and Grammar Errors

Instructions: Start Word. Open the document, Make It Right 1-1 New York Tour Flyer, from the Data Files for Students. See the inside back cover of this book for instructions on downloading the Data Files for Students, or contact your instructor for information on accessing the required files.

The document is a flyer that contains spelling and grammar errors, as shown in Figure 1–91. You are to correct each spelling (red wavy underline) and grammar error (green wavy underline) by right-clicking the flagged text and then clicking the appropriate correction on the shortcut menu. If your screen does not display the wavy underlines, click the Office Button and then click the Word Options button. When the Word Options dialog box is displayed, click Proofing, be sure the 'Hide spelling errors in this document only' and 'Hide grammar errors in this document only' check boxes do not have check marks, and then click the OK button. If your screen still does not display the wavy under-lines, redisplay the Word Options dialog box, click Proofing, and then click the Recheck Document button.

Change the document properties, including keywords, as specified by your instructor. Save the revised document with a new file name and then submit it in the format specified by your instructor.

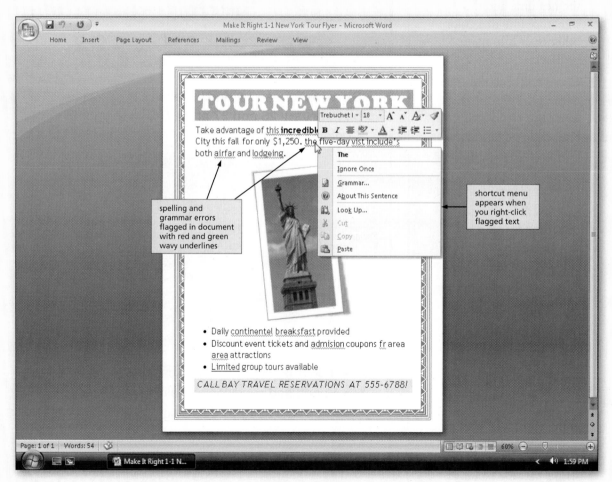

Figure 1–91

In the Lab

Design and/or create a document using the guidelines, concepts, and skills presented in this chapter. Labs are listed in order of increasing difficulty.

Lab 1: Creating a Flyer with a Picture

Problem: You work part-time at Scenic Air. Your boss has asked you to prepare a flyer that advertises aerial tours over the city of Campton. First, you prepare the unformatted flyer shown in Figure 1–92a, and then you format it so that it looks like Figure 1–92b on the next page. *Hint:* Remember, if you make a mistake while formatting the flyer, you can click the Undo button on the Quick Access Toolbar to undo your last action.

Instructions: Perform the following tasks:

1. Display formatting marks on the screen.
2. Type the flyer text, unformatted, as shown in Figure 1–92a. If Word flags any misspelled words as you type, check the spelling of these words and correct them.
3. Save the document on a USB flash drive using the file name, Lab 1-1 Airplane Rides Flyer.
4. Apply the Heading 1 style to the headline. Apply the Heading 2 style to the signature line.
5. Center the headline and the signature line.
6. Change the font and font size of the headline to 48-point Arial Rounded MT Bold, or a similar font.
7. Change the font size of body copy between the headline and the signature line to 22 point.
8. Change the font size of the signature line to 28 point.
9. Bullet the three lines (paragraphs) of text above the signature line.
10. Bold the text, change your view.
11. Italicize the word, aerial.

Airplane Rides

Gain an entirely new vision of Campton by taking an aerial tour. Visitor or local, business or pleasure, the trip will change your view of the city.

Pilots are licensed and experienced

15-, 30-, or 60-minute tours available during daylight hours

Individual and group rates

Call Scenic Air at 555-9883!

Figure 1–92a

Continued >

In the Lab continued

12. Underline the word, and, in the first bulleted paragraph.

13. Change the style set to Formal.

14. Change the theme fonts to the Metro font set.

15. Change the zoom to 50 percent so the entire page is visible in the document window.

16. Change the spacing before the headline to 0 point. Change the spacing after the first paragraph of body copy to 0 point. Change the spacing before the first bulleted paragraph to 12 point.

17. Insert the picture centered on the blank line above the bulleted list. The picture is called Airplane Ride over City and is available on the Data Files for Students. Apply the Relaxed Perspective, White picture style to the inserted picture.

18. The entire flyer should fit on a single page. If it flows to two pages, resize the picture or decrease spacing before and after paragraphs until the entire flyer text fits on a single page.

19. Change the document properties, including keywords, as specified by your instructor.

20. Save the flyer again with the same file name.

21. Submit the document, shown in Figure 1–92b, in the format specified by your instructor.

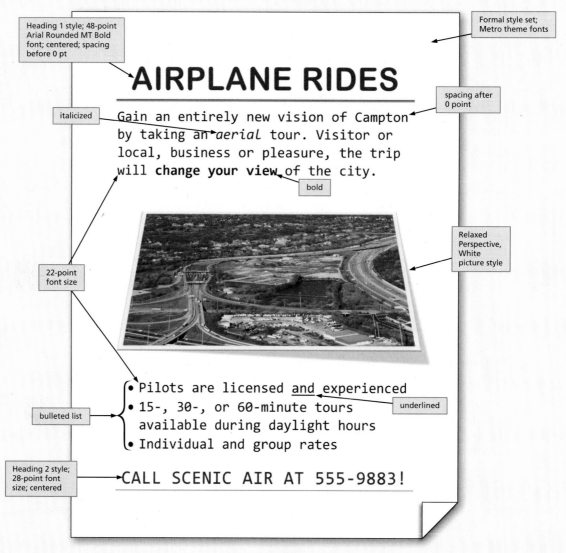

Figure 1–92b

In the Lab

Lab 2: Creating a Flyer with a Picture and a Border

Problem: Your boss at Danvers Nursery has asked you to prepare a flyer that promotes its expanded greenhouses and grounds. You prepare the flyer shown in Figure 1–93. *Hint:* Remember, if you make a mistake while formatting the flyer, you can click the Undo button on the Quick Access Toolbar to undo your last action.

Instructions: Perform the following tasks:

1. Display formatting marks on the screen.

2. Type the flyer text, unformatted. If Word flags any misspelled words as you type, check the spelling of these words and correct them.

3. Save the document on a USB flash drive using the file name, Lab 1-2 Nursery Expansion Flyer.

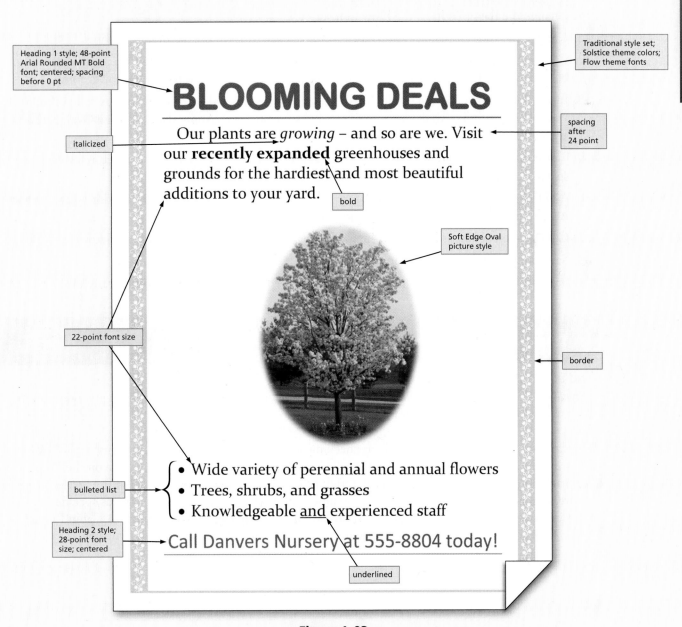

Figure 1–93

Continued >

In the Lab *continued*

4. Apply the Heading 1 style to the headline. Apply the Heading 2 style to the signature line.

5. Center the headline and the signature line.

6. Change the font and font size of the headline to 48-point Arial Rounded MT Bold, or a similar font.

7. Change the font size of body copy between the headline and the signature line to 22 point.

8. Change the font size of the signature line to 28 point.

9. Bullet the three lines (paragraphs) of text above the signature line.

10. Italicize the word, growing.

11. Bold the text, recently expanded.

12. Underline the word, and, in the third bulleted paragraph.

13. Change the style set to Traditional.

14. Change the theme colors to the Solstice color scheme.

15. Change the theme fonts to the Flow font set.

16. Change the zoom to 50 percent so the entire page is visible in the document window.

17. Change the spacing before the headline to 0 point. Change the spacing after the first paragraph of body copy to 24 point. Change the spacing before the first bulleted paragraph to 12 point.

18. Insert the picture centered on the blank line above the bulleted list. The picture is called Bradford Pear in Bloom and is available on the Data Files for Students. Apply the Soft Edge Oval picture style to the inserted picture.

19. The entire flyer should fit on a single page. If it flows to two pages, resize the picture or decrease spacing before and after paragraphs until the entire flyer text fits on a single page.

20. Add the graphic border, shown in Figure 1–93 on the previous page (about one-third down in the Art gallery). Change the color of the border to Tan, Background 2.

21. Change the document properties, including keywords, as specified by your instructor.

22. Save the flyer again with the same file name.

23. Submit the document, shown in Figure 1–93, in the format specified by your instructor.

In the Lab

Lab 3: Creating a Flyer with a Picture and Resized Border Art

Problem: Your neighbor has asked you to prepare a flyer that promotes her cabin rental business. You prepare the flyer shown in Figure 1–94.

Instructions: Enter the text in the flyer, checking spelling as you type, and then format it as shown in Figure 1–94. The picture to be inserted is called Paddle Boat on Lake and is available on the Data Files for Students. After adding the page border, reduce the point size of its width so that the border is not so predominant on the page. Change the document properties, including keywords, as specified by your instructor. Save the document on a USB flash drive using the file name, Lab 1-3 Cabin Rentals Flyer. Submit the document, shown in Figure 1–94, in the format specified by your instructor.

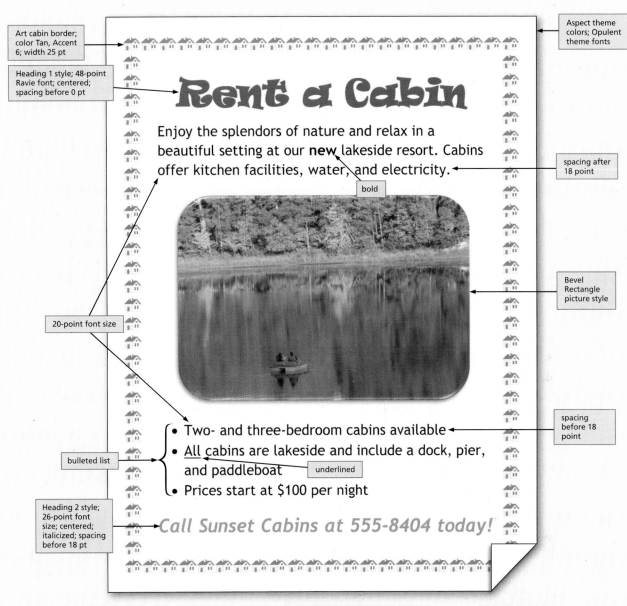

Aspect theme colors; Opulent theme fonts

Art cabin border; color Tan, Accent 6; width 25 pt

Heading 1 style; 48-point Ravie font; centered; spacing before 0 pt

spacing after 18 point

bold

Bevel Rectangle picture style

20-point font size

spacing before 18 point

bulleted list

underlined

Heading 2 style; 26-point font size; centered; italicized; spacing before 18 pt

Figure 1–94

Cases and Places

Apply your creative thinking and problem solving skills to design and implement a solution.

• EASIER   •• MORE DIFFICULT

• 1: Design and Create a Grand Reopening Flyer

Your friend owns the Craft Barn, a large, year-round craft fair. She recently has renovated and remodeled the facility and is planning a grand reopening. She has asked you to create a flyer advertising this fact. The flyer should contain the following headline: Craft Barn. The first paragraph of text below the headline should read: Pick up a jar of homemade jam or a handcrafted gift at the completely remodeled and renovated Craft Barn, located at 8701 County Road 300 West. Insert the photograph named, Barn and Silo, which is available on the Data Files for Students. The bullet items

Continued >

Cases and Places *continued*

under the photograph should read as follows: first bullet – Expanded and paved parking; second bullet – More than 150 booths; and third bullet – Open Monday through Saturday, 10:00 a.m. to 7:00 p.m. The last line should read: Call 555-5709 for more information! Use the concepts and techniques presented in this chapter to create and format this flyer. Be sure to check spelling and grammar.

• 2: Design and Create a Property Advertisement Flyer

As a part-time employee of Markum Realty, you have been assigned the task of preparing a flyer advertising lakefront property. The headline should read: Lakefront Lot. The first paragraph of text should read as follows: Build the house of your dreams or a weekend getaway on this beautiful lakeside property located on the north side of Lake Pleasant. Insert the photograph named, Lake at Sunset, which is available on the Data Files for Students. Below the photograph, insert the following bullet items: first bullet — City sewer and water available; second bullet – Lot size 110 × 300; third bullet – List price $65,000. The last line should read: Call Markum Realty at 555-0995 for a tour! Use the concepts and techniques presented in this chapter to create and format this flyer. Be sure to check spelling and grammar.

•• 3: Design and Create a Flyer for the Sale of a Business

After 25 years, your Uncle Mitch has decided to sell his ice cream shop and wants you to help him create a sales flyer. The shop is in a choice location at the corner of 135th and Main Street and has an established customer base. The building has an adjacent, paved parking lot, as well as an outdoor seating area. He wants to sell the store and all its contents, including the equipment, tables, booths, and chairs. The 1200-square-foot shop recently was appraised at $200,000, and your uncle is willing to sell for cash or on contract. Use the concepts and techniques presented in this chapter to create and format a sales flyer. Include a headline, descriptive body copy, a signature line, an appropriate photograph or clip art image, a bulleted list, a decorative underline, and if appropriate, a page border. Be sure to check spelling and grammar in the flyer.

•• 4: Design and Create a Flyer that Advertises You

Make It Personal

Everyone has at least one skill, talent, or special capability, which if shared with others, can lead to opportunity for growth, experience, and personal reward. Perhaps you play a musical instrument. If so, you could offer lessons. Maybe you are a skilled carpenter or other tradesman who could advertise your services. If you speak a second language, you could offer tutoring. Budding athletes might harbor a desire to pass on their knowledge by coaching a youth sports team. You may have a special knack for singing, sewing, knitting, photography, typing, housecleaning, or pet care. Carefully consider your own personal capabilities, skills, and talents and then use the concepts and techniques presented in this chapter to create a flyer advertising a service you can provide. Include a headline, descriptive body copy, a signature line, an appropriate photograph or clip art image, a bulleted list, a decorative underline, and if appropriate, a page border. Be sure to check spelling and grammar in the flyer.

•• 5: Redesign and Enhance a Poorly Designed Flyer

Working Together

Public locations, such as stores, schools, and libraries, have bulletin boards or windows for people to post flyers. Often, these bulletin boards or windows have so many flyers that some go unnoticed. Locate a posted flyer on a bulletin board or window that you think might be overlooked. Copy the text from the flyer and distribute it to each team member. Each member then independently should use this text, together with the techniques presented in this chapter, to create a flyer that would be more likely to catch the attention of passersby. Be sure to check spelling and grammar. As a group, critique each flyer and have team members redesign their flyer based on the group's recommendations. Hand in each team member's original and final flyers.

1 Creating a Worksheet and an Embedded Chart

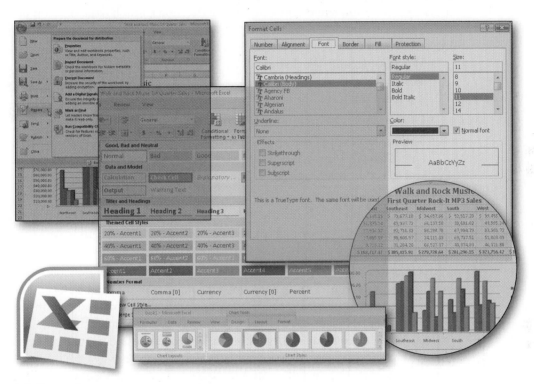

Objectives

You will have mastered the material in this chapter when you can:

- Start and quit Excel
- Describe the Excel worksheet
- Enter text and numbers
- Use the Sum button to sum a range of cells
- Copy the contents of a cell to a range of cells using the fill handle
- Save a workbook
- Format cells in a worksheet
- Create a 3-D Clustered Column chart

- Change document properties
- Save a workbook a second time using the same file name
- Print a worksheet
- Open a workbook
- Use the AutoCalculate area to determine statistics
- Correct errors on a worksheet
- Use Excel Help to answer questions

1 Creating a Worksheet and an Embedded Chart

What Is Microsoft Office Excel 2007?

Microsoft Office Excel 2007 is a powerful spreadsheet program that allows users to organize data, complete calculations, make decisions, graph data, develop professional looking reports (Figure 1–1), publish organized data to the Web, and access real-time data from Web sites. The four major parts of Excel are:

- **Workbooks and Worksheets** Workbooks are a collection of worksheets. Worksheets allow users to enter, calculate, manipulate, and analyze data such as numbers and text. The terms worksheet and spreadsheet are interchangeable.

- **Charts** Excel can draw a variety of charts.

- **Tables** Tables organize and store data within worksheets. For example, once a user enters data into a worksheet, an Excel table can sort the data, search for specific data, and select data that satisfies defined criteria.

- **Web Support** Web support allows users to save Excel worksheets or parts of a worksheet in HTML format, so a user can view and manipulate the worksheet using a browser. Excel Web support also provides access to real-time data, such as stock quotes, using Web queries.

This latest version of Excel makes it much easier than in previous versions to perform common functions by introducing a new style of user interface. It also offers the capability of creating larger worksheets, improved formatting and printing, improved charting and table functionality, industry-standard XML support that simplifies the sharing of data within and outside an organization, improved business intelligence functionality, and the capability of performing complex tasks on a server.

In this chapter, you will create a worksheet that includes a chart. The data in the worksheet and chart includes sales data for several stores that a company owns and operates.

Project Planning Guidelines

The process of developing a worksheet that communicates specific information requires careful analysis and planning. As a starting point, establish why the worksheet is needed. Once the purpose is determined, analyze the intended users of the worksheet and their unique needs. Then, gather information about the topic and decide what to include in the worksheet. Finally, determine the worksheet design and style that will be most successful at delivering the message. Details of these guidelines are provided in Appendix A. In addition, each project developed in this book provides practical applications of these planning considerations.

Project — Worksheet with an Embedded Chart

The project in this chapter follows proper design guidelines and uses Excel to create the worksheet shown in Figure 1–1. The worksheet contains sales data for Walk and Rock Music stores. The Walk and Rock Music product line includes a variety of MP3 music players, called Rock-It MP3, including players that show pictures and video, as well as a complete line of headphones and other accessories. The company sells its products at kiosks in several malls throughout the United States. By concentrating its stores near colleges and universities and keeping the newest items in stock, the Walk and Rock Music stores quickly became trendy. As sales continued to grow in the past year, senior management requested an easy-to-read worksheet that shows product sales for the first quarter by region. In addition, they asked for a chart showing first quarter sales, because the president of the company likes to have a graphical representation of sales that allows him quickly to identify stronger and weaker product types by region.

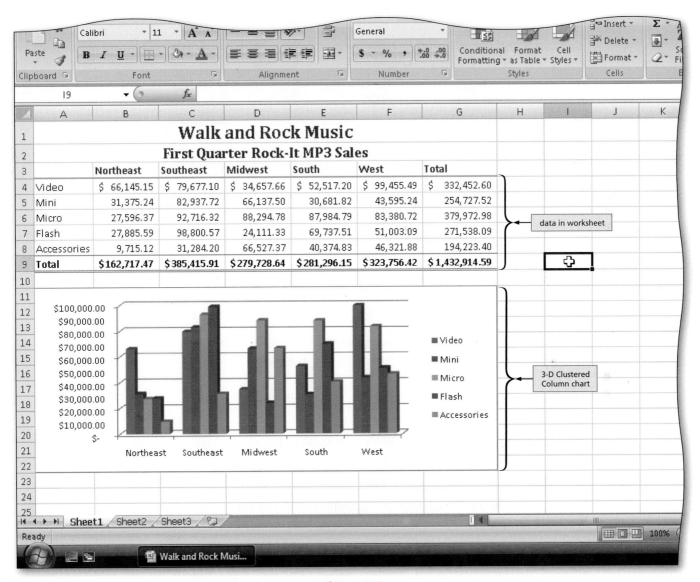

Figure 1–1

The first step in creating an effective worksheet is to make sure you understand what is required. The person or persons requesting the worksheet should supply their requirements in a requirements document. A **requirements document** includes a needs

BTW

Excel 2007 Features
With its what-if
analysis tools, research
capabilities, collaboration
tools, streamlined user
interface, smart tags,
charting features, Web
capabilities, hundreds of
functions, and enhanced
formatting capabilities,
Excel 2007 is one of the
easier and more powerful
spreadsheet packages
available.

statement, source of data, summary of calculations, and any other special requirements for the worksheet, such as charting and Web support. Figure 1–2 shows the requirements document for the new workbook to be created in this chapter.

requirements
document →

REQUEST FOR NEW WORKBOOK

Date Submitted:	April 15, 2008
Submitted By:	Trisha Samuels
Worksheet Title:	Walk and Rock Music First Quarter Sales
Needs:	An easy-to-read worksheet that shows Walk and Rock Music's first quarter sales for each of our sales regions in which we operate (Northeast, Southeast, Midwest, South, West). The worksheet also should include total sales for each region, total sales for each product type, and total company sales for the first quarter.
Source of Data:	The data for the worksheet is available for the end of the first quarter from the chief financial officer (CFO) of Walk and Rock Music.
Calculations:	The following calculations must be made for the worksheet: (a) total first quarter sales for each of the five regions; (b) total first quarter sales for each of the five product types; and (c) total first quarter sales for the company.
Chart Requirements:	Below the data in the worksheet, construct a 3-D Clustered Column chart that compares the total sales for each region within each type of product.

Approvals

Approval Status:	X	Approved
		Rejected
Approved By:	Stan Maderbek	
Date:	April 22, 2008	
Assigned To:	J. Quasney, Spreadsheet Specialist	

Figure 1–2

BTW

Worksheet Development Cycle
Spreadsheet specialists
do not sit down and
start entering text,
formulas, and data into
a blank Excel worksheet
as soon as they have a
spreadsheet assignment.
Instead, they follow
an organized plan,
or methodology, that
breaks the development
cycle into a series of
tasks. The recommended
methodology for creating
worksheets includes:
(1) analyze requirements
(supplied in a requirements
document); (2) design
solution; (3) validate
design; (4) implement
design; (5) test solution;
and (6) document
solution.

Overview

As you read this chapter, you will learn how to create the worksheet shown in Figure 1–1 by performing these general tasks:

- Enter text in the worksheet
- Add totals to the worksheet
- Save the workbook that contains the worksheet
- Format the text in the worksheet
- Insert a chart in the worksheet
- Save the workbook a second time using the same file name
- Print the worksheet

**Plan
Ahead**

General Project Guidelines

While creating an Excel worksheet, you need to make several decisions that will determine the appearance and characteristics of the finished worksheet. As you create the worksheet shown in Figure 1–1, you should follow these general guidelines:

1. **Select titles and subtitles for the worksheet.** Follow the *less is more* guideline. The less text in the titles and subtitles, the more impact the titles and subtitles will have. Use the fewest words possible to specify the information presented in the worksheet to the intended audience.

(continued)

sketch of worksheet

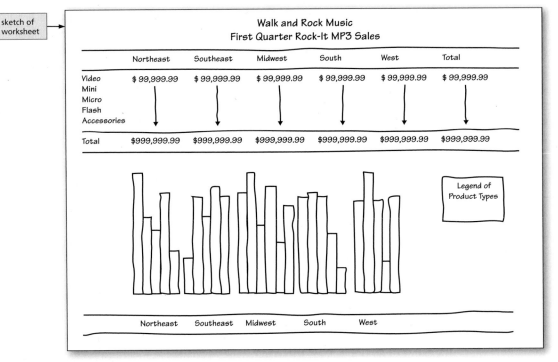

Figure 1–3

Plan Ahead

(continued)

2. **Determine the contents for rows and columns.** Rows typically contain information that is analogous to items in a list, such as the products sold by a company. Columns typically contain descriptive information about items in rows or contain information that helps to group the data in the worksheet, such as company regions.

3. **Determine the calculations that are needed.** You can decide to total data in a variety of ways, such as across rows or in columns. You also can include a grand total.

4. **Determine where to save the workbook.** You can store a workbook permanently, or **save** it, on a variety of storage media including a hard disk, USB flash drive, or CD. You also can indicate a specific location on the storage media for saving the workbook.

5. **Identify how to format various elements of the worksheet.** The overall appearance of a worksheet significantly affects its ability to communicate clearly. Examples of how you can modify the appearance, or **format**, of text include changing its shape, size, color, and position on the worksheet.

6. **Decide on the type of chart needed.** Excel includes the capability of creating many different types of charts, such as bar charts and pie charts. Each chart type relays a different message about the data in the worksheet. Choose a chart type that relays the message that you want to convey.

7. **Establish where to position and how to format the chart.** The position and format of the chart should command the attention of the intended audience. If possible, position the chart so that it prints with the worksheet data on a single page.

When necessary, more specific details concerning the above guidelines are presented at appropriate points in the chapter. The chapter also will identify the actions performed and decisions made regarding these guidelines during the creation of the worksheet shown in Figure 1–1 on page EX 3.

After carefully reviewing the requirements document (Figure 1–2 on page EX 4) and necessary decisions, the next step is to design a solution or draw a sketch of the worksheet based on the requirements, including titles, column and row headings, location of data values, and the 3-D Clustered Column chart, as shown in Figure 1–3 on page EX 5. The dollar signs, 9s, and commas that you see in the sketch of the worksheet indicate formatted numeric values.

With a good understanding of the requirements document, an understanding of the necessary decisions, and a sketch of the worksheet, the next step is to use Excel to create the worksheet and chart.

Starting Excel

If you are using a computer to step through the project in this chapter and you want your screen to match the figures in this book, you should change your computer's resolution to 1024 × 768. For information about how to change a computer's resolution, read Appendix E.

To Start Excel

The following steps, which assume Windows Vista is running, start Excel based on a typical installation of Microsoft Office on your computer. You may need to ask your instructor how to start Excel for your computer.

Note: If you are using Windows XP, see Appendix F for alternate steps.

1

- Click the Start button on the Windows Vista taskbar to display the Start menu.

- Click All Programs at the bottom of left pane on the the Start menu to display the All Programs list.

- Click Microsoft Office in the All Programs list to display the Microsoft Office list (Figure 1–4).

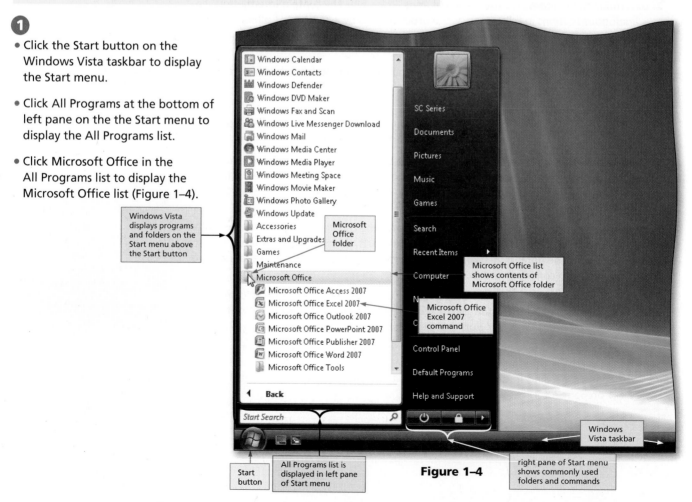

Figure 1–4

2

- Click Microsoft Office Excel 2007 to start Excel and display a new blank workbook titled Book1 in the Excel window (Figure 1–5).

- If the Excel window is not maximized, click the Maximize button next to the Close button on its title bar to maximize the window.

- If the worksheet window in Excel is not maximized, click the Maximize button next to the Close button on its title bar to maximize the worksheet window within Excel.

Q&A

What is a maximized window?

A maximized window fills the entire screen. When you maximize a window, the Maximize button changes to a Restore Down button. When you restore a maximized window, the window returns to its previous size and the Restore Down button changes to a Maximize button.

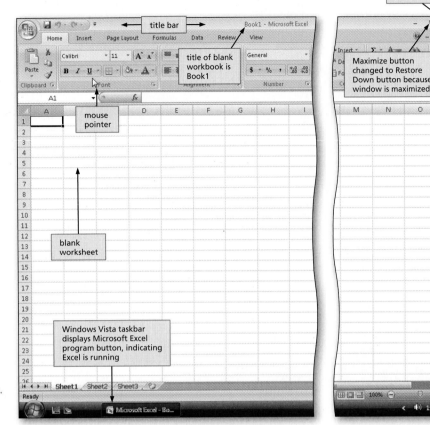

Figure 1–5

Other Ways

1. Double-click Excel 2007 icon on desktop, if one is present

2. Click Microsoft Office Excel 2007 on Start menu

The Excel Workbook

The Excel window consists of a variety of components to make your work more efficient and worksheets more professional. These include the document window, Ribbon, Mini toolbar and shortcut menus, Quick Access Toolbar, and Office Button. Some of these components are common to other Microsoft Office 2007 programs; others are unique to Excel.

When Excel starts, it creates a new blank workbook, called Book1. The **workbook** (Figure 1–6) is like a notebook. Inside the workbook are sheets, each of which is called a **worksheet**. Excel opens a new workbook with three worksheets.

If necessary, you can add additional worksheets as long as your computer has enough memory to accommodate them. Each worksheet has a sheet name that appears on a **sheet tab** at the bottom of the workbook. For example, Sheet1 is the name of the active worksheet displayed in the Book1 workbook. If you click the sheet tab labeled Sheet2, Excel displays the Sheet2 worksheet. The project in this chapter uses only the Sheet1 worksheet.

The Worksheet

The worksheet is organized into a rectangular grid containing vertical columns and horizontal rows. A column letter above the grid, also called the **column heading**, identifies each column. A row number on the left side of the grid, also called the **row heading**, identifies

BTW

Excel Help
Help with Excel is no further away than the Help button on the right side of the Ribbon. Click the Help button, type help in the 'Type words to search for' box, and then press the ENTER key. Excel responds with a list of topics you can click to learn about obtaining Help on any Excel-related topic. To find out what is new in Excel 2007, type what is new in Excel in the 'Type words to search for' box.

each row. With the screen resolution set to 1024 × 768 and the Excel window maximized, Excel displays 15 columns (A through O) and 25 rows (1 through 25) of the worksheet on the screen, as shown in Figure 1–6.

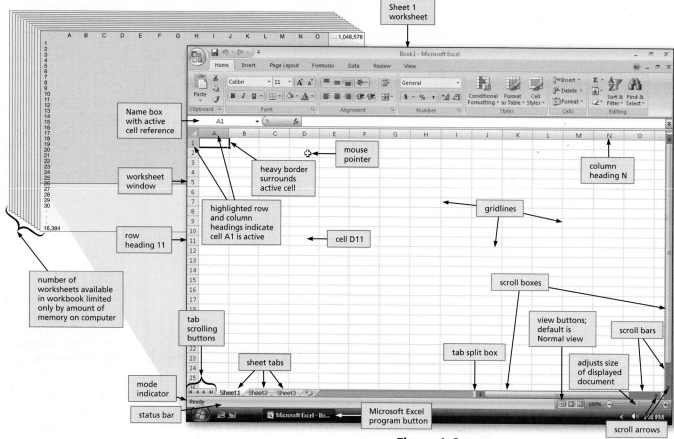

Sheet 1 worksheet

Name box with active cell reference

worksheet window

row heading 11

number of worksheets available in workbook limited only by amount of memory on computer

mode indicator

status bar

mouse pointer

heavy border surrounds active cell

highlighted row and column headings indicate cell A1 is active

cell D11

column heading N

gridlines

scroll boxes

view buttons; default is Normal view

scroll bars

tab split box

adjusts size of displayed document

tab scrolling buttons

sheet tabs

Microsoft Excel program button

scroll arrows

Figure 1–6

BTW

Worksheet Development
The key to developing a useful worksheet is careful planning. Careful planning can reduce your effort significantly and result in a worksheet that is accurate, easy to read, flexible, and useful. When analyzing a problem and designing a worksheet solution, you should follow these steps: (1) define the problem, including need, source of data, calculations, charting, and Web or special requirements; (2) design the worksheet; (3) enter the data and formulas; and (4) test the worksheet.

The intersection of each column and row is a cell. A **cell** is the basic unit of a worksheet into which you enter data. Each worksheet in a workbook has 16,384 columns and 1,048,576 rows for a total of 17,179,869,180 cells. Only a small fraction of the active worksheet appears on the screen at one time.

A cell is referred to by its unique address, or **cell reference**, which is the coordinates of the intersection of a column and a row. To identify a cell, specify the column letter first, followed by the row number. For example, cell reference D11 refers to the cell located at the intersection of column D and row 11 (Figure 1–6).

One cell on the worksheet, designated the **active cell**, is the one into which you can enter data. The active cell in Figure 1–6 is A1. The active cell is identified in three ways. First, a heavy border surrounds the cell; second, the active cell reference shows immediately above column A in the Name box; and third, the column heading A and row heading 1 are highlighted so it is easy to see which cell is active (Figure 1–6).

The horizontal and vertical lines on the worksheet itself are called **gridlines**. Gridlines make it easier to see and identify each cell in the worksheet. If desired, you can turn the gridlines off so they do not show on the worksheet, but it is recommended that you leave them on for now.

The mouse pointer in Figure 1–6 has the shape of a block plus sign. The mouse pointer appears as a block plus sign whenever it is located in a cell on the worksheet. Another common shape of the mouse pointer is the block arrow. The mouse pointer turns into the block arrow whenever you move it outside the worksheet or when you drag cell contents between rows or columns. The other mouse pointer shapes are described when they appear on the screen.

Worksheet Window

You view the portion of the worksheet displayed on the screen through a **worksheet window** (Figure 1–6). The default (preset) view is **normal view**. Below and to the right of the worksheet window are **scroll bars**, **scroll arrows**, and **scroll boxes** that you can use to move the worksheet window around to view different parts of the active worksheet. To the right of the sheet tabs at the bottom of the screen is the tab split box. You can drag the **tab split box** to increase or decrease the view of the sheet tabs (Figure 1–6). When you decrease the view of the sheet tabs, you increase the length of the horizontal scroll bar, and vice versa.

Status Bar

The status bar is located immediately above the Windows Vista taskbar at the bottom of the screen (Figure 1–6). The **status bar** presents information about the worksheet, the function of the button the mouse pointer is pointing to, or the mode of Excel. **Mode indicators**, such as Enter and Ready, appear on the status bar and specify the current mode of Excel. When the mode is **Ready**, Excel is ready to accept the next command or data entry. When the mode indicator reads **Enter**, Excel is in the process of accepting data through the keyboard into the active cell.

Keyboard indicators, such as Scroll Lock, show which toggle keys are engaged. Keyboard indicators appear to the right of the mode indicator. Toward the right edge of the status bar are buttons and controls you can use to change the view of a document and adjust the size of the displayed document.

Ribbon

The **Ribbon**, located near the top of the Excel window, is the control center in Excel (Figure 1–7a). The Ribbon provides easy, central access to the tasks you perform while creating a worksheet. The Ribbon consists of tabs, groups, and commands. Each **tab** surrounds a collection of groups, and each **group** contains related commands.

BTW

The Worksheet Size and Window
Excel's 16,384 columns and 1,048,576 rows make for a huge worksheet that – if you could imagine – takes up the entire side of a building to display in its entirety. Your computer screen, by comparison, is a small window that allows you to view only a minute area of the worksheet at one time. While you cannot see the entire worksheet, you can move the window over the worksheet to view any part of it.

BTW

Increasing the Viewing Area
You can increase the size of the Excel window or viewing area to show more of the worksheet. Two ways exist to increase what you can see in the viewing area: (1) on the View tab on the Ribbon, click Full Screen; and (2) change to a higher resolution. See Appendix E for information about how to change to a higher resolution.

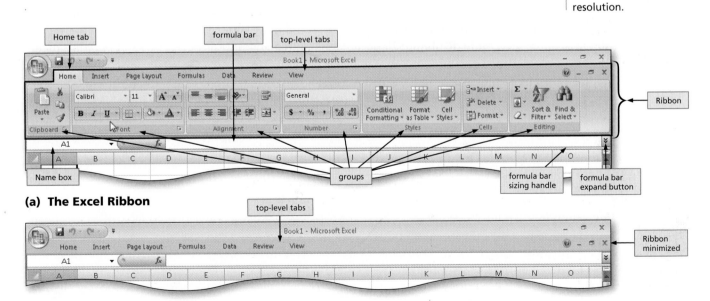

(a) The Excel Ribbon

(b) The Excel Ribbon Minimized

Figure 1–7

BTW

Minimizing the Ribbon
If you want to minimize the Ribbon, right-click the Ribbon and then click Minimize the Ribbon on the shortcut menu, double-click the active tab, or press CTRL+F1. To restore a minimized Ribbon, right-click the Ribbon and then click Minimize the Ribbon on the shortcut menu, double-click any top-level tab, or press CTRL+F1. To use commands on a minimized Ribbon, click the top-level tab.

When you start Excel, the Ribbon displays seven top-level tabs: Home, Insert, Page Layout, Formulas, Data, Review, and View. The **Home tab**, called the primary tab, contains groups with the more frequently used commands. To display a different tab on the Ribbon, click the top-level tab. That is, to display the Insert tab, click Insert on the Ribbon. To return to the Home tab, click Home on the Ribbon. The tab currently displayed is called the **active tab**.

To display more of the document in the document window, some users prefer to minimize the Ribbon, which hides the groups on the Ribbon and displays only the top-level tabs (Figure 1–7b). To use commands on a minimized Ribbon, click the top-level tab.

Each time you start Excel, the Ribbon appears the same way it did the last time you used Excel. The chapters in this book, however, begin with the Ribbon appearing as it did at the initial installation of the software. If you are stepping through this chapter on a computer and you want your Ribbon to match the figures in this book, read Appendix E.

In addition to the top-level tabs, Excel displays other tabs, called **contextual tabs**, when you perform certain tasks or work with objects such as charts or tables. If you insert a chart in the worksheet, for example, the Chart Tools tab and its related subordinate tabs appear (Figure 1–8). When you are finished working with the chart, the Chart Tools and subordinate tabs disappear from the Ribbon. Excel determines when contextual tabs should appear and disappear, based on the tasks you perform.

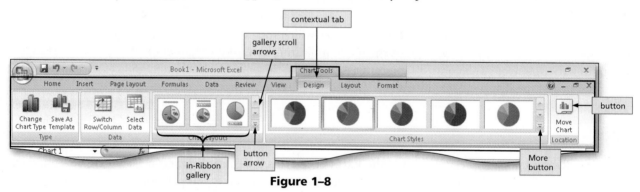

Figure 1–8

Ribbon commands include buttons, boxes (text boxes, check boxes, etc.), and galleries (Figure 1–8). A **gallery** is a set of choices, often graphical, arranged in a grid or in a list. You can scroll through choices on an in-Ribbon gallery by clicking the gallery's scroll arrows. An **in-Ribbon** gallery shows common gallery choices on the Ribbon rather than in a dropdown list. Or, you can click a gallery's More button to view more gallery options on the screen at a time. Some buttons and boxes have arrows that, when clicked, also display a gallery; others always cause a gallery to be displayed when clicked. Most galleries support **live preview**, which is a feature that allows you to point to a gallery choice and see its effect in the worksheet without actually selecting the choice (Figure 1–9).

Some commands on the Ribbon display an image to help you remember their function. When you point to a command on the Ribbon, all or part of the command glows in shades of yellow and orange, and an Enhanced ScreenTip appears on the screen. An **Enhanced ScreenTip** is an on-screen note that provides the name of the command, available keyboard shortcut(s), a description of the command, and sometimes instructions for how to obtain Help about the command (Figure 1–10). Enhanced ScreenTips are more detailed than a typical **ScreenTip**, which usually displays only the name of the command.

The lower-right corner of some groups on the Ribbon has a small arrow, called a **Dialog Box Launcher**, that when clicked displays a dialog box or a task pane (Figure 1–11). A **dialog box** contains additional commands and options for the group. When presented with a dialog box, you make selections and must close the dialog box before returning to the worksheet. A **task pane**, by contrast, is a window that contains additional commands and can stay open and visible while you work on the worksheet.

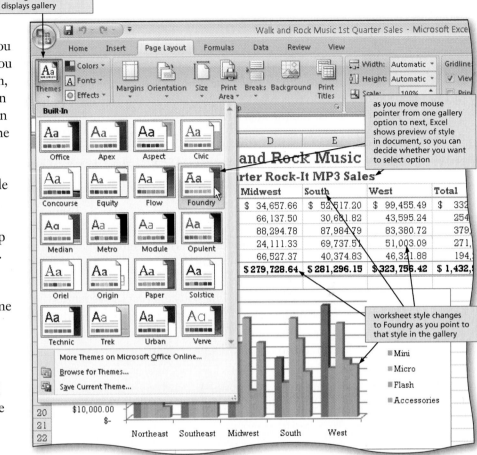

Figure 1–9

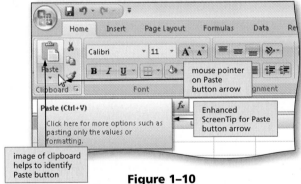

Figure 1–10

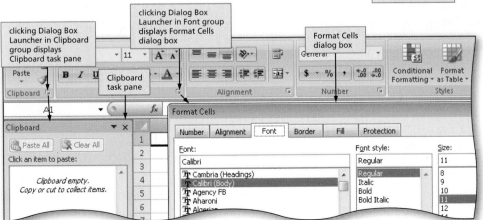

Figure 1–11

Formula Bar

The formula bar appears below the Ribbon (Figure 1–12a). As you type, Excel displays the entry in the **formula bar**. You can make the formula bar larger by dragging the sizing handle (Figure 1–7) on the formula bar or clicking the expand button to the right of the formula bar. Excel also displays the active cell reference in the **Name box** on the left side of the formula bar.

Mini Toolbar and Shortcut Menus

The **Mini toolbar**, which appears automatically based on tasks you perform (such as selecting text), contains commands related to changing the appearance of text in a worksheet. All commands on the Mini toolbar also exist on the Ribbon. The purpose of the Mini toolbar is to minimize mouse movement. For example, if you want to format text using a command that currently is not displayed on the active tab, you can use the command on the Mini toolbar — instead of switching to a different tab to use the command.

When the Mini toolbar appears, it initially is transparent (Figure 1–12a). If you do not use the transparent Mini toolbar, it disappears from the screen. To use the Mini toolbar, move the mouse pointer into the toolbar, which causes the Mini toolbar to change from a transparent to a bright appearance (Figure 1–12b).

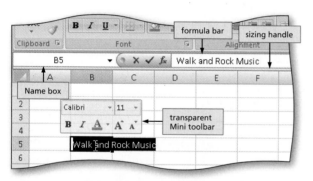

(a) Transparent Mini Toolbar

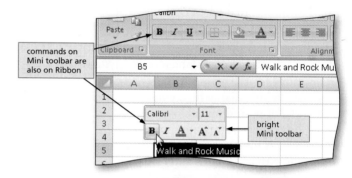

(b) Bright Mini Toolbar

Figure 1–12

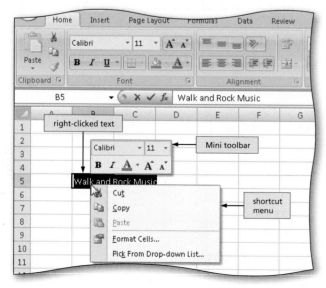

A **shortcut menu**, which appears when you right-click an object, is a list of frequently used commands that relate to the right-clicked object. If you right-click an item in the document window such as a cell, Excel displays both the Mini toolbar and a shortcut menu (Figure 1–13).

Figure 1–13

Quick Access Toolbar

The **Quick Access Toolbar**, located by default above the Ribbon, provides easy access to frequently used commands (Figure 1–14a). The commands on the Quick Access Toolbar always are available, regardless of the task you are performing. Initially, the Quick Access Toolbar contains the Save, Undo, and Redo buttons. If you click the Customize Quick Access Toolbar button, Excel provides a list of commands you quickly can add to and remove from the Quick Access Toolbar (Figure 1–14b).

You also can add other commands to or delete commands from the Quick Access Toolbar so that it contains the commands you use most often. As you add commands to the Quick Access Toolbar, its commands may interfere with the workbook title on the title bar. For this reason, Excel provides an option of displaying the Quick Access Toolbar below the Ribbon (Figure 1–14c).

BTW

Quick Access Toolbar Commands
To add a Ribbon command as a button to the Quick Access Toolbar, right-click the command on the Ribbon and then click Add to Quick Access Toolbar on the shortcut menu. To delete a button from the Quick Access Toolbar, right-click the button on the Quick Access Toolbar and then click Remove from Quick Access Toolbar on the shortcut menu. To display the Quick Access Toolbar below the Ribbon, right-click the Quick Access Toolbar and then click Show Quick Access Toolbar Below the Ribbon on the shortcut menu.

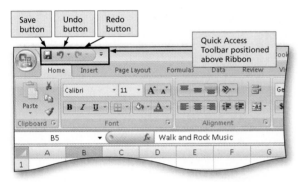

(a) Quick Access Toolbar above Ribbon

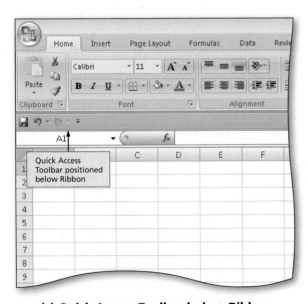

(c) Quick Access Toolbar below Ribbon

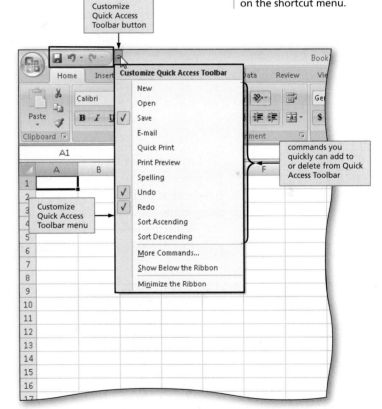

(b) Customize Quick Access Toolbar Menu

Figure 1–14

Each time you start Excel, the Quick Access Toolbar appears the same way it did the last time you used Excel. The chapters in this book, however, begin with the Quick Access Toolbar appearing as it did at the initial installation of the software. If you are stepping through this chapter on a computer and you want your Quick Access Toolbar to match the figures in this book, you should reset your Quick Access Toolbar. For more information about how to reset the Quick Access Toolbar, read Appendix E.

Office Button

While the Ribbon is a control center for creating worksheets, the **Office Button** is a central location for managing and sharing workbooks. When you click the Office Button, located in the upper-left corner of the window, Excel displays the Office Button menu (Figure 1–15). A **menu** contains a list of commands.

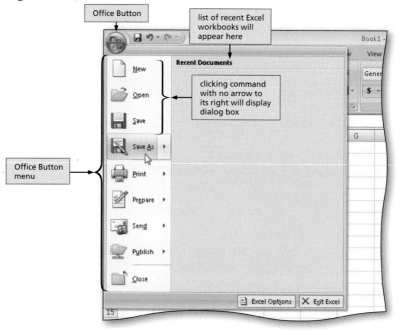

Figure 1–15

When you click the New, Open, Save As, and Print commands on the Office Button menu, Excel displays a dialog box with additional options. The Save As, Print, Prepare, Send, and Publish commands have an arrow to their right. If you point to a button that includes an arrow, Excel displays a **submenu**, which is a list of additional commands associated with the selected command (Figure 1–16). For the Prepare, Send, and Publish commands that do not display a dialog box when clicked, you can point either to the command or the arrow to display the submenu.

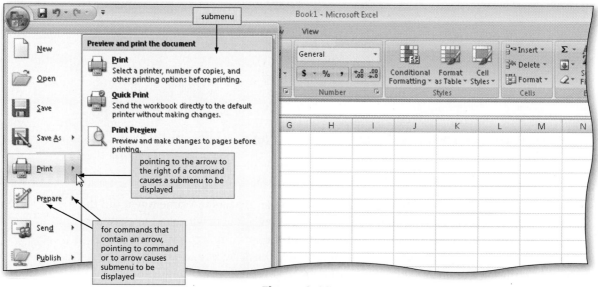

Figure 1–16

Key Tips

If you prefer using the keyboard, instead of the mouse, you can press the ALT key on the keyboard to display a **Key Tip badge**, or keyboard code icon, for certain commands (Figure 1–17). To select a command using the keyboard, press its displayed code letter, or **Key Tip**. When you press a Key Tip, additional Key Tips related to the selected command appear. For example, to select the New command on the Office Button menu, press the ALT key, then press the F key, then press the N key.

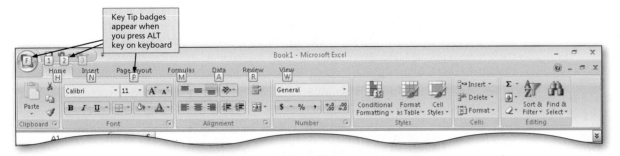

Figure 1–17

To remove the Key Tip badges from the screen, press the ALT key or the ESC key on the keyboard until all Key Tip badges disappear or click the mouse anywhere in the Excel window.

Selecting a Cell

To enter data into a cell, you first must select it. The easiest way **to select a cell** (make it active) is to use the mouse to move the block plus sign mouse pointer to the cell and then click.

An alternative method is to use the arrow keys that are located just to the right of the typewriter keys on the keyboard. An arrow key selects the cell adjacent to the active cell in the direction of the arrow on the key.

You know a cell is selected, or active, when a heavy border surrounds the cell and the active cell reference appears in the Name box on the left side of the formula bar. Excel also changes the active cell's column heading and row heading to a gold color.

Entering Text

In Excel, any set of characters containing a letter, hyphen (as in a telephone number), or space is considered text. **Text** is used to place titles, such as worksheet titles, column titles, and row titles, on the worksheet.

Plan Ahead	**Select titles and subtitles for the worksheet.**
	As previously stated, worksheet titles and subtitles should be as brief and meaningful as possible. As shown in Figure 1–18, the worksheet title, Walk and Rock Music, identifies the company for whom the worksheet is being created in Chapter 1. The worksheet subtitle, First Quarter Rock-It MP3 Sales, identifies the type of report.

Plan Ahead	**Determine the contents of rows and columns.**
	As previously mentioned, rows typically contain information that is similar to items in a list. For the Walk and Rock Music sales data, the list of product types meets this criterion. It is more likely that in the future, the company will add more product types as opposed to more regions. Each product type, therefore, should be placed in its own row. The row titles in column A (Video, Mini, Micro, Flash, Accessories, and Total) identify the numbers in each row.
	Columns typically contain descriptive information about items in rows or contain information that helps to group the data in the worksheet. In the case of the Walk and Rock Music sales data, the regions classify the sales of each product type. The regions, therefore, are placed in columns. The column titles in row 3 (Northeast, Southeast, Midwest, South, West, and Total) identify the numbers in each column.

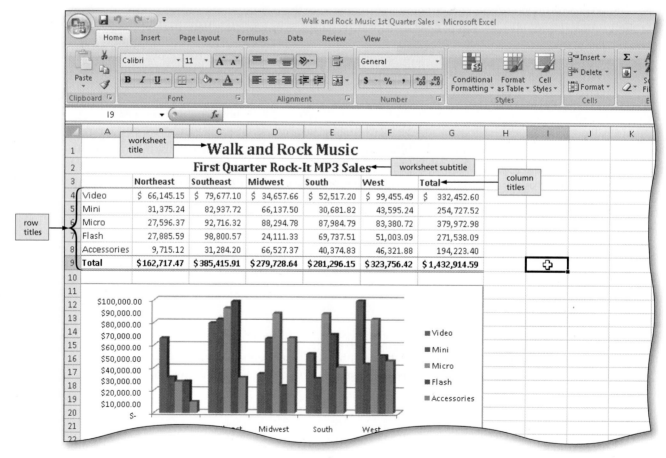

Figure 1–18

To Enter the Worksheet Titles

The following steps show how to enter the worksheet titles in cells A1 and A2. Later in this chapter, the worksheet titles will be formatted so they appear as shown in Figure 1–18.

1

• Click cell A1 to make cell A1 the active cell (Figure 1–19).

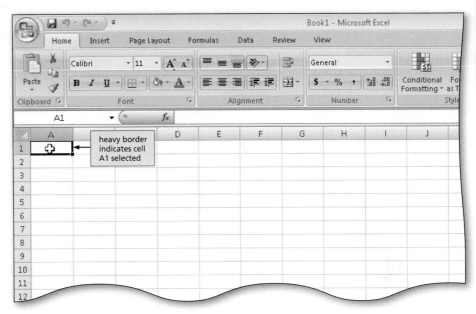

Figure 1–19

2

• Type Walk and Rock Music in cell A1, and then point to the Enter box in the formula bar.

Q&A

Why did the appearance of the formula bar change?

Excel displays the title in the formula bar and in cell A1. When you begin typing a cell entry, Excel displays two additional boxes in the formula bar: the Cancel box and the Enter box. Clicking the **Enter box** completes an entry. Clicking the **Cancel box** cancels an entry.

Q&A

What is the vertical line in cell A1?

In Figure 1–20, the text in cell A1 is followed by the insertion point. The **insertion point** is a blinking vertical line that indicates where the next typed character will appear.

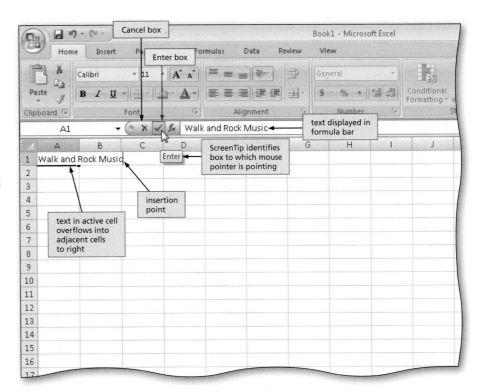

Figure 1–20

- Click the Enter box to complete the entry and enter the worksheet title in cell A1 (Figure 1–21).

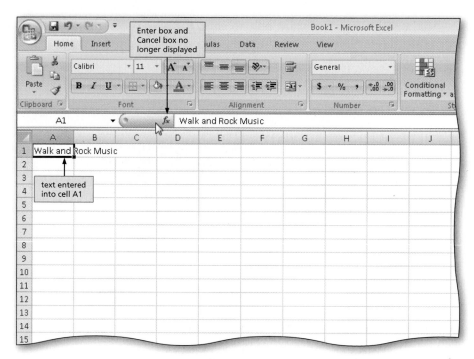

Figure 1–21

- Click cell A2 to select it.

- Type First Quarter Rock-It MP3 Sales as the cell entry.

- Click the Enter box to complete the entry and enter the worksheet subtitle in cell A2 (Figure 1–22).

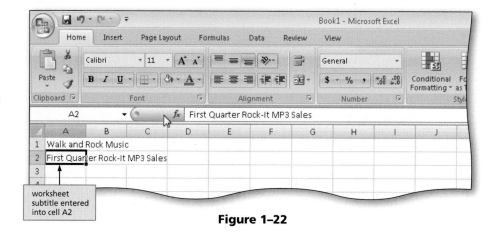

Figure 1–22

Other Ways

1. To complete entry, click any cell other than active cell

2. To complete entry, press ENTER key

3. To complete entry, press HOME, PAGE UP, PAGE DOWN, or END key

4. To complete entry, press UP, DOWN, LEFT, or RIGHT key.

Entering Text in a Cell

When you complete a text entry into a cell, a series of events occurs. First, Excel positions the text left-aligned in the cell. **Left-aligned** means the cell entry is positioned at the far left in the cell. Therefore, the W in the worksheet title, Walk and Rock Music, begins in the leftmost position of cell A1.

Second, when the text is longer than the width of a column, Excel displays the overflow characters in adjacent cells to the right as long as these adjacent cells contain no data. In Figure 1–22, the width of cell A1 is approximately nine characters. The text consists of 19 characters. Therefore, Excel displays the overflow characters from cell A1 in cells B1 and C1, because cells B1 and C1 are empty. If cell B1 contained data, Excel would hide the overflow characters, so that only the first nine characters in cell A1 would appear on the worksheet. Excel stores the overflow characters in cell A1 and displays them in the formula bar whenever cell A1 is the active cell.

Third, when you complete an entry by clicking the Enter box, the cell in which the text is entered remains the active cell.

Correcting a Mistake while Typing

If you type the wrong letter and notice the error before clicking the Enter box or pressing the ENTER key, use the BACKSPACE key to delete all the characters back to and including the incorrect letter. To cancel the entire entry before entering it into the cell, click the Cancel box in the formula bar or press the ESC key. If you see an error in a cell after entering the text, select the cell and retype the entry. Later in this chapter, additional error-correction techniques are discussed.

AutoCorrect

The **AutoCorrect feature** of Excel works behind the scenes, correcting common mistakes when you complete a text entry in a cell. AutoCorrect makes three types of corrections for you:

1. Corrects two initial capital letters by changing the second letter to lowercase.

2. Capitalizes the first letter in the names of days.

3. Replaces commonly misspelled words with their correct spelling. For example, it will change the misspelled word *recieve* to *receive* when you complete the entry. AutoCorrect will correct the spelling of hundreds of commonly misspelled words automatically.

BTW

The ENTER Key
When you first install Excel, the ENTER key not only completes the entry, but it also moves the selection to an adjacent cell. You can instruct Excel not to move the selection after pressing the ENTER key by clicking the Excel Options button on the Office Button menu, clicking the Advanced option, removing the checkmark from the 'After pressing Enter, move selection' check box, and then clicking the OK button.

To Enter Column Titles

To enter the column titles in row 3, select the appropriate cell and then enter the text. The following steps enter the column titles in row 3.

- Click cell B3 to make cell B3 the active cell (Figure 1–23).

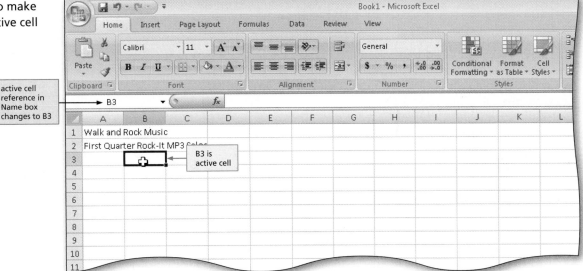

Figure 1–23

- Type Northeast in cell B3 (Figure 1–24).

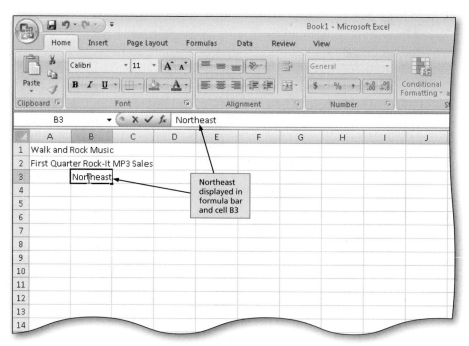

Figure 1–24

- Press the RIGHT ARROW key to enter the column title, Northeast, in cell B3 and make cell C3 the active cell (Figure 1–25).

Why is the RIGHT ARROW key used to complete the entry in the cell?

If the next entry is in an adjacent cell, use the arrow keys to complete the entry in a cell. When you press an arrow key to complete an entry, the adjacent cell in the direction of the arrow (up, down, left, or right) becomes the active cell. If the next entry is in a nonadjacent cell, complete an entry by clicking the next cell in which you plan to enter data. You also can click the Enter box or press the ENTER key and then click the appropriate cell for the next entry.

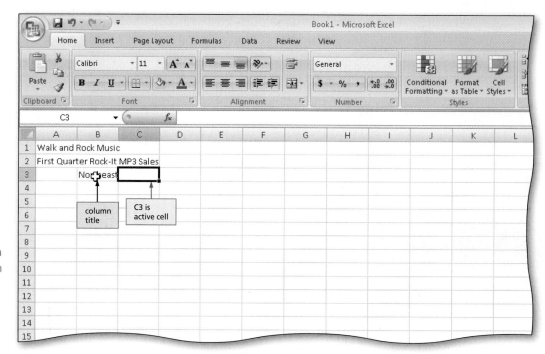

Figure 1–25

4

* Repeat Steps 2 and 3 to enter the remaining column titles in row 3; that is, enter Southeast in cell C3, Midwest in cell D3, South in cell E3, West in cell F3, and Total in cell G3 (complete the last entry in cell G3 by clicking the Enter box in the formula bar) (Figure 1–26).

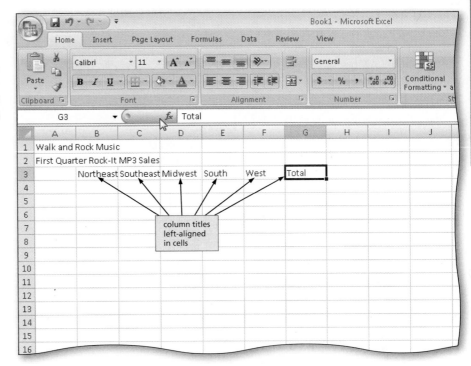

Figure 1–26

To Enter Row Titles

The next step in developing the worksheet for this project is to enter the row titles in column A. This process is similar to entering the column titles. The following steps enter the row titles in the worksheet.

1

* Click cell A4 to select it.

* Type Video and then press the DOWN ARROW key to enter the row title and make cell A5 the active cell (Figure 1–27).

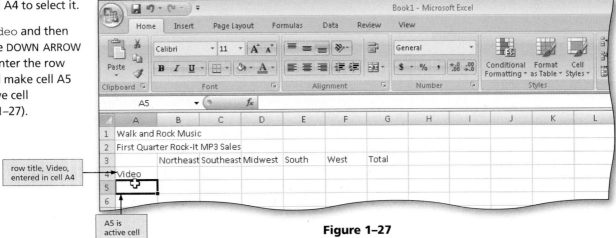

Figure 1–27

2

- Repeat Step 1 to enter the remaining row titles in column A; that is, enter Mini in cell A5, Micro in cell A6, Flash in cell A7, Accessories in cell A8, and Total in cell A9 (Figure 1–28).

Q&A

Why is the text left-aligned in the cells?

When you enter text, Excel automatically left-aligns the text in the cell. Excel treats any combination of numbers, spaces, and nonnumeric characters as text. For example, the following entries are text:

401AX21, 921-231, 619 321, 883XTY

You can change the text alignment in a cell by realigning it. Several alignment techniques are discussed later in the chapter.

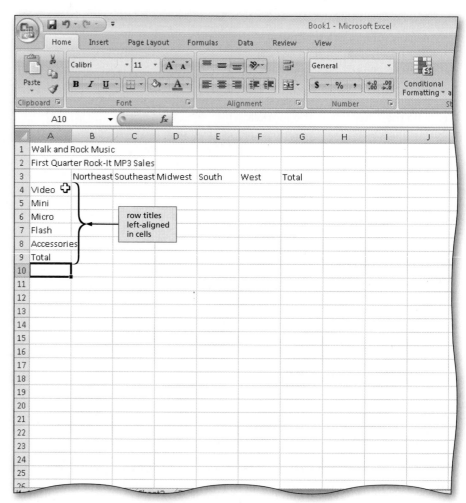

Figure 1–28

Entering Numbers

In Excel, you can enter numbers into cells to represent amounts. A **number** can contain only the following characters:

$$0\ 1\ 2\ 3\ 4\ 5\ 6\ 7\ 8\ 9\ +\ -\ (\ )\ ,\ /\ .\ \$\ \%\ E\ e$$

If a cell entry contains any other keyboard character (including spaces), Excel interprets the entry as text and treats it accordingly. The use of the special characters is explained when they are used in this book.

To Enter Numbers

The Walk and Rock Music First Quarter Rock-It MP3 Sales numbers used in Chapter 1 are summarized in Table 1–1. These numbers, which represent sales revenue for each of the product types and regions, must be entered in rows 4, 5, 6, 7, and 8.

Table 1–1 Walk and Rock Music First Quarter Rock-It MP3 Sales					
	Northeast	**Southeast**	**Midwest**	**South**	**West**
Video	66145.15	79677.10	34657.66	52517.20	99455.49
Mini	31375.24	82937.72	66137.50	30681.82	43595.24
Micro	27596.37	92716.32	88294.78	87984.79	83380.72
Flash	27885.59	98800.57	24111.33	69737.51	51003.09
Accessories	9715.12	31284.20	66527.37	40374.83	46321.88

The following steps enter the numbers in Table 1–1 one row at a time.

1

• Click cell B4.

• Type 66145.15 and then press the RIGHT ARROW key to enter the data in cell B4 and make cell C4 the active cell (Figure 1–29).

Q&A

Do I need to enter dollar signs, commas, or trailing zeros for the quarterly sales numbers?

You are not required to type dollar signs, commas, or trailing zeros. When you enter a dollar value that has cents, however, you must add the decimal point and the numbers representing the cents. Later in this chapter, the numbers will be formatted to use dollar signs, commas, and trailing zeros to improve the appearance and readability of the numbers.

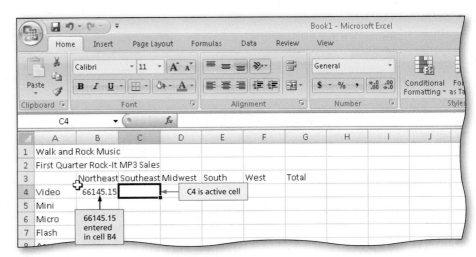

Figure 1–29

2

• Enter 79677.1 in cell C4, 34657.66 in cell D4, 52517.2 in cell E4, and 99455.49 in cell F4 (Figure 1–30).

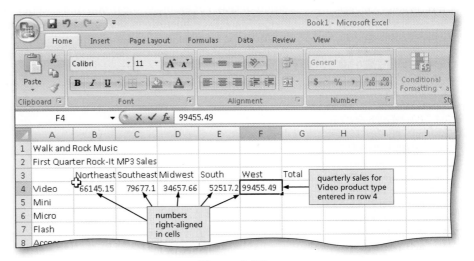

Figure 1–30

3

- Click cell B5.

- Enter the remaining first quarter sales numbers provided in Table 1–1 for each of the four remaining offerings in rows 5, 6, 7, and 8 to display the quarterly sales in the worksheet (Figure 1–31).

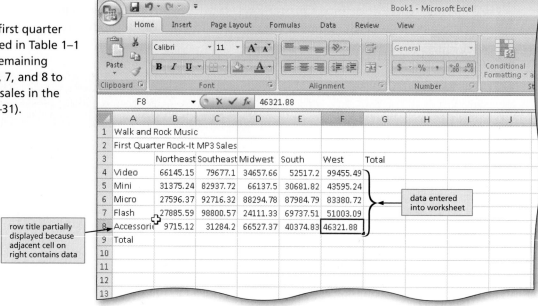

Figure 1–31

Calculating a Sum

The next step in creating the worksheet is to perform any necessary calculations, such as calculating the column and row totals.

Determine calculations that are needed.
As stated in the requirements document in Figure 1–2 on page EX 4, totals are required for each region, each product type, and the company. The first calculation is to determine the quarterly sales for the stores in the Northeast region in column B. To calculate this value in cell B9, Excel must add, or sum, the numbers in cells B4, B5, B6, B7, and B8. Excel's **SUM function**, which adds all of the numbers in a range of cells, provides a convenient means to accomplish this task.

A **range** is a series of two or more adjacent cells in a column or row or a rectangular group of cells. For example, the group of adjacent cells B4, B5, B6, B7, and B8 is called a range. Many Excel operations, such as summing numbers, take place on a range of cells.

After the total quarterly sales for the stores in the Northeast region in column B is determined, the totals for the remaining regions and totals for each product type will be determined.

To Sum a Column of Numbers

The following steps sum the numbers in column B.

1

- Click cell B9 to make it the active cell and then point to the Sum button on the Ribbon (Figure 1–32).

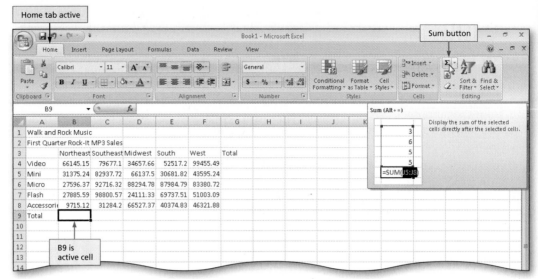

Figure 1–32

2

- Click the Sum button on the Ribbon to display =SUM(B4: B8) in the formula bar and in the active cell B9 (Figure 1–33).

Q&A

How does Excel know which cells to sum?

When you enter the SUM function using the Sum button, Excel automatically selects what it considers to be your choice of the range to sum. When proposing the range to sum, Excel first looks for a range of cells with numbers above the active cell and then to the left. If Excel proposes the wrong range, you can correct it by dragging through the correct range before pressing the ENTER key. You also can enter the correct range by typing the beginning cell reference, a colon (:), and the ending cell reference.

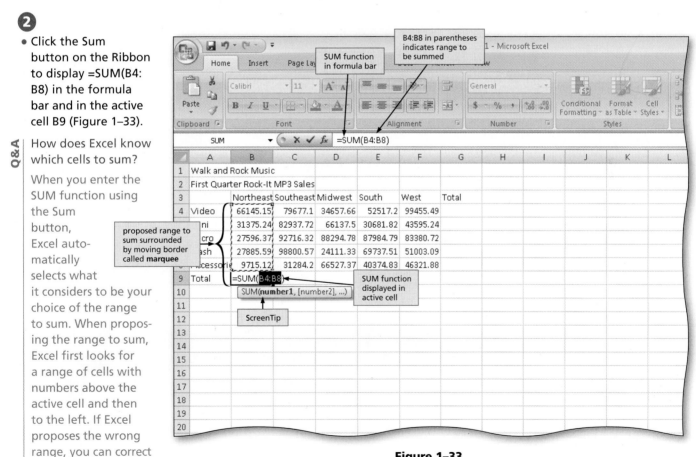

Figure 1–33

3

- Click the Enter box in the formula bar to enter the sum of the first quarter sales for the five product types for the Northeast region in cell B9 (Figure 1-34).

Q&A

What is the purpose of the Sum button arrow?

If you click the Sum button arrow on the right side of the Sum button (Figure 1–34), Excel displays a list of often-used functions from which you can choose. The list includes functions that allow you to determine the average, the number of items in the selected range, the minimum value, or the maximum value of a range of numbers.

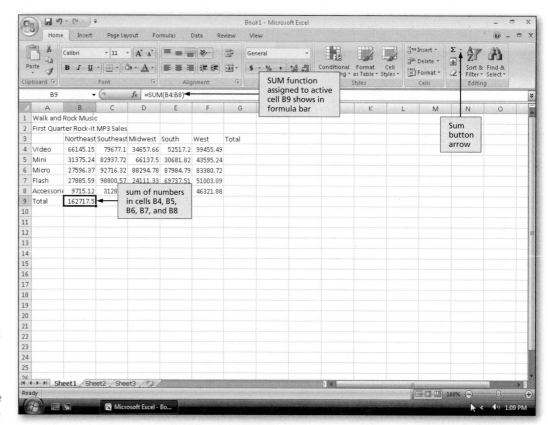

Figure 1–34

Other Ways

1. Click Insert Function button in formula bar, select SUM in Select a function list, click OK button, select range, click OK button

2. Click Sum button arrow on Ribbon, click More Functions, select SUM in Select a function list, click OK button, select range, click OK button

3. Type = s in cell, select SUM from list, select range

4. Press ALT + EQUAL SIGN (=) twice

Using the Fill Handle to Copy a Cell to Adjacent Cells

Excel also must calculate the totals for the Southeast in cell C9, the Midwest in cell D9, the South in cell E9, and for the West in cell F9. Table 1–2 illustrates the similarities between the entry in cell B9 and the entries required to sum the totals in cells C9, D9, E9, and F9.

Table 1–2 Sum Function Entries in Row 9		
Cell	**Sum Function Entries**	**Remark**
B9	=SUM(B4:B8)	Sums cells B4, B5, B6, B7, and B8
C9	=SUM(C4:C8)	Sums cells C4, C5, C6, C7, and C8
D9	=SUM(D4:D8)	Sums cells D4, D5, D6, D7, and D8
E9	=SUM(E4:E8)	Sums cells E4, E5, E6, E7, and E8
F9	=SUM(F4:F8)	Sums cells F4, F5, F6, F7, and F8

To place the SUM functions in cells C9, D9, E9, and F9, you could follow the same steps shown previously in Figures 1–32 through 1–34. A second, more efficient method is to copy the SUM function from cell B9 to the range C9:F9. The cell being copied is called the **source area** or **copy area**. The range of cells receiving the copy is called the **destination area** or **paste area**.

Although the SUM function entries in Table 1–2 are similar, they are not exact copies. The range in each SUM function entry uses cell references that are one column to the right of the previous column. When you copy cell references, Excel automatically adjusts them for each new position, resulting in the SUM function entries illustrated in Table 1–2. Each adjusted cell reference is called a **relative reference**.

To Copy a Cell to Adjacent Cells in a Row

The easiest way to copy the SUM formula from cell B9 to cells C9, D9, E9, and F9 is to use the fill handle. The **fill handle** is the small black square located in the lower-right corner of the heavy border around the active cell. The following steps use the fill handle to copy cell B9 to the adjacent cells C9:F9.

1

- With cell B9 active, point to the fill handle (Figure 1–35).

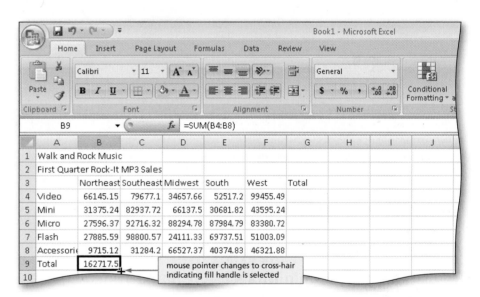

Figure 1–35

2

- Drag the fill handle to select the destination area, range C9:F9, to display a shaded border around the destination area, range C9:F9, and the source area, cell B9 (Figure 1–36). Do not release the mouse button.

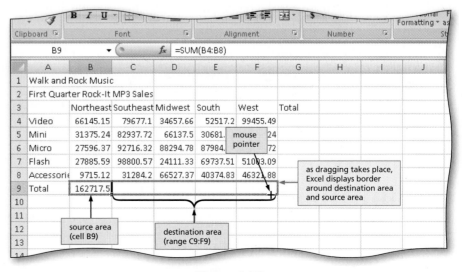

Figure 1–36

3

- Release the mouse button to copy the SUM function in cell B9 to the range C9:F9 (Figure 1–37) and calculate the sums in cells C9, D9, E9, and F9.

Q&A

What is the purpose of the Auto Fill Options button?

When you copy one range to another, Excel displays an Auto Fill Options button (Figure 1–37). The Auto Fill Options button allows you to choose whether you want to copy the values from the source area to the destination area with formatting, without formatting, or copy only the format. To view the available fill options, click the Auto Fill Options button. The Auto Fill Options button disappears when you begin another activity.

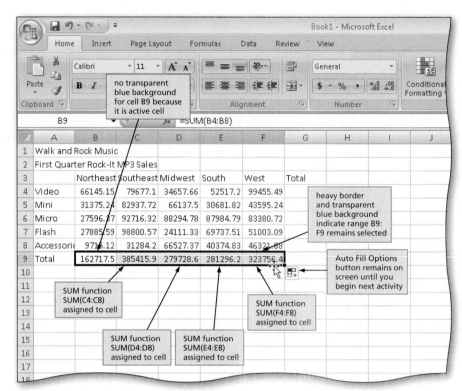

Figure 1–37

Other Ways

1. Select source area, click Copy button on Ribbon, select destination area, click Paste button on Ribbon

2. Right-click source area, click Copy on shortcut menu, right-click destination area, click Paste on shortcut menu

3. Select source area and then point to border of range; while holding down CTRL key, drag source area to destination area

To Determine Multiple Totals at the Same Time

The next step in building the worksheet is to determine the quarterly sales for each product type and total quarterly sales for the company in column G. To calculate these totals, you can use the SUM function much as it was used to total the quarterly sales by region in row 9. In this example, however, Excel will determine totals for all of the rows at the same time. The following steps illustrate this process.

1

- Click cell G4 to make it the active cell (Figure 1–38).

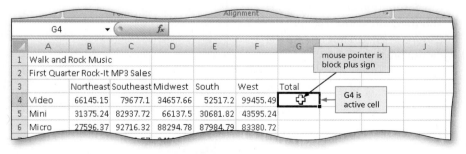

Figure 1–38

2

- With the mouse pointer in cell G4 and in the shape of a block plus sign, drag the mouse pointer down to cell G9 to highlight the range G4:G9 with a transparent view (Figure 1–39).

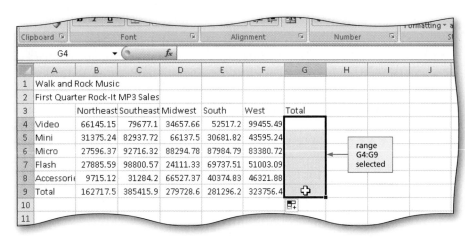

Figure 1–39

3

- Click the Sum button on the Ribbon to calculate and display the sums of the corresponding rows of sales in cells G4, G5, G6, G7, G8, and G9 (Figure 1–40).

4

- Select cell A10 to deselect the range G4:G9.

Q&A

Why does Excel create totals for each row?

If each cell in a selected range is next to a row of numbers, Excel assigns the SUM function to each cell when you click the Sum button.

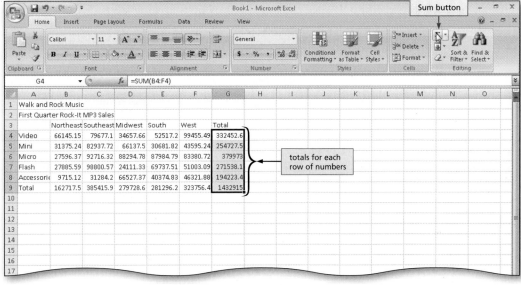

Figure 1–40

Saving the Project

While you are building a worksheet in a workbook, the computer stores it in memory. When you save a workbook, the computer places it on a storage medium such as a USB flash drive, CD, or hard disk. A saved workbook is referred to as a **file**. A **file name** is the name assigned to a file when it is saved. It is important to save the workbook frequently for the following reasons:

- The worksheet in memory will be lost if the computer is turned off or you lose electrical power while Excel is open.
- If you run out of time before completing your workbook, you may finish your worksheet at a future time without starting over.

BTW

Saving
Excel allows you to save a workbook in more than 30 different file formats. Choose the file format by clicking the 'Save as type' box arrow at the bottom of the Save As dialog box (Figure 1–41 on the next page). Excel Workbook is the default file format.

Plan Ahead	**Determine where to save the workbook.**
	When saving a workbook, you must decide which storage medium to use.
	• If you always work on the same computer and have no need to transport your projects to a different location, then your computer's hard drive will suffice as a storage location. It is a good idea, however, to save a backup copy of your projects on a separate medium in case the file becomes corrupted or the computer's hard drive fails.
	• If you plan to work on your workbooks in various locations or on multiple computers, then you should save your workbooks on a portable medium, such as a USB flash drive or CD. The workbooks used in this book are saved to a USB flash drive, which saves files quickly and reliably and can be reused. CDs are easily portable and serve as good backups for the final versions of workbooks because they generally can save files only one time.

To Save a Workbook

You have performed many tasks while creating this project and do not want to risk losing the work completed thus far. Accordingly, you should save the workbook. The following steps save a workbook on a USB flash drive using the file name, Walk and Rock Music 1st Quarter Sales.

Note: If you are using Windows XP, see Appendix F for alternate steps.

1

- With a USB flash drive connected to one of the computer's USB ports, click the Save button on the Quick Access Toolbar to display the Save As dialog box (Figure 1–41).

- If the Navigation pane is not displayed in the Save As dialog box, click the Browse Folders button to expand the dialog box.

- If a Folders list is displayed below the Folders button, click the Folders button to remove the Folders list.

Q&A Do I have to save to a USB flash drive?

No. You can save to any device or folder. A **folder** is a specific location on a storage medium. You can save to the default folder or a different folder. You also can create your own folders, which is explained later in this book.

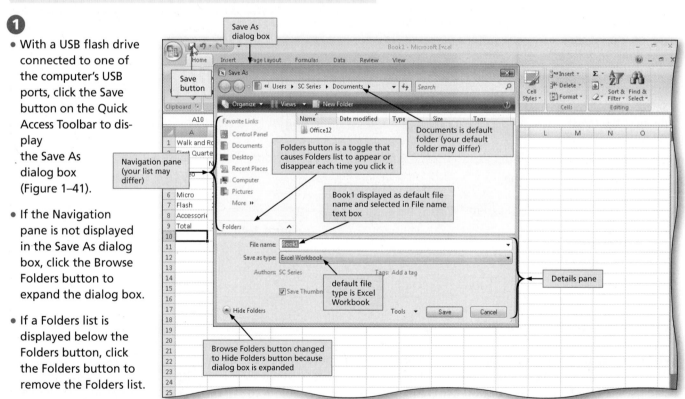

Figure 1–41

2

- Type Walk and Rock Music 1st Quarter Sales in the File name text box to change the file name. Do not press the ENTER key after typing the file name (Figure 1–42).

Q&A What characters can I use in a file name?

A file name can have a maximum of 255 characters, including spaces. The only invalid characters are the backslash (\ ), slash (/), colon (:), asterisk (*), question mark (?), quotation mark ("), less than symbol (<), greater than symbol (>), and vertical bar (|).

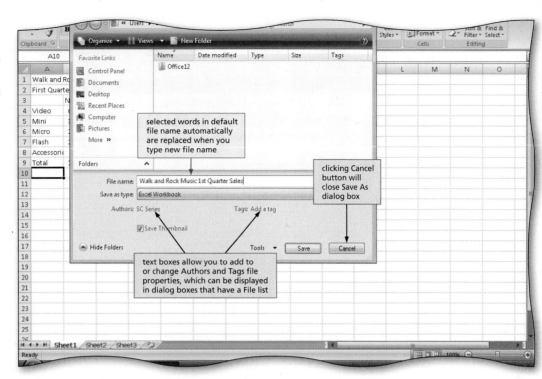

Figure 1–42

3

- If Computer is not displayed in the Favorite Links section, drag the top or bottom edge of the Save As dialog box until Computer is displayed.

- Click Computer in the Favorite Links section to display a list of available drives (Figure 1–43).

- If necessary, scroll until UDISK 2.0 (E :) appears in the list of available drives.

Q&A Why is my list of files, folders, and drives arranged and named differently from those shown in the figure?

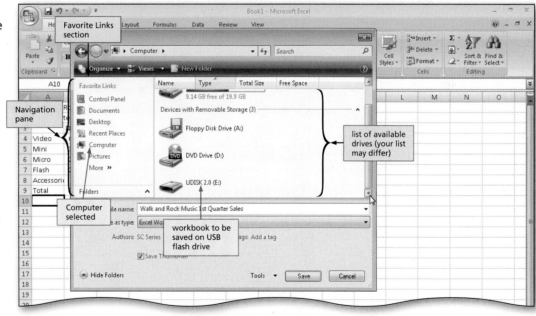

Figure 1–43

Your computer's configuration determines how the list of files and folders is displayed and how drives are named. You can change the save location by clicking links on the **Favorite Links section**.

Q&A How do I save the file if I am not using a USB flash drive?

Use the same process, but be certain to select your device in the list of available drives.

4

- Double-click UDISK 2.0 (E:) in the Save in list to select the USB flash drive, Drive E in this case, as the new save location (Figure 1–44).

Q&A

What if my USB flash drive has a different name or letter?

It is very likely that your USB flash drive will have a different name and drive letter and be connected to a different port.

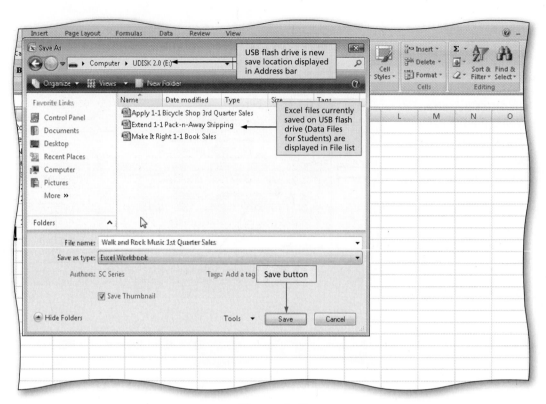

Figure 1–44

5

- Click the Save button in the Save As dialog box to save the workbook on the USB flash drive with the file name, Walk and Rock Music 1st Quarter Sales (Figure 1–45).

Q&A

How do I know that Excel saved the workbook?

While Excel is saving your file, it briefly displays a message on the status bar indicating the amount of the file saved. In addition, your USB drive may have a light that flashes during the save process.

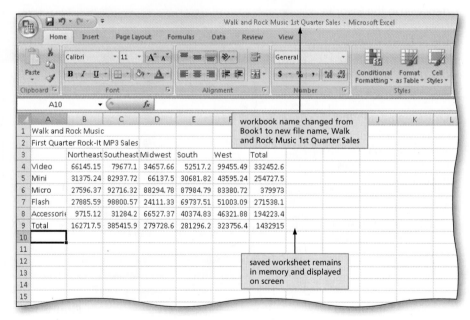

Figure 1–45

Other Ways

1. Click Office Button, click Save, type file name, select drive or folder, click Save button
2. Press CTRL+S or press SHIFT+F12, type file name, select drive or folder, click Save button

Formatting the Worksheet

The text, numeric entries, and functions for the worksheet now are complete. The next step is to format the worksheet. You **format** a worksheet to emphasize certain entries and make the worksheet easier to read and understand.

Figure 1–46a shows the worksheet before formatting. Figure 1–46b shows the worksheet after formatting. As you can see from the two figures, a worksheet that is formatted not only is easier to read but also looks more professional.

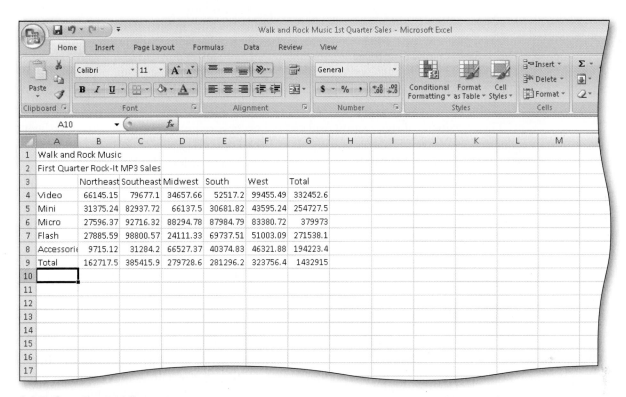

(a) Before Formatting

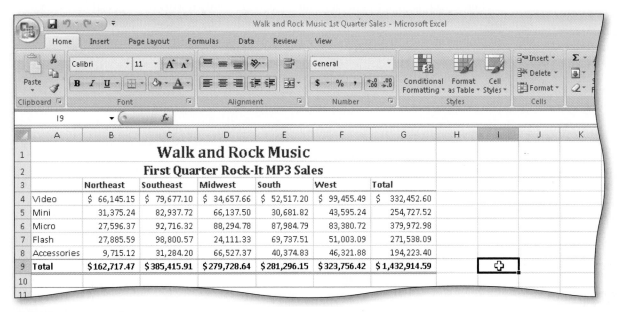

(b) After Formatting

Figure 1–46

Plan Ahead

Identify how to format various elements of the worksheet.
To change the unformatted worksheet in Figure 1–46a to the formatted worksheet in Figure 1–46b, the following tasks must be completed:

1. Change the font type, change the font style to bold, increase the font size, and change the font color of the worksheet titles in cells A1 and A2. These changes make the worksheet title prominently display to the user and inform the user of the purpose of the worksheet.

2. Center the worksheet titles in cells A1 and A2 across columns A through G.

3. Format the body of the worksheet. The body of the worksheet, range A3:G9, includes the column titles, row titles, and numbers. Formatting the body of the worksheet changes the numbers to use a dollars-and-cents format, with dollar signs in the first row (row 4) and the total row (row 9); adds underlining that emphasizes portions of the worksheet; and modifies the column widths to make the text and numbers readable.

The remainder of this section explains the process required to format the worksheet. Although the format procedures are explained in the order described above, you should be aware that you could make these format changes in any order. Modifying the column widths, however, usually is done last.

Font Type, Style, Size, and Color

The characters that Excel displays on the screen are a specific font type, style, size, and color. The **font type**, or font face, defines the appearance and shape of the letters, numbers, and special characters. Examples of font types include Calibri, Cambria, Times New Roman, Arial, and Courier. **Font style** indicates how the characters are emphasized. Common font styles include regular, bold, underline, or italic. The **font size** specifies the size of the characters on the screen. Font size is gauged by a measurement system called points. A single point is about 1/72 of one inch in height. Thus, a character with a **point size** of 10 is about 10/72 of one inch in height. The **font color** defines the color of the characters. Excel can display characters in a wide variety of colors, including black, red, orange, and blue.

When Excel begins, the preset font type for the entire workbook is Calibri, with a font size, font style, and font color of 11-point regular black. Excel allows you to change the font characteristics in a single cell, a range of cells, the entire worksheet, or the entire workbook.

BTW

Fonts
In general, use no more than two font types in a worksheet.

BTW

Fonts and Themes
Excel uses default recommended fonts based on the workbook's theme. A theme is a collection of fonts and color schemes. The default theme is named Office, and the two recommended fonts for the Office theme are Calibri and Cambria. Excel, however, allows you to apply any font to a cell or range as long as the font is installed on your computer.

To Change a Cell Style

Excel includes the capability of changing several characteristics of a cell, such as font type, font size, and font color, all at once by assigning a predefined cell style to a cell. The following steps assign the Title cell style to the worksheet title in cell A1.

1
- Click cell A1 to make cell A1 the active cell.

- Click the Cell Styles button on the Ribbon to display the Cell Styles gallery (Figure 1–47).

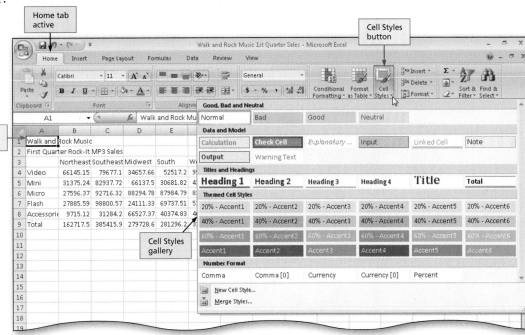

Figure 1–47

2
- Point to the Title cell style in the Titles and Headings area of the Cell Styles gallery to see a live preview of the cell style in cell A1 (Figure 1–48).

Experiment
- Point to several other cell styles in the Cell Styles gallery to see a live preview of other cell styles in cell A1.

Q&A

Why does the font type, font size, and font color change in cell A1 when I point to it?

The change in cell A1 is a result of live preview. Live preview is a feature of Excel 2007 that allows you to preview cell styles as you point to them in the Cell Styles gallery.

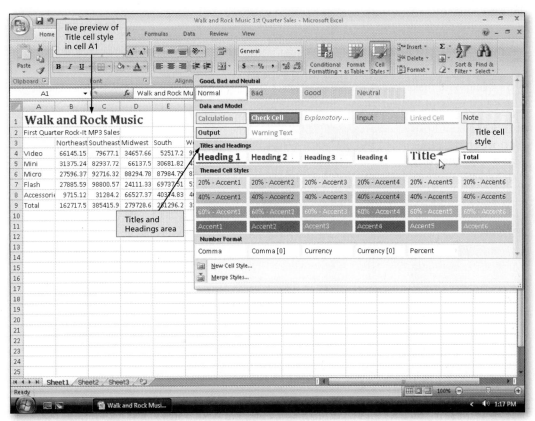

Figure 1–48

3

- Click the Title cell style to apply the cell style to cell A1 (Figure 1–49).

Q&A

Why do several items in the Font group on the Ribbon change?

The changes to the Font box, Bold button, and Font Size box indicate the font changes applied to the active cell, cell A1, as a result of applying the Title cell style.

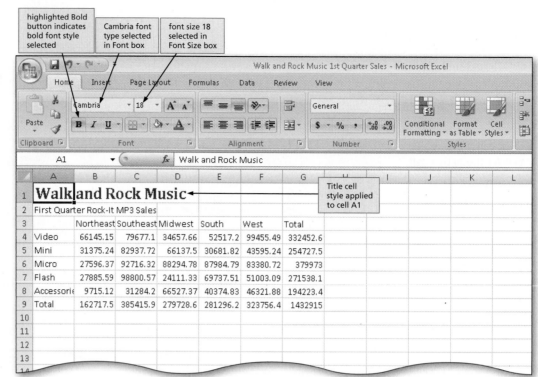

Figure 1–49

To Change the Font Type

Different font types often are used in a worksheet to make it more appealing to the reader. The following steps show how to change the worksheet subtitle's font type from Calibri to Cambria.

1

- Click cell A2 to make cell A2 the active cell.

- Click the Font box arrow on the Ribbon to display the Font gallery (Figure 1–50).

Q&A

Which fonts are displayed in the Font gallery?

Because many applications supply additional font types beyond what comes with the Windows Vista operating system, the number of font types available on your computer will depend on the applications installed. This book uses only font types that come with the Windows Vista operating system and Microsoft Office.

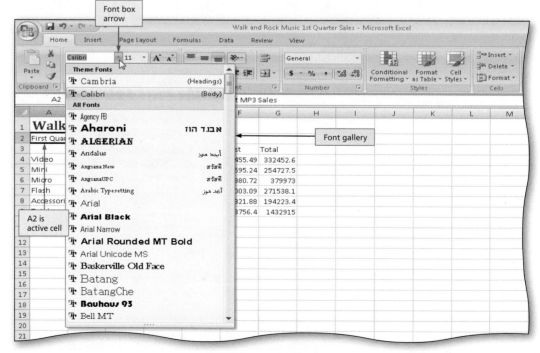

Figure 1–50

2

- Point to Cambria in the Theme Fonts area of the Font gallery to see a live preview of the Cambria font in cell A2 (Figure 1–51).

Experiment

- Point to several other fonts in the Font gallery to see a live preview of other fonts in cell A2.

Q&A What is the Theme Fonts area?

Excel applies the same default theme to any new workbook that you start. A **theme** is a collection of cell styles and other styles that have common characteristics, such as a color scheme and font type. The default theme for an Excel workbook is the Office theme. The Theme Fonts area of the Font gallery includes the fonts included in the default Office theme. Cambria is recommended for headings and Calibri is recommended for cells in the body of the worksheet (Figure 1–51).

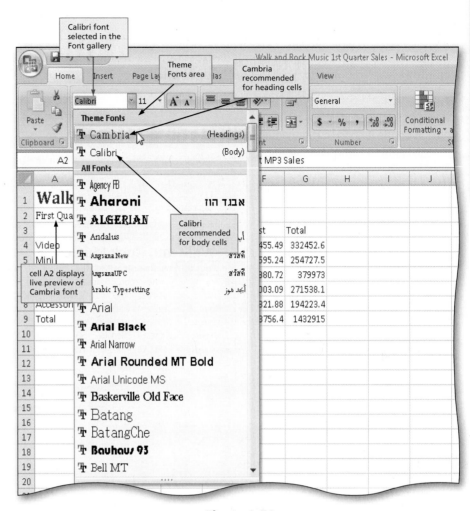

Figure 1–51

3

- Click Cambria in the Theme Fonts area to change the font type of the worksheet subtitle in cell A2 from Calibri to Cambria (Figure 1–52).

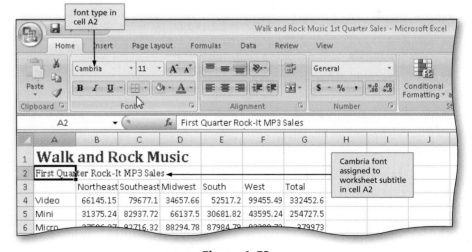

Figure 1–52

Other Ways

1. Select font type from Font list on Mini toolbar
2. Right-click cell, click Format Cells on shortcut menu, click Font tab, click desired font type, click OK button

To Bold a Cell

You **bold** an entry in a cell to emphasize it or make it stand out from the rest of the worksheet. The following step shows how to bold the worksheet subtitle in cell A2.

1

- With cell A2 active, click the Bold button on the Ribbon to change the font style of the worksheet subtitle to bold (Figure 1–53).

Q&A What if a cell already includes a bold style?

If the active cell is already bold, then Excel displays the Bold button with a transparent orange background.

Q&A How do I remove the bold style from a cell?

Clicking the Bold button a second time removes the bold font style.

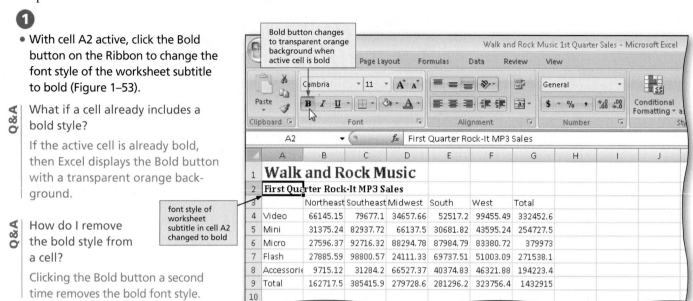

Figure 1–53

Other Ways

1. Click Bold button on Mini toolbar
2. Right-click cell, click Format Cells on shortcut menu,
   click Font tab, click Bold, click OK button
3. Press CTRL+B

To Increase the Font Size of a Cell Entry

Increasing the font size is the next step in formatting the worksheet subtitle. You increase the font size of a cell so the entry stands out and is easier to read. The following steps increase the font size of the worksheet subtitle in cell A2.

1

- With cell A2 selected, click the Font Size box arrow on the Ribbon to display the Font Size list.

- Point to 14 in the Font Size list to see a live preview of cell A2 with a font size of 14 (Figure 1–54).

Experiment

- Point to several other font sizes in the Font Size list to see a live preview of other font sizes in cell A2.

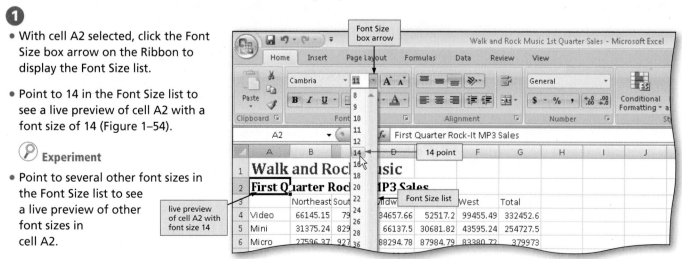

Figure 1–54

2

- Click 14 in the Font Size list to change the font in cell A2 from 11 point to 14 point (Figure 1–55).

Q&A Can I assign a font size that is not in the Font Size list?

Yes. An alternative to clicking a font size in the Font Size list is to click the Font Size box, type the font size, and then press the ENTER key. This procedure allows you to assign a font size not available in the Font Size list to a selected cell entry.

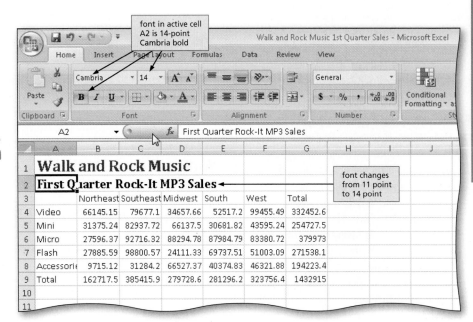

Figure 1–55

Other Ways

1. Click Increase Font Size button or Decrease Font Size button on Ribbon

2. Select font size from Font Size list on Mini toolbar

3. Right-click cell, click Format Cells on shortcut menu, click Font tab, select font size in Size box, click OK button

To Change the Font Color of a Cell Entry

The next step is to change the color of the font in cell A2 from black to dark blue. The following steps change the font color of a cell entry.

1

- With cell A2 selected, click the Font Color button arrow on the Ribbon to display the Font Color palette.

- Point to Dark Blue, Text 2 (dark blue color in column 4, row 1) in the Theme Colors area of the Font Color palette to see a live preview of the font color in cell A2 (Figure 1–56).

Experiment

- Point to several other colors in the Font Color palette to see a live preview of other font colors in cell A2.

Q&A Which colors does Excel make available on the Font Color palette?

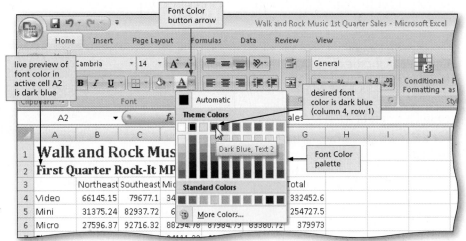

Figure 1–56

You can choose from more than 60 different font colors on the Font Color palette (Figure 1–56). Your Font Color palette may have more or fewer colors, depending on color settings of your operating system. The Theme Colors area includes colors that are included in the current workbook's theme.

2

- Click Dark Blue, Text 2 (column 4, row 1) on the Font Color palette to change the font of the worksheet subtitle in cell A2 from black to dark blue (Figure 1–57).

Q&A

Why does the Font Color button change after I select the new font color?

When you choose a color on the Font Color palette, Excel changes the Font Color button on the Formatting toolbar to the chosen color. Thus, to change the font color of the cell entry in another cell to the same color, you need only to select the cell and then click the Font Color button.

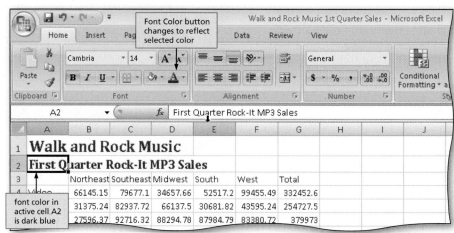

Figure 1–57

Other Ways

1. Select font color from Font Color list on Mini toolbar

2. Right-click cell, click Format Cells on shortcut menu, click Font tab, select color on Font Color palette, click OK button

To Center Cell Entries across Columns by Merging Cells

The final step in formatting the worksheet title and subtitle is to center them across columns A through G. Centering a title across the columns used in the body of the worksheet improves the worksheet's appearance. To do this, the seven cells in the range A1:G1 are combined, or merged, into a single cell that is the width of the columns in the body of the worksheet. The seven cells in the range A2:G2 also are merged in a similar manner. **Merging cells** involves creating a single cell by combining two or more selected cells. The following steps center the worksheet title and subtitle across columns by merging cells.

1

- Select cell A1 and then drag to cell G1 to highlight the range A1:G1 (Figure 1–58).

Q&A

What if a cell in the range B1:G1 contained data?

For the Merge & Center button to work properly, all the cells except the leftmost cell in the selected range must be empty.

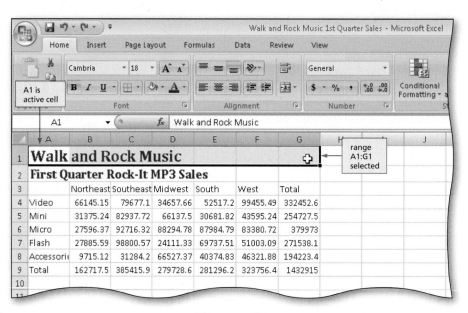

Figure 1–58

2

- Click the Merge & Center button on the Ribbon to merge cells A1 through G1 and center the contents of cell A1 across columns A through G (Figure 1–59).

Q&A

What happened to cells B1 through G1?

After the merge, cells B1 through G1 no longer exist. Cell A1 now extends across columns A through G.

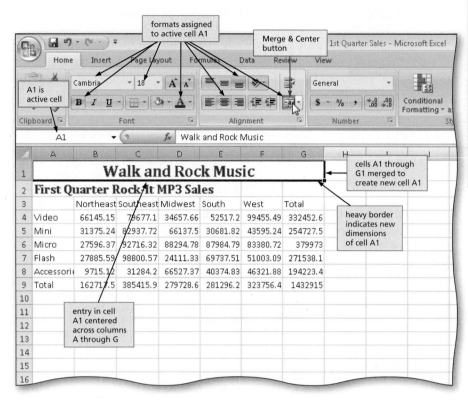

Figure 1–59

3

- Repeat Steps 1 and 2 to merge and center the worksheet subtitle across cells A2 through G2 (Figure 1–60).

Q&A

Are cells B1 through G1 and B2 through G2 lost forever?

No. The opposite of merging cells is **splitting a merged cell**. After you have merged multiple cells to create one merged cell, you can unmerge, or split, the merged cell to display the original cells on the worksheet. You split a merged cell by selecting it and clicking the Merge & Center button. For example, if you click the Merge & Center button a second time in Step 2, it will split the merged cell A1 to cells A1, B1, C1, D1, E1, F1, and G1.

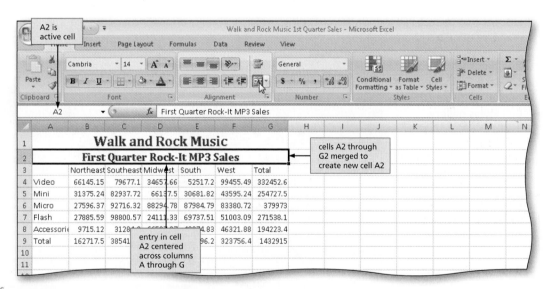

Figure 1–60

Other Ways

1. Right-click selection, click Merge & Center button on Mini toolbar

2. Right-click selection, click Format Cells on shortcut menu, click Alignment tab, select Center Across Selection in Horizontal list, click OK button

To Format Column Titles and the Total Row

The next step to format the worksheet is to format the column titles in row 3 and the total row, row 9. Column titles and the total row should be formatted so anyone who views the worksheet can quickly distinguish the column titles and total row from the data in the body of the worksheet. The following steps format the column titles and total row using cell styles in the default worksheet theme.

- Click cell A3 and then drag the mouse pointer to cell G3 to select the range A3:G3.

- Point to the Cell Styles button on the Ribbon (Figure 1–61).

Q&A

Why is cell A3 selected in the range for the column headings?

The style to be applied to the column headings includes an underline that will help to distinguish the column headings from the rest of the worksheet. Including cell A3 in the range ensures that the cell will include the underline, which is visually appealing and further helps to separate the data in the worksheet.

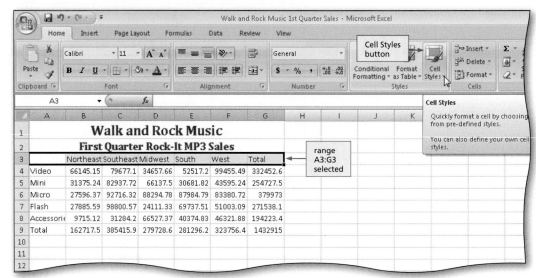

Figure 1–61

- Click the Cell Styles button to display the Cell Styles gallery.

- Point to the Heading 3 cell style in the Titles and Headings area of the Cell Styles gallery to see a live preview of the cell style in the range A3:G3 (Figure 1–62).

Experiment

- Point to other cell styles in the Titles and Headings area of the Cell Styles gallery to see a live preview of other cell styles in the range A3:G3.

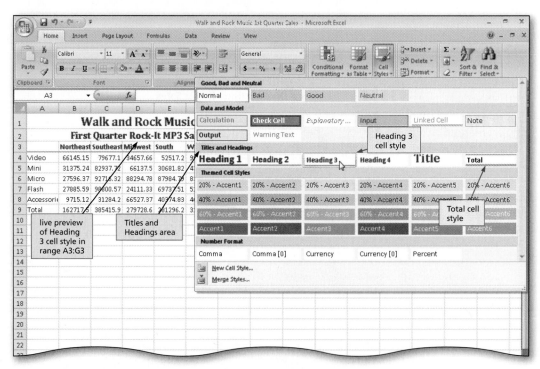

Figure 1–62

3

- Click the Heading 3 cell style to apply the cell style to the range A3:G3.

- Click cell A9 and then drag the mouse pointer to cell G9 to select the range A9:G9.

- Point to the Cell Styles button on the Ribbon (Figure 1–63).

Q&A

Why should I choose Heading 3 instead of another heading cell style?

Excel includes many types of headings, such as Heading 1 and Heading 2, because worksheets often include many levels of headings above columns. In the case of the worksheet created for this project, the Heading 3 title includes formatting that makes the column titles' font size smaller than the title and subtitle and makes the column titles stand out from the data in the body of the worksheet.

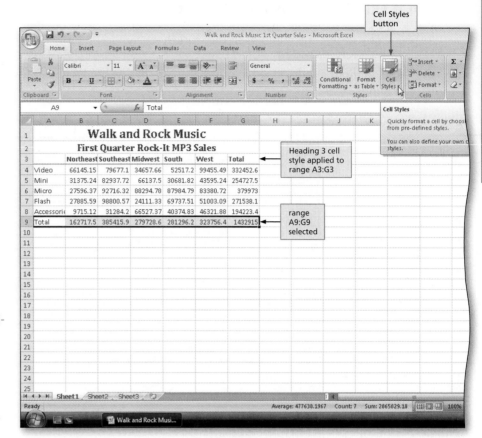

Figure 1–63

4

- Click the Cell Styles button on the Ribbon to display the Cell Styles gallery and then click the Total cell style in the Titles and Headings area to apply the Total cell style to the cells in the range A9:G9.

- Click cell A11 to select the cell (Figure 1–64).

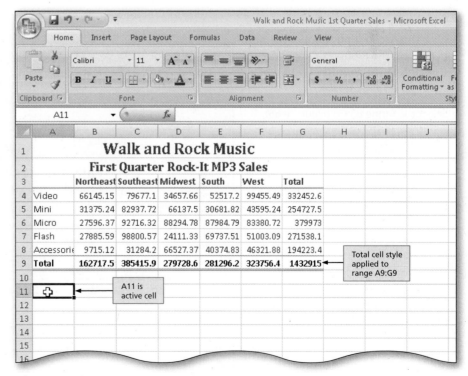

Figure 1–64

To Format Numbers in the Worksheet

As previously noted, the numbers in the worksheet should be formatted to use a dollar-and-cents format, with dollar signs in the first row (row 4) and the total row (row 9). Excel allows you to format numbers in a variety of ways, and these methods are discussed in other chapters in this book. The following steps use buttons on the Ribbon to format the numbers in the worksheet.

- Select cell B4 and drag the mouse pointer to cell G4 to select the range B4:G4.

- Point to the Accounting Number Format button on the Ribbon to display the Enhanced ScreenTip (Figure 1–65).

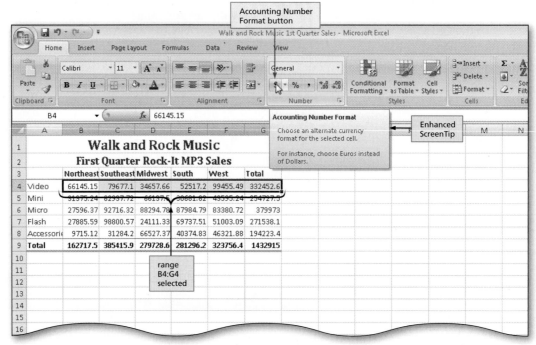

Figure 1–65

- Click the Accounting Number Format button on the Ribbon to apply the Accounting Number format to the cells in the range B4:G4.

- Select the range B5:G8 (Figure 1–66).

Q&A What effect does the Accounting Number format have on the selected cells?

The Accounting Number format causes the cells to display with two decimal places so that decimal places in cells below the selected cells align vertically. Cell widths are automatically adjusted to accommodate the new formatting.

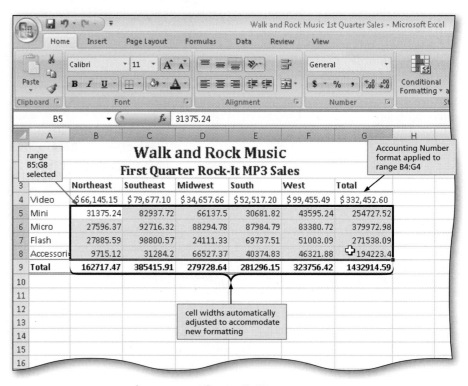

Figure 1–66

3
- Click the Comma Style button on the Ribbon to apply the Comma Style to the range B5:G8.

- Select the range B9:G9 (Figure 1–67).

What effect does the Comma Style format have on the selected cells?

The Comma Style format causes the cells to display with two decimal places and commas as thousands separators.

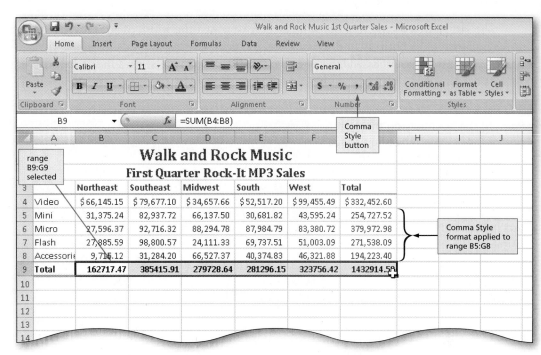

Figure 1–67

4
- Click the Accounting Number Format button on the Ribbon to apply the Accounting Number format to the cells in the range B9:G9.

- Select cell A11 (Figure 1-68).

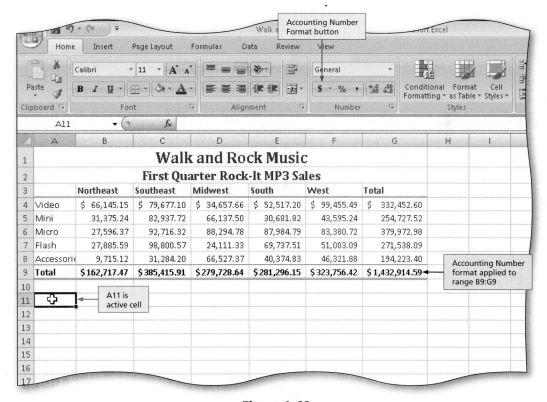

Figure 1–68

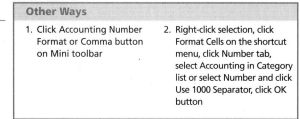

Other Ways
1. Click Accounting Number Format or Comma button on Mini toolbar	2. Right-click selection, click Format Cells on the shortcut menu, click Number tab, select Accounting in Category list or select Number and click Use 1000 Separator, click OK button

To Adjust the Column Width

The last step in formatting the worksheet is to adjust the width of column A so that the word Accessories in cell A8 is shown in its entirety in the cell. Excel includes several methods for adjusting cell widths and row heights, and these methods are discussed later in this book. The following steps adjust the width of column A so that the contents of cell A8 are displayed in the cell.

1

• Point to the boundary on the right side of the column A heading above row 1 to change the mouse pointer to a split double arrow (Figure 1–69).

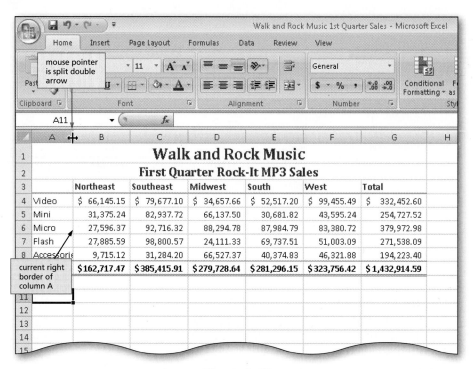

Figure 1–69

2

• Double-click on the boundary to adjust the width of column A to the width of the largest item in the column (Figure 1–70).

What if none of the items in column A extended through the entire width of the column?

If all of the items in column A were shorter in length than the width of the column when you double-click the right side of the column A heading, then Excel still would adjust the column width to the largest item in the column. That is, Excel would reduce the width of the column to the largest item.

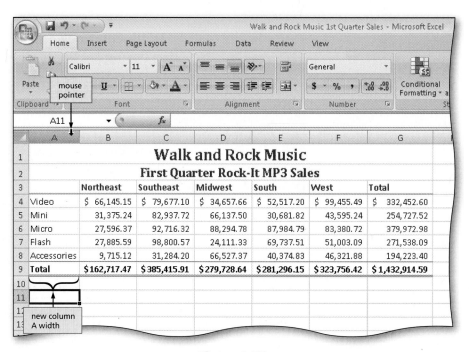

Figure 1–70

Using the Name Box to Select a Cell

The next step is to chart the quarterly sales for the five product types sold by the company. To create the chart, you must select the cell in the upper-left corner of the range to chart (cell A3). Rather than clicking cell A3 to select it, the next section describes how to use the Name box to select the cell.

To Use the Name Box to Select a Cell

As previously noted, the Name box is located on the left side of the formula bar. To select any cell, click the Name box and enter the cell reference of the cell you want to select. The following steps select cell A3.

1

• Click the Name box in the formula bar and then type a3 as the cell to select (Figure 1–71).

Q&A Why is cell A11 still selected?

Even though cell A11 is the active cell, Excel displays the typed cell reference a3 in the Name box until you press the ENTER key.

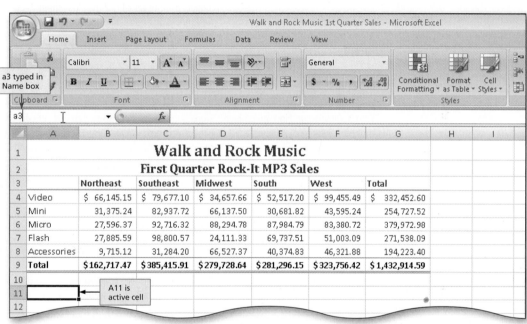

Figure 1–71

2

• Press the ENTER key to change the active cell from A11 to cell A3 (Figure 1–72).

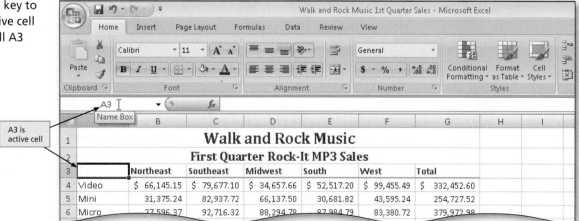

Figure 1–72

Other Ways to Select Cells

As you will see in later chapters, in addition to using the Name box to select any cell in a worksheet, you also can use it to assign names to a cell or range of cells. Excel supports several additional ways to select a cell, as summarized in Table 1–3.

BTW

Find & Select
You can find and select cells based on their content. Click the Find & Select button on the Home tab on the Ribbon. Then, click the Go To Special command. Choose your desired option in the Select area of the Go To Special dialog box and then click the OK button.

Table 1–3 Selecting Cells in Excel

Key, Box, or Command	Function
ALT+PAGE DOWN	Selects the cell one worksheet window to the right and moves the worksheet window accordingly.
ALT+PAGE UP	Selects the cell one worksheet window to the left and moves the worksheet window accordingly.
ARROW	Selects the adjacent cell in the direction of the arrow on the key.
CTRL+ARROW	Selects the border cell of the worksheet in combination with the arrow keys and moves the worksheet window accordingly. For example, to select the rightmost cell in the row that contains the active cell, press CTRL+RIGHT ARROW. You also can press the END key, release it, and then press the appropriate arrow key to accomplish the same task.
CTRL+HOME	Selects cell A1 or the cell one column and one row below and to the right of frozen titles and moves the worksheet window accordingly.
Find command on Find and Select menu or SHIFT+F5	Finds and selects a cell that contains specific contents that you enter in the Find dialog box. If necessary, Excel moves the worksheet window to display the cell. You also can press CTRL+F to display the Find dialog box.
Go To command on Find and Select menu or F5	Selects the cell that corresponds to the cell reference you enter in the Go To dialog box and moves the worksheet window accordingly. You also can press CTRL+G to display the Go To dialog box.
HOME	Selects the cell at the beginning of the row that contains the active cell and moves the worksheet window accordingly.
Name box	Selects the cell in the workbook that corresponds to the cell reference you enter in the Name box.
PAGE DOWN	Selects the cell down one worksheet window from the active cell and moves the worksheet window accordingly.
PAGE UP	Selects the cell up one worksheet window from the active cell and moves the worksheet window accordingly.

Plan Ahead

Decide on the type of chart needed.
Excel includes 11 chart types from which you can choose including column, line, pie, bar, area, X Y (scatter), stock, surface, doughnut, bubble, and radar. The type of chart you choose depends on the type of data that you have, how much data you have, and the message you want to convey.

A column chart is a good way to compare values side-by-side. A Clustered Column chart can go even further in comparing values across categories. In the case of the Walk and Rock Music quarterly sales data, comparisons of product types within each region can be made side-by-side with a Clustered Column chart.

Establish where to position and how to format the chart.

• When possible, try to position charts so that both the data and chart appear on the screen on the worksheet together and so that the data and chart can be printed in the most readable manner possible. By placing the chart below the data on the Walk and Rock Music 1st Quarter Sales worksheet, both of these goals are accomplished.

• When choosing/selecting colors for a chart, consider the color scheme of the rest of the worksheet. The chart should not present colors that are in stark contrast to the rest of the worksheet. If the chart will be printed in color, minimize the amount of dark colors on the chart so that the chart both prints quickly and preserves ink.

Adding a 3-D Clustered Column Chart to the Worksheet

As outlined in the requirements document in Figure 1–2 on page EX 4, the worksheet should include a 3-D Clustered Column chart to graphically represent quarterly sales for each product type that the company sells. The 3-D Clustered Column chart shown in Figure 1–73 is called an **embedded chart** because it is drawn on the same worksheet as the data.

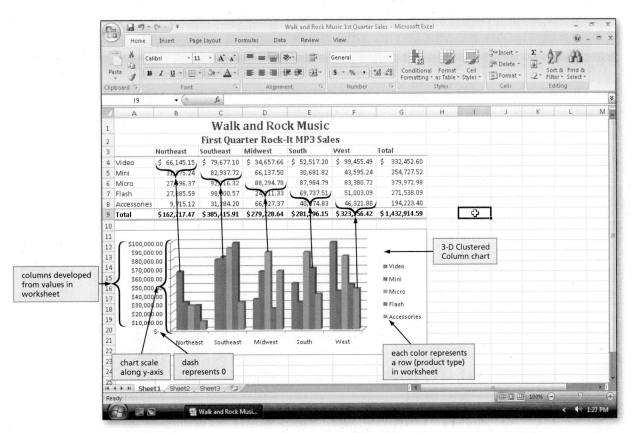

Figure 1–73

The chart uses different colored columns to represent sales for different product types. Each region uses the same color scheme for identifying product types, which allows for easy identification and comparison. For the Northeast sales region, for example, the dark blue column representing Video products shows quarterly sales of $66,145.15; for the Southeast sales region, the maroon column representing Mini products shows quarterly sales of $82,937.72; for the Midwest sales region, the pale green column representing Micro products shows quarterly sales of $88,294.78; for the South sales region, the violet column representing Flash products shows quarterly sales of $69,737.51; and for the West sales region, the light blue column representing Accessories shows quarterly sales of $46,321.88. Because the same color scheme is used in each region to represent the five product types, you easily can compare sales of product types among the sales regions. The totals from the worksheet are not represented, because the totals are not in the range specified for charting.

BTW

Cell Values and Charting
When you change a cell value on which a chart is dependent, Excel redraws the chart instantaneously, unless automatic recalculation is disabled. If automatic recalculation is disabled, then you must press the F9 key to redraw the chart. To enable or disable automatic recalculation, click the Calculations Options button on the Formulas tab on the Ribbon.

Excel derives the chart scale based on the values in the worksheet and then displays the scale along the vertical axis (also called the **y-axis** or **value axis**) of the chart. For example, no value in the range B4:F8 is less than 0 or greater than $100,000.00, so the scale ranges from 0 to $100,000.00. Excel also determines the $10,000.00 increments of the scale automatically. For the numbers along the y-axis, Excel uses a format that includes representing the 0 value with a dash (Figure 1–73 on the previous page).

To Add a 3-D Clustered Column Chart to the Worksheet

The commands to insert a chart are located on the Insert tab. With the range to chart selected, you click the Column button on the Ribbon to initiate drawing the chart. The area on the worksheet where the chart appears is called the chart location. As shown in Figure 1–73, the chart location in this worksheet is the range A11:G22, immediately below the worksheet data.

The following steps draw a 3-D Clustered Column chart that compares the quarterly sales by product type for the five sales regions.

- Click cell A3 and then drag the mouse pointer to the cell F8 to select the range A3:F8 (Figure 1–74).

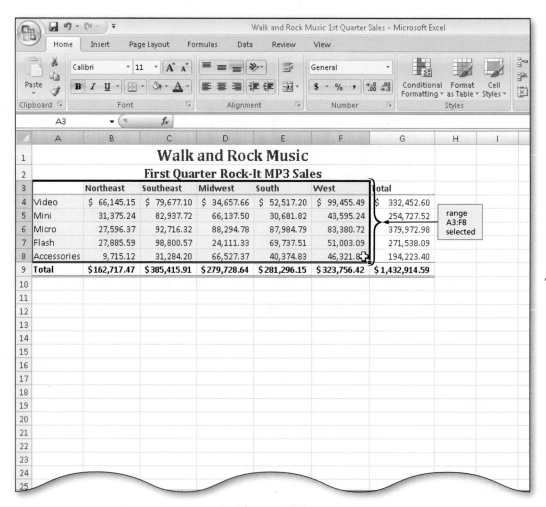

Figure 1–74

2

- Click the Insert tab to make the Insert tab the active tab (Figure 1–75).

Q&A

What tasks can I perform with the Insert tab?

The Insert tab includes commands that allow you to insert various objects, such as shapes, tables, illustrations, and charts, into a worksheet. These objects will be discussed as they are used throughout this book.

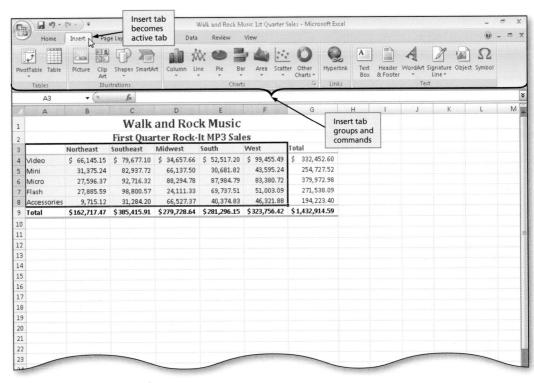

Figure 1–75

3

- Click the Column button on the Ribbon to display the Column gallery.

- Point to the 3-D Clustered Column chart type in the 3-D Column area of the Column gallery (Figure 1–76).

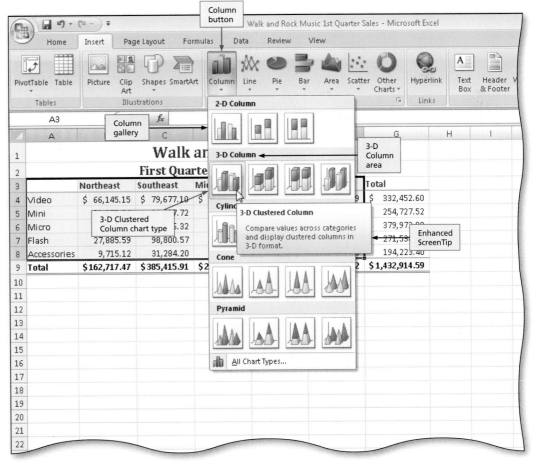

Figure 1–76

4

- Click the 3-D Clustered Column chart type in the 3-D Column area of the Column gallery to add a 3-D Clustered Column chart to the middle of the worksheet in a selection rectangle.

- Click the top-right edge of the selection rectangle but do not release the mouse to grab the chart and change the mouse pointer to a crosshair with four arrowheads (Figure 1–77).

Q&A Why is a new tab displayed on the Ribbon?

When you select objects such as shapes or charts, Excel displays contextual tabs that include special commands that are used to work with the type of object selected. Because a chart is selected, Excel displays the Chart Tools contextual tab. The three tabs below the Chart Tools contextual tab, Design, Layout, and Format, are tabs that include commands to work with charts.

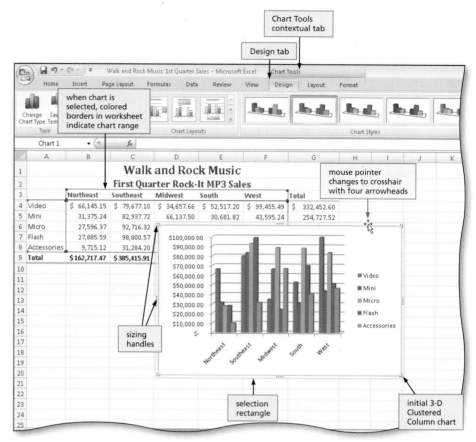

Figure 1–77

5

- Continue holding down the left mouse button while dragging the chart down and to the left to position the upper-left corner of the dotted line rectangle over the upper-left corner of cell A11. Release the mouse button to complete the move of the chart.

- Click the middle sizing handle on the right edge of the chart and do not release the mouse button (Figure 1–78).

Q&A How does Excel know how to create the chart?

Excel automatically selects the entries in the topmost row of the chart range (row 3) as the titles for the horizontal axis (also called the **x-axis** or **category axis**) and draws a column for each of the 25 cells in the range containing numbers.

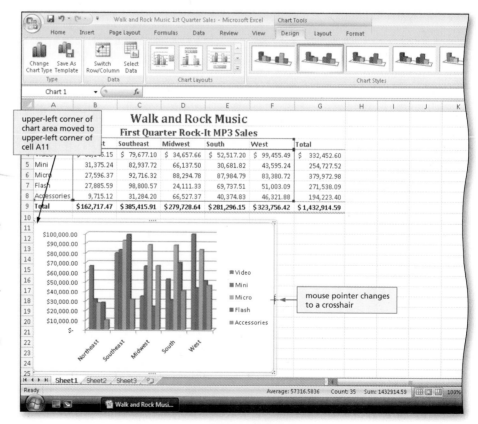

Figure 1–78

6

- While continuing to hold down the mouse button, press the ALT key and drag the right edge of the chart to the right edge of column G and then release the mouse button to resize the chart.

- Point to the middle sizing handle on the bottom edge of the selection rectangle and do not release the mouse button (Figure 1–79).

Q&A

Why should I hold the ALT key down while I resize a chart?

Holding down the ALT key while you drag a chart **snaps** (aligns) the edge of the chart area to the worksheet gridlines. If you do not hold down the ALT key, then you can place an edge of a chart in the middle of a column or row.

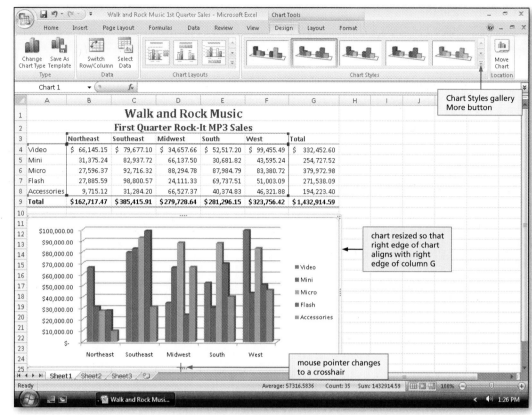

Figure 1–79

7

- While continuing to hold down the mouse button, press the ALT key and drag the bottom edge of the chart up to the bottom edge of row 22 and then release the mouse button to resize the chart.

- Click the More button in the Chart Styles gallery to expand the gallery and point to Style 2 in the gallery (column 2, row 1) (Figure 1–80).

Figure 1–80

8

- Click Style 2 in the Chart Styles gallery to apply the chart style Style 2 to the chart.

Experiment

- Select other chart styles in the Chart Styles gallery to apply other chart styles to the chart, but select Style 2 as your final choice.

- Click cell I9 to deselect the chart and complete the worksheet (Figure 1–81).

Q&A

What is the purpose of the items on the right side of the chart?

The items to the right of the column chart in Figure 1–81 are the **legend**, which identifies the colors assigned to each bar in the chart. Excel automatically selects the entries in the leftmost column of the chart range (column A) as titles within the legend.

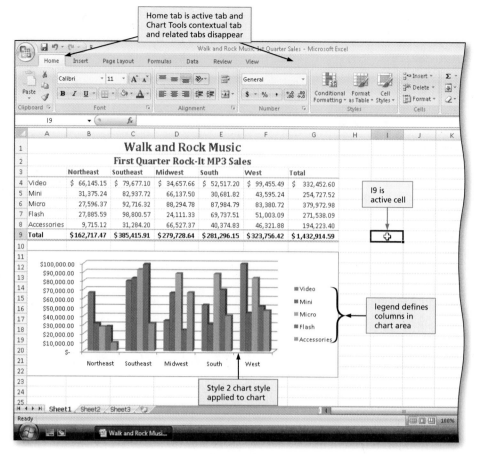

Figure 1–81

Changing Document Properties and Saving Again

BTW

Document Properties
Excel allows you to assign additional document properties by clicking the Document Properties button arrow in the Document Information Panel and then clicking Advanced Properties. You can assign custom properties, such as Department, Purpose, and Editor. Or, you can create your own document properties.

Excel helps you organize and identify your files by using **document properties**, which are the details about a file. Document properties, also known as **metadata**, can include such information as the project author, title, or subject. **Keywords** are words or phrases that further describe the document. For example, a class name or worksheet topic can describe the file's purpose or content. Document properties are valuable for a variety of reasons:

- Users can save time locating a particular file because they can view a document's properties without opening the workbook.

- By creating consistent properties for files having similar content, users can better organize their workbooks.

- Some organizations require Excel users to add document properties so that other employees can view details about these files.

Five different types of document properties exist, but the more common ones used in this book are standard and automatically updated properties. **Standard properties** are associated with all Microsoft Office documents and include author, title, and subject. **Automatically updated properties** include file system properties, such as the date you create or change a file, and statistics, such as the file size.

To Change Document Properties

The **Document Information Panel** contains areas where you can view and enter document properties. You can view and change information in this panel at any time while you are creating your workbook. Before saving the workbook again, you want to add your name and class name as document properties. The following steps use the Document Information Panel to change document properties.

1

- Click the Office Button to display the Office Button menu.

- Point to Prepare on the Office Button menu to display the Prepare submenu (Figure 1–82).

Q&A

What other types of actions besides changing properties can you take to prepare a document for distribution?

The Prepare submenu provides commands related to sharing a document with others, such as allowing or restricting people to view and modify your document, checking to see if your worksheet will work in earlier versions of Excel, and searching for hidden personal information.

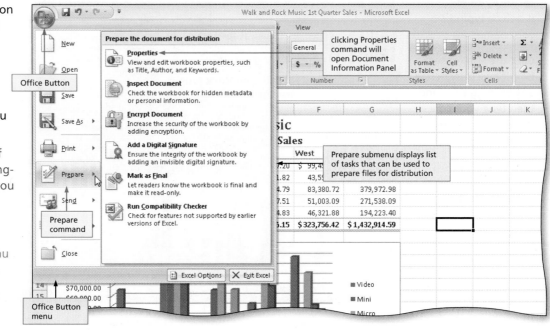

Figure 1–82

2

- Click Properties on the Prepare submenu to display the Document Information Panel (Figure 1–83).

Q&A

Why are some of the document properties in my Document Information Panel already filled in?

The person who installed Microsoft Office 2007 on your computer or network may have set or customized the properties.

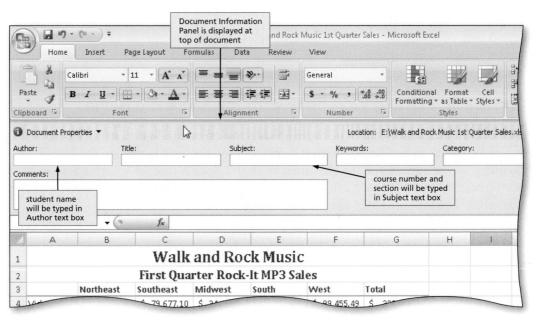

Figure 1–83

3

- Click the Author text box and then type your name as the Author property. If a name already is displayed in the Author text box, delete it before typing your name.

- Click the Subject text box, if necessary delete any existing text, and then type your course and section as the Subject property.

- Click the Keywords text box, if necessary delete any existing text, and then type First Quarter Rock-It MP3 Sales (Figure 1-84).

Q&A

What types of document properties does Excel collect automatically?

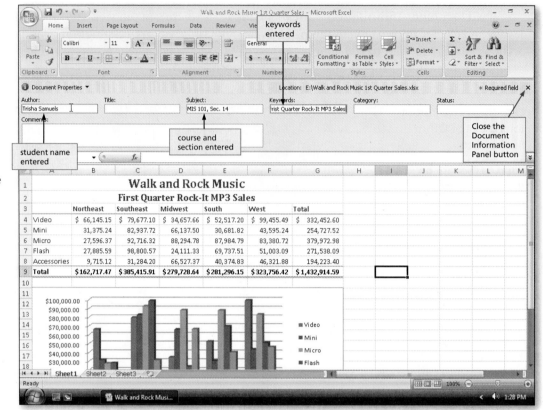

Figure 1–84

Excel records such details as how long you worked at creating your project, how many times you revised the document, and what fonts and themes are used.

4

- Click the Close the Document Information Panel button so that the Document Information Panel no longer is displayed.

To Save an Existing Workbook with the Same File Name

Saving frequently cannot be overemphasized. Several modifications have been made to the workbook since it was saved earlier in the chapter. Earlier in this chapter, the Save button on the Quick Access Toolbar caused the Save As dialog box to appear, and the file name, Walk and Rock Music 1st Quarter Sales, was entered. Clicking the Save button on the Quick Access Toolbar causes Excel to save the changes made to the workbook since the last time it was saved. The following step saves the workbook again.

Q&A

1

- With your USB flash drive connected to one of the computer's USB ports, click the Save button on the Quick Access Toolbar to overwrite the previous Walk and Rock Music 1st Quarter Sales file on the USB flash drive (Figure 1–85).

Why did the Save As dialog box not appear?

Excel overwrites the document using the settings specified the first time the document was saved. To save the file with a different file name or on different media, display the Save As dialog box by clicking the Office Button and then clicking Save As on the Office Button menu. Then, fill in the Save As dialog box as described in Steps 2 through 5 on pages EX 31 and EX 32.

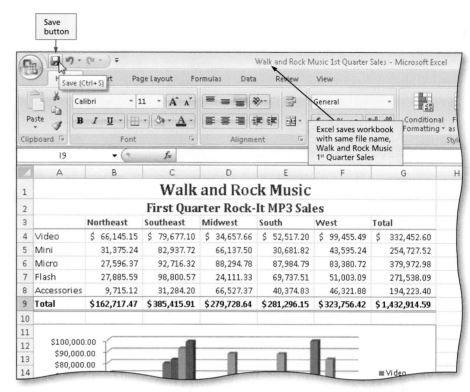

Figure 1–85

Other Ways

1. Press CTRL+S or press SHIFT+F12, press ENTER

Printing a Worksheet

After you create a worksheet, you often want to print it. A printed version of the worksheet is called a **hard copy** or **printout**. Printed copies of your worksheet can be useful for the following reasons:

- Many people prefer proofreading a hard copy of the worksheet rather than viewing the worksheet on the screen to check for errors and readability.

- Someone without computer access can view the worksheet's content.

- Copies can be distributed as handouts to people during a meeting or presentation.

- Hard copies can serve as reference material if your storage medium is lost or becomes corrupted and you need to recreate the worksheet.

   It is a good practice to save a workbook before printing it, in the event you experience difficulties with the printer.

To Print a Worksheet

With the completed worksheet saved, you may want to print it. The following steps print the worksheet in the saved Walk and Rock Music 1st Quarter Sales workbook.

- Click the Office Button to display the Office Button menu.

- Point to Print on the Office Button menu to display the Print submenu (Figure 1–86).

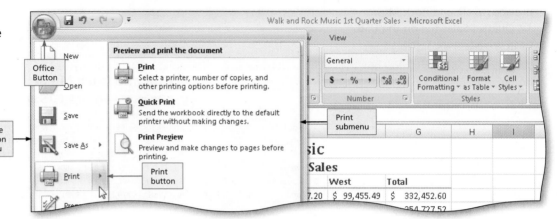

Figure 1–86

- Click Quick Print on the Print submenu to print the worksheet (Figure 1–87).

Q&A

Can I print my worksheet in black and white to conserve ink or toner?

Yes. Click the Office Button and then click the Excel Options button on the Office Button menu. When the Excel Options dialog box is displayed, click Advanced, scroll to the Print area, place a check mark in the Use draft quality check box if it is displayed, and then click the OK button and then click the Close Print Preview button on the Ribbon. Click the Office Button, point to Print, and then click Quick Print.

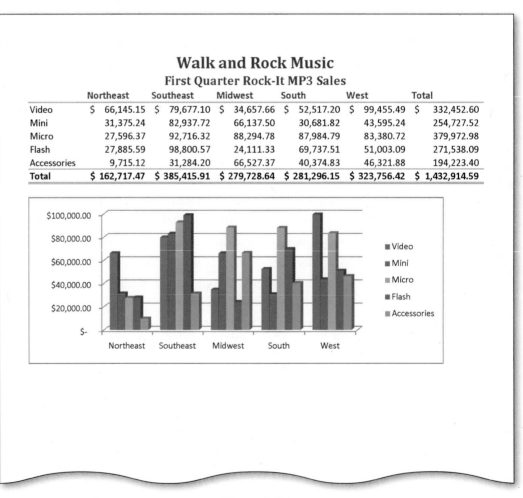

Figure 1–87

Other Ways

1. Press CTRL+P, press ENTER

Quitting Excel

When you quit Excel, if you have made changes to a workbook since the last time the file was saved, Excel displays a dialog box asking if you want to save the changes you made to the file before it closes that window. The dialog box contains three buttons with these resulting actions:

- Yes button — Saves the changes and then quits Excel
- No button — Quits Excel without saving changes
- Cancel button — Closes the dialog box and redisplays the worksheet without saving the changes

If no changes have been made to an open workbook since the last time the file was saved, Excel will close the window without displaying a dialog box.

To Quit Excel with One Workbook Open

The Walk and Rock 1st Quarter Sales worksheet is complete. The following steps quit Excel if only one workbook is open.

1
- Point to the Close button on the right side of the Excel title bar (Figure 1–88).

2
- Click the Close button to quit Excel.

Q&A

What if I have more than one Excel workbook open?

You would click the Close button on the Excel title bar for each open workbook. When you click the Close button with the last workbook open, Excel also quits. As an alternative, you could click the Office Button and then click the Exit Excel button on the Office Button menu, which closes all open workbooks and then quits Excel.

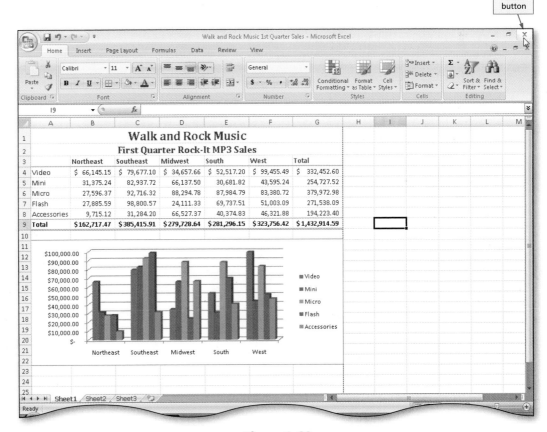

Figure 1–88

Other Ways

1. Double-click Office Button

2. With multiple workbooks open, click Office Button, click Exit Excel on Office Button menu

3. Right-click Microsoft Excel button on Windows Vista taskbar, click Close on shortcut menu

4. Press ALT+F4

BTW

Print Preview
You can preview the printout on your screen using the Print Preview command on the Print submenu (Figure 1–86 on page EX 58), make adjustments to the worksheet, and then print it only when it appears exactly as you want. Each time you preview rather than print, you save both ink and paper.

Starting Excel and Opening a Workbook

Once you have created and saved a workbook, you may need to retrieve it from your storage medium. For example, you might want to revise a worksheet or reprint it. Opening a workbook requires that Excel is running on your computer.

To Start Excel

The following steps, which assume Windows Vista is running, start Excel.

Note: If you are using Windows XP, please see Appendix F for alternate steps.

1 Click the Start button on the Windows Vista taskbar to display the Start menu.

2 Click All Programs at the bottom of the left pane on the Start menu to display the All Programs list and then click Microsoft Office in the All Programs list to display the Microsoft Office list.

3 Click Microsoft Office Excel 2007 in the Microsoft Office list to start Excel and display a new blank worksheet in the Excel window.

4 If the Excel window is not maximized, click the Maximize button on its title bar to maximize the window.

To Open a Workbook from Excel

Earlier in this chapter, the workbook was saved on a USB flash drive using the file name, Walk and Rock Music 1st Quarter Sales. The following steps open the Walk and Rock Music 1st Quarter Sales file from the USB flash drive.

1

- With your USB flash drive connected to one of the computer's USB ports, click the Office Button to display the Office Button menu (Figure 1–89).

Q&A

What files are shown in the Recent Documents list?

Excel displays the most recently opened document file names in this list. If the name of the file you want to open appears in the Recent Documents list, you could double-click it to open the file.

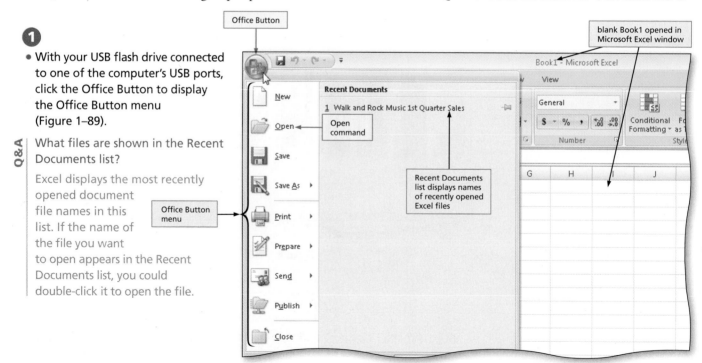

Figure 1–89

2

- Click Open on the Office Button menu to display the Open dialog box.

- If the Folders list is displayed below the Folders button, click the Folders button to remove the Folders list.

- If necessary, click Computer in the Favorite Links section and then scroll until UDISK 2.0 (E:) appears in the list of available drives.

- Double-click UDISK 2.0 (E:) to select the USB flash drive, Drive E in this case, as the new open location.

- Click Walk and Rock Music 1st Quarter Sales to select the file name (Figure 1–90).

Q&A How do I open the file if I am not using a USB flash drive?

Use the same process, but be certain to select your device in the Computer list.

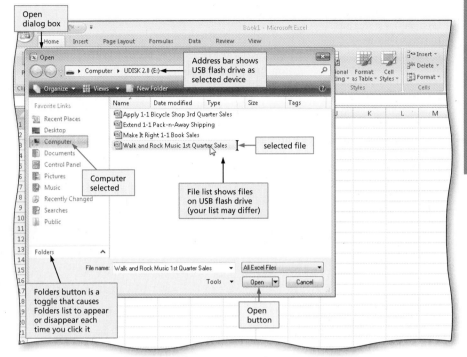

Figure 1–90

3

- Click the Open button to open the selected file and display the worksheet in the Excel window (Figure 1–91).

Q&A Why do I see the Microsoft Excel icon and name on the Windows Vista taskbar?

When you open an Excel file, the application name (Microsoft Excel) is displayed on a selected button on the Windows Vista taskbar. If you point to this button, the file name also appears in a ScreenTip.

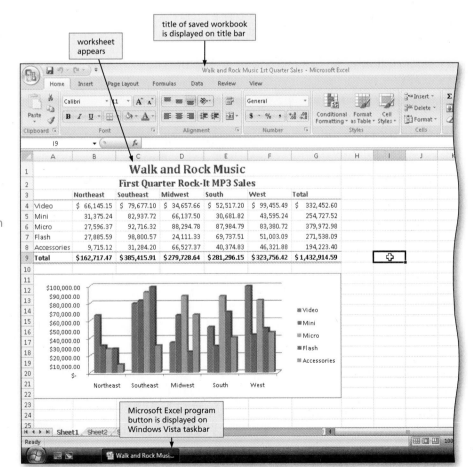

Figure 1–91

Other Ways

1. Click Office Button, double-click file name in Recent Documents list

2. Press CTRL+O, select file name, press ENTER

BTW

AutoCalculate
Use the AutoCalculate area on the status bar to check your work as you enter data in a worksheet. If you enter large amounts of data, you select a range of data and then check the AutoCalculate area to provide insight into statistics about the data you entered. Often, you will have an intuitive feel for whether the numbers are accurate or if you may have made a mistake while entering the data.

AutoCalculate

You easily can obtain a total, an average, or other information about the numbers in a range by using the **AutoCalculate area** on the status bar. First, select the range of cells containing the numbers you want to check. Next, right-click the AutoCalculate area to display the Status Bar Configuration shortcut menu (Figure 1–92). The check mark to the left of the active functions (Average, Count, and Sum) indicates that the sum, count, and average of the selected range are displayed in the AutoCalculate area on the status bar. The functions of the AutoCalculate commands on the Status Bar Configuration shortcut menu are described in Table 1–4.

Table 1–4 AutoCalculate Shortcut Menu Commands

Command	Function
Average	AutoCalculate area displays the average of the numbers in the selected range
Count	AutoCalculate area displays the number of nonblank cells in the selected range
Numerical Count	AutoCalculate area displays the number of cells containing numbers in the selected range
Minimum	AutoCalculate area displays the lowest value in the selected range
Maximum	AutoCalculate area displays the highest value in the selected range
Sum	AutoCalculate area displays the sum of the numbers in the selected range

To Use the AutoCalculate Area to Determine a Maximum

The following steps show how to display the largest quarterly sales for any region for the Micro product type.

1

- Select the range B6:F6 and then right-click the AutoCalculate area on the status bar to display the Status Bar Configuration shortcut menu (Figure 1–92).

Q&A

What is displayed on the Status Bar Configuration shortcut menu?

This shortcut menu includes several commands that allow you to control the items displayed on the Customize Status Bar shortcut menu. The AutoCalculate area of the shortcut menu includes six commands as well as the result of the associated calculation on the right side of the menu.

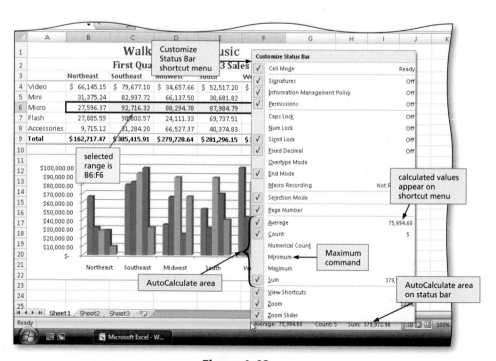

Figure 1–92

2

- Click Maximum on the shortcut menu to display the Maximum value in the range B6:F6 in the AutoCalculate area of the status bar.

- Click anywhere on the worksheet to cause the shortcut menu to disappear (Figure 1–93).

3

- Right-click the AutoCalculate area and then click Maximum on the shortcut menu to cause the Maximum value to no longer appear in the AutoCalculate area.

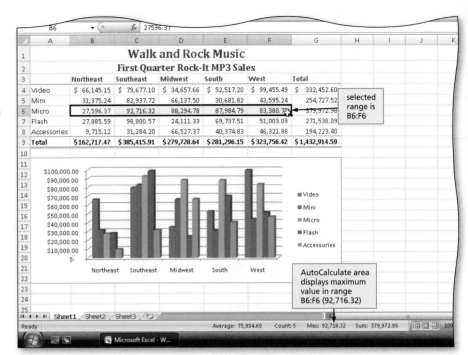

Figure 1–93

Correcting Errors

You can correct errors on a worksheet using one of several methods. The method you choose will depend on the extent of the error and whether you notice it while typing the data or after you have entered the incorrect data into the cell.

Correcting Errors while You Are Typing Data into a Cell

If you notice an error while you are typing data into a cell, press the BACKSPACE key to erase the incorrect characters and then type the correct characters. If the error is a major one, click the Cancel box in the formula bar or press the ESC key to erase the entire entry and then reenter the data from the beginning.

Correcting Errors after Entering Data into a Cell

If you find an error in the worksheet after entering the data, you can correct the error in one of two ways:

1. If the entry is short, select the cell, retype the entry correctly, and then click the Enter box or press the ENTER key. The new entry will replace the old entry.

2. If the entry in the cell is long and the errors are minor, using Edit mode may be a better choice than retyping the cell entry. Use the Edit mode as described below.

   a. Double-click the cell containing the error to switch Excel to Edit mode. In **Edit mode**, Excel displays the active cell entry in the formula bar and a flashing

BTW

In-Cell Editing
An alternative to double-clicking the cell to edit it is to select the cell and then press the F2 key.

insertion point in the active cell (Figure 1–94). With Excel in Edit mode, you can edit the contents directly in the cell — a procedure called **in-cell editing**.

b. Make changes using in-cell editing, as indicated below.

(1) To insert new characters between two characters, place the insertion point between the two characters and begin typing. Excel inserts the new characters at the location of the insertion point.

(2) To delete a character in the cell, move the insertion point to the left of the character you want to delete and then press the DELETE key or place the insertion point to the right of the character you want to delete and then press the BACKSPACE key. You also can use the mouse to drag through the character or adjacent characters you want to delete and then press the DELETE key or click the Cut button on the Home tab on the Ribbon.

(3) When you are finished editing an entry, click the Enter box or press the ENTER key.

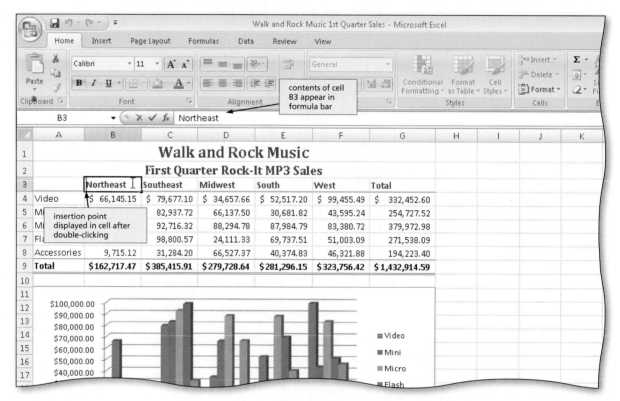

Figure 1–94

When Excel enters the Edit mode, the keyboard usually is in Insert mode. In **Insert mode**, as you type a character, Excel inserts the character and moves all characters to the right of the typed character one position to the right. You can change to Overtype mode by pressing the INSERT key. In **Overtype mode**, Excel overtypes, or replaces, the character to the right of the insertion point. The INSERT key toggles the keyboard between Insert mode and Overtype mode.

While in Edit mode, you may have reason to move the insertion point to various points in the cell, select portions of the data in the cell, or switch from inserting characters to overtyping characters. Table 1–5 summarizes the more common tasks used during in-cell editing.

BTW

Editing the Contents of a Cell
Rather than using in-cell editing, you can select the cell and then click the formula bar to edit the contents.

Table 1–5 Summary of In-Cell Editing Tasks

	Task	Mouse	Keyboard
1	Move the insertion point to the beginning of data in a cell.	Point to the left of the first character and click.	Press HOME
2	Move the insertion point to the end of data in a cell.	Point to the right of the last character and click.	Press END
3	Move the insertion point anywhere in a cell.	Point to the appropriate position and click the character.	Press RIGHT ARROW or LEFT ARROW
4	Highlight one or more adjacent characters.	Drag the mouse pointer through adjacent characters.	Press SHIFT+RIGHT ARROW or SHIFT+LEFT ARROW
5	Select all data in a cell.	Double-click the cell with the insertion point in the cell if there are no spaces in the data in the cell.	
6	Delete selected characters.	Click the Cut button on the Home tab on the Ribbon.	Press DELETE
7	Delete characters to the left of the insertion point.		Press BACKSPACE
8	Delete characters to the right of the insertion point.		Press DELETE
9	Toggle between Insert and Overtype modes.		Press INSERT

Undoing the Last Cell Entry

Excel provides the Undo command on the Quick Access Toolbar (Figure 1–95), which allows you to erase recent cell entries. Thus, if you enter incorrect data in a cell and notice it immediately, click the Undo button and Excel changes the cell entry to what it was prior to the incorrect data entry.

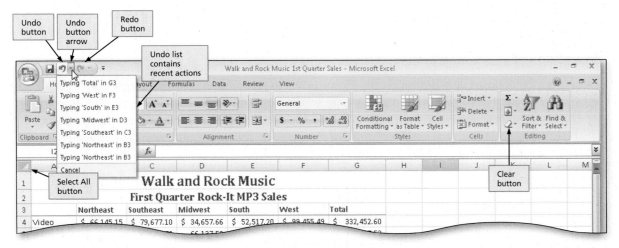

Figure 1–95

Excel remembers the last 100 actions you have completed. Thus, you can undo up to 100 previous actions by clicking the Undo button arrow to display the Undo list and then clicking the action to be undone (Figure 1–95). You can drag through several actions in the Undo list to undo all of them at once. If no actions are available for Excel to undo, then the Undo button is dimmed and inoperative.

The Redo button, next to the Undo button on the Quick Access Toolbar, allows you to repeat previous actions.

BTW

Quick Reference
For a table that lists how to complete the tasks covered in this book using the mouse, Ribbon, shortcut menu, and keyboard, see the Quick Reference Summary at the back of this book, or visit the Excel 2007 Quick Reference Web page (scsite.com/ex2007/qr).

Clearing a Cell or Range of Cells

If you enter data into the wrong cell or range of cells, you can erase, or clear, the data using one of the first four methods listed below. The fifth method clears the formatting from the selected cells.

To Clear Cell Entries Using the Fill Handle

1. Select the cell or range of cells and then point to the fill handle so the mouse pointer changes to a crosshair.
2. Drag the fill handle back into the selected cell or range until a shadow covers the cell or cells you want to erase. Release the mouse button.

To Clear Cell Entries Using the Shortcut Menu

1. Select the cell or range of cells to be cleared.
2. Right-click the selection.
3. Click Clear Contents on the shortcut menu.

To Clear Cell Entries Using the delete Key

1. Select the cell or range of cells to be cleared.
2. Press the DELETE key.

BTW

Certification
The Microsoft Certified Application Specialist (MCAS) program provides an opportunity for you to obtain a valuable industry credential – proof that you have the Excel 2007 skills required by employers. For more information, see Appendix G or visit the Excel 2007 Certification Web page (scsite.com/ex2007/cert).

To Clear Cell Entries and Formatting Using the Clear Button

1. Select the cell or range of cells to be cleared.
2. Click the Clear button on the Home tab (Figure 1–95 on the previous page).
3. Click Clear Contents on the menu.

To Clear Formatting Using the Cell Styles Button

1. Select the cell or range of cells from which you want to remove the formatting.
2. Click the Cell Styles button on the Home tab and point to Normal.
3. Click Normal in the Cell Styles Gallery.

The Clear button on the Home tab is the only command that clears both the cell entry and the cell formatting. As you are clearing cell entries, always remember that you should *never press the* SPACEBAR *to clear a cell.* Pressing the SPACEBAR enters a blank character. A blank character is text and is different from an empty cell, even though the cell may appear empty.

BTW

Getting Back to Normal
If you accidentally assign unwanted formats to a range of cells, you can use the Normal cell style selection in the Cell Styles gallery. Click Cell Styles on the Home tab on the Ribbon and then click Normal. Doing so changes the format to Normal style. To view the characteristics of the Normal style, right-click the style in the Cell Styles gallery and then click Modify, or press ALT+APOSTROPHE (').

Clearing the Entire Worksheet

If required worksheet edits are extremely extensive, you may want to clear the entire worksheet and start over. To clear the worksheet or delete an embedded chart, use the following steps.

To Clear the Entire Worksheet

1. Click the Select All button on the worksheet (Figure 1–95).
2. Click the Clear button on the Home tab to delete both the entries and formats.

The Select All button selects the entire worksheet. Instead of clicking the Select All button, you also can press CTRL+A. To clear an unsaved workbook, click the workbook's Close Window button or click the Close command on the Office Button menu. Click the No button if the Microsoft Excel dialog box asks if you want to save changes. To start a new, blank workbook, click the New command on the Office Button menu.

To delete an embedded chart, complete the following steps.

To Delete an Embedded Chart
1. Click the chart to select it.
2. Press the DELETE key.

BTW

Excel Help
The best way to become familiar with Excel Help is to use it. Appendix C includes detailed information about Excel Help and exercises that will help you gain confidence in using it.

Excel Help

At any time while using Excel, you can find answers to questions and display information about various topics through **Excel Help**. This section introduces you to Excel Help.

To Search for Excel Help

Using Excel Help, you can search for information based on phrases such as save a workbook or format a chart, or key terms such as copy, save, or format. Excel Help responds with a list of search results displayed as links to a variety of resources. The following steps, which use Excel Help to search for information about formatting a chart, assume you are connected to the Internet.

- Click the Microsoft Office Excel Help button near the upper-right corner of the Excel window to open the Excel Help window.

- Type format a chart in the Type words to search for text box at the top of the Excel Help window (Figure 1–96).

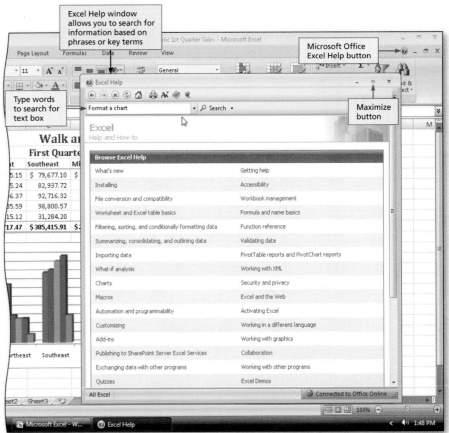

Figure 1–96

2

- Press the ENTER key to display the search results.

- Click the Maximize button on the Excel Help window title bar to maximize the Help window (Figure 1–97).

Q&A

Where is the Excel window with the Walk and Rock Music 1st Quarter Sales worksheet?

Excel is open in the background, but the Excel Help window is overlaid on top of the Microsoft Excel window. When the Excel Help window is closed, the worksheet will reappear.

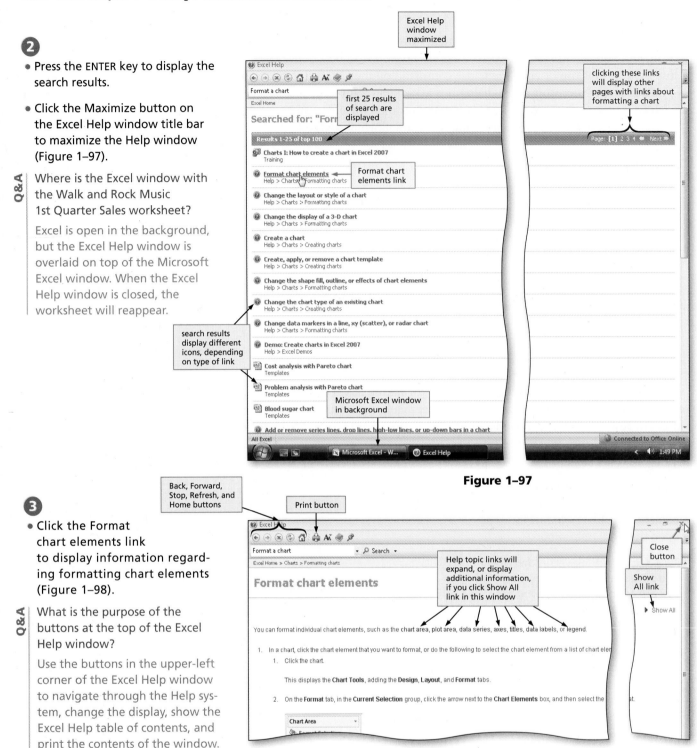

Figure 1–97

3

- Click the Format chart elements link to display information regarding formatting chart elements (Figure 1–98).

Q&A

What is the purpose of the buttons at the top of the Excel Help window?

Use the buttons in the upper-left corner of the Excel Help window to navigate through the Help system, change the display, show the Excel Help table of contents, and print the contents of the window.

Figure 1–98

4

- Click the Close button on the Excel Help window title bar to close the Excel Help window and make Excel active.

Other Ways

1. Press F1

To Quit Excel

The following steps quit Excel.

1 Click the Close button on the right side of the title bar to quit Excel; or if you have multiple Excel workbooks open, click the Office Button and then click the Exit Excel button on the Office Button menu to close all open workbooks and quit Excel.

2 If necessary, click the No button in the Microsoft Office Excel dialog box so that any changes you have made are not saved.

BTW

Quitting Excel
Do not forget to remove your USB flash drive from the USB port after quitting Excel, especially if you are working in a laboratory environment. Nothing can be more frustrating than leaving all of your hard work behind on a USB flash drive for the next user.

Chapter Summary

In this chapter you have learned about the Excel window, how to enter text and numbers to create a worksheet, how to select a range, how to use the Sum button, save a workbook, format cells, insert a chart, print a worksheet, quit Excel, and use Excel Help. The items listed below include all the new Excel skills you have learned in this chapter.

1. Start Excel (EX 6)
2. Enter the Worksheet Titles (EX 17)
3. Enter Column Titles (EX 19)
4. Enter Row Titles (EX 21)
5. Enter Numbers (EX 23)
6. Sum a Column of Numbers (EX 25)
7. Copy a Cell to Adjacent Cells in a Row (EX 27)
8. Determine Multiple Totals at the Same Time (EX 28)
9. Save a Workbook (EX 30)
10. Change a Cell Style (EX 35)
11. Change the Font Type (EX 36)
12. Bold a Cell (EX 38)
13. Increase the Font Size of a Cell Entry (EX 38)
14. Change the Font Color of a Cell Entry (EX 39)
15. Center Cell Entries across Columns by Merging Cells (EX 40)
16. Format Column Titles and the Total Row (EX 42)
17. Format Numbers in the Worksheet (EX 44)
18. Adjust the Column Width (EX 46)
19. Use the Name Box to Select a Cell (EX 47)
20. Add a 3-D Clustered Column Chart to the Worksheet (EX 50)
21. Change Document Properties (EX 55)
22. Save an Existing Workbook with the Same File Name (EX 58)
23. Print a Worksheet (EX 58)
24. Quit Excel with One Workbook Open (EX 59)
25. Open a Workbook from Excel (EX 60)
26. Use the AutoCalculate Area to Determine a Maximum (EX 62)
27. Clear Cell Entries Using the Fill Handle (EX 66)
28. Clear Cell Entries Using the Shortcut Menu (EX 66)
29. Clear Cell Entries Using the DELETE Key (EX 66)
30. Clear Cell Entries and Formatting Using the Clear Button (EX 66)
31. Clear Formatting Using the Cell Styles Button (EX 66)
32. Clear the Entire Worksheet (EX 66)
33. Delete an Embedded Chart (EX 67)
34. Search for Excel Help (EX 67)

If you have a SAM user profile, you may have access to hands-on instruction, practice, and assessment. Log in to your SAM account (http://sam2007.course.com) to launch any assigned training activities or exams that relate to the skills covered in this chapter.

Learn It Online

Test your knowledge of chapter content and key terms.

Instructions: To complete the Learn It Online exercises, start your browser, click the Address bar, and then enter the Web address scsite.com/ex2007/learn. When the Excel 2007 Learn It Online page is displayed, click the link for the exercise you want to complete and then read the instructions.

Chapter Reinforcement TF, MC, and SA
A series of true/false, multiple choice, and short answer questions that test your knowledge of the chapter content.

Flash Cards
An interactive learning environment where you identify chapter key terms associated with displayed definitions.

Practice Test
A series of multiple choice questions that test your knowledge of chapter content and key terms.

Who Wants To Be a Computer Genius?
An interactive game that challenges your knowledge of chapter content in the style of a television quiz show.

Wheel of Terms
An interactive game that challenges your knowledge of chapter key terms in the style of the television show *Wheel of Fortune*.

Crossword Puzzle Challenge
A crossword puzzle that challenges your knowledge of key terms presented in the chapter.

Apply Your Knowledge

Reinforce the skills and apply the concepts you learned in this chapter.

Changing the Values in a Worksheet
Instructions: Start Excel. Open the workbook Apply 1-1 Bicycle Shop 3rd Quarter Sales (Figure 1–99a). See the inside back cover of this book for instructions for downloading the Data Files for Students, or see your instructor for information on accessing the files required in this book.

1. Make the changes to the worksheet described in Table 1–6 so that the worksheet appears as shown in Figure 1–99b. As you edit the values in the cells containing numeric data, watch the totals in row 8, the totals in column G, and the chart change.

2. Change the worksheet title in cell A1 to the Title cell style and then merge and center it across columns A through G. Use commands in the Font group on the Home tab on the Ribbon to change the worksheet subtitle in cell A2 to 16-point Corbel red, bold font and then center it across columns A through G. Use the Accent 1 theme color (column 5, row 1 on the Font Color palette) for the red font color.

3. Update the document properties with your name, course number, and name for the workbook. Save the workbook using the file name, Apply 1-1 Spoke-Up Bicycle Shop 3rd Quarter Sales. Submit the assignment as requested by your instructor.

Table 1–6 New Worksheet Data	
Cell	**Change Cell Contents To**
A1	Spoke-Up Bicycle Shop
B4	11869.2
E4	9157.83
D6	5217.92
F6	6239.46
B7	3437.64

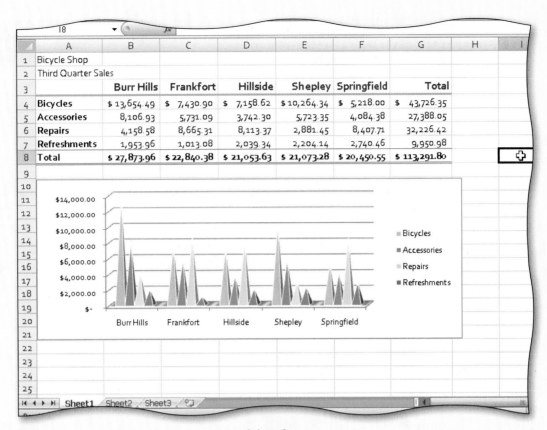

(a) Before

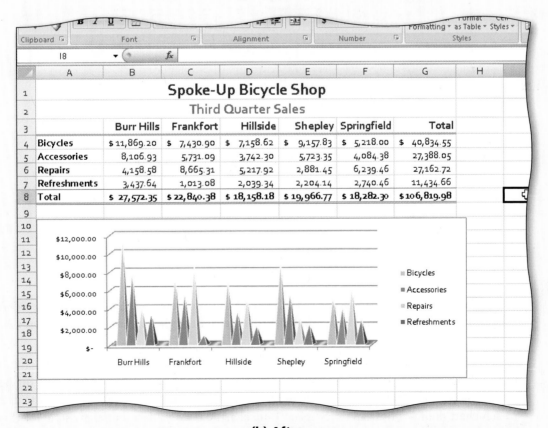

(b) After

Figure 1–99

Extend Your Knowledge

Extend the skills you learned in this chapter and experiment with new skills. You may need to use Help to complete the assignment.

Formatting Cells and Inserting Multiple Charts

Instructions: Start Excel. Open the workbook Extend 1-1 Pack-n-Away Shipping. See the inside back cover of this book for instructions for downloading the Data Files for Students, or see your instructor for information on accessing the files required in this book. Perform the following tasks to format cells in the worksheet and to add two charts to the worksheet.

1. Use the commands in the Font group on the Home tab on the Ribbon to change the font of the title in cell A1 to 24-point Arial, red; bold and subtitle of the worksheet to 16-point Arial Narrow, blue, bold.

2. Select the range A3:E8, click the Insert tab on the Ribbon, and then click the Dialog Box Launcher in the Charts group on the Ribbon to open the Insert Chart dialog box (Figure 1–100).

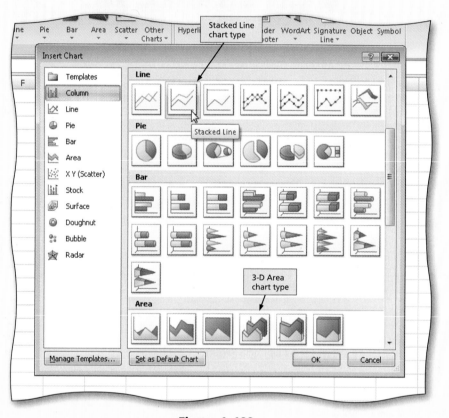

Figure 1–100

3. Insert a Stacked Line chart by clicking the Stacked Line chart in the gallery and then clicking the OK button. Move the chart either below or to the right of the data in the worksheet. Click the Design tab and apply a chart style to the chart.

4. If necessary, reselect the range A3:E8 and follow Step 3 above to insert a 3-D Area chart in the worksheet. You may need to use the scroll box on the right side of the Insert Chart dialog box to view the Area charts in the gallery. Move the chart either below or to the right of the data so that each chart does not overlap the Stacked Line chart. Choose a different chart style for this chart than the one you selected for the Stacked Line chart.

5. Resize each chart so that each snaps to the worksheet gridlines. Make certain that both charts are visible with the worksheet data without the need to scroll the worksheet.

6. Update the document properties with your name, course number, and name for the workbook.

7. Save the workbook using the file name, Extend 1-1 Pack-n-Away Shipping Charts. Submit the assignment as requested by your instructor.

Make It Right

Analyze a workbook and correct all errors and/or improve the design.

Correcting Formatting and Values in a Worksheet

Instructions: Start Excel. Open the workbook Make It Right 1-1 Book Sales. See the inside back cover of this book for instructions for downloading the Data Files for Students, or see your instructor for information on accessing the files required for this book. Correct the following formatting problems and data errors (Figure 1–101) in the worksheet, while keeping in mind the guidelines presented in this chapter.

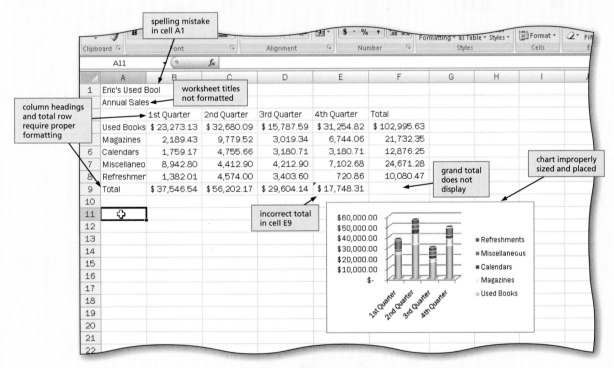

Figure 1–101

1. Merge and center the worksheet title and subtitle appropriately.

2. Format the worksheet title with a cell style appropriate for a worksheet title.

3. Format the subtitle using commands in the Font group on the Ribbon.

4. Correct the spelling mistake in cell A1 by changing Bool to Books.

5. Apply proper formatting to the column headers and total row.

Continued >

Make It Right *continued*

6. Adjust column sizes so that all data in each column is visible.

7. Use the SUM function to create the grand total for annual sales.

8. The SUM function in cell E9 does not sum all of the numbers in the column. Correct this error by editing the range for the SUM function in the cell.

9. Resize and move the chart so that it is below the worksheet data and does not extend past the right edge of the worksheet data. Be certain to snap the chart to the worksheet gridlines by holding down the ALT key as you resize the chart.

10. Update the document properties with your name, course number, and name for the workbook. Save the workbook using the file name, Make It Right 1-1 Eric's Used Books Annual Sales. Submit the assignment as requested by your instructor.

In the Lab

Design and/or create a workbook using the guidelines, concepts, and skills presented in this chapter. Labs 1, 2, and 3 are listed in order of increasing difficulty.

Lab 1: Annual Cost of Goods Worksheet

Problem: You work part-time as a spreadsheet specialist for Kona's Expresso Coffee, one of the up-and-coming coffee franchises in the United States. Your manager has asked you to develop an annual cost of goods analysis worksheet similar to the one shown in Figure 1–102.

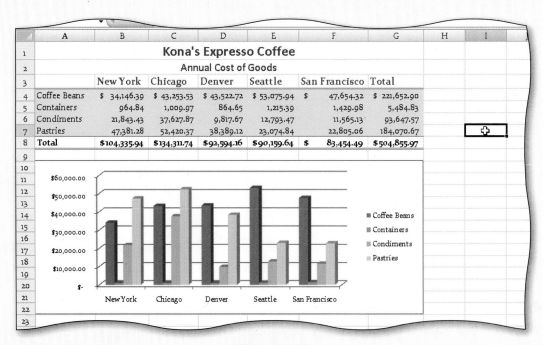

Figure 1–102

Instructions: Perform the following tasks.

1. Start Excel. Enter the worksheet title, Kona's Expresso Coffee, in cell A1 and the wor subtitle, Annual Cost of Goods, in cell A2. Beginning in row 3, enter the store locat′ goods, and supplies categories shown in Table 1–7.

Table 1–7 Kona's Expresso Coffee Annual Cost of Goods					
	New York	**Chicago**	**Denver**	**Seattle**	**San Franscisco**
Coffee Beans	34146.39	43253.53	43522.72	53075.94	47654.32
Containers	964.84	1009.97	864.65	1215.39	1429.98
Condiments	21843.43	37627.87	9817.67	12793.47	11565.13
Pastries	47381.28	52420.37	38389.12	23074.84	22805.06

2. Use the SUM function to determine the totals for each store location, type of supply, and company grand total.

3. Use Cell Styles in the Styles group on the Home tab on the Ribbon to format the worksheet title with the Title cell style. Center the title across columns A through G. Do not be concerned if the edges of the worksheet title are not displayed.

4. Use buttons in the Font group on the Home tab on the Ribbon to format the worksheet subtitle to 14-point Calibri dark blue, bold font, and center it across columns A through G.

5. Use Cell Styles in the Styles group on the Home tab on the Ribbon to format the range A3:G3 with the Heading 2 cell style, the range A4:G7 with the 20% - Accent1 cell style, and the range A8:G8 with the Total cell style. Use the buttons in the Number group on the Home tab on the Ribbon to apply the Accounting Number format to the range B4:G4 and the range B8:G8. Use the buttons in the Number group on the Home tab on the Ribbon to apply the Comma Style to the range B5:G7. Adjust any column widths to the widest text entry in each column.

6. Select the range A3:F7 and then insert a 3-D Clustered Column chart. Apply the Style 5 chart style to the chart. Move and resize the chart so that it appears in the range A10:G22. If the labels along the horizontal axis (x-axis) do not appear as shown in Figure 1-102, then drag the right side of the chart so that it is displayed in the range A10:G22.

7. Update the document properties with your name, course number, and name for the workbook.

8. Save the workbook using the file name Lab 1-1 Konas Expresso Coffee Annual Cost of Goods.

9. Print the worksheet.

10. Make the following two corrections to the sales amounts: $9,648.12 for Seattle Condiments (cell E6), $12,844.79 for Chicago Pastries (cell C7). After you enter the corrections, the company totals in cell G8 should equal $462,135.04.

11. Print the revised worksheet. Close the workbook without saving the changes. Submit the assignment as requested by your instructor.

In the Lab

Lab 2: Annual Sales Analysis Worksheet

Problem: As the chief accountant for Scissors Office Supply, Inc., you have been asked by the sales manager to create a worksheet to analyze the annual sales for the company by location and customer type category (Figure 1–103). The office locations and corresponding sales by customer type for the year are shown in Table 1–8.

Continued >

In the Lab *continued*

Instructions: Perform the following tasks.
1. Create the worksheet shown in Figure 1–103 using the data in Table 1–8.
2. Use the SUM function to determine totals sales for the four offices, the totals for each customer type, and the company total. Add column and row headings for the totals row and totals column, as appropriate.

Table 1–8 Scissors Office Supply Annual Sales				
	Boston	**Miami**	**St. Louis**	**Santa Fe**
Consumer	206348.81	113861.40	69854.13	242286.82
Small Business	235573.28	133511.24	199158.35	228365.51
Large Business	237317.55	234036.08	126519.10	111773.38
Government	178798.04	144548.80	135470.86	132599.75
Nonprofit	15180.63	28837.75	63924.48	21361.42

3. Format the worksheet title with the Title cell style and center it across columns A through F. Use the Font group on the Ribbon to format the worksheet subtitle to 16-point Cambria green, and bold font. Center the title across columns A through F.

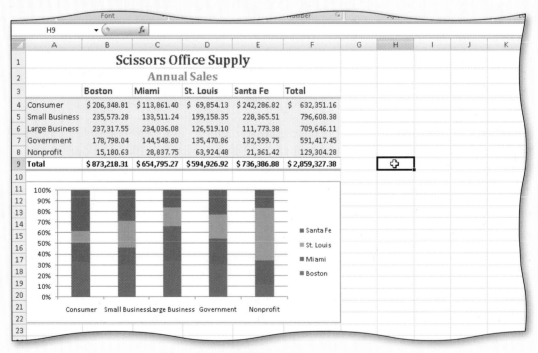

Figure 1–103

4. Format the range A3:F3 with the Heading 2 cell style, the range A4:F8 with the 20% - Accent3 cell style, and the range A9:F9 with the Total cell style. Use the Number group on the Ribbon to format cells B4:F4 and B9:F9 with the Accounting Number Format and cells B5:F8 with the Comma Style numeric format. Adjust the width of column A in order to fit contents of the column.
5. Chart the range A3:E8. Insert a 100% Stacked Column chart for the range A3:E8, as shown in Figure 1–103, by using the Column button on the Insert tab on the Ribbon. Use the chart location A11:F22.

6. Update the document properties with your name, course number, and name for the workbook.

7. Save the workbook using the file name, Lab 1-2 Scissors Office Supply Annual Sales. Print the worksheet.

8. Two corrections to the figures were sent in from the accounting department. The correct sales are $98,342.16 for Miami's annual Small Business sales (cell C5) and $48,933.75 for St. Louis's annual Nonprofit sales (cell D8). After you enter the two corrections, the company total in cell F9 should equal $2,809,167.57. Print the revised worksheet.

9. Use the Undo button to change the worksheet back to the original numbers in Table 1–8. Use the Redo button to change the worksheet back to the revised state.

10. Close Excel without saving the latest changes. Start Excel and open the workbook saved in Step 7. Double-click cell E6 and use in-cell editing to change the Santa Fe annual Large Business sales (cell E6) to $154,108.49. Write the company total in cell F9 at the top of the first printout. Click the Undo button.

11. Click cell A1 and then click the Merge & Center button to split cell A1 into cells A1, B1, C1, D1, E1, and F1. To merge the cells into one again, select the range A1:F1 and then click the Merge & Center button on the Home tab on the Ribbon.

12. Close the workbook without saving the changes. Submit the assignment as requested by your instructor.

In the Lab

Lab 3: College Cost and Financial Support Worksheet

Problem: Attending college is an expensive proposition and your resources are limited. To plan for your four-year college career, you have decided to organize your anticipated resources and costs in a worksheet. The data required to prepare your worksheet is shown in Table 1–9.

Table 1–9 College Cost and Resources

Cost	Freshman	Sophomore	Junior	Senior
Books	450.00	477.00	505.62	535.95
Room & Board	7500.00	7950.00	8427.00	8932.62
Tuition	8200.00	8692.00	9213.52	9766.33
Entertainment	1325.00	1404.50	1488.77	1578.10
Miscellaneous	950.00	1007.00	1067.42	1131.47
Clothes	725.00	768.50	814.61	863.49

Financial Support	Freshman	Sophomore	Junior	Senior
Job	3400.00	3604.00	3820.24	4049.45
Savings	4350.00	4611.00	4887.66	5180.92
Parents	4700.00	4982.00	5280.92	5597.78
Financial Aid	5500.00	5830.00	6179.80	6550.59
Other	1200.00	1272.00	1348.32	1429.22

Continued >

ab continued

Instructions Part 1:   Using the numbers in Table 1–9, create the worksheet shown in columns A through F in Figure 1–104. Format the worksheet title as Calibri 24-point bold red. Merge and center the worksheet title in cell A1 across columns A through F. Format the worksheet subtitles in cells A2 and A11 as Calibri 16-point bold green. Format the ranges A3:F3 and A12:F12 with the Heading 2 cell style, the ranges A4:F9 and A13:F17 with the 20% - Accent1 cell style, and the ranges A10:F10 and A18:F18 with the Total cell style.

Update the document properties, including the addition of at least one keyword to the properties, and save the workbook using the file name, Lab 1-3 Part 1 College Cost and Financial Support. Print the worksheet. Submit the assignment as requested by your instructor.

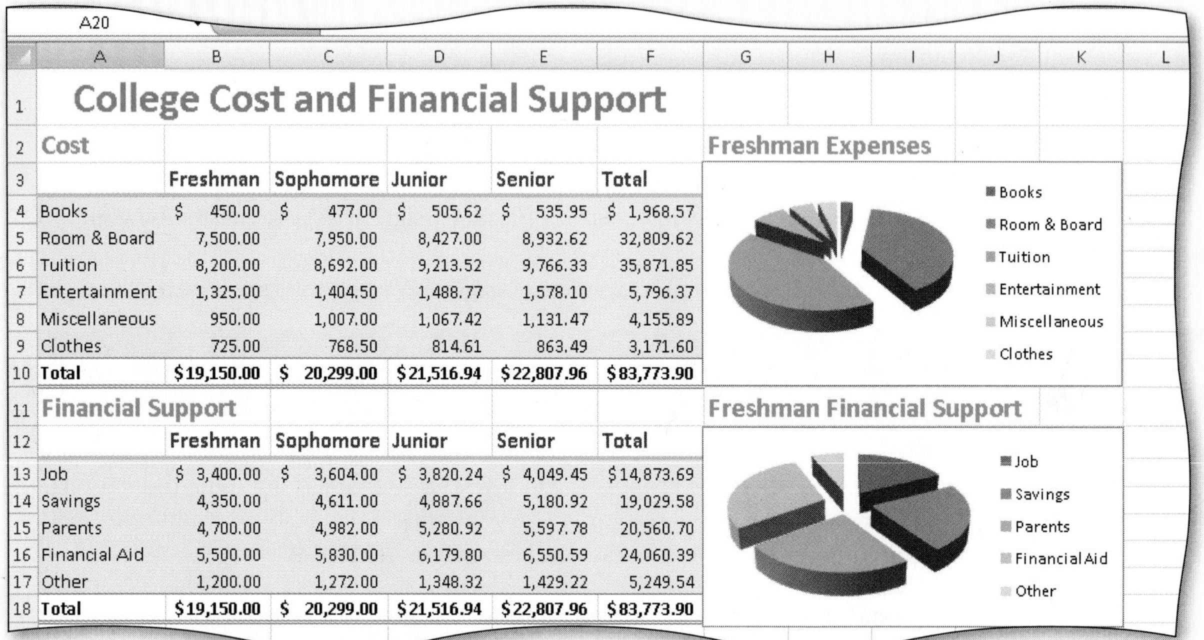

Figure 1–104

After reviewing the numbers, you realize you need to increase manually each of the Junior-year expenses in column D by $600. Change the Junior-year expenses to reflect this change. Manually change the financial aid for the Junior year in cell D16 by the amount required to cover the increase in costs. The totals in cells F10 and F18 should equal $87,373.90. Print the worksheet. Close the workbook without saving changes.

Instructions Part 2:   Open the workbook Lab 1-3 Part 1 College Cost and Financial Support and then save the workbook using the file name, Lab 1-3 Part 2 College Cost and Financial Support. Insert an Exploded pie in 3-D chart in the range G3:K10 to show the contribution of each category of cost for the Freshman year. Chart the range A4:B9 and apply the Style 8 chart style to the chart. Add the Pie chart title as shown in cell G2 in Figure 1–104. Insert an Exploded pie in 3-D chart in the range G12:K18 to show the contribution of each category of financial support for the Freshman year. Chart the range A13:B17 and apply the Style 8 chart style to the chart. Add the Pie chart title shown in cell G11 in Figure 1–104. Update the identification area with the exercise part number and save the workbook. Print the worksheet. Submit the assignment as requested by your instructor.

Instructions Part 3:   Open the workbook Lab 1-3 Part 2 College Cost and Financial Support. Do not save the workbook in this part. A close inspection of Table 1–9 shows that both cost and financial support figures increase 6% each year. Use Excel Help to learn how to enter the data for the last three years using a formula and the Copy and Paste buttons on the Home tab on the Ribbon. For example, the formula to enter in cell C4 is =B4*1.06. Enter formulas to replace all the numbers in the range C4:E9 and C13:E17. If necessary, reformat the tables, as described in Part 1. The worksheet should appear as shown in Figure 1–104, except that some of the totals will be off by 0.01 due to rounding errors. Save the worksheet using the file name, Lab 1-3 Part 3 College Cost and Financial Support. Print the worksheet. Press CTRL+ACCENT MARK (`) to display the formulas. Print the formulas version. Submit the assignment as requested by your instructor. Close the workbook without saving changes.

Cases and Places

Apply your creative thinking and problem solving skills to design and implement a solution.

● EASIER   ●● MORE DIFFICULT

● 1: Design and Create a Workbook to Analyze Yearly Sales

You are working as a summer intern for Hit-the-Road Mobile Services. Your manager has asked you to prepare a worksheet to help her analyze historical yearly sales by type of product (Table 1–10). Use the concepts and techniques presented in this chapter to create the worksheet and an embedded 3-D Clustered Column chart.

Table 1–10 Hit-the-Road Mobile Services Sales

	2005	2006	2007	2008
Standard Mobile Phones	87598	99087	129791	188785
Camera Phones	71035	75909	96886	100512
Music Phones	65942	24923	34590	15696
Wireless PDAs	67604	58793	44483	35095
Satellite Radios	15161	27293	34763	43367
Headsets	9549	6264	2600	4048
Other Accessories	47963	108059	100025	62367

● 2: Design and Create a Worksheet and Chart to Analyze a Budget

To estimate the funds needed by your school's Environmental Club to make it through the upcoming year, you decide to create a budget for the club itemizing the expected quarterly expenses. The anticipated expenses are listed in Table 1–11. Use the concepts and techniques presented in this chapter to create the worksheet and an embedded 3-D Column chart using an appropriate chart style that compares the quarterly cost of each expense. Use the AutoCalculate area to determine the average amount spent per quarter on each expense. Manually insert the averages with appropriate titles in an empty area on the worksheet.

Table 1–11 Quarterly Environmental Club Budget

	Jan – Mar	April – June	July – Sept	Oct – Dec
Meeting Room Rent	300	300	150	450
Copies and Supplies	390	725	325	640
Travel	450	755	275	850
Refreshments	105	85	215	155
Speaker Fees	200	200	0	500
Miscellaneous	125	110	75	215

Continued >

Cases and Places *continued*

•• 3: Create a 3-D Pie Chart to Analyze Quarterly Revenue

In-the-Villa DVD Rental is a DVD movie rental store. The owner of the store is trying to decide if it is feasible to hire more employees during certain times of the year. You have been asked to develop a worksheet totaling all the revenue received last year by quarter. The revenue per quarter is: Quarter 1, $52,699.23; Quarter 2, $111,244.32; Quarter 3, $70,905.03; and Quarter 4, $87,560.10. Create a 3-D Pie chart to illustrate quarterly revenue contribution by quarter. Use the AutoCalculate area to find the average, maximum, and minimum quarterly revenue and manually enter them and their corresponding identifiers in an empty area of the worksheet.

•• 4: Design and Create a Workbook to Analyze Your Field of Interest

Make It Personal

Based on your college major, area of interest, or career, use an Internet search engine or other research material to determine the total number of people employed in your chosen field of interest in the country over the past five years. For each year, break the yearly number down into two or more categories. For example, the number for each year can be broken into management and nonmanagement employees. Create an Excel worksheet that includes this data. Place the data in appropriate rows and columns for each year and category. Create totals for each row, totals for each column, and a grand total. Format the worksheet title, column headings, and data using the concepts presented in this chapter. Create a properly formatted Clustered Cone chart for the data and place it below the data in the worksheet. Make certain that years are on the X axis and number of employees is on the Y axis.

•• 5: Design and Create a Workbook to Analyze Your School

Working Together

Visit the registrar's office at your school and obtain data, such as age, gender, and full-time versus part-time status, for the students majoring in at least six different academic departments this semester. Have each member of your team divide the data into different categories. For example, separate the data by:

1. Age, divided into four different age groups

2. Gender, divided into male and female

3. Status, divided into full-time and part-time

After coordinating the data as a group, have each member independently use the concepts and techniques presented in this chapter to create a worksheet and appropriate chart to show the total students by characteristics by academic department. As a group, critique each worksheet and have each member modify his or her worksheet based on the group recommendations.

1 Creating and Using a Database

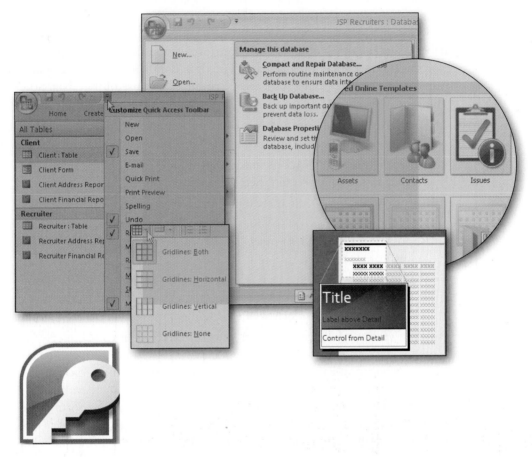

Objectives

You will have mastered the material in this chapter when you can:

- Describe databases and database management systems
- Design a database to satisfy a collection of requirements
- Start Access
- Describe the features of the Access window
- Create a database
- Create a table and add records

- Close a table
- Close a database and quit Access
- Open a database
- Print the contents of a table
- Create and print custom reports
- Create and use a split form
- Use the Access Help system

1 | Creating and Using a Database

What Is Microsoft Office Access 2007?

Microsoft Office Access 2007, usually referred to as simply Access, is a database management system. A database management system, such as Access, is a software tool that allows you to use a computer to create a database; add, change, and delete data in the database; sort the data in the database; retrieve data in the database; and create forms and reports using the data in the database. The term **database** describes a collection of data organized in a manner that allows access, retrieval, and use of that data. Some of the key features in Access are:

- **Data entry and update** Access provides easy mechanisms for adding, changing, and deleting data, including the capability of making mass changes in a single operation.
- **Queries (questions)** Access makes it possible to ask complex questions concerning the data in the database and then receive instant answers.
- **Forms** Access allows the user to produce attractive and useful forms for viewing and updating data.
- **Reports** Access includes report creation tools that make it easy to produce sophisticated reports for presenting data.
- **Web support** Access allows you to save objects, reports, and tables in HTML format so they can be viewed using a browser. You also can import and export documents in XML format as well as share data with others using SharePoint Services.

This latest version of Access has many new features to help you be more productive. Like the other Office applications, it features a new, improved interface utilizing the Ribbon. The new Navigation Pane makes navigating among the various objects in a database easier and more intuitive than in the past. The new version includes several professionally designed templates that you can use to quickly create a database. Sorting and filtering has been enhanced in this version. The new Layout view allows you to make changes to the design of forms and reports at the same time you are browsing the data. Datasheet view also has been enhanced to make creating tables more intuitive. Split form, a new form object, combines both a datasheet and a form as a single unit. Memo fields now support rich text, and there is a new Attachment data type. Using the Attachment data type, a field can contain an attached file, such as a document, image, or spreadsheet.

Project Planning Guidelines

The process of developing a database that communicates specific information requires careful analysis and planning. As a starting point, establish why the database is needed. Once the purpose is determined, analyze the intended users of the database and their unique needs. Then, gather information about the topic and decide what to include in the database. Finally, determine the database design and style that will be most successful at delivering the message. Details of these guidelines are provided in Appendix A. In addition, each project in this book provides practical applications of these planning considerations.

Project — Database Creation

JSP Recruiters is a recruiting firm that specializes in job placement for health care professionals. Because the recruiters at JSP have previous experience in the health care industry, the firm is able to provide quality candidates for employment in hospitals, clinics, medical laboratories, doctors' offices, and other health care facilities.

JSP Recruiters works with clients in need of health care professionals. It assigns each client to a specific recruiter. The recruiter works with the client to determine the necessary qualifications for each job candidate. The recruiter then contacts and does a preliminary review of the qualifications for each candidate before setting up a job interview between the client and the candidate. If the candidate is hired, the client pays a percentage of the new employee's annual salary to the recruiting firm, which then distributes a percentage of that client fee to the recruiter.

To ensure that operations run smoothly, JSP Recruiters organizes data on its clients and recruiters in a database, managed by Access. In this way, JSP keeps its data current and accurate while the firm's management can analyze the data for trends and produce a variety of useful reports.

In Access, a database consists of a collection of tables, each of which contains information on a specific subject. Figure 1–1 shows the database for JSP Recruiters. It consists of two tables. The Client table (Figure 1–1a) contains information about the clients to whom JSP provides services. The Recruiter table (Figure 1–1b) contains information about the recruiters to whom these clients are assigned.

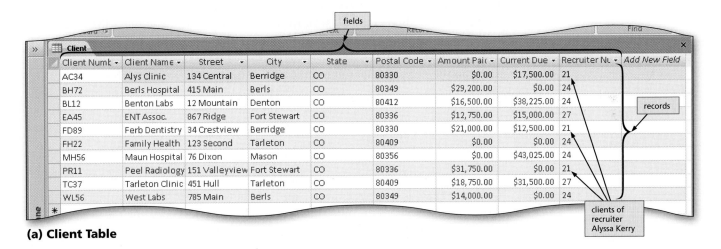

(a) Client Table

Client Number	Client Name	Street	City	State	Postal Code	Amount Paid	Current Due	Recruiter Number
AC34	Alys Clinic	134 Central	Berridge	CO	80330	$0.00	$17,500.00	21
BH72	Berls Hospital	415 Main	Berls	CO	80349	$29,200.00	$0.00	24
BL12	Benton Labs	12 Mountain	Denton	CO	80412	$16,500.00	$38,225.00	24
EA45	ENT Assoc.	867 Ridge	Fort Stewart	CO	80336	$12,750.00	$15,000.00	27
FD89	Ferb Dentistry	34 Crestview	Berridge	CO	80330	$21,000.00	$12,500.00	21
FH22	Family Health	123 Second	Tarleton	CO	80409	$0.00	$0.00	24
MH56	Maun Hospital	76 Dixon	Mason	CO	80356	$0.00	$43,025.00	24
PR11	Peel Radiology	151 Valleyview	Fort Stewart	CO	80336	$31,750.00	$0.00	21
TC37	Tarleton Clinic	451 Hull	Tarleton	CO	80409	$18,750.00	$31,500.00	27
WL56	West Labs	785 Main	Berls	CO	80349	$14,000.00	$0.00	24

(b) Recruiter Table

Recruiter Number	Last Name	First Name	Street	City	State	Postal Code	Rate	Commission
21	Kerry	Alyssa	261 Pointer	Tourin	CO	80416	0.10	$17,600.00
24	Reeves	Camden	3135 Brill	Denton	CO	80412	0.10	$19,900.00
27	Fernandez	Jaime	265 Maxwell	Charleston	CO	80380	0.09	$9,450.00
34	Lee	Jan	1827 Oak	Denton	CO	80413	0.08	$0.00

Figure 1–1

The rows in the tables are called **records**. A record contains information about a given person, product, or event. A row in the Client table, for example, contains information about a specific client.

The columns in the tables are called fields. A **field** contains a specific piece of information within a record. In the Client table, for example, the fourth field, City, contains the city where the client is located.

The first field in the Client table is the Client Number. JSP Recruiters assigns a number to each client. As is common to the way in which many organizations format client numbers, JSP Recruiters calls it a *number*, although it actually contains letters. The JSP client numbers consist of two uppercase letters followed by a two-digit number.

These numbers are unique; that is, no two clients are assigned the same number. Such a field can be used as a **unique identifier**. This simply means that a given client number will appear only in a single record in the table. Only one record exists, for example, in which the client number is BH72. A unique identifier also is called a **primary key**. Thus, the Client Number field is the primary key for the Client table.

The next seven fields in the Client table are Client Name, Street, City, State, Postal Code, Amount Paid, and Current Due. Note that the default width of the columns cuts off the names of some of the columns. The Amount Paid column contains the amount that the client has paid JSP Recruiters year to date (YTD) prior to the current period. The Current Due column contains the amount due to JSP for the current period. For example, client BL12 is Benton Labs. The address is 12 Mountain in Denton, Colorado. The postal code is 80412. The client has paid $16,500 for recruiting services so far this year. The amount due for the current period is $38,225.

JSP assigns each client a single recruiter. The last column in the Client table, Recruiter Number, gives the number of the client's recruiter.

The first field in the Recruiter table, Recruiter Number, is the number JSP Recruiters assigns to the recruiter. These numbers are unique, so Recruiter Number is the primary key of the Recruiter table.

The other fields in the Recruiter table are Last Name, First Name, Street, City, State, Postal Code, Rate, and Commission. The Rate field contains the percentage of the client fee that the recruiter earns, and the Commission field contains the total amount that JSP has paid the recruiter so far this year. For example, Recruiter 27 is Jaime Fernandez. His address is 265 Maxwell in Charleston, Colorado. The Postal Code is 80380. His commission rate is .09 (9%), and his commission is $9,450.

The recruiter number appears in both the Client table and the Recruiter table. It relates clients and recruiters. For example, in the Client table, you see that the recruiter number for client BL12 is 24. To find the name of this recruiter, look for the row in the Recruiter table that contains 24 in the Recruiter Number column. After you have found it, you know the client is assigned to Camden Reeves. To find all the clients assigned to Camden Reeves, you must look through the Client table for all the clients that contain 24 in the Recruiter Number column. His clients are BH72 (Berls Hospital), BL12 (Benton Labs), FH22 (Family Health), MH56 (Maun Hospital), and WL56 (West Labs).

The last recruiter in the Recruiter table, Jan Lee, has not been assigned any clients yet; therefore, her recruiter number, 34, does not appear on any row in the Client table.

Overview

As you read this chapter, you will learn how to create the database shown in Figure 1–1 on the previous page by performing these general tasks:

- Design the database.
- Create a new blank database.

- Create a table and add the records.
- Preview and print the contents of a table.
- Create a second table and add the records.
- Create four reports.
- Create a form.

Plan
Ahead

Database design guidelines.

Database design refers to the arrangement of data into tables and fields. In the example in this chapter the design is specified, but in many cases, you will have to determine the design based on what you want the system to accomplish.

When designing a database, the actions you take and the decisions you make will determine the tables and fields that will be included in the database. As you create a database, such as the project shown in Figure 1–1 on page AC 3, you should follow these general guidelines:

1. **Identify the tables.** Examine the requirements for the database in order to identify the main objects that are involved. There will be a table for each object you identified.

   In one database, for example, the main objects might be departments and employees. Thus, there would be two tables: one for departments and the other for employees. In another database, the main objects might be clients and recruiters. In this case, there would also be two tables: one for clients and the other for recruiters. In still another database, the main objects might be books, publishers, and authors. Here there would be three tables: one for books, a second for publishers, and a third for authors.

2. **Determine the primary keys.** Recall that the primary key is the unique identifier for records in the table. For each table, determine the unique identifier, if there is one. For a Department table, for example, the unique identifier might be the Department Code. For a Book table, the unique identifier might be the ISBN number.

3. **Determine the additional fields.** The primary key will be a field or combination of fields in a table. There typically will be many additional fields, each of which contains a type of data. Examine the project requirements to determine these additional fields. For example, in an Employee table, the additional fields might include such fields as Employee Name, Street Address, City, State, Postal Code, Date Hired, Salary, and so on.

4. **Determine relationships among the tables.** Examine the list of tables you have created to see which tables are related. When you determine two tables are related, include matching fields in the two tables. For example, in a database containing employees and departments, there is a relationship between the two tables because one department can have many employees assigned to it. Department Code could be the matching field in the two tables.

5. **Determine data types for the fields.** For each field, determine the type of data the field can contain. One field, for example, might contain only numbers. Another field might contain currency amounts, while a third field might contain only dates. Some fields contain text data, meaning any combination of letters, numbers and special characters (!, ;, ', &, and so on). For example, in an Employee table, the Date Hired field would contain dates, the Salary field would contain currency amounts, and the Hours Worked field would contain numbers. The other fields in the Employee table would contain text data, such as Employee Name and Department Code.

6. **Identify and remove any unwanted redundancy.** Redundancy is the storing of a piece of data in more than one place. Redundancy usually, but not always, causes problems, such as wasted space, difficulties with update, and possible data inconsistency. Examine each table you have created to see if it contains redundancy and, if so, determine whether the redundancy causes these problems. If it does, remove the redundancy by splitting the table into two tables. For example, you may have a single table of employees. In addition to typical employee data (name, address, earnings, and so on), the table might contain Department Number and Department Name. If so, the Department Name could repeat multiple times.

(continued)

(continued)

Every employee whose department number is 12, for example, would have the same department name. It would be better to split the table into two tables, one for Employees and one for Department. In the Department table, the Department Name is stored only once.

7. **Determine a location for the database. The database you have designed will be stored in a single file. You need to determine a location in which to store the file.**

When necessary, more specific details concerning the above guidelines are presented at appropriate points in the chapter. The chapter also will identify the actions performed and decisions made regarding these guidelines during the creation of the database shown in Figure 1–1 on page AC 3.

BTW

Database Design
For more information on database design methods and for techniques for identifying and eliminating redundancy, visit the Access 2007 Database Design Web page (scsite.com/ac2007/dbdesign).

Designing a Database

This section illustrates the database design process by showing how you would design the database for JSP Recruiters from a set of requirements. In this section, you will use a commonly accepted shorthand to represent the tables and fields that make up the database as well as the primary keys for the tables. For each table, you give the name of the table followed by a set of parentheses. Within the parentheses is a list of the fields in the table separated by commas. You underline the primary key. For example,

Product (<u>Product Code</u>, Description, On Hand, Price)

represents a table called Product. The Product table contains four fields: Product Code, Description, On Hand, and Price. The Product Code field is the primary key.

Database Requirements

JSP Recruiters needs to maintain information on both clients and recruiters. It currently keeps this data in the two Word tables and two Excel workbooks shown in Figure 1–2. They use Word tables for address information and Excel workbooks for financial information.

Client Number	Client Name	Street	City	State	Postal Code
AC34	Alys Clinic	134 Central	Berridge	CO	80330
BH72	Berls Hospital	415 Main	Berls	CO	80349
BL12	Benton Labs	12 Mountain	Denton	CO	80412
EA45	ENT Assoc.	867 Ridge	Fort Stewart	CO	80336
FD89	Ferb Dentistry	34 Crestview	Berridge	CO	80330
FH22	Family Health	123 Second	Tarleton	CO	80409
MH56	Maun Hospital	76 Dixon	Mason	CO	80356
PR11	Peel Radiology	151 Valleyview	Fort Stewart	CO	80336
TC37	Tarleton Clinic	451 Hull	Tarleton	CO	80409
WL56	West Labs	785 Main	Berls	CO	80349

**(a)
Client Address
Information
(Word Table)**

Figure 1–2

**(b)
Client
Financial
Information
(Excel
Workbook)**

	A	B	C	D
1	Client Number	Client Name	Amount Paid	Current Due
2	AC34	Alys Clinic	$0.00	$17,500.00
3	BH72	Berls Hospital	$29,200.00	$0.00
4	BL12	Benton Labs	$16,500.00	$38,225.00
5	EA45	ENT Assoc.	$12,750.00	$15,000.00
6	FD89	Ferb Dentistry	$21,000.00	$12,500.00
7	FH22	Family Health	$0.00	$0.00
8	MH56	Maun Hospital	$0.00	$43,025.00
9	PR11	Peel Radiology	$31,750.00	$0.00
10	TC37	Tarleton Clinic	$18,750.00	$31,500.00
11	WL56	West Labs	$14,000.00	$0.00

**(c)
Recruiter
Address
Information
(Word Table)**

Recruiter Number	Last Name	First Name	Street	City	State	Postal Code
21	Kerry	Alyssa	261 Pointer	Tourin	CO	80416
24	Reeves	Camden	3135 Brill	Denton	CO	80412
27	Fernandez	Jaime	265 Maxwell	Charleston	CO	80380
34	Lee	Jan	1827 Oak	Denton	CO	80413

**(d)
Recruiter
Financial
Information
(Excel
Workbook)**

	A	B	C	D	E
1	Recruiter Number	Last Name	First Name	Rate	Commission
2	21	Kerry	Alyssa	0.10	$17,600.00
3	24	Reeves	Camden	0.10	$19,900.00
4	27	Fernandez	Jaime	0.09	$9,450.00
5	34	Lee	Jan	0.08	$0.00

Figure 1–2 (continued)

For clients, JSP needs to maintain address data. It currently keeps this address data in a Word table (Figure 1–2a). It also maintains financial data for each client. This includes the amount paid and the current due from the client. It keeps these amounts along with the client name and number in the Excel workbook shown in Figure 1–2b.

JSP keeps recruiter address data in a Word table as shown in Figure 1–2c. Just as with clients, it keeps financial data for recruiters, including their rate and commission, in a separate Excel workbook, as shown in Figure 1–2d.

Finally, it keeps track of which clients are assigned to which recruiters. Currently, for example, clients AC34 (Alys Clinic), FD89 (Ferb Dentistry), and PR11 (Peel Radiology) are assigned to recruiter 21 (Alyssa Kerry). Clients BH72 (Berls Hospital), BL12 (Benton Labs), FH22 (Family Health), MH56 (Maun Hospital), and WL56 (West Labs) are assigned to recruiter 24 (Camden Reeves). Clients EA45 (ENT Assoc.) and TC37 (Tarleton Clinic) are assigned to recruiter 27 (Jaime Fernandez). JSP has an additional recruiter, Jan Lee, whose number has been assigned as 34, but who has not yet been assigned any clients.

Naming Tables and Fields

In designing your database, you must name the tables and fields. Thus, before beginning the design process, you must understand the rules for table and field names, which are:

1. Names can be up to 64 characters in length.
2. Names can contain letters, digits, and spaces, as well as most of the punctuation symbols.
3. Names cannot contain periods (.), exclamation points (!), accent graves (`), or square brackets ([ ]).
4. The same name cannot be used for two different fields in the same table.

The approach to naming tables and fields used in this text is to begin the names with an uppercase letter and to use lowercase for the other letters. In multiple-word names, each word begins with an uppercase letter, and there is a space between words (for example, Client Number). You should know that there are other approaches. Some people omit the space (ClientNumber). Still others use an underscore in place of the space (Client_Number). Finally, some use an underscore in place of a space, but use the same case for all letters (CLIENT_NUMBER or client_number).

Identifying the Tables

Now that you know the rules for naming tables and fields, you are ready to begin the design process. The first step is to identify the main objects involved in the requirements. For the JSP Recruiters database, the main objects are clients and recruiters. This leads to two tables, which you must name. Reasonable names for these two tables are:

Client
Recruiter

Determining the Primary Keys

The next step is to identify the fields that will be the primary keys. Client numbers uniquely identify clients, and recruiter numbers uniquely identify recruiters. Thus, the primary key for the Client table is the client number, and the primary key for the Recruiter table is the recruiter number. Reasonable names for these fields would be Client Number and Recruiter Number, respectively. Adding these primary keys to the tables gives:

Client (<u>Client Number</u>)
Recruiter (<u>Recruiter Number</u>)

Determining Additional Fields

After identifying the primary keys, you need to determine and name the additional fields. In addition to the client number, the Client Address Information shown in Figure 1–2a on page AC 6 contains the client name, street, city, state, and postal code. These would be fields in the Client table. The Client Financial Information shown in Figure 1–2b also contains the client number and client name, which are already included in the Client table. The financial information also contains the amount paid and the current due. Adding the amount paid and current due fields to those already identified in the Client table and assigning reasonable names gives:

Client (<u>Client Number</u>, Client Name, Street, City, State, Postal Code,
    Amount Paid, Current Due)

Similarly, examining the Recruiter Address Information in Figure 1–2c on page AC 7 adds the last name, first name, street, city, state, and postal code fields to the Recruiter table. In addition to the recruiter number, last name, and first name, the Recruiter Financial Information in Figure 1–2d would add the rate and commission. Adding these fields to the Recruiter table and assigning reasonable names gives:

Recruiter (<u>Recruiter Number</u>, Last Name, First Name, Street, City,
   State, Postal Code, Rate, Commission)

Determining and Implementing Relationships Between the Tables

Plan
Ahead

Determine relationships among the tables.
The most common type of relationship you will encounter between tables is the **one-to-many relationship**. This means that each row in the first table may be associated with *many* rows in the second table, but each row in the second table is associated with only *one* row in the first. The first table is called the "one" table and the second is called the "many" table. For example, there may be a relationship between departments and employees, in which each department can have many employees, but each employee is assigned to only one department. In this relationship, there would be two tables, Department and Employee. The Department table would be the "one" table in the relationship. The Employee table would be the "many" table.
   To determine relationships among tables, you can follow these general guidelines:

1. Identify the "one" table.

2. Identify the "many" table.

3. Include the primary key from the "one" table as a field in the "many" table.

According to the requirements, each client has one recruiter, but each recruiter can have many clients. Thus, the Recruiter table is the "one" table, and the Client table is the "many" table. To implement this one-to-many relationship between recruiters and clients, add the Recruiter Number field (the primary key of the Recruiter table) to the Client table. This produces:

Client (<u>Client Number</u>, Client Name, Street, City, State, Postal Code, Amount Paid,
   Current Due, Recruiter Number)

Recruiter (<u>Recruiter Number</u>, Last Name, First Name, Street, City, State, Postal
   Code, Rate, Commission)

Determining Data Types for the Fields

Each field has a **data type**. This indicates the type of data that can be stored in the field. Three of the most commonly used data types are:

1. **Text** — The field can contain any characters. A maximum number of 255 characters is allowed in a field whose data type is Text.

2. **Number** — The field can contain only numbers. The numbers either can be positive or negative. Fields are assigned this type so they can be used in arithmetic operations. Fields that contain numbers but will not be used for arithmetic operations usually are assigned a data type of Text.

3. **Currency** — The field can contain only monetary data. The values will appear with currency symbols, such as dollar signs, commas, and decimal points, and with

BTW

Currency Symbols
To show the symbol for the Euro (€) instead of the dollar sign, change the Format property for the field whose data type is currency. To change the default symbols for currency, change the settings in the operating system using the Control Panel.

BTW

Field Size (Text Fields)
You can restrict the number of characters that can be entered in a text field by changing the field size. For example, if you change the field size for the Client Name field to 25, users will be unable to enter more than 25 characters in the field.

two digits following the decimal point. Like numeric fields, you can use currency fields in arithmetic operations. Access assigns a size to currency fields automatically.

Table 1–1 shows the other data types that are available.

Table 1–1 Additional Data Types	
Data Type	**Description**
Memo	Field can store a variable amount of text or combinations of text and numbers where the total number of characters may exceed 255.
Date/Time	Field can store dates and times.
AutoNumber	Field can store a unique sequential number that Access assigns to a record. Access will increment the number by 1 as each new record is added.
Yes/No	Field can store only one of two values. The choices are Yes/No, True/False, or On/Off.
OLE Object	Field can store an OLE object, which is an object linked to or embedded in the table.
Hyperlink	Field can store text that can be used as a hyperlink address.
Attachment	Field can contain an attached file. Images, spreadsheets, documents, charts, and so on can be attached to this field in a record in the database. You can view and edit the attached file.

In the Client table, because the Client Number, Client Name, Street, City, and State can all contain letters, their data types should be Text. The data type for Postal Code is Text instead of Number, because postal codes are not used in arithmetic operations. You do not add postal codes or find an average postal code, for example. The Amount Paid and Current Due fields both contain monetary data, so their data types should be Currency.

Similarly, in the Recruiter table, the data type for the Recruiter Number, Last Name, First Name, Street, City, State, and Postal Code fields all should be Text. The Commission field contains monetary amounts, so its data type should be Currency. The Rate field contains a number that is not a currency amount, so its data type should be Number.

Identifying and Removing Redundancy

Redundancy means storing the same fact in more than one place. It usually results from placing too many fields in a table — fields that really belong in separate tables — and often causes serious problems. If you had not realized there were two objects, clients and recruiters, for example, you might have placed all the data in a single Client table. Figure 1–3 shows a portion of this table with some sample data. Notice that the data for a given Recruiter (number, name, address, and so on) occurs on more than one record. The data for Camden Reeves is repeated in the figure.

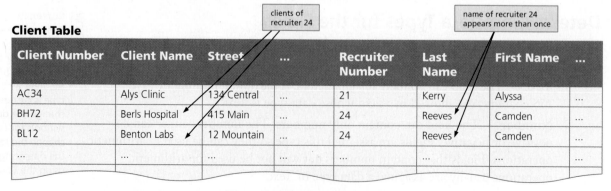

Figure 1–3

Storing this data on multiple records is an example of redundancy, which causes several problems, including:

1. Wasted storage space. The name of Recruiter 24 (Camden Reeves), for example, should be stored only once. Storing this fact several times is wasteful.

2. More difficult database updates. If, for example, Camden Reeves's name is spelled wrong and needs to be changed in the database, his name would need to be changed in several different places.

3. A possibility of inconsistent data. There is nothing to prohibit the recruiter's last name from being Reeves on client BH72's record and Reed on client BL12's record. The data would be inconsistent. In both cases, the recruiter number is 24, but the last names are different.

The solution to the problem is to place the redundant data in a separate table, one in which the data no longer will be redundant. If, for example, you place the data for recruiters in a separate table (Figure 1–4), the data for each recruiter will appear only once.

Client Table

Client Number	Client Name	Street	...	Recruiter Number
AC34	Alys Clinic	134 Central	...	21
BH72	Berls Hospital	415 Main	...	24
BL12	Benton Labs	12 Mountain	...	24
...	...	...	...	...

clients of recruiter 24

Recruiter Table

Recruiter Number	Last Name	First Name	...
21	Kerry	Alyssa	...
24	Reeves	Camden	...
...	...	...	...

name of recruiter 24 appears only once

Figure 1–4

Notice that you need to have the recruiter number in both tables. Without it, there would be no way to tell which recruiter is associated with which client. The remaining recruiter data, however, was removed from the Client table and placed in the Recruiter table. This new arrangement corrects the problems of redundancy in the following ways:

1. Because the data for each recruiter is stored only once, space is not wasted.

2. Changing the name of a recruiter is easy. You have only to change one row in the Recruiter table.

3. Because the data for a recruiter is stored only once, inconsistent data cannot occur. Designing to omit redundancy will help you to produce good and valid database designs.

You should always examine your design to see if it contains redundancy. If it does, you should decide whether you need to remove the redundancy by creating a separate table.

BTW

Postal Codes
Some organizations with many customers spread throughout the country will, in fact, have a separate table of postal codes, cities, and states. If you call such an organization to place an order, they typically will ask you for your postal code (or ZIP code), rather than asking for your city, state, and postal code. They then will indicate the city and state that correspond to that postal code and ask you if that is correct.

If you examine your design, you'll see that there is one area of redundancy (see the data in Figure 1–1 on page AC 3). Cities and states are both repeated. Every client whose postal code is 80330, for example, has Berridge as the city and CO as the state. To remove this redundancy, you would create a table whose primary key is Postal Code and that contains City and State as additional fields. City and State would be removed from the Client table. Having City, State, and Postal Code in a table is very common, however, and usually you would not take such action. There is no other redundancy in your tables.

Starting Access

If you are using a computer to step through the project in this chapter, and you want your screen to match the figures in this book, you should change your screen's resolution to 1024 × 768. For information about how to change a computer's resolution, read Appendix E.

Note: If you are using Windows XP, see Appendix F for alternate steps.

To Start Access

The following steps, which assume Windows Vista is running, start Access based on a typical installation. You may need to ask your instructor how to start Access for your computer.

1
- Click the Start button on the Windows Vista taskbar to display the Start menu.
- Click All Programs at the bottom of the left pane on the Start menu to display the All Programs list.
- Click Microsoft Office in the All Programs list to display the Microsoft Office list (Figure 1–5).

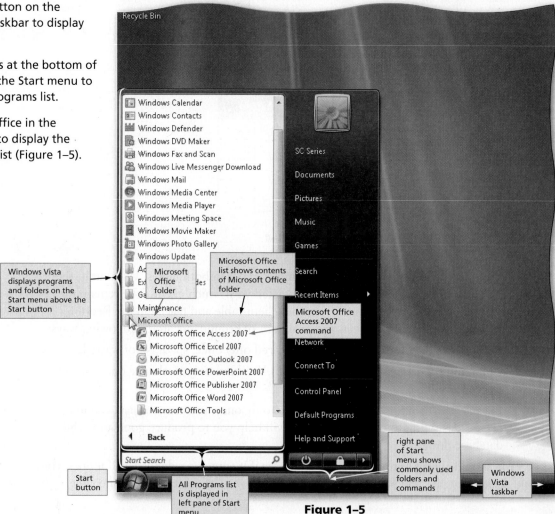

Figure 1–5

2

- Click Microsoft Office Access 2007 to start Access and display the Getting Started with Microsoft Office Access screen (Figure 1–6).

- If the Access window is not maximized, click the Maximize button next to the Close button on its title bar to maximize the window.

Q&A

What is a maximized window?

A maximized window fills the entire screen. When you maximize a window, the Maximize button changes to a Restore Down button.

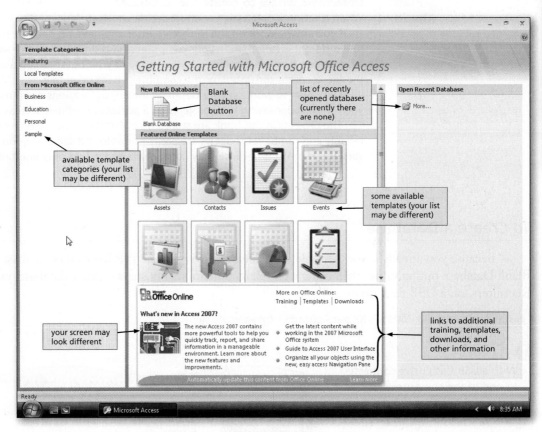

Figure 1–6

Other Ways

1. Double-click Access icon on desktop, if one is present
2. Click Microsoft Office Access 2007 on Start menu

Creating a Database

In Access, all the tables, reports, forms, and queries that you create are stored in a single file called a database. Thus, before creating any of these objects, you first must create the database that will hold them. You can use either the Blank Database option or a template to create a new database. If you already know the tables and fields you want in your database, you would use the Blank Database option. If not, you can use a template. Templates can guide you by suggesting some commonly used databases. If you choose to create a database using a template, you would use the following steps.

TO CREATE A DATABASE USING A TEMPLATE

1. If the template you wish to use is not already visible on the Getting Started with Microsoft Office Access page, double-click the links in the Template Categories pane to display the desired template.
2. Click the template you wish to use.
3. Enter a file name (or accept the suggested file name) and select a location for the database.
4. Click the Create button to create the database or the Download button to download the database and create the database, if necessary.

When you create a database, the computer places it on a storage medium, such as a USB flash drive, CD, or hard disk. A saved database is referred to as a **file**. A **file name** is the name assigned to a file when it is saved.

BTW

Naming Files
File names can be a maximum of 260 characters including the file extension. The file extension for Access 2007 is .accdb. You can use either uppercase or lowercase letters in file names.

Plan Ahead	**Determine where to create the database.**
	When creating a database, you must decide which storage medium to use.
	If you always work on the same computer and have no need to transport your database to a different location, then your computer's hard drive will suffice as a storage location. It is a good idea, however, to save a backup copy of your database on a separate medium in case the file becomes corrupted, or the computer's hard drive fails.
	If you plan to work on your database in various locations or on multiple computers, then you can consider saving your projects on a portable medium, such as a USB flash drive or CD. The projects in this book are stored on a USB flash drive, which saves files quickly and reliably and can be reused. CDs are easily portable and serve as good backups for the final versions of projects because they generally can save files only one time.

To Create a Database

Because you already know the tables and fields you want in the JSP Recruiters database, you would use the Blank Database option rather than using a template. The following steps create a database, using the file name JSP Recruiters, on a USB flash drive.

Note: If you are using Windows XP, see Appendix F for alternate steps.

1

- With a USB flash drive connected to one of the computer's USB ports, click Blank Database to create a new blank database (Figure 1–7).

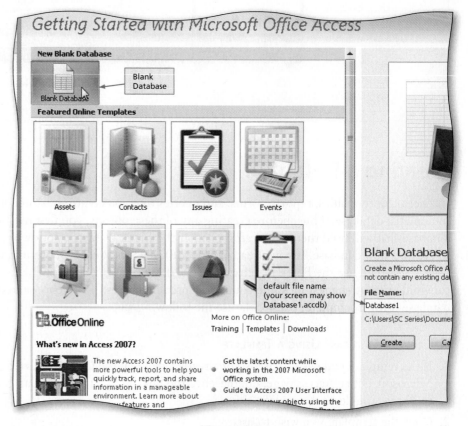

Figure 1–7

2

- Repeatedly press the DELETE key to delete the default name of Database1.

- Type JSP Recruiters in the File Name text box to replace the default file name of Database1 (your screen may show Database1.accdb). Do not press the ENTER key after typing the file name (Figure 1–8).

Q&A What characters can I use in a file name?

A file name can have a maximum of 260 characters, including spaces. The only invalid characters are the back-slash (\), slash (/), colon (:), asterisk (*), question mark (?), quotation mark ("), less than symbol (<), greater than symbol (>), and vertical bar (|).

3

- Click the 'Browse for a location to put your database' button to display the File New Database dialog box.

- If the Navigation Pane is not displayed in the Save As dialog box, click the Browse Folders button to expand the dialog box.

- If a Folders list is displayed below the Folders button, click the Folders button to remove the Folders list (Figure 1-9).

Q&A Do I have to save to a USB flash drive?

No. You can save to any device or folder. A **folder** is a specific location on a storage medium. You can save to the default folder or a differ-ent folder. You also can create your own folders, which is explained later in this book.

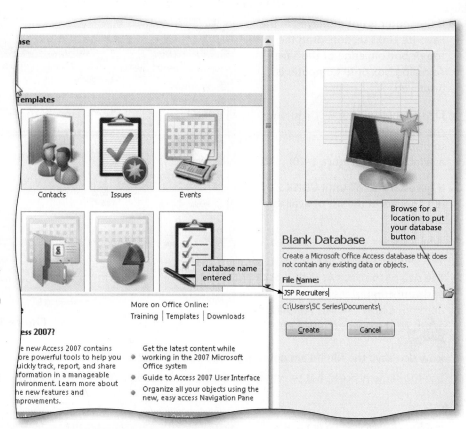

Figure 1–8

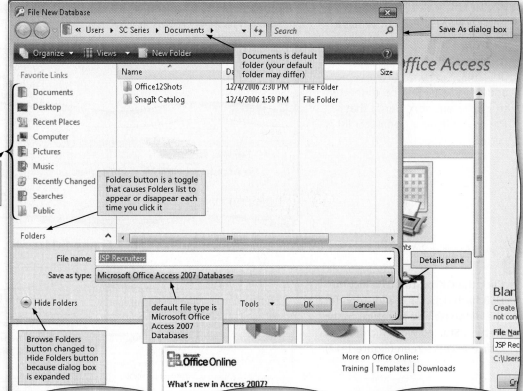

Figure 1–9

- If Computer is not displayed in the Favorite Links section, drag the top or bottom edge of the Save As dialog box until Computer is displayed.

- Click Computer in the Favorite Links section to display a list of available drives (Figure 1–10).

- If necessary, scroll until UDISK 2.0 (E:) appears in the list of available drives.

 Q&A

Why is my list of drives arranged and named differently?

The size of the Save As dialog box and your computer's configuration determine how the list is displayed and how the drives are named.

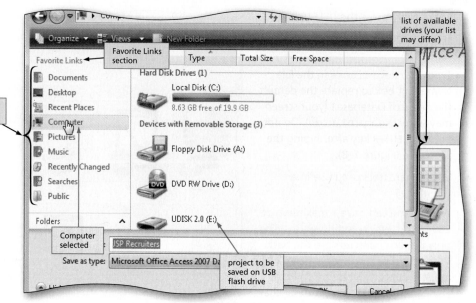

Figure 1–10

Q&A

How do I save the file if I am not using a USB flash drive?

Use the same process, but select your desired save location in the Favorite Links section.

- Double-click UDISK 2.0 (E:) in the Computer list to select the USB flash drive, Drive E in this case, as the new save location (Figure 1–11).

Q&A

What if my USB flash drive has a different name or letter?

It is very likely that your USB flash drive will have a different name and drive letter and be connected to a different port. Verify that the device in your Computer list is correct.

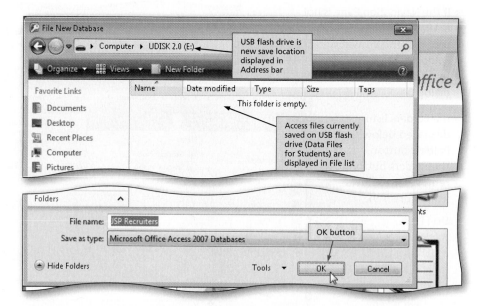

Figure 1–11

- Click the OK button to select the USB flash drive as the location for the database and to return to the Getting Started with Microsoft Office Access screen (Figure 1–12).

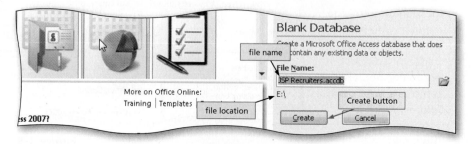

Figure 1–12

7

- Click the Create button to create the database on the USB flash drive with the file name, JSP Recruiters (Figure 1–13).

 Q&A

How do I know that the JSP Recruiters database is created?

The name of the database appears in the title bar.

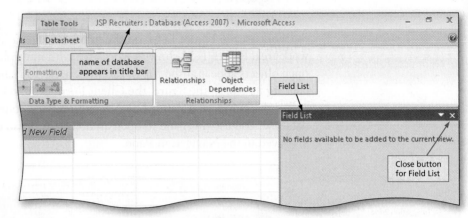

Figure 1–13

8

- If a Field List appears, click its Close button to remove the Field List from the screen (Figure 1–14).

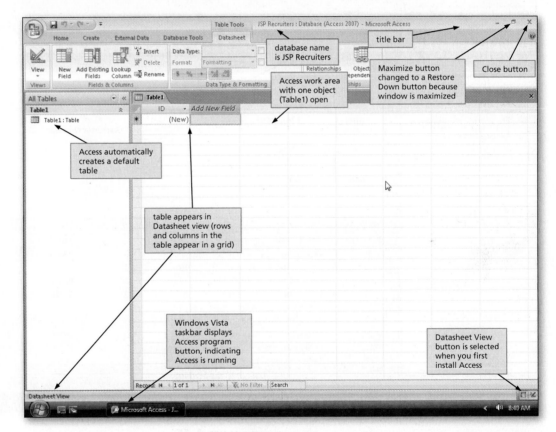

Figure 1–14

Other Ways

1. Click Office Button, click Save, type file name, click Computer, select drive or folder, click Save button

2. Press CTRL+S or press SHIFT+F12, type file name, click Computer, select drive or folder, click Save button

The Access Window

The Access window consists of a variety of components to make your work more efficient and documents more professional. These include the Navigation Pane, Access work area, Ribbon, Mini toolbar and shortcut menus, Quick Access Toolbar, and Office Button. Some of these components are common to other Microsoft Office 2007 programs; others are unique to Access.

Navigation Pane and Access Work Area

You work on objects such as tables, forms, and reports in the **Access work area**. In the work area in Figure 1–14 on the previous page, a single table, Table1, is open in the work area. Figure 1–15 shows a work area with multiple objects open. **Object tabs** for the open objects appear at the top of the work area. You can select one of the open objects by clicking its tab. In the figure, the Client Form is the selected object. To the left of the work area is the Navigation Pane. The Navigation Pane contains a list of all the objects in the database. You use this pane to open an object. You also can customize the way objects are displayed in the Navigation Pane.

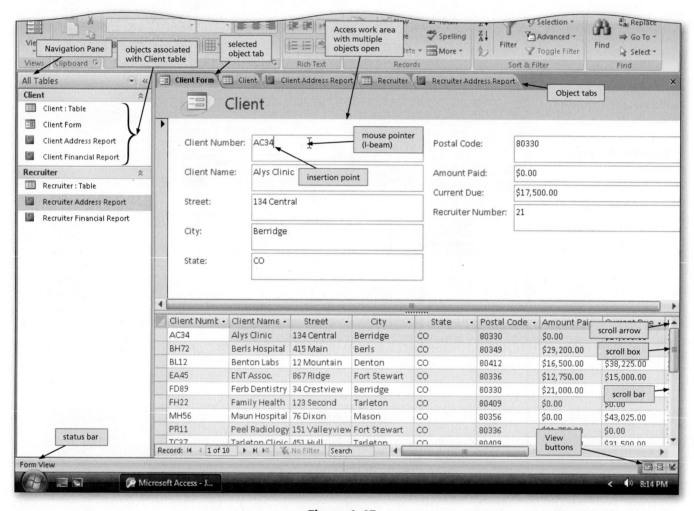

Figure 1–15

The Access work area in Figure 1–15 contains an insertion point, mouse pointer, scroll bar, and status bar. Other elements that may appear in the work area are discussed later in this and subsequent chapters.

Insertion Point   The **insertion point** is a blinking vertical bar that indicates where text, graphics, and other items will be inserted. As you type, the insertion point moves to the right.

Mouse Pointer   The **mouse pointer** becomes different shapes depending on the task you are performing in Access and the pointer's location on the screen. The mouse pointer in Figure 1–15 is the shape of an I-beam.

Scroll Bar   You use a **scroll bar** to display different portions of a database object in the Access window. At the right edge of the window is a **vertical scroll bar**. If an object is too wide to fit in the Access window, a **horizontal scroll bar** also appears at the bottom of the window. On a scroll bar, the position of the **scroll box** reflects the location of the portion of the database object that is displayed in the Access window. A **scroll arrow** is located at each end of a scroll bar. To scroll through, or display different portions of the object in the Access window, you can click a scroll arrow or drag the scroll box.

Status Bar   The **status bar**, located at the bottom of the Access window above the Windows Vista taskbar, presents information about the database object, the progress of current tasks, and the status of certain commands and keys; it also provides controls for viewing the object. As you type text or perform certain commands, various indicators may appear on the status bar.

The left edge of the status bar in Figure 1–15 shows that the form object is open in Form view. Toward the right edge are View buttons, which you can use to change the view that is currently displayed.

Ribbon

The **Ribbon**, located near the top of the Access window, is the control center in Access (Figure 1–16a). The Ribbon provides easy, central access to the tasks you perform while creating a database object. The Ribbon consists of tabs, groups, and commands. Each **tab** surrounds a collection of groups, and each group contains related commands.

When you start Access, the Ribbon displays four top-level tabs: Home, Create, External Data, and Database Tools. The **Home tab**, called the primary tab, contains the more frequently used commands. To display a different tab on the Ribbon, click the top-level tab. That is, to display the Create tab, click Create on the Ribbon. To return to the Home tab, click Home on the Ribbon. The tab currently displayed is called the **active tab**.

To allow more space in the Access work area, some users prefer to minimize the Ribbon, which hides the groups on the Ribbon and displays only the top-level tabs (Figure 1–16b). To use commands on a minimized Ribbon, click the top-level tab.

Each time you start Access, the Ribbon appears the same way it did the last time you used Access. The chapters in this book, however, begin with the Ribbon appearing as it did at the initial installation of the software. If you are stepping through this chapter on a computer and you want your Ribbon to match the figures in this book, read Appendix E.

BTW

Minimizing the Ribbon
If you want to minimize the Ribbon, right-click the Ribbon and then click Minimize the Ribbon on the shortcut menu, double-click the active tab, or press CTRL+F1. To restore a minimized Ribbon, right-click the Ribbon and then click Minimize the Ribbon on the shortcut menu, double-click any top-level tab, or press CTRL+F1. To use commands on a minimized Ribbon, click the top-level tab.

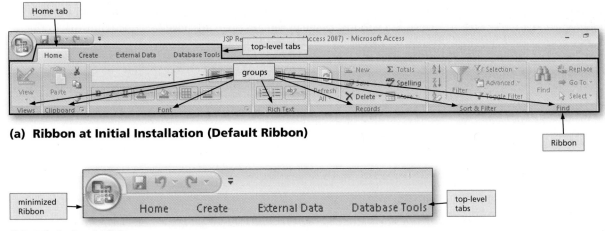

(a) Ribbon at Initial Installation (Default Ribbon)

(b) Minimized Ribbon

Figure 1–16

In addition to the top-level tabs, Access displays other tabs, called **contextual tabs**, when you perform certain tasks or work with objects such as datasheets. If you are working with a table in Datasheet view, for example, the Table Tools tab and its related subordinate Datasheet tab appear (Figure 1–17). When you are finished working with the table, the Table Tools and Datasheet tabs disappear from the Ribbon. Access determines when contextual tabs should appear and disappear based on tasks you perform. Some contextual tabs have more than one related subordinate tab.

Figure 1–17

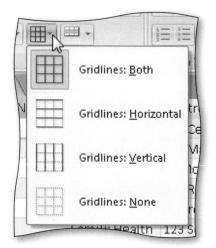

Figure 1–18

Commands on the Ribbon include buttons, boxes (text boxes, check boxes, etc.), and galleries (Figure 1–18). A **gallery** is a set of choices, often graphical, arranged in a grid or in a list. You can scroll through choices on an in-Ribbon gallery by clicking the gallery's scroll arrows. Or, you can click a gallery's More button to view more gallery options on the screen at a time. Some buttons and boxes have arrows that, when clicked, also display a gallery; others always cause a gallery to be displayed when clicked. Many galleries support **live preview**, which is a feature that allows you to point to a gallery choice and see its effect in the database object — without actually selecting the choice.

Some commands on the Ribbon display an image to help you remember their function. When you point to a command on the Ribbon, all or part of the command glows in shades of yellow and orange, and an Enhanced ScreenTip appears on the screen. An **Enhanced ScreenTip** is an on-screen note that provides the name of the command, available keyboard shortcut(s), a description of the command, and sometimes instructions for how to obtain help about the command (Figure 1–19). Enhanced ScreenTips are more detailed than a typical ScreenTip, which usually only displays the name of the command.

The lower-right corner of some groups on the Ribbon has a small arrow, called a **Dialog Box Launcher**, which, when clicked, displays a dialog box or a task pane with additional options for the group (Figure 1–20). When presented with a dialog box, you make selections and must close the dialog box before returning to the database object. A **task pane**, by contrast, is a window that can remain open and visible while you work in the database object.

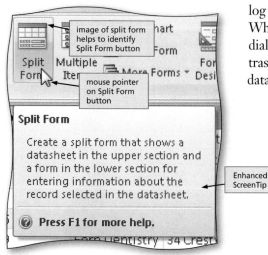

Figure 1–19

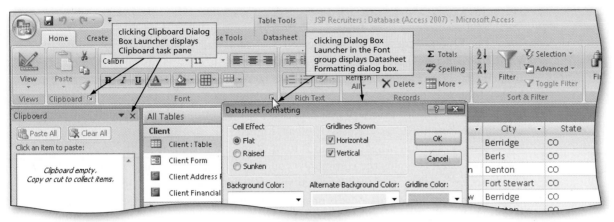

Figure 1–20

Mini Toolbar and Shortcut Menus

The **Mini toolbar**, which appears automatically based on tasks you perform, contains commands related to changing the appearance of text in a database object. All commands on the Mini toolbar also exist on the Ribbon. The purpose of the Mini toolbar is to minimize mouse movement. For example, if you want to use a command that currently is not displayed on the active tab, you can use the command on the Mini toolbar — instead of switching to a different tab to use the command.

When the Mini toolbar appears, it initially is transparent (Figure 1–21a). If you do not use the transparent Mini toolbar, it disappears from the screen. To use the Mini toolbar, move the mouse pointer into the toolbar, which causes the Mini toolbar to change from a transparent to bright appearance (Figure 1–21b).

A **shortcut menu**, which appears when you right-click an object, is a list of frequently used commands that relate to the right-clicked object. When you right-click a table, for example, a shortcut menu appears with commands related to the table (Figure 1–21c).

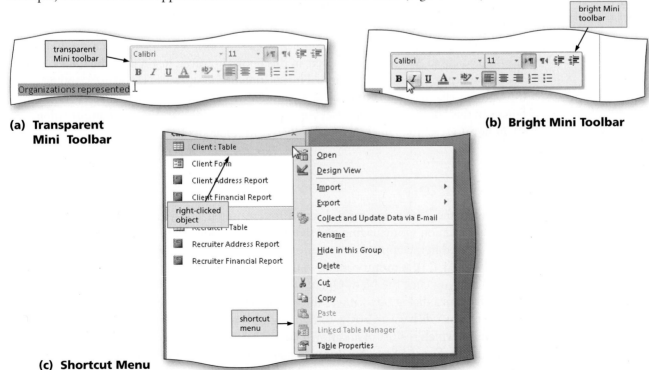

(a) Transparent Mini Toolbar

(b) Bright Mini Toolbar

(c) Shortcut Menu

Figure 1–21

Quick Access Toolbar

The **Quick Access Toolbar**, located by default above the Ribbon, provides easy access to frequently used commands (Figure 1–22a). The commands on the Quick Access Toolbar always are available, regardless of the task you are performing. Initially, the Quick Access Toolbar contains the Save, Undo, and Redo commands. If you click the Customize Quick Access Toolbar button, Access provides a list of commands you quickly can add to and remove from the Quick Access Toolbar (Figure 1–22b).

You also can add other commands to or delete commands from the Quick Access Toolbar so that it contains the commands you use most often. As you add commands to the Quick Access Toolbar, its commands may interfere with the title of the database object on the title bar. For this reason, Access provides an option of displaying the Quick Access Toolbar below the Ribbon (Figure 1–22c).

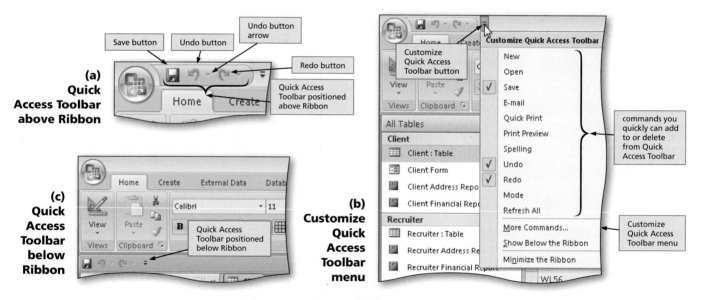

Figure 1–22

Each time you start Access, the Quick Access Toolbar appears the same way it did the last time you used Access. The chapters in this book, however, begin with the Quick Access Toolbar appearing as it did at the initial installation of the software. If you are stepping through this chapter on a computer, and you want your Quick Access Toolbar to match the figures in this book, you should reset your Quick Access Toolbar. For more information about how to reset the Quick Access Toolbar, read Appendix E.

Office Button

While the Ribbon is a control center for creating database objects, the **Office Button** is a central location for managing and sharing database objects. When you click the Office Button, located in the upper-left corner of the window, Access displays the Office Button menu (Figure 1–23). A **menu** contains a list of commands.

When you click the New, Open, and Print commands on the Office Button menu, Access displays a dialog box with additional options. The Save As, Print, Manage, and Publish commands have an arrow to their right. If you point to this arrow, Access displays a **submenu**, which is a list of additional commands associated with the selected command (Figure 1–24). For the Save As, Print, Manage, and Publish commands that do not display a dialog box when clicked, you can point either to the command or the arrow to display the submenu.

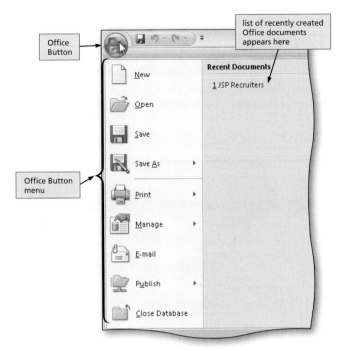

Figure 1–23

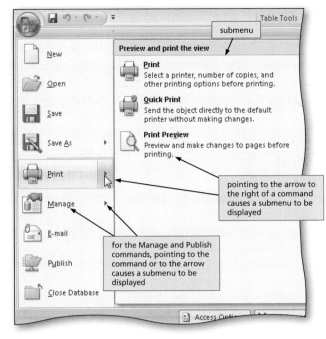

Figure 1–24

Key Tips

If you prefer using the keyboard instead of the mouse, you can press the ALT key on the keyboard to display a **Key Tip badge**, or keyboard code icon, for certain commands (Figure 1–25). To select a command using the keyboard, press its displayed code letter, or **Key Tip**. When you press a Key Tip, additional Key Tips related to the selected command may appear. For example, to select the New command on the Office Button menu, press the ALT key, then press the F key, then press the N key.

To remove the Key Tip badges from the screen, press the ALT key or the ESC key until all Key Tip badges disappear, or click the mouse anywhere in the Access window.

Figure 1–25

Creating a Table

When you first create your database, Access automatically creates a table for you. You can immediately begin defining the fields. If, for whatever reason, you do not have this table or inadvertently delete it, you can create the table by clicking Create on the Ribbon and then clicking the Table button on the Create tab. In either case, you are ready to define the fields.

BTW

Using Design View
The steps on pages AC 24 through AC 29 create the Client table using Datasheet view. To create the Client table using Design view, follow the steps in the PDF document located with the Data Files for Students on scsite.com. See the inside back cover of this book for instructions on accessing those files.

To Define the Fields in a Table

With the table already created, the next step is to define the fields in the table and to assign them data types. The fields in the Client table are Client Number, Client Name, Street, City, State, Postal Code, Amount Paid, Current Due, and Recruiter Number. The data type for the Amount Paid and Current Due fields is Currency. The data type for all other fields is Text. The following steps define the fields in the table.

* Right-click Add New Field to display a shortcut menu (Figure 1–26).

Q&A Why don't I delete the ID field first, before adding other fields?

You cannot delete the primary key in Datasheet view; you only can delete it in Design view. After adding the other fields, you will move to Design view, delete the ID field, and then make the Client Number the primary key.

Q&A Why does my shortcut menu look different?

You right-clicked within the column instead of right-clicking the column heading.

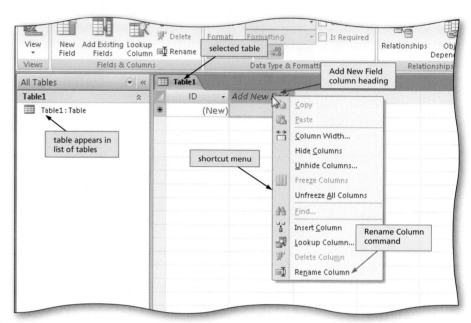

Figure 1–26

* Click Rename Column on the shortcut menu to display an insertion point.

* Type `Client Number` to assign a name to the new field.

* Press the DOWN ARROW key to complete the addition of the field (Figure 1–27).

Q&A Why doesn't the whole name appear?

The default column size is not large enough for Client Number to appear in its entirety. Later in this book, you will learn how to resize columns so that the entire name can appear.

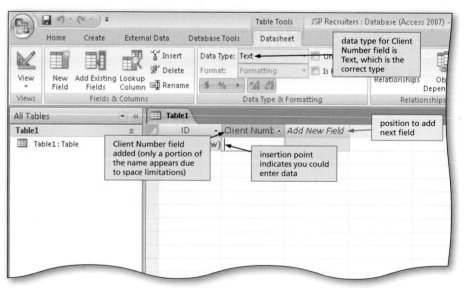

Figure 1–27

3

- Right-click Add New Field to display a shortcut menu, click Rename Column on the shortcut menu to display an insertion point, type `Client Name` to assign a name to the new field, and then press the DOWN ARROW key to complete the addition of the field.

 Did I have to press the DOWN ARROW key? Couldn't I have just moved to the next field or pressed the ENTER key?

You could have pressed the TAB key or the ENTER key to move to the column heading for the

next field. Pressing the DOWN ARROW key, however, completes the entry of the Client Number field and allows you to ensure that the column is assigned the correct data type.

- Using the same technique add the fields in the Client table up through and including the Amount Paid field.

- Click the Data Type box arrow to display the Data Type box menu (Figure 1–28).

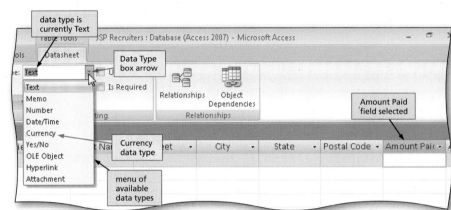

Figure 1–28

4

- Click Currency to select Currency as the data type for the Amount Paid field (Figure 1–29).

 Why does Currency appear twice?

The second Currency is the format, which indicates how the data will be displayed. For the Currency data type, Access automatically sets the format to Currency, which is usually what you would want. You could change it to something else, if desired, by clicking the arrow and selecting the desired format.

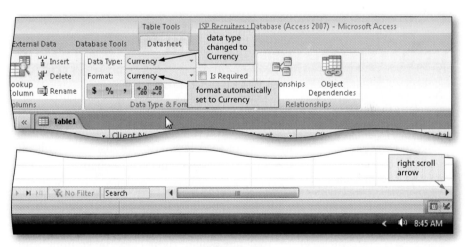

Figure 1–29

5

- Click the right scroll arrow to shift the fields to the left and display the Add New Field column (Figure 1–30).

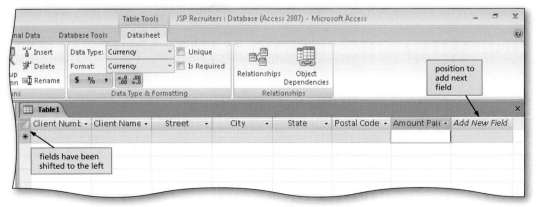

Figure 1–30

6

• Make the remaining entries from the Client table structure shown in Figure 1–31 to complete the structure. Be sure to select Currency as the data type for the Current Due field.

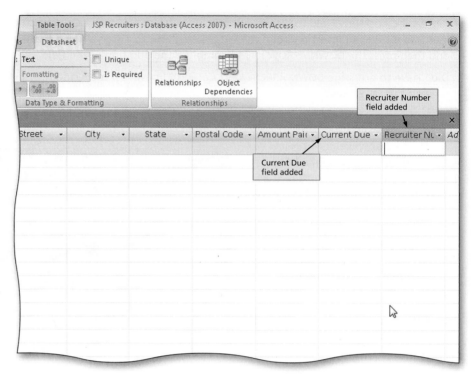

Figure 1–31

Creating a Table: Table Templates
Access includes table templates that assist you in creating some commonly used tables and fields. To use a template, click Create on the Ribbon and then click the Table Templates button on the Create tab. Click the desired template, make any adjustments you wish to the table that Access creates, and then save the table.

Making Changes to the Structure

When creating a table, check the entries carefully to ensure they are correct. If you discover a mistake while still typing the entry, you can correct the error by repeatedly pressing the BACKSPACE key until the incorrect characters are removed. Then, type the correct characters. If you do not discover a mistake until later, you can use the following techniques to make the necessary changes to the structure:

• To undo your most recent change, click the Undo button on the Quick Access Toolbar. If there is nothing that Access can undo, this button will be dim, and clicking it will have no effect.

• To delete a field, right-click the column heading for the field (the position containing the field name), and then click Delete Column on the shortcut menu.

• To change the name of a field, right-click the column heading for the field, click Rename Column on the shortcut menu, and then type the desired field name.

• To insert a field as the last field, right-click the Add New Field column heading, click Rename Column on the shortcut menu, type the desired field name, click the down arrow, and then ensure the correct data type is already selected.

• To insert a field between existing fields, right-click the column heading for the field that will follow the new field, and then click Insert Column on the shortcut menu. You then proceed just as you do when you insert a field as the last field.

As an alternative to these steps, you may want to start over. To do so, click the Close button for the window containing the table, and then click the No button in the Microsoft Office Access dialog box. Click Create on the Ribbon and then click the Table button to create a table. You then can repeat the process you used earlier to define the fields in the table.

To Save a Table

The Client table structure now is complete. The final step is to save and close the table within the database. At this time, you should give the table a name.

The following steps save the table, giving it the name, Client.

- Click the Save button on the Quick Access Toolbar to save the structure of the table (Figure 1–32).

I have an extra row between the row containing the field names and the row that begins with the asterisk. What happened? Is this a problem? If so, how do I fix it?

You inadvertently added a record to the table by pressing some key after you pressed the DOWN ARROW key. Even pressing the Spacebar would add a record. You now have a record you do not want and it will cause problems when you attempt to assign a different primary key. To fix it, you need to delete the record, which you will do in Step 3.

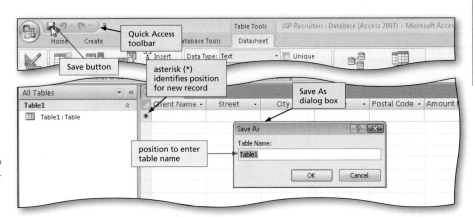

Figure 1–32

- Type `Client` to change the name to be assigned to the table (Figure 1–33).

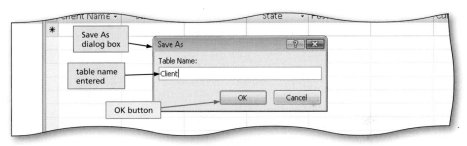

Figure 1–33

- Click the OK button to save the structure with the name, Client (Figure 1–34).

- If you have an additional record between the field names and the aster-isk, click the record selector (the box at the beginning of the record), press the DELETE key, and then click the Yes button when Access asks you if you want to delete the record.

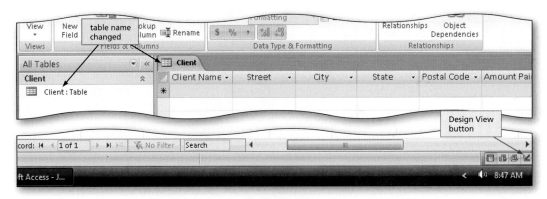

Figure 1–34

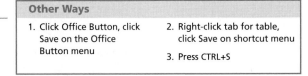

Other Ways

1. Click Office Button, click Save on the Office Button menu
2. Right-click tab for table, click Save on shortcut menu
3. Press CTRL+S

To Change the Primary Key

To change the primary key, you must first delete the ID field that Access created automatically. You then can designate the Client Number field as the primary key (see page AC 8). To delete the ID field, the table must appear in Design view rather than Datasheet view. You also can designate the Client Number field as the primary key within Design view. As you define or modify the fields, the **row selector**, the small box or bar that, when you click it, selects the entire row, indicates the field you currently are describing. The following steps move to Design view and then change the primary key.

- Click the Design View button on the status bar to move to Design view.

- Confirm that your data types match those shown in the figure. Make any necessary corrections to the data types (Figure 1-35).

Q&A Did I have to save the table before moving to Design view?

Yes. If you had not saved it yourself, Access would have asked you to save it.

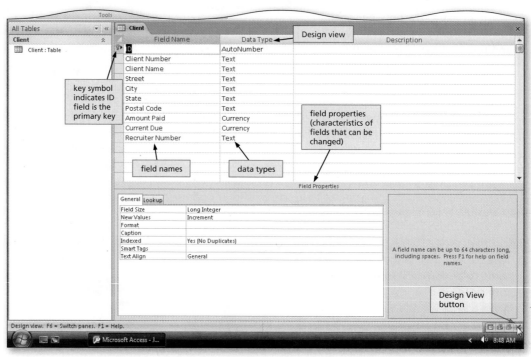

Figure 1–35

- Click the row selector for the ID field to select the field.

- Press the DELETE key to delete the field (Figure 1–36).

Q&A What if I click the row selector for the wrong field before pressing the DELETE key?

Click the No button in the Microsoft Office Access dialog box. If you inadvertently clicked the Yes button, you have deleted the wrong field. You can fix this by clicking the Close button for the Client table, and then clicking the No button when asked if you want to save your changes.

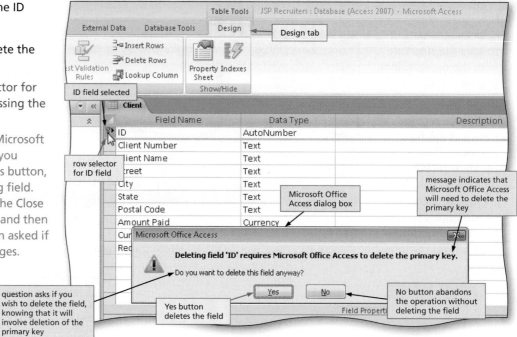

Figure 1–36

3

- Click the Yes button to complete the deletion of the field.

- With the Client Number field selected, click the Primary Key button to designate the Client Number field as the primary key.

- Click the Save button to save the changes (Figure 1–37).

Q&A When I attempted to save the table I got an error message that indicates index or primary key cannot contain a null value. What did I do wrong and how do I fix it?

You inadvertently added a record to the table by pressing some key after you pressed the DOWN ARROW key. To fix it, click the OK button (you will need to do it twice) and then click the Primary Key button to remove the primary key. Click the Save button to save the table and then click the View button near the upper-left corner of the screen to return to datasheet view. Click the little box immediately to the left of the record you added and press the DELETE key. Click the Yes button when Access asks if it is OK to delete the record. Click the View button again and continue with these steps.

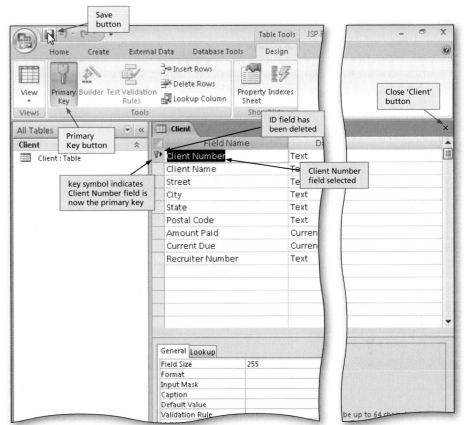

Figure 1–37

4

- Close the Client table by clicking the Close 'Client' button (Figure 1–38).

Q&A What other changes can I make in Design view?

There are many. Two of the most common are changing the field size and adding a description. You can restrict the number of characters users can enter in a Text field by changing the field size. You also can enter a description for a field, which will appear on the Status bar when users are attempting to enter data in the field.

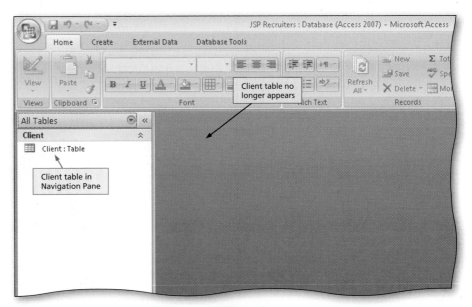

Figure 1–38

To Add Records to a Table

Creating a table by building the structure and saving the table is the first step in a two-step process. The second step is to add records to the table. To add records to a table, the table must be open. When making changes to tables, you work in Datasheet view. In **Datasheet view**, the table is represented as a collection of rows and columns called a **datasheet**.

You often add records in phases. You may, for example, not have enough time to add all the records in one session. The following steps open the Client table in Datasheet view and then add the first two records in the Client table (Figure 1–39).

Client Numb ▾	Client Name ▾	Street ▾	City ▾	State ▾	Postal Code ▾	Amount Paic ▾	Current Due ▾	Recruiter Nu ▾
AC34	Alys Clinic	134 Central	Berridge	CO	80330	$0.00	$17,500.00	21
BH72	Berls Hospital	415 Main	Berls	CO	80349	$29,200.00	$0.00	24

Figure 1–39

1

• Right-click the Client table in the Navigation Pane to display the shortcut menu (Figure 1–40).

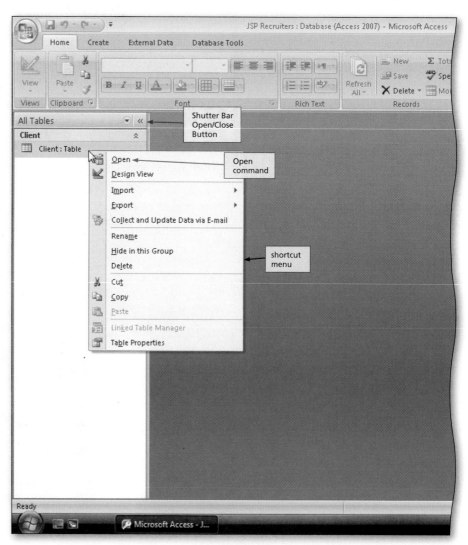

Figure 1–40

2

- Click Open on the shortcut menu to open the Client table in Datasheet view.

Q&A

What if I want to return to Design view?

There are two ways to get to Design view. You could click Design View on the shortcut menu. Alternatively, you could click Open on the shortcut menu to open the table in Datasheet view and then click the Design View button on the Access status bar.

- Click the Shutter Bar Open/Close Button to hide the Navigation Pane (Figure 1–41).

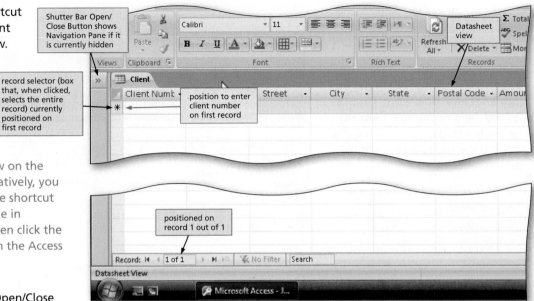

Figure 1–41

3

- Click in the Client Number field and type AC34 to enter the first client number. Be sure you type the letters in uppercase so they are entered in the database correctly (Figure 1–42).

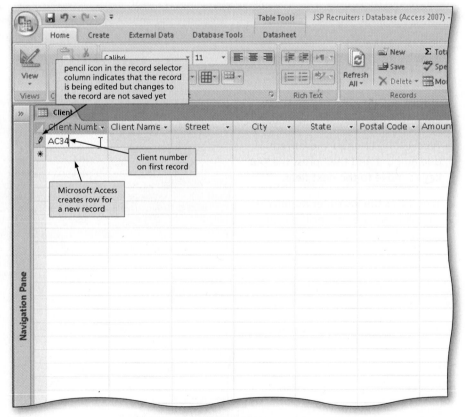

Figure 1–42

4

- Press the TAB key to complete the entry for the Client Number field.

- Enter the client name, street, city, state, and postal code by typing the following entries, pressing the TAB key after each one: `Alys Clinic` as the client name, `134 Central` as the street, `Berridge` as the city, `CO` as the state, and `80330` as the postal code.

- Type `0` to enter the amount paid (Figure 1–43).

 Q&A

Do I need to type a dollar sign?

You do not need to type dollar signs or commas. In addition, because the digits to the right of the decimal point are both zeros, you do not need to type either the decimal point or the zeros.

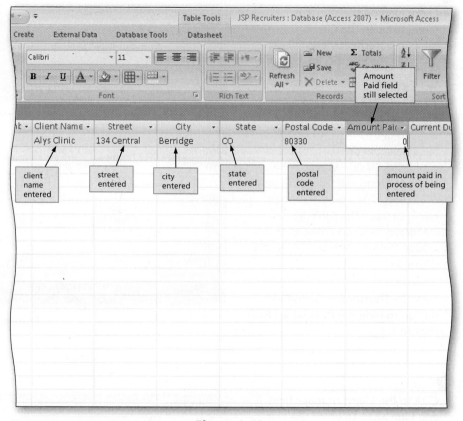

Figure 1–43

5

- Press the TAB key to complete the entry for the Amount Paid field.

- Type `17500` to enter the current due amount and then press the TAB key to move to the next field.

- Type `21` as the Recruiter number to complete data entry for the record (Figure 1–44).

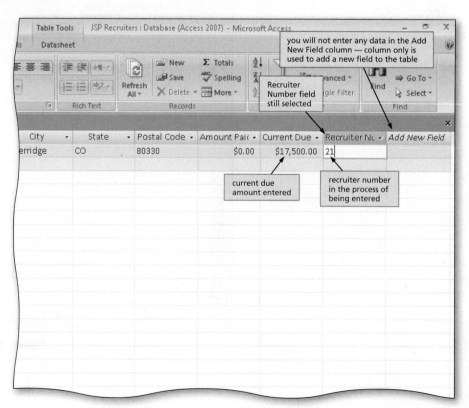

Figure 1–44

6
- Press the TAB key to complete the entry of the first record (Figure 1–45).

How and when do I save the record?

As soon as you have entered or modified a record and moved to another record, the original record is saved. This is different from other applications. The rows entered in an Excel worksheet, for example, are not saved until the entire worksheet is saved.

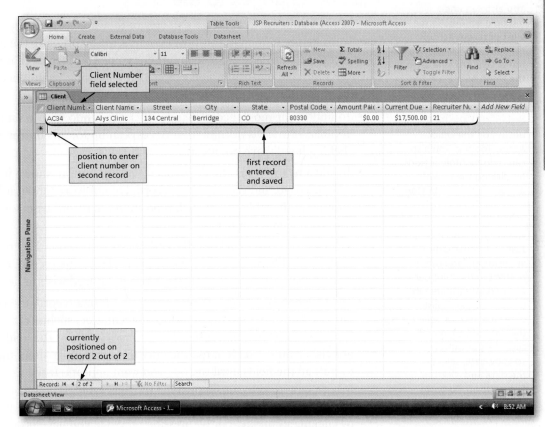

Figure 1–45

7
- Use the techniques shown in Steps 3 through 6 to enter the data for the second record in the Client table (Figure 1–46).

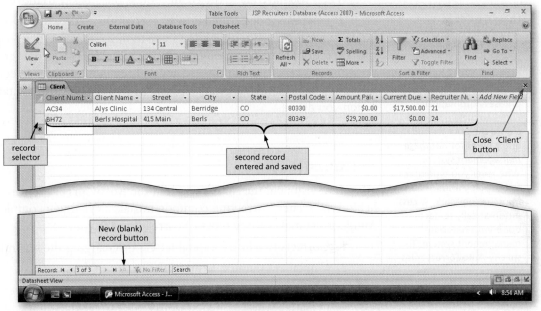

Figure 1–46

BTW

Undo and Redo
You also can undo multiple actions. To see a list of recent actions that you can undo, click the down arrow next to the Undo button on the Quick Access Toolbar. To redo the most recent action, click the Redo button on the Quick Access Toolbar. You also can redo multiple actions by clicking the down arrow next to the button.

BTW

Cut, Copy, and Paste
Just as in other Office applications, you can use buttons in the Clipboard group on the Home tab to cut, copy, and paste data. To cut data, select the data to be cut and click the Cut button. To copy data, select the data and click the Copy button. To paste data, select the desired location and click the Paste button.

BTW

AutoCorrect Options
Using the Office AutoCorrect feature, you can create entries that will replace abbreviations with spelled-out names and phrases automatically. For example, you can create the abbreviated entry *dbms* for *database management system*. Whenever you type dbms followed by a space or punctuation mark, Access automatically replaces dbms with database management system. To specify AutoCorrect rules and exceptions to the rules, click Access Options on the Office Button menu and then click Proofing in the Access Options dialog box.

Making Changes to the Data

Check your entries carefully to ensure they are correct. If you make a mistake and discover it before you press the TAB key, correct it by pressing the BACKSPACE key until the incorrect characters are removed and then typing the correct characters. If you do not discover a mistake until later, you can use the following techniques to make the necessary corrections to the data:

- To undo your most recent change, click the Undo button on the Quick Access Toolbar. If there is nothing that Access can undo, this button will be dim, and clicking it will have no effect.

- To add a record, click the New (blank) record button, shown in Figure 1–46 on the previous page, and then add the record. Do not worry about it being in the correct position in the table. Access will reposition the record based on the primary key, in this case, the Client Number.

- To delete a record, click the Record selector, shown in Figure 1–46, for the record to be deleted. Then press the DELETE key to delete the record, and click the Yes button when Access asks you to verify that you do indeed wish to delete the record.

- To change the contents of one or more fields in a record, the record must be on the screen. If it is not, use any appropriate technique, such as the UP ARROW and DOWN ARROW keys or the vertical scroll bar, to move to it. If the field you want to correct is not visible on the screen, use the horizontal scroll bar along the bottom of the screen to shift all the fields until the one you want appears. If the value in the field is currently highlighted, you can simply type the new value. If you would rather edit the existing value, you must have an insertion point in the field. You can place the insertion point by clicking in the field or by pressing F2. Once you have produced an insertion point, you can use the arrow keys, the DELETE key, and the BACKSPACE key in making the correction. You also can use the INSERT key to switch between Insert and Overtype mode. When you have made the change, press the TAB key to move to the next field.

If you cannot determine how to correct the data, you may find that you are "stuck" on the record. Access neither allows you to move to any other record until you have made the correction, nor allows you to close the table. If you encounter this situation, simply press the ESC key. Pressing the ESC key will remove from the screen the record you are trying to add. You then can move to any other record, close the table, or take any other action you desire.

AutoCorrect

Not visible in the Access window, the **AutoCorrect** feature of Access works behind the scenes, correcting common mistakes when you complete a text entry in a cell. AutoCorrect makes three types of corrections for you:

1. Corrects two initial capital letters by changing the second letter to lowercase.

2. Capitalizes the first letter in the names of days.

3. Replaces commonly misspelled words with their correct spelling. For example, it changes the misspelled word *recieve* to *receive* when you complete the entry. AutoCorrect will correct the spelling automatically of more than 400 commonly misspelled words.

To Close a Table

It is a good idea to close a table as soon as you have finished working with it. It keeps the screen from getting cluttered and prevents you from making accidental changes to the data in the table. The following steps close the Client table.

- Click the Close 'Client' button, shown in Figure 1–46 on page AC 33, to close the table (Figure 1–47).

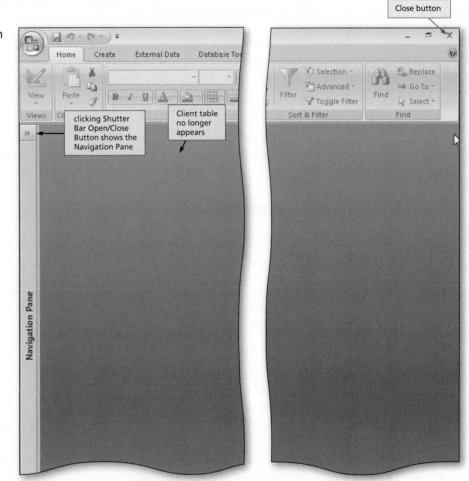

Figure 1–47

Other Ways

1. Right-click tab for table, click Close on shortcut menu

Quitting Access

If you save the object on which you are currently working and then quit Access, all Access windows close. If you have made changes to an object since the last time the object was saved, Access displays a dialog box asking if you want to save the changes you made before it closes that window. The dialog box contains three buttons with these resulting actions:

- Yes button — Saves the changes and then quits Access
- No button — Quits Access without saving changes
- Cancel button — Closes the dialog box and redisplays the database without saving the changes

If no changes have been made to any object since the last time the object was saved, Access will close all windows without displaying any dialog boxes.

To Quit Access

You saved your changes to the table and did not make any additional changes. You are ready to quit Access. The following step quits Access.

1 Click the Close button on the right side of the Access title bar, shown in Figure 1–47 on the previous page, to quit Access.

Starting Access and Opening a Database

Once you have created and later closed a database, you will need to open it in the future in order to use it. Opening a database requires that Access is running on your computer.

Note: If you are using Windows XP, see Appendix F for alternate steps.

To Start Access

The following steps, which assume Windows Vista is running, start Access.

1 Click the Start button on the Windows Vista taskbar to display the Start menu.

2 Click All Programs at the bottom of the left pane on the Start menu to display the All Programs list and then click Microsoft Office in the All Programs list to display the Microsoft Office list.

3 Click Microsoft Office Access 2007 on the Microsoft Office submenu to start Access and display the Getting Started with Microsoft Office Access window (Figure 1–48).

4 If the Access window is not maximized, click the Maximize button on its title bar to maximize the window.

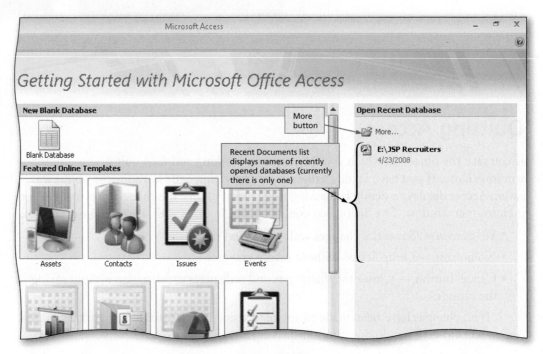

Figure 1–48

To Open a Database from Access

Note: If you are using Windows XP, see Appendix F for alternate steps.

Earlier in this chapter you created your database on a USB flash drive using the file name, JSP Recruiters. There are two ways to open the file containing your database. If the file you created appears in the Recent Documents list, you could click it to open the file. If not, you can use the More button to open the file. The following steps use the More button to open the JSP Recruiters database from the USB flash drive.

1

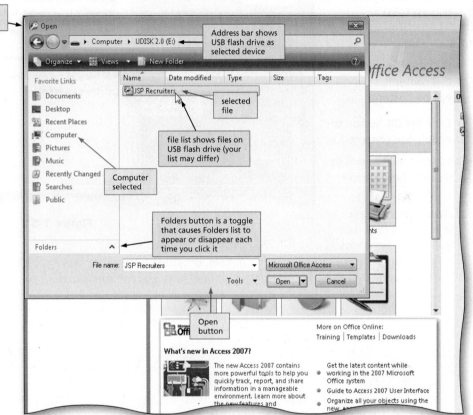

- With your USB flash drive connected to one of the computer's USB ports, click the More button, shown in Figure 1–48, to display the Open dialog box.

- If the Folders list is displayed below the Folders button, click the Folders button to remove the Folders list.

- If necessary, click Computer in the Favorite Links section.

- Double-click UDISK 2.0 (E:) to select the USB flash drive, Drive E in this case, as the new open location.

- Click JSP Recruiters to select the file name (Figure 1–49).

 Q&A How do I open the file if I am not using a USB flash drive?

Use the same process, but be certain to select your device in the Look in list. You might need to open multiple folders.

Figure 1–49

2

- Click the Open button to open the database (Figure 1–50).

Q&A Why do I see the Access icon and name on the Windows Vista taskbar?

When you open an Access database, an Access program button is displayed on the taskbar. If the contents of a button cannot fit in the allotted button space, an ellipsis appears. If you point to a program button, its entire contents appear in a ScreenTip, which in this case would be the program name followed by the file name.

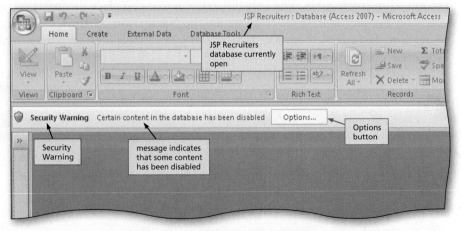

Figure 1–50

- If a Security Warning appears, as shown in Figure 1–50 on the previous page, click the Options button to display the Microsoft Office Security Options dialog box (Figure 1–51).

- Click the 'Enable this content' option button.

- Click the OK button to enable the content.

Q&A

When would I want to disable the content?

You would want to disable the content if you suspected that your database might contain harmful content or damaging macros. Because you are the one who created the database and no one else has used it, you should have no such suspicions.

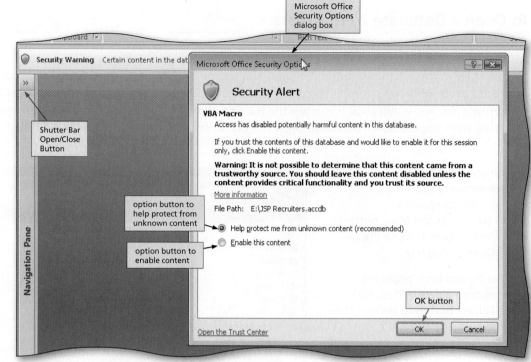

Figure 1–51

Other Ways

1. Click Office Button, double-click file name in Recent Documents list

2. Press CTRL+O, select file name, press ENTER

To Add Additional Records to a Table

You can add records to a table that already contains data using a process almost identical to that used to add records to an empty table. The only difference is that you place the insertion point after the last data record before you enter the additional data. To do so, use the **Navigation buttons**, which are buttons used to move within a table, found near the lower-left corner of the screen when a table is open. The purpose of each of the Navigation buttons is described in Table 1–2.

Table 1–2 Navigation Buttons in Datasheet View	
Button	**Purpose**
First record	Moves to the first record in the table
Previous record	Moves to the previous record
Next record	Moves to the next record
Last record	Moves to the last record in the table
New (blank) record	Moves to the end of the table to a position for entering a new record

The following steps add the remaining records (Figure 1–52) to the Client table.

Client Numb ▾	Client Name ▾	Street ▾	City ▾	State ▾	Postal Code ▾	Amount Paic ▾	Current Due ▾	Recruiter Nu ▾
BL12	Benton Labs	12 Mountain	Denton	CO	80412	$16,500.00	$38,225.00	24
EA45	ENT Assoc.	867 Ridge	Fort Stewart	CO	80336	$12,750.00	$15,000.00	27
FD89	Ferb Dentistry	34 Crestview	Berridge	CO	80330	$21,000.00	$12,500.00	21
FH22	Family Health	123 Second	Tarleton	CO	80409	$0.00	$0.00	24
MH56	Maun Hospital	76 Dixon	Mason	CO	80356	$0.00	$43,025.00	24
PR11	Peel Radiology	151 Valleyview	Fort Stewart	CO	80336	$31,750.00	$0.00	21
TC37	Tarleton Clinic	451 Hull	Tarleton	CO	80409	$18,750.00	$31,500.00	27
WL56	West Labs	785 Main	Berls	CO	80349	$14,000.00	$0.00	24

Figure 1–52

1

- If the Navigation Pane is hidden, click the Shutter Bar Open/Close Button, shown in Figure 1–47, to show the Navigation Pane (Figure 1–53).

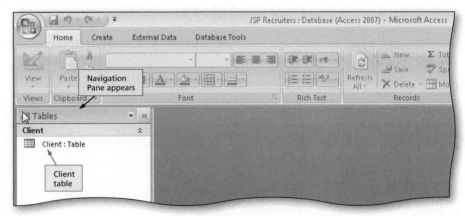

Figure 1–53

2

- Right-click the Client table in the Navigation Pane to display a shortcut menu.
- Click Open on the shortcut menu to open the Client table in Datasheet view.
- Hide the Navigation Pane by clicking the Shutter Bar Open/Close button (Figure 1–54).

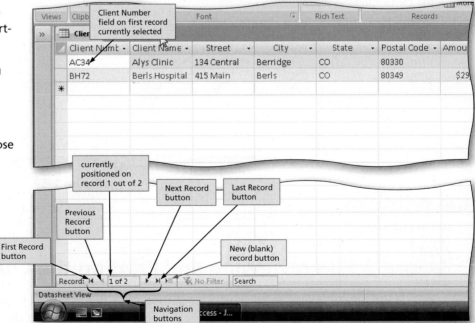

Figure 1–54

3

Q&A

- Click the New (blank) record button to move to a position to enter a new record (Figure 1–55).

Why click the New (blank) record button? Could you just click the Client Number on the first open record and then add the record?

You could click the Client Number on the first open record, provided that record appears on the screen. With only two records in the table, this is not a problem. Once a table contains more records than will fit on the screen, it is easier to click the New (blank) record button.

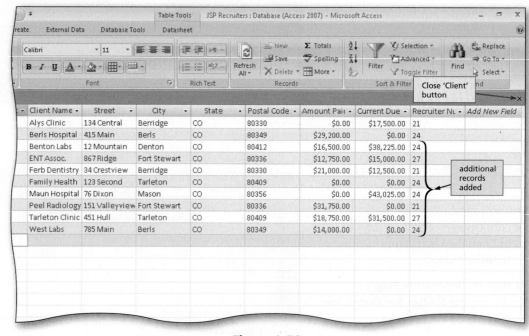

Figure 1–55

4

- Add the records shown in Figure 1–52 on the previous page, using the same techniques you used to add the first two records (Figure 1–56).

5

- Click the Close 'Client' button to close the table.

Figure 1–56

Other Ways

1. Click New button in Records group on Ribbon
2. Press CTRL+PLUS SIGN (+)

Previewing and Printing the Contents of a Table

When working with a database, you often will need to print a copy of the table contents. Figure 1–57 shows a printed copy of the contents of the Client table. (Yours may look slightly different, depending on your printer.) Because the Client table is wider substantially than the screen, it also will be wider than the normal printed page in portrait orientation. **Portrait orientation** means the printout is across the width of the page.

Client Number	Client Name	Street	City	State	Postal Code	Amount Paid	Current Due	Recruiter Numb
AC34	Alys Clinic	134 Central	Berridge	CO	80330	$0.00	$17,500.00	21
BH72	Berls Hospital	415 Main	Berls	CO	80349	$29,200.00	$0.00	24
BL12	Benton Labs	12 Mountain	Denton	CO	80412	$16,500.00	$38,225.00	24
EA45	ENT Assoc.	867 Ridge	Fort Stewart	CO	80336	$12,750.00	$15,000.00	27
FD89	Ferb Dentistry	34 Crestview	Berridge	CO	80330	$21,000.00	$12,500.00	21
FH22	Family Health	123 Second	Tarleton	CO	80409	$0.00	$0.00	24
MH56	Maun Hospital	76 Dixon	Mason	CO	80356	$0.00	$43,025.00	24
PR11	Peel Radiology	151 Valleyview	Fort Stewart	CO	80336	$31,750.00	$0.00	21
TC37	Tarleton Clinic	451 Hull	Tarleton	CO	80409	$18,750.00	$31,500.00	27
WL56	West Labs	785 Main	Berls	CO	80349	$14,000.00	$0.00	24

Client   4/23/2008

Figure 1–57

Landscape orientation means the printout is across the length (height) of the page. Thus, to print the wide database table, use landscape orientation. If you are printing the contents of a table that fit on the screen, you will not need landscape orientation. A convenient way to change to landscape orientation is to preview what the printed copy will look like by using Print Preview. This allows you to determine whether landscape orientation is necessary and, if it is, to change the orientation easily to landscape. In addition, you also can use Print Preview to determine whether any adjustments are necessary to the page margins.

To Preview and Print the Contents of a Table

The following steps use Print Preview to preview and then print the Client table.

1

- If the Navigation Pane is hidden, show the Navigation Pane by clicking the Shutter Bar Open/Close Button.

- Be sure the Client table is selected (Figure 1–58).

Q&A Why do I have to be sure the Client table is selected? It is the only object in the database.

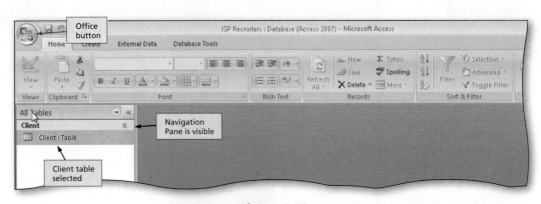

Figure 1–58

There is no issue when the database contains only one object. Ensuring that the correct object is selected is a good habit to form, however, to make sure that the object you print is the one you want.

2

- Click the Office Button to display the Office Button menu.

- Point to the Print command arrow to display the Print submenu (Figure 1–59).

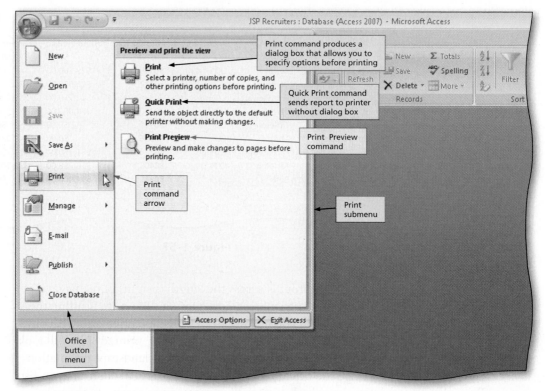

Figure 1–59

3

- Click Print Preview on the Print submenu to display a preview of the report (Figure 1–60).

Q&A

I can't read the report. Can I magnify a portion of the report?

Yes. Point the mouse pointer, whose shape will change to a magnifying glass, at the portion of the report that you wish to magnify, and then click. You can return the view of the report to the one shown in the figure by clicking a second time.

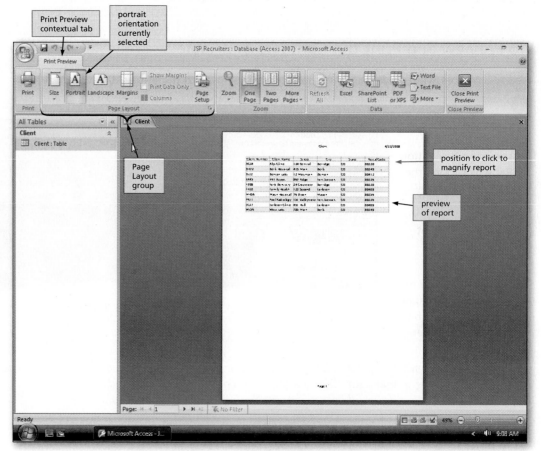

Figure 1–60

4

- Click the mouse pointer in the position shown in Figure 1–60 to magnify the upper-right section of the report (Figure 1–61).

Q&A My report was already magnified in a different area. How can I see the area shown in the figure?

There are two ways. You can use the scroll bars to move to the desired portion of the report. You also can click the mouse pointer anywhere in the report to produce a screen like the one in Figure 1–60, and then click in the location shown in the figure.

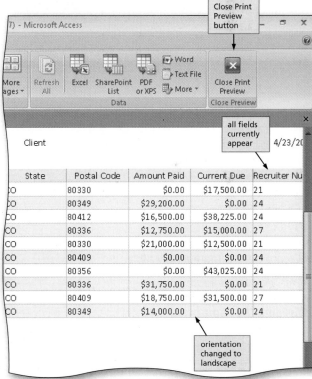

Figure 1–61

5

- Click the Landscape button to change to landscape orientation (Figure 1–62).

6

- Click the Print button on the Print Preview tab to print the report.

- When the printer stops, retrieve the hard copy of the Client table.

- Click the Close Print Preview button to close the Print Preview window.

Q&A How can I print multiple copies of my document other than clicking the Print button multiple times?

Click the Office Button, point to the arrow next to Print on the Office Button menu, click Print on the Print submenu, increase the number in the Number of Copies: box, and then click the OK button.

Q&A How can I print a range of pages rather than printing the whole report?

Click the Office Button, point to the arrow next to Print on the Office Button menu, click Print on the Print submenu, click the Pages option button in the Print Range box, enter the desired page range, and then click the OK button.

Figure 1–62

Other Ways

1. Press CTRL+P, press ENTER

BTW

Using Design View
The steps on pages AC 44 through AC 48 create the Recruiter table using Datasheet view. To create the Recruiter table using Design view, follow the steps in the PDF document located with the Data Files for Students on scsite.com. See the inside back cover of this book for instructions on accessing those files.

Creating Additional Tables

The JSP Recruiters database contains two tables, the Client table and the Recruiter table. You need to create the Recruiter table and add records to it. Because you already used the default table that Access created when you created the database, you will need to first create the table. You can then add fields as you did with the Client table.

To Create an Additional Table

The fields to be added are Recruiter Number, Last Name, First Name, Street, City, State, Postal Code, Rate, and Commission. The data type for the Rate field is Number, and the data type for the Commission field is Currency. The data type for all other fields is Text. The following steps create the Recruiter table.

 1

- Click Create on the Ribbon to display the Create tab (Figure 1–63).

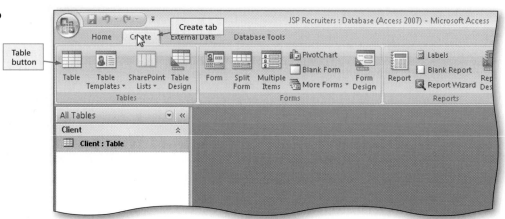

Figure 1–63

 2

- Click the Table button on the Create tab to create a new table (Figure 1–64).

Q&A

Could I save the table now so I can assign it the name I want, rather than Table1?

You certainly can. Be aware, however, that you will still need to save it again once you have added all your fields.

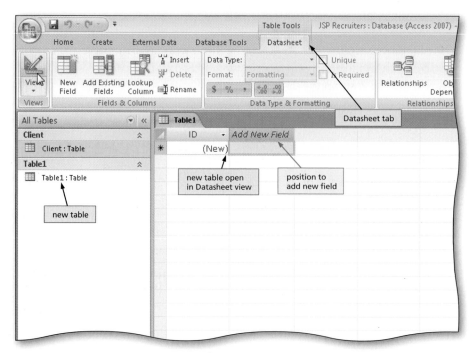

Figure 1–64

- Right-click Add New Field to display a shortcut menu.
- Click Rename Column on the shortcut menu to display an insertion point.
- Type `Recruiter Number` to assign a name to the new field.
- Press the DOWN ARROW key to complete the addition of the field.
- Using the same technique, add the Last Name, First Name, Street, City, State, Postal Code, and Rate fields.
- Click the Data Type box arrow to display the Data Type box menu (Figure 1–65).

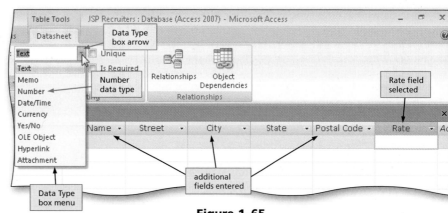

Figure 1–65

- Click Number on the Data Type box menu to select the Number data type and assign the Number data type to the Rate field.
- Add the Commission field and assign it the Currency data type.
- Click the Save button to display the Save As dialog box (Figure 1–66).

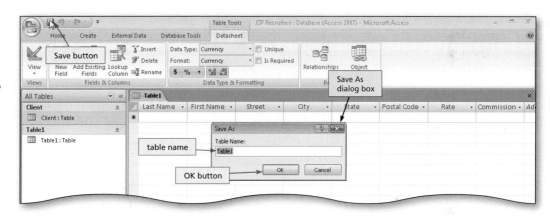

Figure 1–66

- Type `Recruiter` to assign a name to the table.
- Click the OK button (Figure 1–67).

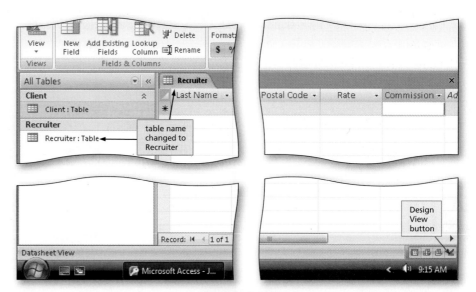

Figure 1–67

To Modify the Primary Key and Field Properties

Fields whose data type is Number often require you to change the field size. Table 1–3 shows the possible field sizes for Number fields.

Table 1–3 Field Sizes for Number Fields	
Field Size	**Description**
Byte	Integer value in the range of 0 to 255.
Integer	Integer value in the range of -32,768 to 32,767.
Long Integer	Integer value in the range of -2,147,483,648 to 2,147,483,647.
Single	Numeric values with decimal places to seven significant digits — requires four bytes of storage.
Double	Numeric values with decimal places to more accuracy than Single — requires eight bytes of storage.
Replication ID	Special identifier required for replication.
Decimal	Numeric values with decimal places to more accuracy than Single — requires 12 bytes of storage.

Because the values in the Rate field have decimal places, only Single, Double, or Decimal would be possible choices. The difference between these choices concerns the amount of accuracy. Double is more accurate than Single, for example, but requires more storage space. Because the rates are only two decimal places, Single is a perfectly acceptable choice.

In addition to changing the field size, you should also change the format to Fixed (a fixed number of decimal places) and the number of decimal places to 2.

The following steps move to Design view, delete the ID field, and make the Recruiter Number field the primary key. They then change the field size of the Rate field to Single, the format to Fixed, and the number of decimal places to 2.

- Click the Design View button on the status bar to move to Design view (Figure 1–68).

Figure 1–68

2

- Click the row selector for the ID field to select the field.

- Press the DELETE key to delete the field.

- Click the Yes button to complete the deletion of the field.

- With the Recruiter Number field selected, click the Primary Key button to designate the Recruiter Number field as the primary key.

- Click the row selector for the Rate field to select the field (Figure 1–69).

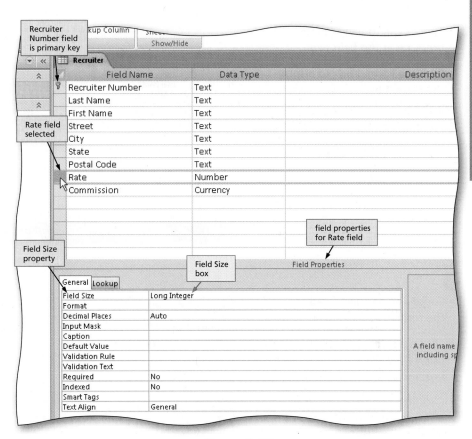

Figure 1–69

3

- Click the Field Size box to display the Field Size box arrow.

- Click the Field Size box arrow to display the Field Size box menu (Figure 1–70).

Q&A What would happen if I left the field size set to Long Integer?

If the field size is Long Integer, no decimal places can be stored. Thus a value of .10 would be stored as 0. If you enter your rates and the values all appear as 0, chances are you did not change the field size.

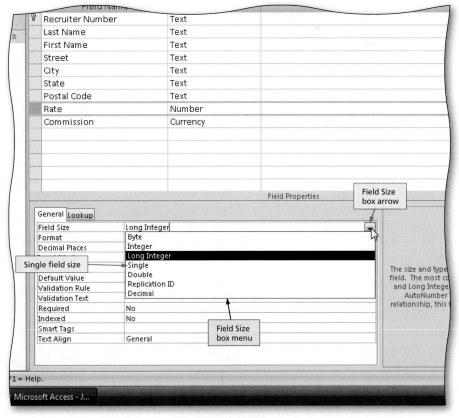

Figure 1–70

4

- Click Single to select single precision as the field size.

- Click the Format box to display the Format box arrow (Figure 1–71).

- Click the Format box arrow to open the Format box menu.

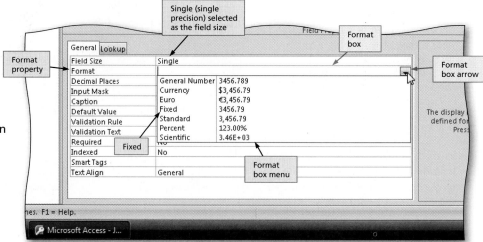

Figure 1–71

5

- Click Fixed to select fixed as the format.

- Click the Decimal Places box to display the Decimal Places box arrow.

- Click the Decimal Places box arrow to enter the number of decimal places.

- Click 2 to select 2 as the number of decimal places.

- Click the Save button to save your changes (Figure 1–72).

Q&A What is the purpose of the error checking button?

You changed the number of decimal places. The error checking button gives you a quick way of making the same change everywhere Rate appears. So far, you have not added any data, nor have you created any forms or reports that use the Rate field, so no such changes are necessary.

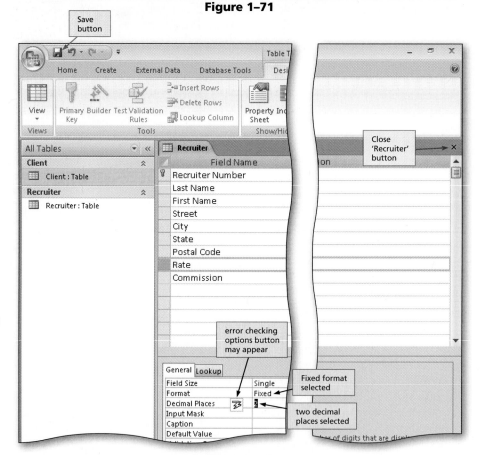

Figure 1–72

6

- Close the Recruiter table by clicking the Close 'Recruiter' button (Figure 1–73).

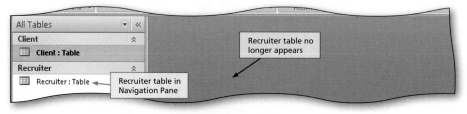

Figure 1–73

To Add Records to an Additional Table

The following steps add the records shown in Figure 1–74 to the Recruiter table.

Recruiter Nu ▾	Last Name ▾	First Name ▾	Street ▾	City ▾	State ▾	Postal Code ▾	Rate ▾	Commission ▾
21	Kerry	Alyssa	261 Pointer	Tourin	CO	80416	0.10	$17,600.00
24	Reeves	Camden	3135 Brill	Denton	CO	80412	0.10	$19,900.00
27	Fernandez	Jaime	265 Maxwell	Charleston	CO	80380	0.09	$9,450.00
34	Lee	Jan	1827 Oak	Denton	CO	80413	0.08	$0.00

Figure 1–74

- Open the Recruiter table in Datasheet view and then hide the Navigation Pane.

- Enter the Recruiter data from Figure 1–74 (Figure 1–75).

Experiment

- Click in the Rate field on any of the records. Be sure the Datasheet tab is selected. Click the Format box arrow and then click each of the formats in the Format box menu to see the effect on the values in the Rate field. When finished, click Fixed in the Format box menu.

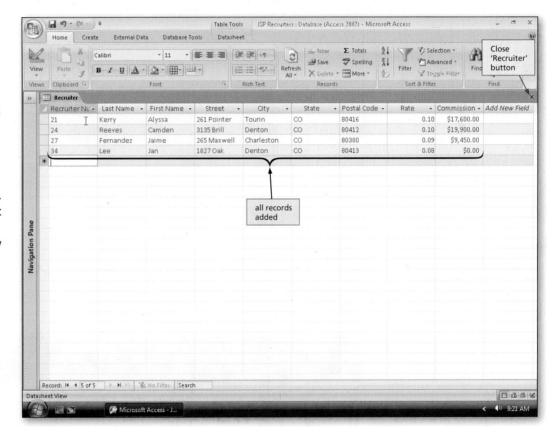

Figure 1–75

- Click the Close 'Recruiter' button to close the table and remove the datasheet from the screen.

Creating a Report

JSP Recruiters needs the following reports. You will create the four reports shown in Figure 1–76 in this section.

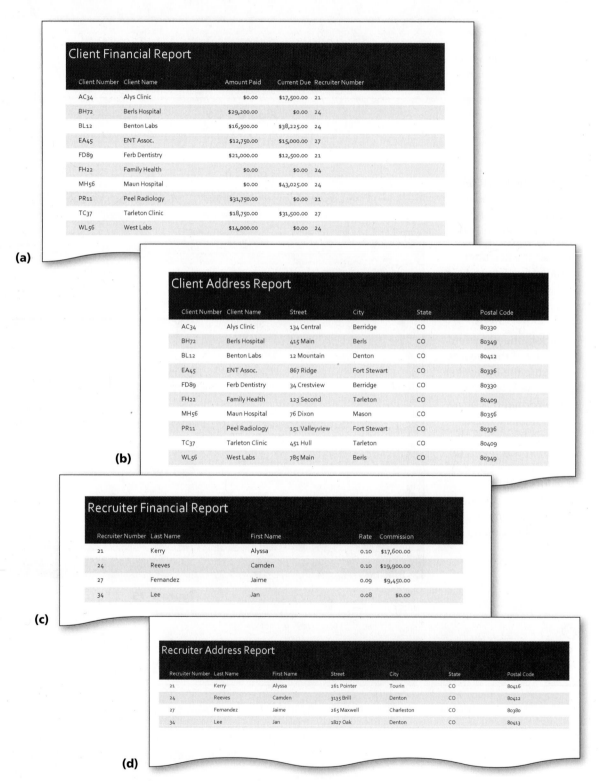

Figure 1–76

To Create a Report

You will first create the report shown in Figure 1–76a. The records in the report are sorted (ordered) by Client Number. To ensure that the records appear in this order, you will specify that the records are to be sorted on the Client Number field. The following steps create the report in Figure 1–76a.

1

- Be sure the Client table is selected in the Navigation Pane.

- Click Create on the Ribbon to display the Create tab.

- Click the Report Wizard button to display the Report Wizard dialog box (Figure 1–77).

Q&A What would have happened if the Recruiter table were selected instead of the Client table?

The list of available fields would have contained fields from the Recruiter table rather than the Client table.

Q&A If the list contained Recruiter table fields, how could I make it contain Client table fields?

Click the arrow in the Tables/ Queries box and then click the Client table in the list that appears.

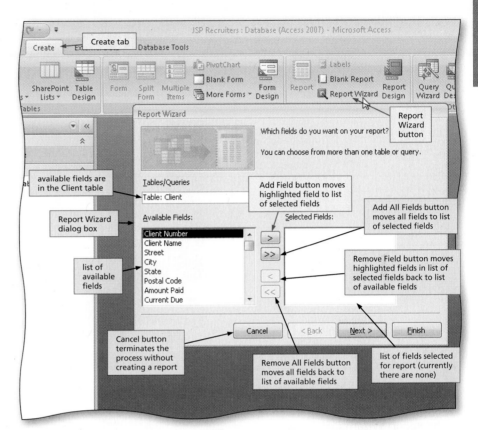

Figure 1–77

2

- Click the Add Field button to add the Client Number field.

- Click the Add Field button to add the Client Name field.

- Click the Amount Paid field, and then click the Add Field button to add the Amount Paid field.

- Click the Add Field button to add the Current Due field.

- Click the Add Field button to add the Recruiter Number field (Figure 1–78).

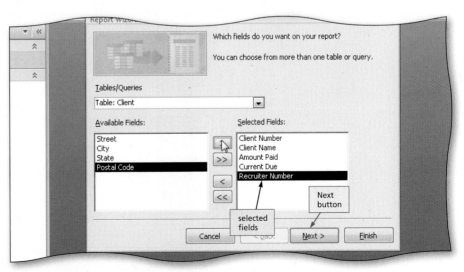

Figure 1–78

● Click the Next button to display the next Report Wizard screen (Figure 1–79).

Q&A

What is grouping?

Grouping means creating separate collections of records sharing some common characteristic. For example, you might want to group clients in the same Postal code or that have the same recruiter.

Q&A

What if I realize that I have selected the wrong fields?

You can click the Back button to return to the previous screen and then correct the list of fields. You also could click the Cancel button and start over.

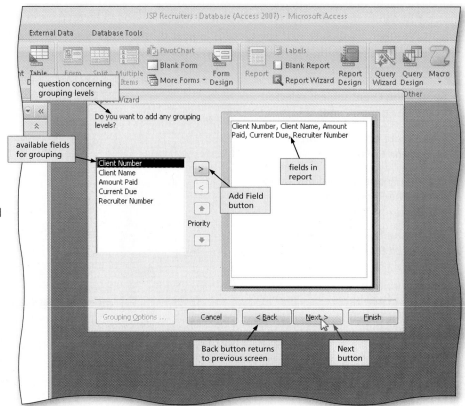

Figure 1–79

● Because you will not specify any grouping, click the Next button in the Report Wizard dialog box to display the next Report Wizard screen.

● Click the box arrow in the text box labeled 1 to display a list of available fields for sorting (Figure 1–80).

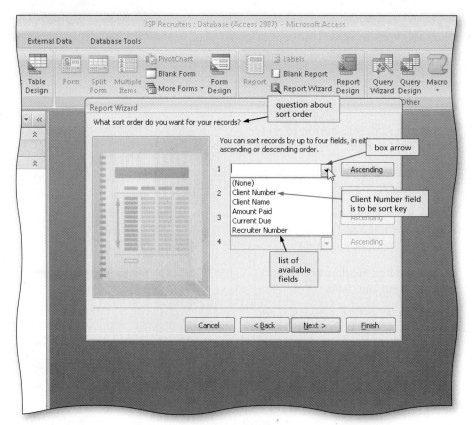

Figure 1–80

5

- Click the Client Number field to select the field as the sort key (Figure 1–81).

What if I want Descending order?

Click the Ascending button next to the sort key to change Ascending order to Descending. If you decide you want Ascending after all, click the button a second time.

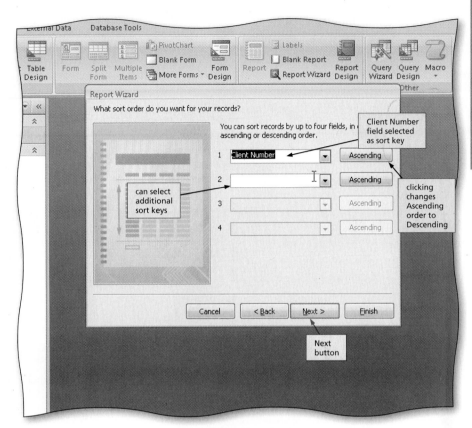

Figure 1–81

6

- Click the Next button to display the next Report Wizard screen (Figure 1–82).

 Experiment

- Click different layouts and observe the effect on the sample report. When you have finished experimenting, click the Tabular option button for the layout and the Portrait option button for the orientation.

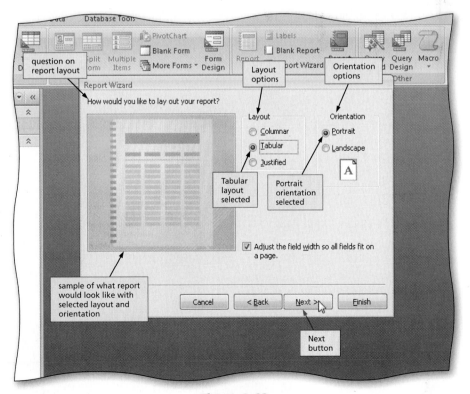

Figure 1–82

7

- Make sure that Tabular is selected as the Layout. (If it is not, click the Tabular option button to select Tabular layout.)

- Make sure Portrait is selected as the Orientation. (If it is not, click the Portrait option button to select Portrait orientation.)

- Click the Next button to display the next Report Wizard screen (Figure 1–83).

Experiment

- Click different styles and observe the effect on the sample report. When you have finished experimenting, click the Module style.

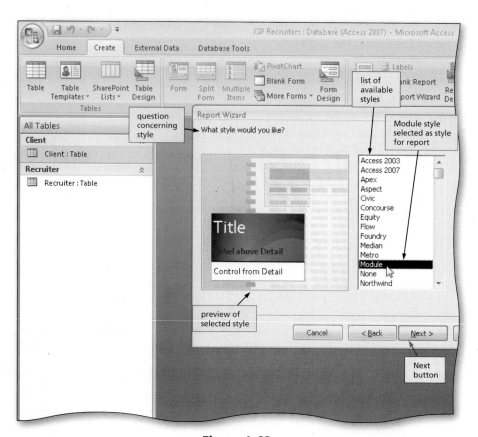

Figure 1–83

8

- Be sure the Module style is selected. (If it is not, click Module to select the Module style.)

- Click the Next button to display the next Report Wizard screen (Figure 1–84).

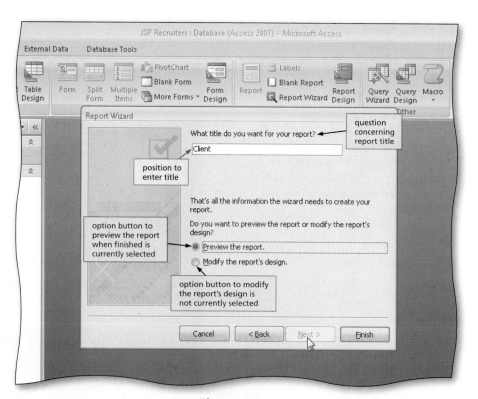

Figure 1–84

9

- Erase the current title, and then type Client Financial Report as the new title (Figure 1–85).

Q&A How do I erase the title?

You can highlight the existing title and then press the DELETE key. You can click at the end of the title and repeatedly press the BACKSPACE key. You can click at the beginning of the title and repeatedly press the DELETE key.

Q&A Could I just click after the word, Client, press the Spacebar, and then type Financial Report?

Yes. In general, you can edit the current title to produce the new title using the method with which you are most comfortable.

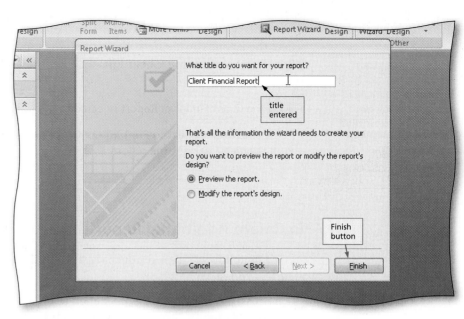

Figure 1–85

- Click the Finish button to produce the report (Figure 1–86).

10

- Click the Close 'Client Financial Report' button to remove the report from the screen.

Q&A Why didn't I have to save the report?

The Report Wizard saves the report automatically.

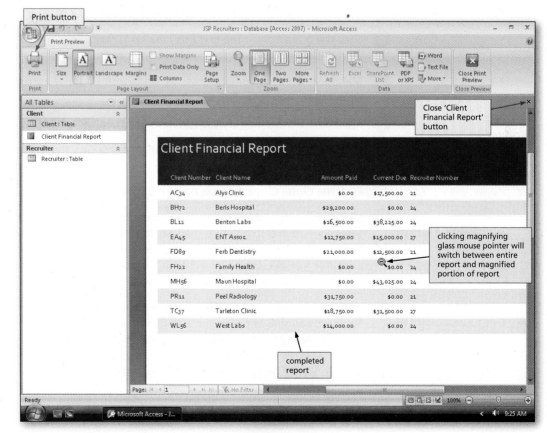

Figure 1–86

BTW

Quick Reference
For a table that lists how to complete the tasks covered in this book using the mouse, Ribbon, shortcut menu, and keyboard, see the Quick Reference Summary at the back of this book, or visit the Access 2007 Quick Reference Web page (scsite.com/ ac2007/qr).

To Print a Report

Once you have created a report, you can print it at any time. The printed layout will reflect the layout you created. The data in the report will always reflect current data. The following step prints the Client Financial Report.

1

- With the Client Financial Report selected in the Navigation Pane, click the Office Button.

- Point to the arrow next to Print on the Office Button menu and then click Quick Print on the Print submenu to print the report.

To Create Additional Reports

The following steps produce the reports shown in Figure 1–76b, Figure 1–76c, and Figure 1–76d on page AC 50.

1 If necessary, click Create on the Ribbon to display the Create tab, and then click the Report Wizard button to display the Report Wizard dialog box.

2 Add the Client Number, Client Name, Street, City, State, and Postal Code fields by clicking each field and then clicking the Add Field button.

3 Click the Next button to move to the screen asking about grouping, and then click the Next button a second time to move to the screen asking about sort order.

4 Click the box arrow in the text box labeled 1, click the Client Number field to select the field as the sort key, and then click the Next button.

5 Make sure that Tabular is selected as the Layout and that Portrait is selected as the Orientation, and then click the Next button.

6 Make sure the Module style is selected, and then click the Next button.

7 Enter `Client Address Report` as the title and click the Finish button to produce the report.

8 Click the Close 'Client Address Report' button to close the Print Preview window.

9 Click the Recruiter table in the Navigation Pane, and then use the techniques shown in Steps 1 through 8 to produce the Recruiter Financial Report. The report is to contain the Recruiter Number, Last Name, First Name, Rate, and Commission fields. It is to be sorted by Recruiter Number. It is to have tabular layout, portrait orientation, and the Module Style. The title is to be Recruiter Financial Report.

10 With the Recruiter table selected in the Navigation Pane, use the techniques shown in Steps 1 through 8 to produce the Recruiter Address Report. The report is to contain the Recruiter Number, Last Name, First Name, Street, City, State, and Postal Code fields. It is to be sorted by Recruiter Number. It is to have tabular layout, landscape orientation, and the Module Style. The title is to be Recruiter Address Report.

11 Click the Close 'Recruiter Address Report' button to close the Print Preview window.

Using a Form to View Data

In Datasheet view, you can view many records at once. If there are many fields, however, only some of the fields in each record might be visible at a time. In **Form view**, where data is displayed in a form on the screen, you usually can see all the fields, but only for one record. To get the advantages from both, many database management systems allow you to easily switch between Datasheet view and Form view while maintaining position within the database. In Access 2007, you can view both a datasheet and a form simultaneously using a split form.

To Create a Split Form

A **split form** combines both a datasheet and a form, thus giving the advantages of both views. The following steps create a split form.

1

- Select the Client table in the Navigation Pane.

- If necessary, click Create on the Ribbon to display the Create tab (Figure 1–87).

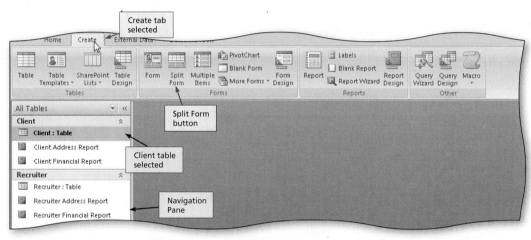

Figure 1–87

2

- Click the Split Form button to create a split form. If a Field List appears, click its Close button to remove the Field List from the screen (Figure 1–88).

 Q&A

Is the form automatically saved the way the report was created when I used the Report Wizard?

No. You must take specific action if you wish to save the form.

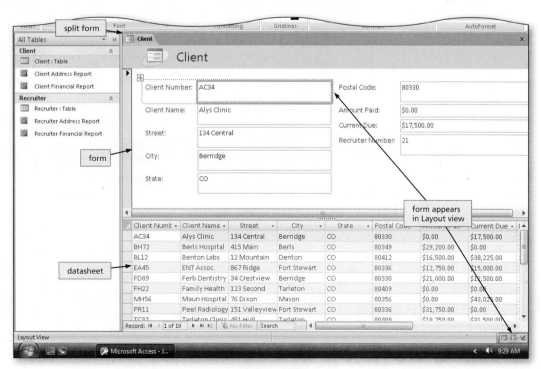

Figure 1–88

- Click the Save button to display the Save As dialog box (Figure 1–89).

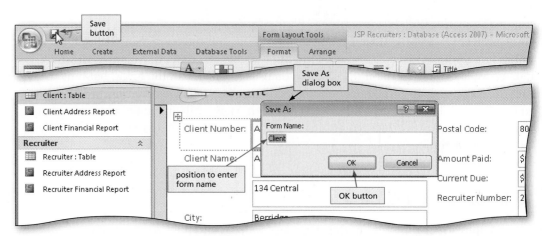

Figure 1–89

- Type Client Form as the form name, and then click the OK button to save the form.

- If the form appears in Layout view, click the Form View button on the Access status bar to display the form in Form view (Figure 1–90).

Q&A

How can I recognize Layout view?

There are three ways. The left end of the Status bar will contain the words Layout View. There will be shading around the outside of the selected field in the form. The Layout View button will be selected in the right end of the Status bar.

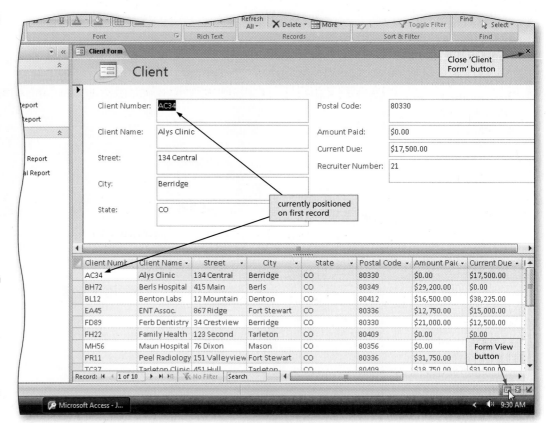

Figure 1–90

To Use a Split Form

After you have saved a form, you can use it at any time by right-clicking the form in the Navigation Pane and then clicking Open in the shortcut menu. If you plan to use the form to enter data, you must ensure you are viewing the form in Form view.

1

- Click the Next Record button four times to move to record 5 (Figure 1–91).

Q&A I inadvertently closed the form at the end of the previous steps. What should I do?

Right-click the form in the Navigation Pane and then click Open on the shortcut menu.

Q&A Do I have to take any special action for the form to be positioned on the same record as the datasheet?

No. The advantage to the split form is that changing the position on either the datasheet or the form automatically changes the position on the other.

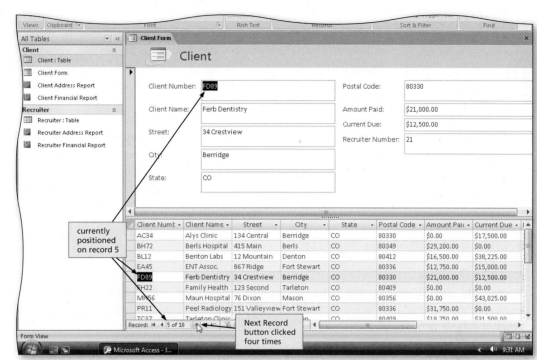

Figure 1–91

2

- Click the Postal Code field on the second record in the datasheet to select the second record in both the datasheet and the form (Figure 1–92).

Experiment

- Click several fields in various records in the datasheet and observe the effect on the form.

3

- Click the Close 'Client Form' button to remove the form from the screen.

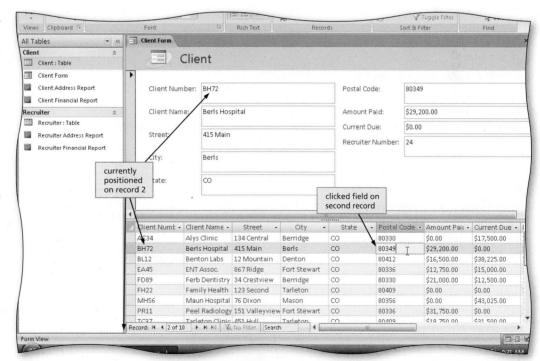

Figure 1–92

BTW

Certification
The Microsoft Certified Application Specialist (MCAS) program provides an opportunity for you to obtain a valuable industry credential — proof that you have the Access 2007 skills required by employers. For more information see Appendix G or visit the Access 2007 Certification Web page (scsite.com/ac2007/cert).

Changing Database Properties

Access helps you organize and identify your databases by using **database properties,** which are the details about a file. Database properties, also known as **metadata,** can include such information as the project author, title, or subject. **Keywords** are words or phrases that further describe the database. For example, a class name or database topic can describe the file's purpose or content.

Five different types of document properties exist, but the more common ones used in this book are standard and automatically updated properties. **Standard properties** are associated with all Microsoft Office documents and include author, title, and subject. **Automatically updated properties** include file system properties, such as the date you create or change a file, and statistics, such as the file size.

To Change Database Properties

The Database Properties dialog box contains areas where you can view and enter document properties. You can view and change information in this dialog box at any time while you are working on your database. It is a good idea to add your name and class name as database properties. The following steps use the Properties dialog box to change database properties.

- Click the Office Button to display the Office Button menu.

- Point to Manage on the Office Button menu to display the Manage submenu (Figure 1–93).

Q&A What other types of actions besides changing properties can you take to prepare a database for distribution?

The Manage submenu provides commands to compact and repair a database as well as to back up a database.

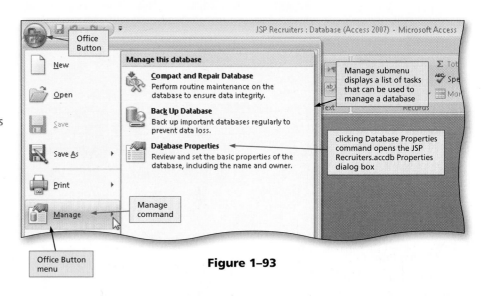

Figure 1–93

- Click Database Properties on the Manage submenu to display the JSP Recruiters.accdb Properties dialog box (Figure 1–94).

Q&A Why are some of the document properties in my Properties dialog box already filled in?

The person who installed Microsoft Office 2007 on your computer or network may have set or customized the properties.

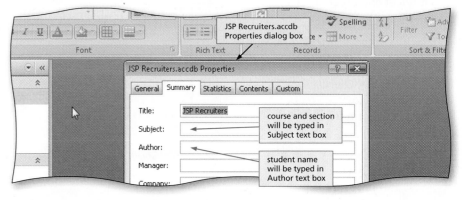

Figure 1–94

3

- If necessary, click the Summary tab.

- Click the Author text box and then type your name as the Author property. If a name already is displayed in the Author text box, delete it before typing your name.

- Click the Subject text box, if necessary delete any existing text, and then type your course and section as the Subject property.

- Click the Keywords text box, if necessary delete any existing text, and then type Healthcare, Recruiter as the Keywords property (Figure 1–95).

 Q&A

What types of properties does Access collect automatically?

Access records such details as when the database was created, when it was last modified, total editing time, and the various objects contained in the database.

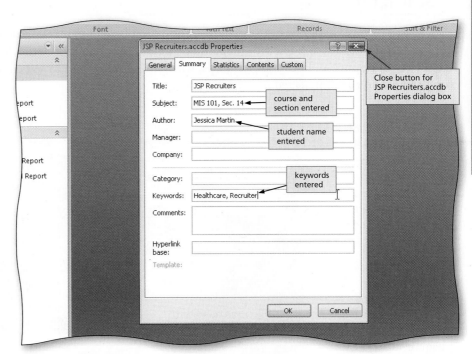

Figure 1–95

4

- Click the OK button to save your changes and remove the JSP Recruiters.accdb Properties dialog box from the screen.

Access Help

At any time while using Access, you can find answers to questions and display information about various topics through **Access Help**. Used properly, this form of assistance can increase your productivity and reduce your frustrations by minimizing the time you spend learning how to use Access.

This section introduces you to Access Help. Additional information about using Access Help is available in Appendix C.

To Search for Access Help

Using Access Help, you can search for information based on phrases, such as create a form or change a data type, or key terms, such as copy, save, or format. Access Help responds with a list of search results displayed as links to a variety of resources. The following steps, which use Access Help to search for information about creating a form, assume you are connected to the Internet.

- Click the Microsoft Office Access Help button near the upper-right corner of the Access window to open the Access Help window.

- Type create a form in the 'Type words to search for' text box at the top of the Access Help window (Figure 1–96).

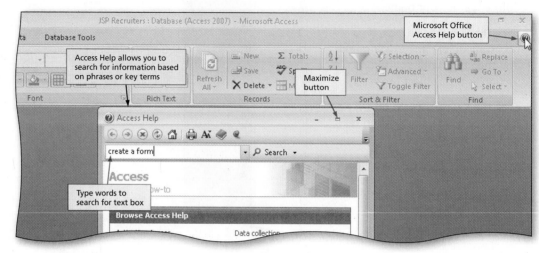

Figure 1–96

- Press the ENTER key to display the search results.

- Click the Maximize button on the Access Help window title bar to maximize the Help window unless it is already maximized (Figure 1–97).

Q&A

Where is the Access window with the JSP Recruiters database?

Access is open in the background, but the Access Help window sits on top of the Microsoft Access window. When the Access Help window is closed, the database will reappear.

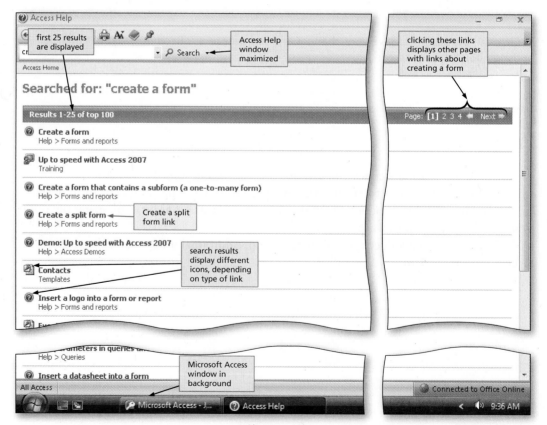

Figure 1–97

❸

- Click the 'Create a split form' link to display information regarding creating a split form (Figure 1–98).

Q&A

What is the purpose of the buttons at the top of the Access Help window?

Use the buttons in the upper-left corner of the Access Help window to navigate through the Help system, change the display, show the Access Help table of contents, and print the contents of the window.

❹

- Click the Close button on the Access Help window title bar to close the Access Help window and make the database active.

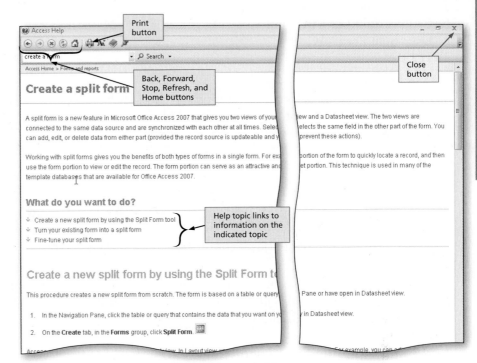

Figure 1–98

Other Ways
1. Press F1

To Quit Access

You saved all your changes and are ready to quit Access. The following step quits Access.

❶ Click the Close button on the right side of the Access title bar to quit Access.

Chapter Summary

In this chapter you have learned to design a database, create an Access database, create tables and add records to them, print the contents of tables, create reports, and create forms. The items listed below include all the new Access skills you have learned in this chapter.

1. Start Access (AC 12)
2. Create a Database Using a Template (AC 13)
3. Create a Database (AC 14)
4. Define the Fields in a Table (AC 24)
5. Create a Table Using a Template (AC 26)
6. Save a Table (AC 27)
7. Change the Primary Key (AC 28)
8. Add Records to a Table (AC 30)
9. Close a Table (AC 35)
10. Quit Access (AC 36)
11. Start Access (AC 36)
12. Open a Database from Access (AC 37)
13. Add Additional Records to a Table (AC 38)
14. Preview and Print the Contents of a Table (AC 41)
15. Create an Additional Table (AC 44)
16. Modify the Primary Key and Field Properties (AC 46)
17. Add Records to an Additional Table (AC 49)
18. Create a Report (AC 51)
19. Print a Report (AC 56)

If you have a SAM user profile, you may have access to hands-on instruction, practice, and assessment. Log in to your SAM account (http://sam2007.course.com) to launch any assigned training activities or exams that relate to the skills covered in this chapter.

Learn It Online

Test your knowledge of chapter content and key terms.

Instructions: To complete the Learn It Online exercises, start your browser, click the Address bar, and then enter the Web address scsite.com/ac2007/learn. When the Access 2007 Learn It Online page is displayed, click the link for the exercise you want to complete and then read the instructions.

Chapter Reinforcement TF, MC, and SA
A series of true/false, multiple choice, and short answer questions that test your knowledge of the chapter content.

Flash Cards
An interactive learning environment where you identify chapter key terms associated with displayed definitions.

Practice Test
A series of multiple choice questions that test your knowledge of chapter content and key terms.

Who Wants To Be a Computer Genius?
An interactive game that challenges your knowledge of chapter content in the style of a television quiz show.

Wheel of Terms
An interactive game that challenges your knowledge of chapter key terms in the style of the television show *Wheel of Fortune*.

Crossword Puzzle Challenge
A crossword puzzle that challenges your knowledge of key terms presented in the chapter.

Apply Your Knowledge

Reinforce the skills and apply the concepts you learned in this chapter.

Changing Data, Creating a Form, and Creating a Report
Instructions: Start Access. Open the The Bike Delivers database. See the inside back cover of this book for instructions for downloading the Data Files for Students, or see your instructor for information on accessing the files required in this book.

The Bike Delivers uses motorbikes to provide courier services for local businesses. The Bike Delivers has a database that keeps track of its couriers and customers. The database has two tables. The Customer table (Figure 1–99a) contains data on the customers who use the services of The Bike Delivers. The Courier table (Figure 1–99b) contains data on the individuals employed by The Bike Delivers.

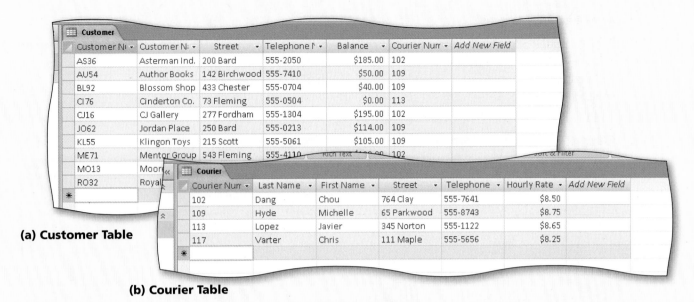

(a) Customer Table

(b) Courier Table

Figure 1–99

Perform the following tasks:

1. Open the Customer table and change the Courier Number for customer KL55 to 113.

2. Close the Customer table.

3. Create a split form for the Courier table. Use the name Courier for the form.

4. Open the form you created and change the street address for Michelle Hyde to 65 Park.

5. Close the Courier form.

6. Create the report shown in Figure 1–100 for the Customer table. The report uses the Module style.

7. Change the database properties, as specified by your instructor. Submit the revised database in the format specified by your instructor.

Figure 1–100

Extend Your Knowledge

Extend the skills you learned in this chapter and experiment with new skills. You may need to use Help to complete the assignment.

Changing Formats and Creating Grouped and Sorted Reports

Instructions: Start Access. Open the Camden Scott College database. See the inside back cover of this book for instructions for downloading the Data Files for Students, or see your instructor for information on accessing the files required in this book.

Continued >

Extend Your Knowledge *continued*

Camden Scott College is a small liberal arts college. The Human Resources Director has created an Access database in which to store information about candidates applying for faculty positions. You will make some changes to the Candidate table so that it looks like that shown in Figure 1–101 and create a report that both groups records and sorts them in ascending order.

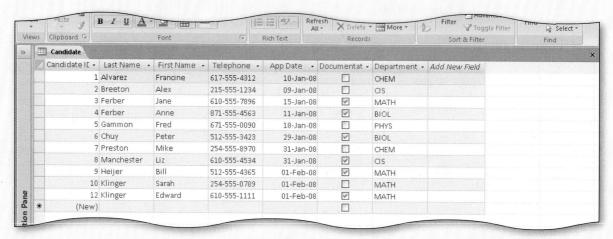

Figure 1–101

Perform the following tasks:

1. Open the Candidate table in Datasheet view and change the column heading for the ID field to Candidate ID.

2. Save the change and open the table in Design view.

3. Select a format for the App Date field that will produce the look shown in Figure 1–101.

4. Change the data type for the Documentation field so that it will match that shown in Figure 1–101.

5. Save the changes.

6. Open the table in Datasheet view. The Human Resources department has received an application from Edward Klinger. Edward applied for the same position as Sarah Klinger on the same date as Sarah. Edward's phone number is 610-555-1111. He did submit all his documentation with his application. Add this record.

7. Add the Quick Print button to the Quick Access Toolbar.

8. Create a report for the Candidate table that lists the Department Code, App Date, Last Name, and First Name. Group the report by Department Code. Sort the report by App Date, Last Name, and then First Name. Choose your own report style and use Candidate by Department as the title of the report.

9. Remove the Quick Print button from the Quick Access Toolbar.

10. Change the database properties, as specified by your instructor. Submit the revised database in the format specified by your instructor.

Make It Right

Analyze a database and correct all errors and/or improve the design.

Correcting Errors in the Table Structure

Instructions: Start Access. Open the SciFi Scene database. See the inside back cover of this book for instructions for downloading the Data Files for Students, or see your instructor for information on accessing the files required in this book.

SciFi Scene is a database containing information on science fiction books. The Book table shown in Figure 1–102 contains a number of errors in the table structure. You are to correct these errors before any additional records can be added to the table. Book Code, not ID, is the primary key for the Book table. The column heading Titel is misspelled. The On Hand field represents the number of books on hand. The field will be used in arithmetic operations. Only whole numbers should be stored in the field. The Price field represents the price of the book. The current data type does not reflect this information.

Change the database properties, as specified by your instructor. Submit the revised database in the format specified by your instructor.

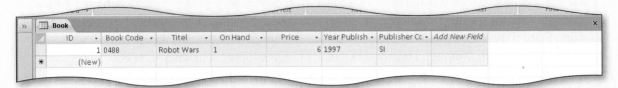

ID	Book Code	Titel	On Hand	Price	Year Publish	Publisher Cc	Add New Field
1	0488	Robot Wars	1		6 1997	SI	
(New)							

Figure 1–102

In the Lab

Design, create, modify, and/or use a database using the guidelines, concepts, and skills presented in this chapter. Labs are listed in order of increasing difficulty.

Lab 1: Creating the JMS TechWizards Database

Problem: JMS TechWizards is a local company that provides technical services to several small businesses in the area. The company currently keeps its records in two Excel workbooks. One Excel workbook (Figure 1–103a) contains information on the clients that JMS TechWizards serves. The other Excel workbook (Figure 1–103b) contains information on the technicians that JMS employs. JMS would like to store this data in a database and has asked for your help.

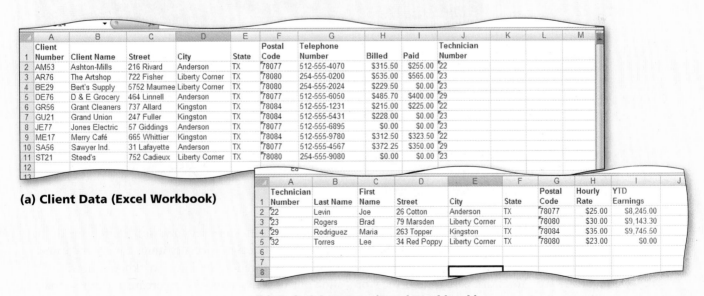

	A	B	C	D	E	F	G	H	I	J	K	L	M
1	Client Number	Client Name	Street	City	State	Postal Code	Telephone Number	Billed	Paid	Technician Number			
2	AM53	Ashton-Mills	216 Rivard	Anderson	TX	78077	512-555-4070	$315.50	$255.00	22			
3	AR76	The Artshop	722 Fisher	Liberty Corner	TX	78080	254-555-0200	$535.00	$565.00	23			
4	BE29	Bert's Supply	5752 Maumee	Liberty Corner	TX	78080	254-555-2024	$229.50	$0.00	23			
5	DE76	D & E Grocery	464 Linnell	Anderson	TX	78077	512-555-6050	$485.70	$400.00	29			
6	GR56	Grant Cleaners	737 Allard	Kingston	TX	78084	512-555-1231	$215.00	$225.00	22			
7	GU21	Grand Union	247 Fuller	Kingston	TX	78084	512-555-5431	$228.00	$0.00	23			
8	JE77	Jones Electric	57 Giddings	Anderson	TX	78077	512-555-6895	$0.00	$0.00	23			
9	ME17	Merry Café	665 Whittier	Kingston	TX	78084	512-555-9780	$312.50	$323.50	22			
10	SA56	Sawyer Ind.	31 Lafayette	Anderson	TX	78077	512-555-4567	$372.25	$350.00	29			
11	ST21	Steed's	752 Cadieux	Liberty Corner	TX	78080	254-555-9080	$0.00	$0.00	23			
12													
13													

(a) Client Data (Excel Workbook)

	A	B	C	D	E	F	G	H	I	J
1	Technician Number	Last Name	First Name	Street	City	State	Postal Code	Hourly Rate	YTD Earnings	
2	22	Levin	Joe	26 Cotton	Anderson	TX	78077	$25.00	$8,245.00	
3	23	Rogers	Brad	79 Marsden	Liberty Corner	TX	78080	$30.00	$9,143.30	
4	29	Rodriguez	Maria	263 Topper	Kingston	TX	78084	$35.00	$9,745.50	
5	32	Torres	Lee	34 Red Poppy	Liberty Corner	TX	78080	$23.00	$0.00	
6										
7										
8										

(b) Technician Data (Excel Workbook)

Figure 1–103

Continued >

In the Lab *continued*

Instructions: Perform the following tasks:

1. Create a new database in which to store all the objects related to the technical services data. Call the database JMS TechWizards.

2. Create a table in which to store the data related to clients. Use the name Client for the table. The fields for the Client table are: Client Number, Client Name, Street, City, State, Postal Code, Telephone Number, Billed, Paid, and Technician Number. Client Number is the primary key. The Billed and Paid fields are currency data type.

3. Create a table in which to store the data related to technicians. Use the name Technician for the table. The fields for the Technician table are: Technician Number, Last Name, First Name, Street, City, State, Postal Code, Hourly Rate, and YTD Earnings. The primary key for the Technician table is Technician Number. Hourly rate and YTD Earnings are currency data type.

4. Add the data from the Client workbook in Figure 1–103a to the Client table.

5. Add the data from the Technician workbook in Figure 1–103b to the Technician table.

6. Create and save the reports shown in Figure 1–104a for the Client table and Figure 1–104b for the Technician table.

7. Change the database properties, as specified by your instructor. Submit the revised database in the format specified by your instructor.

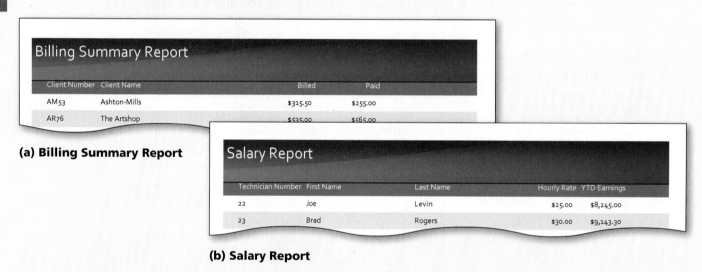

(a) Billing Summary Report

(b) Salary Report

Figure 1–104

In the Lab

Lab 2: Creating the Hockey Fan Zone Database

Problem: Your town has a minor league hockey team. The team store sells a variety of items with the team logo. The store purchases the items from suppliers that deal in specialty items for sports teams. Currently, the information about the items and suppliers is stored in the Excel workbook shown in Figure 1–105. You work part-time at the store, and your boss has asked you to create a database that will store the item and supplier information. You have already determined that you need two tables: an Item table and a Supplier table in which to store the information.

Instructions: Perform the following tasks:

1. Design a new database in which to store all the objects related to the items for sale. Call the database Hockey Fan Zone.

2. Use the information shown in Figure 1–105 to determine the primary keys and determine additional fields. Then, determine the relationships among tables and the data types. (See pages AC 10 and AC 11 for help in designing tables.)

3. Create the Item table using the information shown in Figure 1–105.

4. Create the Supplier table using the information shown in Figure 1–105.

5. Add the appropriate data to the Item table.

6. Add the appropriate data to the Supplier table.

7. Create a split form for the Item table. Use the name Item for the form.

8. Create the report shown in Figure 1–106 for the Item table.

9. Change the database properties, as specified by your instructor. Submit the database in the format specified by your instructor.

	A	B	C	D	E	F	G	H
1	Item Number	Description	On Hand	Cost	Selling Price	Supplier Code	Supplier Name	Telephone Number
2	3663	Ball Cap	30	$11.15	$18.95	LG	Logo Goods	517-555-3853
3	3683	Bumper Sticker	50	$0.95	$1.50	MN	Mary's Novelties	317-555-4747
4	4563	Earrings	10	$4.50	$7.00	LG	Logo Goods	517-555-3853
5	4593	Foam Finger	25	$2.95	$5.00	LG	Logo Goods	517-555-3853
6	5923	Jersey	12	$21.45	$24.75	AC	Ace Clothes	616-555-9228
7	6189	Koozies	35	$2.00	$4.00	MN	Mary's Novelties	317-555-4747
8	6343	Note Cube	7	$5.75	$8.00	MN	Mary's Novelties	317-555-4747
9	7810	Tee Shirt	32	$9.50	$14.95	AC	Ace Clothes	616-555-9228
10	7930	Visor	9	$11.95	$17.00	LG	Logo Goods	517-555-3853
11								

Figure 1–105

Inventory Status Report

Item Number	Description	On Hand	Cost
3663	Ball Cap	30	$11.15
3683	Bumper Sticker	50	$0.95
4563	Earrings	10	$4.50
4593	Foam Finger	25	$2.95
5923	Jersey	12	$21.45
6189	Koozies	35	$2.00
6343	Note Cube	7	$5.75
7810	Tee Shirt	32	$9.50
7930	Visor	9	$11.95

Figure 1–106

In the Lab

Lab 3: Creating the Ada Beauty Supply Database

Problem: A distribution company supplies local beauty salons with items needed in the beauty industry. The distributor employs sales representatives who receive a base salary as well as a commission on sales. Currently, the distributor keeps data on customers and sales reps in two Word documents and two Excel workbooks.

Instructions: Using the data shown in Figure 1–107 on the next page, design the Ada Beauty Supply database. Use the database design guidelines in this chapter to help you in the design process.

Continued >

In the Lab *continued*

Customer Number	Customer Name	Street	Telephone
AM23	Amy's Salon	223 Johnson	555-2150
BB34	Bob the Barber	1939 Jackson	555-1939
BL15	Blondie's	3294 Devon	555-7510
CM09	Cut Mane	3140 Halsted	555-0604
CS12	Curl n Style	1632 Clark	555-0804
EG07	Elegante	1805 Boardway	555-1404
JS34	Just Cuts	2200 Lawrence	555-0313
LB20	Le Beauty	13 Devon	555-5161
NC25	Nancy's Place	1027 Wells	555-4210
RD03	Rose's Day Spa	787 Monroe	555-7657
TT21	Tan and Tone	1939 Congress	555-6554

(a) Customer Address Information (Word table)

E15

	A	B	C	D	E
1	Customer Number	Customer Name	Balance	Amount Paid	Sales Rep Num
2	AM23	Amy's Salon	$195.00	$1,695.00	44
3	BB34	Bob the Barber	$150.00	$0.00	51
4	BL15	Blondie's	$555.00	$1,350.00	49
5	CM09	Cut Mane	$295.00	$1,080.00	51
6	CS12	Curl n Style	$145.00	$710.00	49
7	EG07	Elegante	$0.00	$1,700.00	44
8	JS34	Just Cuts	$360.00	$700.00	49
9	LB20	Le Beauty	$200.00	$1,250.00	51
10	NC25	Nancy's Place	$240.00	$550.00	44
11	RD03	Rose's Day Spa	$0.00	$975.00	51
12	TT21	Tan and Tone	$160.00	$725.00	44
13					
14					
15					
16					

(c) Customer Financial Information (Excel Workbook)

Sales Rep Number	Last Name	First Name	Street	City	State	Postal Code
44	Jones	Pat	43 Third	Lawncrest	WA	98084
49	Gupta	Pinn	678 Hillcrest	Manton	WA	98085
51	Ortiz	Gabe	982 Victoria	Lawncrest	WA	98084
55	Sinson	Terry	45 Elm	Manton	WA	98084

(b) Sales Rep Address Information (Word table)

	A	B	C	D	E	F
1	Sales Rep Number	Last Name	First Name	Salary	Comm Rate	Commission
2	44	Jones	Pat	$ 23,000.00	0.05	$613.50
3	49	Gupta	Pinn	$ 24,000.00	0.06	$616.60
4	51	Ortiz	Gabe	$ 22,500.00	0.05	$492.75
5	55	Sinson	Terry	$ 20,000.00	0.05	$0.00
6						

(d) Sales Rep Financial Information (Excel Workbook)

Figure 1–107

When you have completed the database design, create the database, create the tables, and add the data to the appropriate tables. Be sure to determine the correct data types.

Finally, prepare the Customer Status Report shown in Figure 1–108a and the Sales Rep Salary Report shown in Figure 1–108b. Change the database properties, as specified by your instructor. Submit the database in the format specified by your instructor.

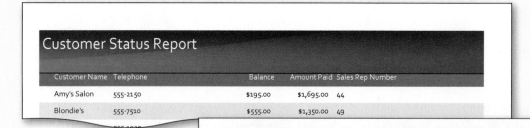

Customer Status Report

Customer Name	Telephone	Balance	Amount Paid	Sales Rep Number
Amy's Salon	555-2150	$195.00	$1,695.00	44
Blondie's	555-7510	$555.00	$1,350.00	49

(a) Customer Status Report

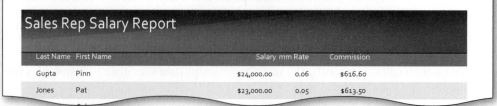

Sales Rep Salary Report

Last Name	First Name	Salary	mm Rate	Commission
Gupta	Pinn	$24,000.00	0.06	$616.60
Jones	Pat	$23,000.00	0.05	$613.50

(b) Sales Rep Salary Report

Figure 1–108

Cases and Places

Apply your creative thinking and problem solving skills to design and implement a solution.

• EASIER •• MORE DIFFICULT

• 1: Design and Create an E-Commerce Database

Students often have very little money to furnish dorm rooms and apartments. You and two of your friends have decided to use the skills you learned in your e-commerce class to create a Web site specifically for college students to buy and sell used household furnishings.

Design and create a database to store the data that you need to manage this new business. Then create the necessary tables and enter the data from the Case 1-1 Second-Hand Goods document. See the inside back cover of this book for instructions for downloading the Data Files for Students, or see your instructor for information on accessing the files required in this book. Submit your assignment in the format specified by your instructor.

• 2: Design and Create a Rental Database

You are a part-time employee of BeachCondo Rentals. BeachCondo Rentals provides a rental service for condo owners who want to rent their units. The company rents units by the week. Currently, the company keeps information about its rentals in an Excel workbook.

Design and create a database to store the rental data. Then create the necessary tables and enter the data from the Case 1-2 BeachCondo Rentals workbook. See the inside back cover of this book for instructions for downloading the Data Files for Students, or see your instructor for information on accessing the files required in this book. Create an Available Rentals Report that lists the unit number, weekly rate, and owner number. Submit your assignment in the format specified by your instructor.

•• 3: Design and Create a Restaurant Database

Your school is sponsoring a conference that will draw participants from a wide geographical area. The conference director has asked for your help in preparing a database of restaurants that might be of interest to the participants. At a minimum, she needs to know the following: the type of restaurant (vegetarian, fast-food, fine dining, and so on), street address, telephone number, and opening and closing times and days. Because most of the participants will stay on campus, she also would like to know the approximate distance from campus. Additionally, she would like to know about any unique or special features the restaurants may have.

Design and create a database to meet the conference director's needs. Create the necessary tables, determine the necessary fields, enter some sample data, and prepare a sample report to show the director. Submit your assignment in the format specified by your instructor.

•• 4: Design and Create a Database to Help You Find a Job

Make It Personal

Conducting a job search requires careful preparation. In addition to preparing a resume and cover letter, you will need to research the companies for which you are interested in working and contact these companies to let them know of your interest and qualifications.

Microsoft Access includes a Contacts table template that can create a table that will help you keep track of your job contacts. Create a database to keep track of the companies that are of interest to you. Submit your assignment in the format specified by your instructor.

Continued >

Cases and Places *continued*

•• 5: Design a Database that Tracks Student Data

Working Together

Keeping track of students is an enormous task for school administrators. Microsoft Access can help school administrators manage student data. The Database Wizard includes a Students template that can create a database that will maintain many different types of data on students, such as allergies, medications, and emergency contact information.

Have each member of your team explore the features of the Database Wizard and determine individually which tables and fields should be included in a Students database. As a group, review your choices and decide on one common design. Prepare a short paper for your instructor that explains why your team chose the particular database design.

After agreeing on the database design, assign one member to create the database using the Database Wizard. Every other team member should contribute data and add the data to the database. Submit your assignment in the format specified by your instructor.

1 | Creating and Editing a Presentation

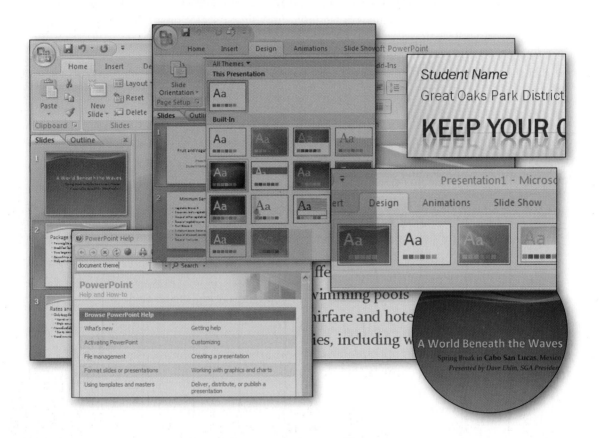

Objectives

You will have mastered the material in this chapter when you can:

- Start and quit PowerPoint

- Describe the PowerPoint window

- Select a document theme

- Create a title slide and text slides with single- and multi-level bulleted lists

- Save a presentation

- Copy elements from one slide to another

- View a presentation in Slide Show view

- Open a presentation

- Display and print a presentation in grayscale

- Check spelling

- Use PowerPoint Help

1 | Creating and Editing a Presentation

What Is Microsoft Office PowerPoint 2007?

Microsoft Office PowerPoint 2007 is a complete presentation graphics program that allows you to produce professional-looking presentations (Figure 1–1). A PowerPoint **presentation** also is called a **slide show**.

PowerPoint contains several features to simplify creating a slide show. For example, the results-oriented user interface can boost productivity by making tasks and options readily accessible. Professionally designed standard layouts help you save time by formatting and creating content. You then can modify these layouts to create custom slides to fit your specific needs. To make your presentation more impressive, you can add diagrams, tables, pictures, video, sound, and animation effects. Additional PowerPoint features include the following:

- **Word processing** — Create bulleted lists, combine words and images, find and replace text, and use multiple fonts and type sizes.
- **Outlining** — Develop your presentation using an outline format. You also can import outlines from Microsoft Word or other word processing programs.
- **Charting** — Create and insert charts into your presentations and then add effects and chart elements.
- **Drawing** — Form and modify diagrams using shapes such as arcs, arrows, cubes, rectangles, stars, and triangles. Then apply Quick Styles to customize and add effects. Arrange these objects by sizing, scaling, and rotating.
- **Inserting multimedia** — Insert artwork and multimedia effects into your slide show. The Microsoft Clip Organizer contains hundreds of media files, including pictures, photos, sounds, and movies.
- **Saving to the Web** — Save presentations or parts of a presentation in HTML format so they can be viewed and manipulated using a browser. You can publish your slide show to the Internet or to an intranet.
- **E-mailing** — Send your entire slide show as an attachment to an e-mail message.
- **Collaborating** — Share your presentation with friends and coworkers. Ask them to review the slides and then insert comments that offer suggestions to enhance the presentation.
- **Preparing delivery** — Rehearse integrating PowerPoint slides into your speech by setting timings, using presentation tools, showing only selected slides in a presentation, and packaging the presentation for a CD.

This latest version of PowerPoint has many new features to increase your productivity. Graphics and other shape effects allow you to add glow, shadowing, 3-D effects, and other appealing visuals. Typography effects enhance the design's impact. PowerPoint themes apply a consistent look to each graphic, font, and table color in an entire presentation. Digital signatures enable you to verify that no one has altered your presentation since you created it, and the Document Inspector removes private data, such as comments and hidden text.

PowerPoint gives you the flexibility to make presentations using a projection device attached to a personal computer or using overhead transparencies. In addition, you can take advantage of the World Wide Web and run virtual presentations on the Internet. PowerPoint also can create paper printouts of the individual slides, outlines, and speaker notes.

The process of developing a presentation that communicates specific information requires careful analysis and planning. As a starting point, establish why the presentation is needed. Next, analyze the intended audience for the presentation and their unique needs. Then, gather information about the topic and decide what to include in the presentation. Finally, determine the presentation design and style that will be most successful at delivering the message. Details of these guidelines are provided in Appendix A. In addition, each project in this book provides practical applications of these planning considerations.

Project Planning Guidlines

Project — Presentation with Bulleted Lists

In Project 1, you will follow proper design guidelines and learn to use PowerPoint to create, save, and print the slides shown in Figures 1–1a through 1–1e on this page and the next. The objective is to produce a presentation, called A World Beneath the Waves, to help the Student Government Association (SGA) President, Dave Ehlin, promote the annual spring break diving and snorkeling trip to Cabo San Lucas, Mexico. This slide show presents the highlights of this trip and promotes the included amenities, tour prices, and the inviting Pacific waters. Some of the text will have formatting and color enhancements. In addition, you will print handouts of your slides to distribute to students.

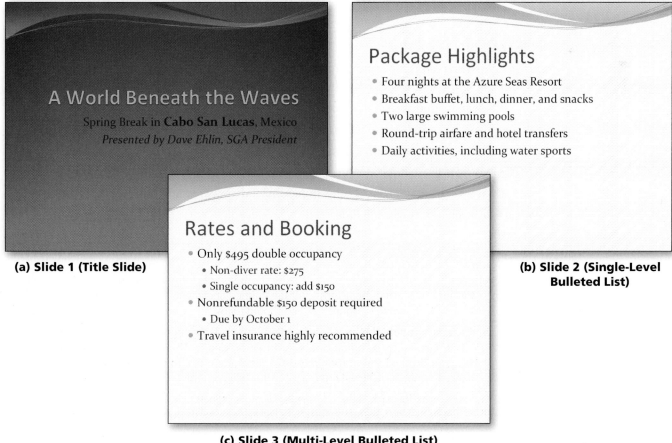

(a) Slide 1 (Title Slide)

(b) Slide 2 (Single-Level Bulleted List)

(c) Slide 3 (Multi-Level Bulleted List)

Figure 1–1

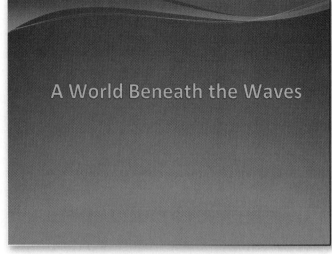

(d) Slide 4 (Multi-Level Bulleted List)   **(e) Slide 5 (Closing Slide)**

Figure 1–1 (continued)

PowerPoint allows you to produce slides to use in an academic, business, or other environment. One of the more common uses of these slides is to enhance an oral presentation. A speaker may desire to convey information, such as urging students to participate in a food drive, explaining first aid, or describing the changes in an employee benefit package. The PowerPoint slides should reinforce the speaker's message and help the audience members retain the information presented. An accompanying handout gives audience members reference notes and review material after the presentation's conclusion.

Overview

As you read this chapter, you will learn how to create the presentation shown in Figure 1–1 by performing these general tasks:

- Select an appropriate document theme.
- Enter titles and text on slides.
- Change the size, color, and style of text.
- View the presentation on your computer.
- Save the presentation so you can modify and view it at a later time.
- Print handouts of your slides.

Plan Ahead

General Project Guidelines

When creating a PowerPoint document, the actions you perform and decisions you make will affect the appearance and characteristics of the finished document. As you create a presentation such as the project shown in Figure 1–1, you should follow these general guidelines:

1. **Find the appropriate theme.** The overall appearance of a presentation significantly affects its capability to communicate information clearly. The slides' graphical appearance should support the presentation's overall message. Colors, fonts, and layouts affect how audience members perceive and react to the slide content.

2. **Choose words for each slide.** Use the less is more principle. The less text, the more likely the slides will enhance your speech. Use the fewest words possible to make a point.

(continued)

When you start PowerPoint, the Ribbon displays seven top-level tabs: Home, Insert, Design, Animations, Slide Show, Review, and View. The **Home tab**, called the primary tab, contains the more frequently used commands. To display a different tab on the Ribbon, click the top-level tab. That is, to display the Insert tab, click Insert on the Ribbon. To return to the Home tab, click Home on the Ribbon. The tab currently displayed is called the **active tab**.

To display more of the document in the document window, some users prefer to minimize the Ribbon, which hides the groups on the Ribbon and displays only the top-level tabs (Figure 1–5b). To use commands on a minimized Ribbon, click the top-level tab.

Each time you start PowerPoint, the Ribbon appears the same way it did the last time you used PowerPoint. The chapters in this book, however, begin with the Ribbon appearing as it did at the initial installation of the software. If you are stepping through this chapter on a computer and you want your Ribbon to match the figures in this book, read Appendix E.

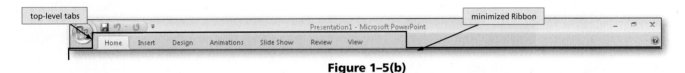

Figure 1–5(b)

In addition to the top-level tabs, PowerPoint displays other tabs, called **contextual tabs**, when you perform certain tasks or work with objects such as pictures or tables. If you insert a picture in a slide, for example, the Picture Tools tab and its related subordinate Format tab appear (Figure 1–6). When you are finished working with the picture, the Picture Tools and Format tabs disappear from the Ribbon. PowerPoint determines when contextual tabs should appear and disappear based on tasks you perform. Some contextual tabs, such as the Chart Tools tab, have more than one related subordinate tab.

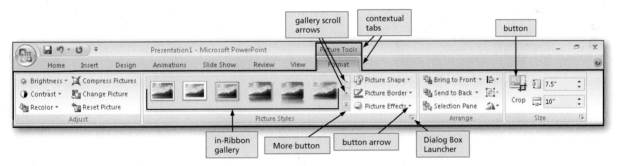

Figure 1–6

Commands on the Ribbon include buttons, boxes (text boxes, check boxes, etc.), and galleries (Figure 1–6). A **gallery** is a set of choices, often graphical, arranged in a grid or in a list. You can scroll through choices on an in-Ribbon gallery by clicking the gallery's scroll arrows. Or, you can click a gallery's More button to view more gallery options on the screen at a time. Some buttons and boxes have arrows that, when clicked, also display a gallery; others always cause a gallery to be displayed when clicked. Most galleries support **live preview**, which is a feature that allows you to point to a gallery choice and see its effect in the document - without actually selecting the choice (Figure 1–7).

BTW

Minimizing the Ribbon
If you want to minimize the Ribbon, right-click the Ribbon and then click Minimize the Ribbon on the shortcut menu, double-click the active tab, or press CTRL+F1. To restore a minimized Ribbon, right-click the Ribbon and then click Minimize the Ribbon on the shortcut menu, double-click any top-level tab, or press CTRL+F1. To use commands on a minimized Ribbon, click the top-level tab.

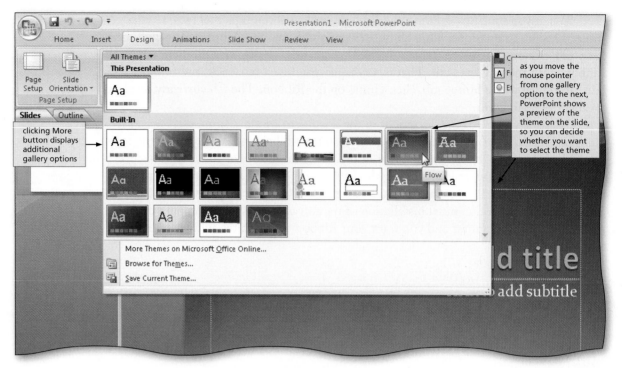

Figure 1–7

Some commands on the Ribbon display an image to help you remember their function. When you point to a command on the Ribbon, all or part of the command glows in shades of yellow and orange, and an Enhanced ScreenTip appears on the screen. An **Enhanced ScreenTip** is an on-screen note that provides the name of the command, available keyboard shortcut(s), a description of the command, and sometimes instructions for how to obtain help about the command (Figure 1–8). Enhanced ScreenTips are more detailed than a typical ScreenTip, which usually only displays the name of the command.

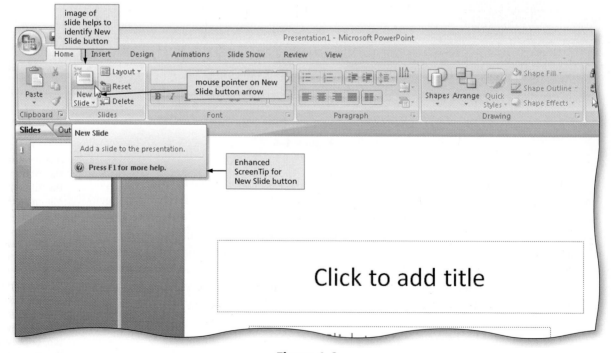

Figure 1–8

The lower-right corner of some groups on the Ribbon has a small arrow, called a **Dialog Box Launcher**, that when clicked displays a dialog box or a task pane with additional options for the group (Figure 1–9). When presented with a dialog box, you make selections and must close the dialog box before returning to the document. A **task pane**, by contrast, is a window that can remain open and visible while you work in the document.

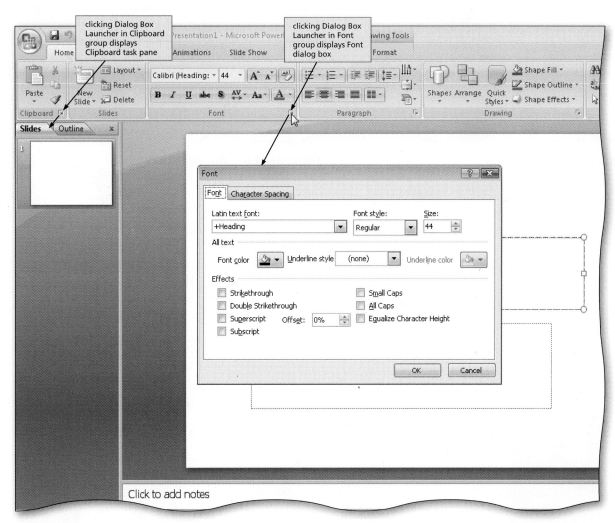

Figure 1–9

Mini Toolbar and Shortcut Menus

The **Mini toolbar**, which appears automatically based on tasks you perform, contains commands related to changing the appearance of text in a slide. All commands on the Mini toolbar also exist on the Ribbon. The purpose of the Mini toolbar is to minimize mouse movement. For example, if you want to use a command that currently is not displayed on the active tab, you can use the command on the Mini toolbar - instead of switching to a different tab to use the command.

When the Mini toolbar appears, it initially is transparent (Figure 1–10a on the next page). If you do not use the transparent Mini toolbar, it disappears from the screen. To use the Mini toolbar, move the mouse pointer into the toolbar, which causes the Mini toolbar to change from a transparent to bright appearance (Figure 1–10b on the next page).

BTW

Turning Off the Mini Toolbar
If you do not want the Mini toolbar to display, click the Office Button, click the PowerPoint Options button on the Office Button menu, and then clear the 'Show Mini Toolbar on selection' check box in the Popular panel.

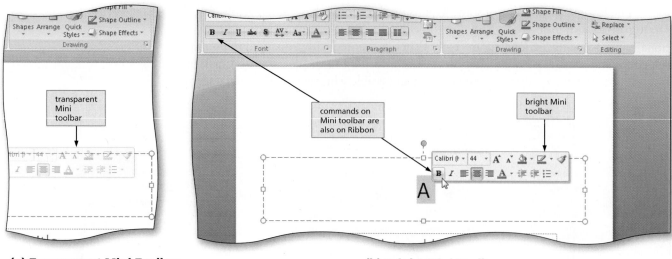

(a) Transparent Mini Toolbar

(b) Bright Mini Toolbar

Figure 1–10

A **shortcut menu**, which appears when you right-click an object, is a list of frequently used commands that relate to the right-clicked object. When you right-click a scroll bar, for example, a shortcut menu appears with commands related to the scroll bar. If you right-click an item in the document window, PowerPoint displays both the Mini toolbar and a shortcut menu (Figure 1–11).

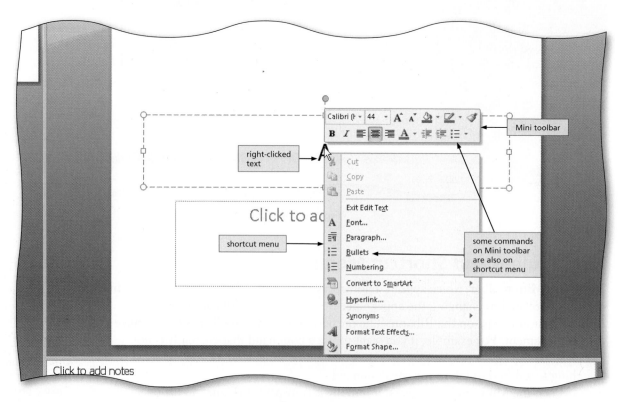

Figure 1–11

Quick Access Toolbar

The **Quick Access Toolbar**, located by default above the Ribbon, provides easy access to frequently used commands (Figure 1–12a). The commands on the Quick Access Toolbar always are available, regardless of the task you are performing. Initially, the Quick Access Toolbar contains the Save, Undo, and Redo commands. If you click the Customize Quick Access Toolbar button, PowerPoint provides a list of commands you quickly can add to and remove from the Quick Access Toolbar (Figure 1–12b).

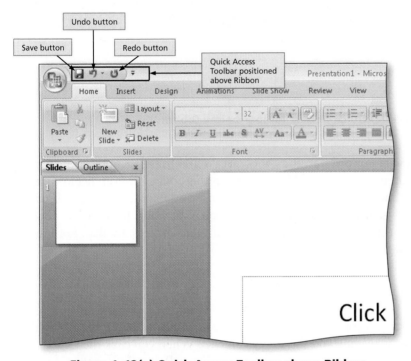

Figure 1–12(a) Quick Access Toolbar above Ribbon

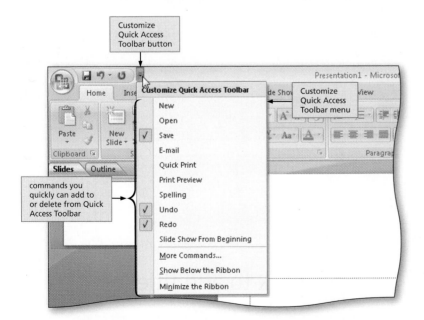

Figure 1–12(b) Customize Quick Access Toolbar

BTW

Quick Access Toolbar Commands
To add a Ribbon command to the Quick Access Toolbar, right-click the command on the Ribbon and then click Add to Quick Access Toolbar on the shortcut menu. To delete a command from the Quick Access Toolbar, right-click the command on the Quick Access Toolbar and then click Remove from Quick Access Toolbar on the shortcut menu. To display the Quick Access Toolbar below the Ribbon, right-click the Quick Access Toolbar and then click Place Quick Access Toolbar below the Ribbon on the shortcut menu.

You also can add other commands to or delete commands from the Quick Access Toolbar so that it contains the commands you use most often. As you add commands to the Quick Access Toolbar, its commands may interfere with the document title on the title bar. For this reason, PowerPoint provides an option of displaying the Quick Access Toolbar below the Ribbon (Figure 1–12c).

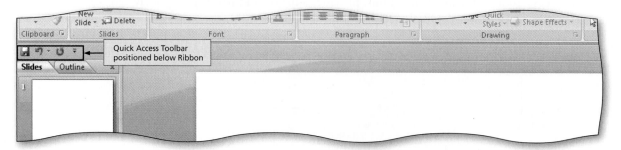

Figure 1–12(c) Quick Access Toolbar below Ribbon

Each time you start PowerPoint, the Quick Access Toolbar appears the same way it did the last time you used PowerPoint. The chapters in this book, however, begin with the Quick Access Toolbar appearing as it did at the initial installation of the software. If you are stepping through this chapter on a computer and you want your Quick Access Toolbar to match the figures in this book, you should reset your Quick Access Toolbar. For more information about how to reset the Quick Access Toolbar, read Appendix E.

Office Button

While the Ribbon is a control center for creating documents, the **Office Button** is a central location for managing and sharing documents. When you click the Office Button, located in the upper-left corner of the window, PowerPoint displays the Office Button menu (Figure 1–13). A **menu** contains a list of commands.

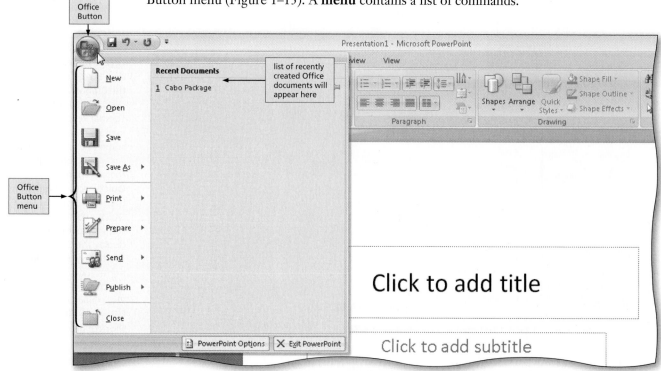

Figure 1–13

When you click the New, Open, Save As, and Print commands on the Office Button menu, PowerPoint displays a dialog box with additional options. The Save As, Print, Prepare, Send, and Publish commands have an arrow to their right. If you point to this arrow, PowerPoint displays a **submenu**, which is a list of additional commands associated with the selected command (Figure 1–14). For the Prepare, Send, and Publish commands that do not display a dialog box when clicked, you can point either to the command or the arrow to display the submenu.

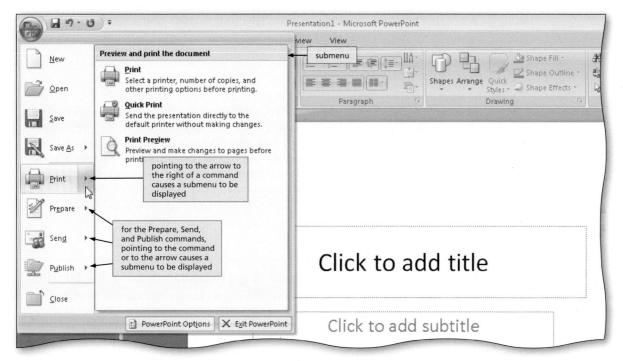

Figure 1–14

Key Tips

If you prefer using the keyboard instead of the mouse, you can press the ALT key on the keyboard to display a **Key Tip badge**, or keyboard code icon, for certain commands (Figure 1–15). To select a command using the keyboard, press its displayed code letter, or **Key Tip**. When you press a Key Tip, additional Key Tips related to the selected command may appear. For example, to select the New command on the Office Button menu, press the ALT key, then press the F key, then press the N key.

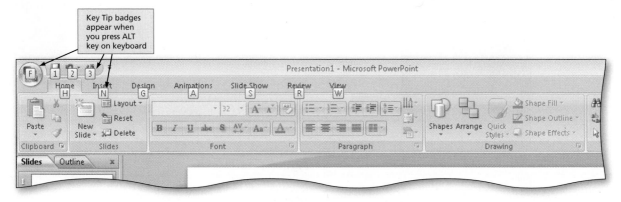

Figure 1–15

To remove the Key Tip badges from the screen, press the ALT key or the ESC key until all Key Tip badges disappear, or click the mouse anywhere in the PowerPoint window.

Choosing a Document Theme

You easily can give a presentation a professional and consistent appearance by using a document theme. This collection of formatting choices includes a set of colors (the color theme), a set of heading and content text fonts (the font theme), and a set of lines and fill effects (the effects theme). These themes allow you to choose and change the appearance of all the slides or individual slides in your presentation.

Plan Ahead

Find the appropriate theme.
In the initial steps of this project, you will select a document theme by locating a particular built-in theme in the Themes group. You could, however, apply a theme at any time while creating the presentation. Some PowerPoint slide show designers create presentations using the default Office Theme. This blank design allows them to concentrate on the words being used to convey the message and does not distract them with colors and various text attributes. Once the text is entered, the designers then select an appropriate document theme.

To Choose a Document Theme

The document theme identifier shows the theme currently used in the slide show. PowerPoint initially uses the **Office Theme** until you select a different theme. The following steps change the theme for this presentation from the Office Theme to the Flow document theme.

- Click Design on the Ribbon to display the Design tab (Figure 1–16).

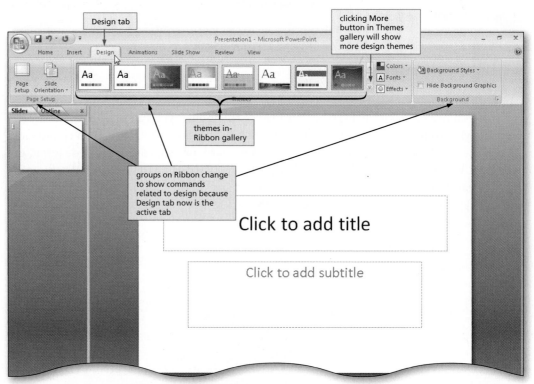

Figure 1–16

2

- Click the More button in the Themes gallery to expand the gallery, which shows more Built-In theme gallery options (Figure 1–17).

Experiment

- Point to various document themes in the Themes gallery and watch the colors and fonts change on the title slide.

Q&A Are the themes displayed in a specific order?

Yes. They are arranged in alphabetical order running from left to right. If you point to a theme, a ScreenTip with the design's name appears on the screen.

Q&A What if I change my mind and do not want to select a new theme?

Click anywhere outside the All Themes gallery to close the gallery.

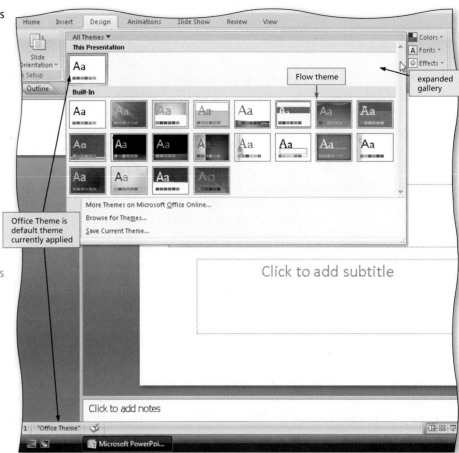

Figure 1–17

3

- Click the Flow theme to apply this theme to Slide 1 (Figure 1–18).

Q&A If I decide at some future time that this design does not fit the theme of my presentation, can I apply a different design?

Yes. You can repeat these steps at any time while creating your presentation.

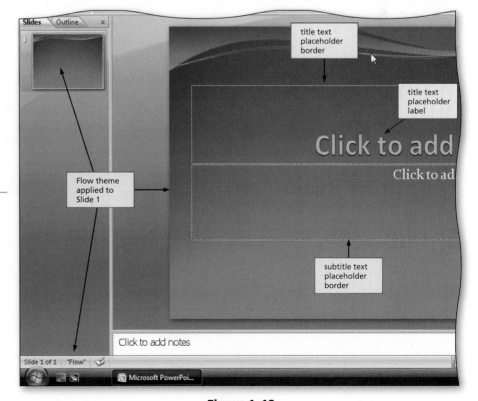

Figure 1–18

Creating a Title Slide

With the exception of a blank slide and a slide with a picture and caption, PowerPoint assumes every new slide has a title. Many of PowerPoint's layouts have both a title text placeholder and at least one content placeholder. To make creating a presentation easier, any text you type after a new slide appears becomes title text in the title text placeholder. The following steps create the title slide for this presentation.

Plan Ahead

> **Choose the words for the slide.**
> No doubt you have heard the phrase, "You get only one chance to make a first impression." The same philosophy holds true for a PowerPoint presentation. The title slide gives your audience an initial sense of what they are about to see and hear. It is, therefore, extremely important to choose the text for this slide carefully. Avoid stating the obvious in the title. Instead, create interest and curiosity using key ideas from the presentation.
> Some PowerPoint users create the title slide as their last step in the design process so that it reflects the tone of the presentation. They begin by planning the final slide in the presentation so that they know where and how they want to end the slide show. All the slides in the presentation should work toward meeting this final slide.

To Enter the Presentation Title

As you begin typing text in the title text placeholder, the title text also is displayed in the Slide 1 thumbnail in the Slides tab. PowerPoint **line wraps** text that exceeds the width of the placeholder. The presentation title for Project 1 is A World Beneath the Waves. This title creates interest by introducing the concept of exploring the life under water. The following step creates the slide show's title.

- Click the label, Click to add title, located inside the title text placeholder to select the placeholder (Figure 1–19).

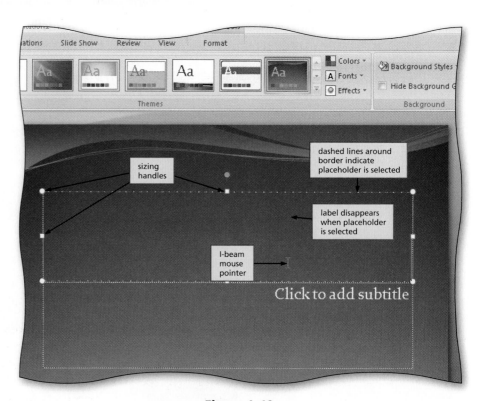

Figure 1–19

2

- Type A World Beneath the Waves in the title text placeholder. Do not press the ENTER key (Figure 1–20).

What if a button with two lines and two arrows appears on the left side of the title text placeholder?

The **AutoFit** button displays because PowerPoint attempts to reduce the size of the letters when the title text does not fit on a single line. If you are creating a slide and need to squeeze an extra line in the text placeholder, you can click this button to resize the existing text in the placeholder so the spillover text will fit on the slide.

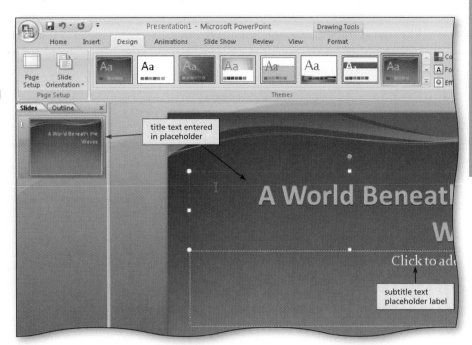

Figure 1–20

Correcting a Mistake When Typing

If you type the wrong letter, press the BACKSPACE key to erase all the characters back to and including the one that is incorrect. If you mistakenly press the ENTER key after typing the title and the insertion point is on the new line, simply press the BACKSPACE key to return the insertion point to the right of the letter s in the word Waves.

When you install PowerPoint, the default setting allows you to reverse up to the last 20 changes by clicking the Undo button on the Quick Access Toolbar. The ScreenTip that appears when you point to the Undo button changes to indicate the type of change just made. For example, if you type text in the title text placeholder and then point to the Undo button, the ScreenTip that appears is Undo Typing. For clarity, when referencing the Undo button in this project, the name displaying in the ScreenTip is referenced. You can reapply a change that you reversed with the Undo button by clicking the Redo button on the Quick Access Toolbar. Clicking the Redo button reverses the last undo action. The ScreenTip name reflects the type of reversal last performed.

Paragraphs

Subtitle text in the subtitle text placeholder supports the title text. It can appear on one or more lines in the placeholder. To create more than one subtitle line, you press the ENTER key after typing some words. PowerPoint creates a new line, which is the second paragraph in the placeholder. A **paragraph** is a segment of text with the same format that begins when you press the ENTER key and ends when you press the ENTER key again. This new paragraph is the same level as the previous paragraph. A **level** is a position within a structure, such as an outline, that indicates the magnitude of importance. PowerPoint allows for five paragraph levels.

To Enter the Presentation Subtitle Paragraph

The first subtitle paragraph links to the title by giving specific details about the vacation location, and the second paragraph gives information about the person who will be speaking to the audience. The following steps enter the presentation subtitle.

- Click the label, Click to add subtitle, located inside the subtitle text place-holder to select the placeholder (Figure 1–21).

Figure 1–21

- **Type** Spring Break in Cabo San Lucas, Mexico **and then press the** ENTER **key.**

- **Type** Presented by Dave Ehlin, SGA President **but do not press the** ENTER **key (Figure 1–22).**

Q&A Why do red wavy lines appear below the words, Cabo and Ehlin?

The lines indicate possible spelling errors.

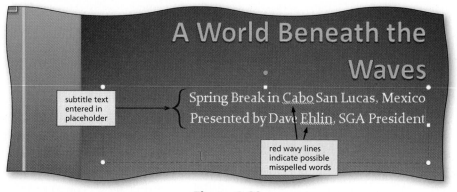

Figure 1–22

Plan Ahead

Identify how to format specific elements of the text.
Most of the time, you use the document theme's text attributes, color scheme, and layout. Occasionally, you may want to change the way a presentation looks, however, and still keep a particular document theme. PowerPoint gives you that flexibility.

Graphic designers use several rules when formatting text.

- Avoid all capital letters, if possible. Audiences have difficulty comprehending sentences typed in all capital letters, especially when the lines exceed seven words. All capital letters leaves no room for emphasis or inflection, so readers get confused about what material deserves particular attention. Some document themes, however, have a default title text style of all capital letters.

- Avoid text with a font size less than 24 point. Audience members generally will sit a maximum of 50 feet from a screen, and at this distance 24-point type is the smallest size text they can read comfortably without straining.

- Make careful color choices. Color evokes emotions, and a careless color choice may elicit the incorrect psychological response. PowerPoint provides a color palette with hundreds of colors. The built-in document themes use complementary colors that work well together. If you stray from these themes and add your own color choices, without a good reason to make the changes, your presentation is apt to become ineffective.

Formatting Characters in a Presentation

Recall that each document theme determines the color scheme, font and font size, and layout of a presentation. You can use a specific document theme and then change the characters' formats any time before, during, or after you type the text.

Fonts and Font Styles

Characters that appear on the screen are a specific shape and size. Examples of how you can modify the appearance, or **format**, of these typed characters on the screen and in print include changing the font, style, size, and color. The **font**, or typeface, defines the appearance and shape of the letters, numbers, punctuation marks, and symbols. **Style** indicates how the characters are formatted. PowerPoint's text font styles include regular, italic, bold, and bold italic. **Size** specifies the height of the characters and is gauged by a measurement system that uses points. A **point** is 1/72 of an inch in height. Thus, a character with a point size of 36 is 36/72 (or 1/2) of an inch in height. **Color** defines the hue of the characters.

This presentation uses the Flow document theme, which uses particular font styles and font sizes. The Flow document theme default title text font is named Calibri. It has a bold style with no special effects, and its size is 56 point. The Flow document theme default subtitle text font is Constantia with a font size of 26 point.

BTW

Formatting Words
To format one word, position the insertion point anywhere in the word. Then make the formatting changes you desire. The entire word does not need to be selected for the change to occur.

To Select a Paragraph

You can use many techniques to format characters. When you want to apply the same formats to multiple words or paragraphs, it is efficient to select the desired text and then make the desired changes to all the characters simultaneously. The first formatting change you will make will apply to the second paragraph of the title slide subtitle. The following step selects this paragraph.

- Triple-click the paragraph, Presented by Dave Ehlin, SGA President, in the subtitle text placeholder to select the paragraph (Figure 1–23).

Can I select the paragraph using a technique other than triple-clicking?

Yes. You can move your mouse pointer to the left of the first paragraph and then drag it to the end of the line.

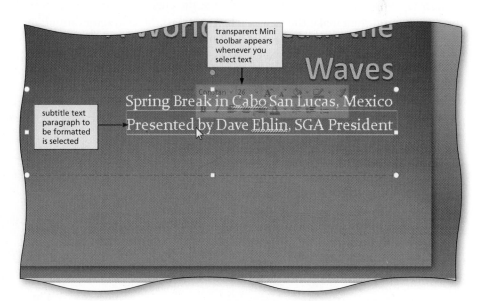

Figure 1–23

To Italicize Text

Different font styles often are used on slides to make them more appealing to the reader and to emphasize particular text. Italic type, used sparingly, draws the readers' eyes to these characters. The following step adds emphasis to the second line of the subtitle text by changing regular text to italic text.

- With the subtitle text still selected, click the Italic button on the Mini toolbar to italicize that text on the slide and on the slide thumbnail (Figure 1–24).

Q&A

If I change my mind and decide not to italicize the text, how can I remove this style?

Select the italicized text and then click the Italic button. As a result, the Italic button will not be selected, and the text will not have the italic font style.

Figure 1–24

Other Ways
1. Right-click selected text, click Font on shortcut menu, click Italic in Font style list   2. Click Home tab, click Italic in Font group   3. Press CTRL+I

To Select Multiple Paragraphs

Each of the subtitle lines is a separate paragraph. As previously discussed, PowerPoint creates a new paragraph each time you press the ENTER key. To change the character formatting in both paragraphs, it is efficient to select the desired text and then make the desired changes to all the characters simultaneously.

The next formatting change you will make will apply to both title slide subtitle paragraphs. The following step selects the first paragraph so that you can format both paragraphs concurrently.

- With the second subtitle text paragraph selected, press the CTRL key and then triple-click the first subtitle text paragraph, Spring Break in Cabo San Lucas, Mexico, to select both paragraphs (Figure 1–25).

Q&A

Can I use a different technique to select both subtitle text paragraphs?

Yes. Click the placeholder border so that it appears as a solid line. When the placeholder is selected in this manner, formatting changes will apply to all text in the placeholder.

Figure 1–25

Identify how to format specific elements of the text.
When selecting text colors, try to limit using red. At least 15 percent of men have difficulty distinguishing varying shades of green or red. They also often see the color purple as blue and the color brown as green. This problem is more pronounced when the colors appear in small areas, such as slide paragraphs or line chart bars.

Plan Ahead

To Change the Text Color

PowerPoint allows you to use one or more text colors in a presentation. To add more emphasis to the title slide subtitle text, you decide to change the color. The following steps add emphasis to both subtitle text paragraphs by changing the font color from white to dark blue.

1

- With both paragraphs selected, click the Font Color arrow on the Mini toolbar to display the palette of Theme Colors and Standard Colors (Figure 1–26).

If the Mini toolbar disappears from the screen, how can I display it once again?

Right-click the text, and the Mini toolbar should appear.

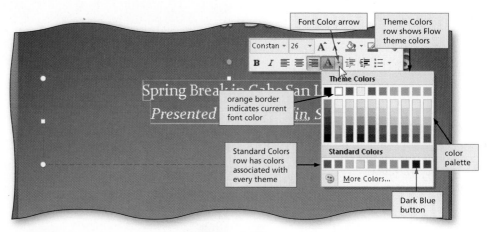

Figure 1–26

2

- Click the Dark Blue button in the Standard Colors row on the Mini toolbar (row 1, column 9) to change the font color to dark blue (Figure 1–27).

Why did I select the color, dark blue?

Dark blue is one of the 10 standard colors associated with every document theme, and it works well with the shades of blue already on the slide. An additional consideration is that dark colors print well.

Figure 1–27

3

- Click outside the selected area to deselect the two paragraphs.

Other Ways

1. Right-click selected text, click Font on shortcut menu, click Font color button, click Dark Blue in Standard Colors row

2. Click Home tab, click Font Color arrow in Font group, click Dark Blue in Standard Colors row

To Select a Group of Words

PowerPoint designers use many techniques to format characters. To apply the same formats to multiple words or paragraphs, they select the desired text and then make the desired changes to all the characters simultaneously.

To add emphasis to the vacation destination, you want to increase the font size and change the font style to bold for the words, Cabo San Lucas. You could perform these actions separately, but it is more efficient to select this group of words and then change the font attributes. The following steps select a group of words.

• Position the mouse pointer immediately to the left of the first character of the text to be selected (in this case, the C in Cabo) (Figure 1–28).

Figure 1–28

• Drag the mouse pointer through the last character of the text to be selected (in this case, the s in Lucas) (Figure 1–29).

Figure 1–29

To Increase Font Size

To add emphasis, you increase the font size for Cabo San Lucas. The Increase Font Size button on the Mini toolbar increases the font size in preset increments. The following step uses this button to increase the font size.

• Click the Increase Font Size button on the Mini toolbar once to increase the font size of the selected text from 26 to 28 point (Figure 1–30).

Other Ways

1. Click Home tab, click Increase Font Size button in Font group
2. Click Home tab, click Font Size box arrow, click new font size
3. Press CTRL+SHIFT+>

Figure 1–30

To Bold Text

Bold characters display somewhat thicker and darker than those that display in a regular font style. Clicking the Bold button on the Mini toolbar is an efficient method of bolding text. To add more emphasis to the vacation destination, you want to bold the words, Cabo San Lucas. The following step bolds this text.

- Click the Bold button on the Mini toolbar to bold the three selected words (Figure 1–31).

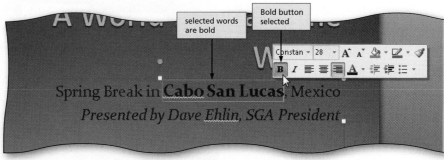

Figure 1–31

Other Ways

1. Click Home tab, click Bold button in Font group
2. Press CTRL+B

Identify how to format specific elements of the text.
Avoid line wraps. Your audience's eyes want to stop at the end of a line. Thus, you must plan your words carefully or adjust the font size so that each point displays on only one line.

Plan Ahead

To Decrease the Title Slide Title Text Font Size

The last word of the title text, Waves, appears on a line by itself. For aesthetic reasons, it is advantageous to have this word appear with the rest of the title on a single line. One way to fit text on one line is to decrease the font size. The process is similar to increasing the font size. Clicking the Decrease Font Size button on the Mini toolbar decreases the size in preset increments. The following steps decrease the font size from 56 to 48 point.

- Select the title slide title text, A World Beneath the Waves (Figure 1–32).

Figure 1–32

2

● Click the Decrease Font Size button on the Mini toolbar twice to decrease the font size from 56 to 48 point (Figure 1–33).

Figure 1–33

Saving the Project

While you are building a presentation, the computer stores it in memory. When you save a presentation, the computer places it on a storage medium such as a USB flash drive, CD, or hard disk. A saved presentation is referred to as a **file**. A **file name** is the name assigned to a file when it is saved.

It is important to save the presentation frequently for the following reasons:

● The presentation in memory will be lost if the computer is turned off or you lose electrical power while PowerPoint is open.

● If you run out of time before completing your project, you may finish your presentation at a future time without starting over.

Plan Ahead

Determine where to save the document.
When saving a document, you must decide which storage medium to use.

● If you always work on the same computer and have no need to transport your projects to a different location, then your computer's hard drive will suffice as a storage location. It is a good idea, however, to save a backup copy of your projects on a separate medium in case the file becomes corrupted or the computer's hard drive fails.

● If you plan to work on your projects in various locations or on multiple computers, then you should save your projects on a portable medium, such as a USB flash drive or CD. The projects in this book use a USB flash drive, which saves files quickly and reliably and can be reused. CDs are easily portable and serve as good backups for the final versions of projects because they generally can save files only one time.

BTW

Saving in a Previous PowerPoint Format
To ensure that your presentation will open in an earlier version of PowerPoint, you must save your file in PowerPoint 97–2003 format. Files saved in this format have the .ppt extension.

To Save a Presentation

You have performed many tasks and do not want to lose the work completed thus far. Thus, you should save the presentation. The following steps save a presentation on a USB flash drive using the file name, Cabo Package.

Note: If you are using Windows XP, see Appendix F for alternate steps.

1

- With a USB flash drive connected to one of the computer's USB ports, click the Save button on the Quick Access Toolbar to display the Save As dialog box. (Figure 1–34).

- If the Navigation pane is not displayed in the Save As dialog box, click the Browse Folders button to expand the dialog box.

- If a Folders list is displayed below the Folders button, click the Folders button to remove the Folders list.

Q&A Do I have to save to a USB flash drive?

No. You can save to any device or folder. A **folder** is a specific location on a storage medium. You can save to the default folder or a different folder. You also can create your own folders, which is explained later in this book.

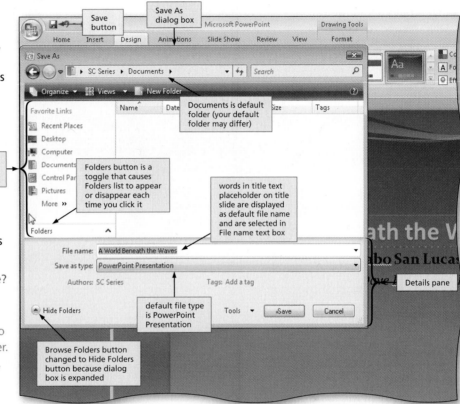

Figure 1–34

2

- Type Cabo Package in the File name box to change the file name. Do not press the ENTER key after typing the file name (Figure 1–35).

Q&A What characters can I use in a file name?

A file name can have a maximum of 260 characters, including spaces. The only invalid characters are the backslash (\), slash (/), colon (:), asterisk (*), question mark (?), quotation mark ("), less than symbol (<), greater than symbol (>), and vertical bar (|).

Q&A What are file properties and tags?

File properties contain information about a file such as the file name, author name, date the file was modified, and tags. A tag is a file property that contains a word or phrase about a file. You can organize and locate files based on their file properties.

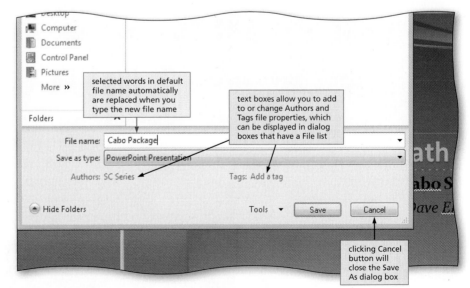

Figure 1–35

3

- If Computer is not displayed in the Favorite Links section, drag the top or bottom edge of the Save As dialog box until Computer is displayed.

- Click Computer in the Favorite Links section to display a list of available drives (Figure 1–36).

- If necessary, scroll until UDISK 2.0 (E:) appears in the list of available drives.

Q&A Why is my list of drives arranged and named differently?

The size of the Save As dialog box and your computer's configuration determine how the list is displayed and how the drives are named.

Q&A How do I save the file if I am not using a USB flash drive?

Use the same process, but select your desired save location in the Favorite Links section.

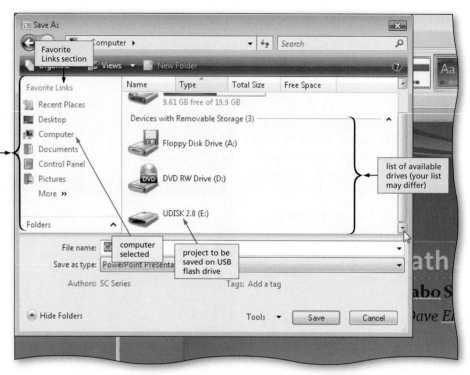

Figure 1–36

4

- Double-click UDISK 2.0 (E:) in the Computer list to select the USB flash drive, Drive E in this case, as the new save location (Figure 1–37).

Q&A What if my USB flash drive has a different name or letter?

It is very likely that your USB flash drive will have a different name and drive letter and be connected to a different port. Verify the device in your Computer list is correct.

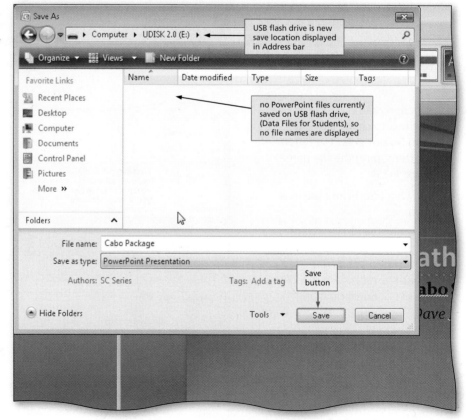

Figure 1–37

5

- Click the Save button in the Save As dialog box to save the presentation on the USB flash drive with the file name, Cabo Package (Figure 1–38).

Q&A How do I know that the project is saved?

While PowerPoint is saving your file, it briefly displays a message on the status bar indicating the amount of the file saved. In addition, your USB drive may have a light that flashes during the save process.

Q&A Why is .pptx displayed immediately to the right of the file name?

Depending on your Windows Vista settings, .pptx may be displayed after you save the file. The file type .pptx is a PowerPoint 2007 document. Previous versions of PowerPoint had a file type of .ppt.

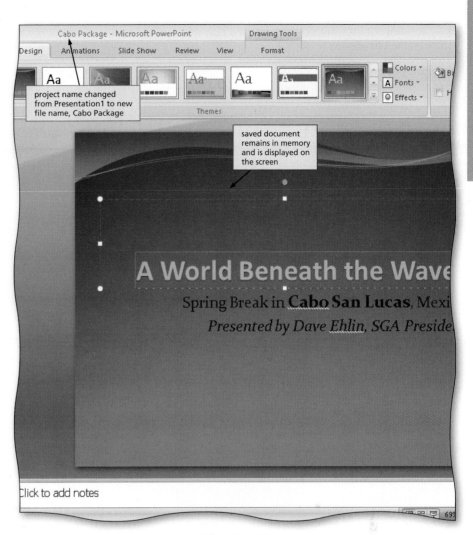

Figure 1–38

Other Ways

1. Click Office Button, click Save, type file name, click Computer, select drive or folder, click Save button
2. Press CTRL+S or press SHIFT+F12, type file name, click Computer, select drive or folder, click Save button

Adding a New Slide to a Presentation

With the title slide for the presentation created, the next step is to add the first text slide immediately after the title slide. Usually, when you create a presentation, you add slides with text, graphics, or charts. Some placeholders allow you to double-click the placeholder and then access other objects, such as media clips, charts, diagrams, and organization charts. You can change the layout for a slide at any time during the creation of a presentation.

To Add a New Text Slide with a Bulleted List

When you add a new slide, PowerPoint uses the Title and Content slide layout. This layout provides a title placeholder and a content area for text, art, charts, and other graphics. A vertical scroll bar appears in the Slide pane when you add the second slide so that you can move from slide to slide easily. A thumbnail of this slide also appears in the Slides tab. The following steps add a new slide with the Title and Content slide layout.

- Click Home on the Ribbon to display the Home tab (Figure 1–39).

Figure 1–39

- Click the New Slide button in the Slides group to insert a new slide with the Title and Content layout (Figure 1–40).

Q&A Why does the bullet character display a blue dot?

The Flow document theme determines the bullet characters. Each paragraph level has an associated bullet character.

Q&A I clicked the New Slide arrow instead of the New Slide button. What should I do?

Click the Title and Content slide thumbnail in the layout gallery.

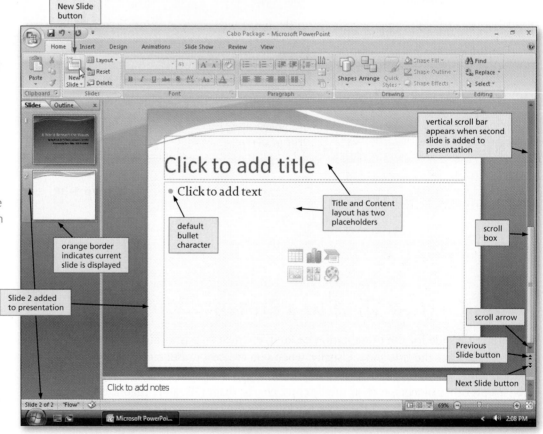

Figure 1–40

Other Ways

1. Press CTRL+M

**Plan
Ahead**

> **Choose the words for the slide.**
> All presentations should follow the 7 × 7 rule which states that each slide should have a maximum of seven lines, and each line should have a maximum of seven words. PowerPoint designers must choose their words carefully and, in turn, help viewers read the slides easily.

Creating a Text Slide with a Single-Level Bulleted List

The information in the Slide 2 text placeholder is presented in a bulleted list. All the bullets appear at the same paragraph level, called the first level.

To Enter a Slide Title

PowerPoint assumes every new slide has a title. The title for Slide 2 is Package Highlights. The following step enters this title.

- Click the label, Click to add title, to select it and then type `Package Highlights` in the placeholder. Do not press the ENTER key (Figure 1–41).

Q&A What are those six icons grouped in the middle of the slide?

You can click one of the icons to insert a specific type of content: table, chart, SmartArt graphic, picture, clip art, or media clip.

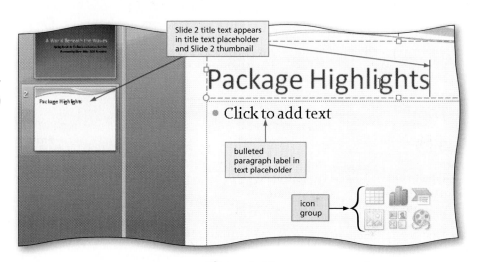

Figure 1–41

To Select a Text Placeholder

Before you can type text into the text placeholder, you first must select it. The following step selects the text placeholder on Slide 2.

- Click the label, Click to add text, to select the text placeholder (Figure 1–42).

Q&A Why does my mouse pointer have a different shape?

If you move the mouse pointer away from the bullet, it will change shape.

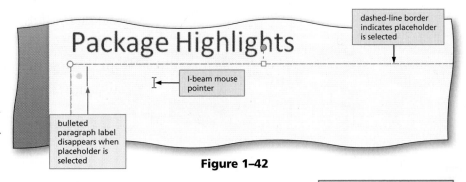

Figure 1–42

Other Ways
1. Press CTRL+ENTER

To Type a Single-Level Bulleted List

The content placeholder provides an area for the text characters. When you click inside a placeholder, you then can type or paste text. If your text exceeds the size of the placeholder, PowerPoint will attempt to make the text fit by reducing the text size and line spacing. **Line spacing** is the amount of vertical space between the lines of text.

As discussed previously, a bulleted list is a list of paragraphs, each of which is preceded by a bullet. A paragraph is a segment of text ended by pressing the ENTER key. The next step is to type the single-level bulleted list, which consists of five paragraphs (Figure 1–1b on page PPT 3). The following steps create a single-level bulleted list.

- **Type** Four nights at the Azure Seas Resort **and then press the** ENTER **key to begin a new bulleted first-level paragraph (Figure 1–43).**

Q&A Can I delete bullets on a slide?

Yes. If you do not want bullets to display on a particular paragraph, click the Bullets button in the Paragraph group on the Home tab or right-click the paragraph and then click the Bullets button on the Mini toolbar.

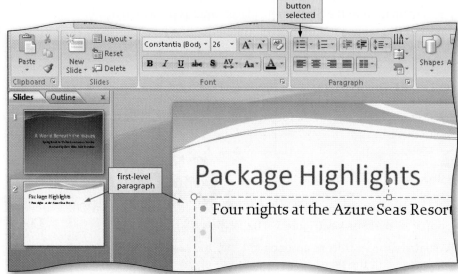

Figure 1–43

- **Type** Breakfast buffet, lunch, dinner, and snacks **and then press the** ENTER **key.**

- **Type** Two large swimming pools **and then press the** ENTER **key.**

- **Type** Round-trip airfare and hotel transfers **and then press the** ENTER **key.**

- **Type** Daily activities, including water sports **but do not press the** ENTER **key (Figure 1–44).**

Q&A I pressed the ENTER key in error, and now a new bullet appears after the last entry on this slide. How can I remove this extra bullet?

Press the BACKSPACE key.

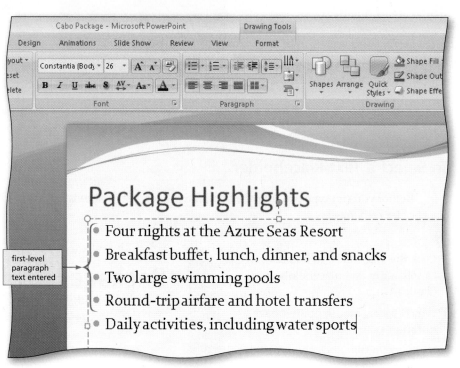

Figure 1–44

Creating a Text Slide with a Multi-Level Bulleted List

Slides 3 and 4 in Figure 1–1 on pages PPT 3–4 contain more than one level of bulleted text. A slide that consists of more than one level of bulleted text is called a **multi-level bulleted list slide**. Beginning with the second level, each paragraph indents to the right of the preceding level and is pushed down to a lower level. For example, if you increase the indent of a first-level paragraph, it becomes a second-level paragraph.

Creating a text slide with a multi-level bulleted list requires several steps. Initially, you enter a slide title in the title text placeholder. Next, you select the content text placeholder. Then, you type the text for the multi-level bulleted list, increasing and decreasing the indents as needed. The next several sections add a slide with a multi-level bulleted list.

To Add a New Slide and Enter a Slide Title

When you add a new slide to a presentation, PowerPoint keeps the same layout used on the previous slide. PowerPoint assumes every new slide has a title. The title for Slide 3 is Rates and Booking. The following steps add a new slide (Slide 3) and enter a title.

- Click the New Slide button in the Slides group on the Home tab to insert a new slide with the Title and Content layout (Figure 1–45).

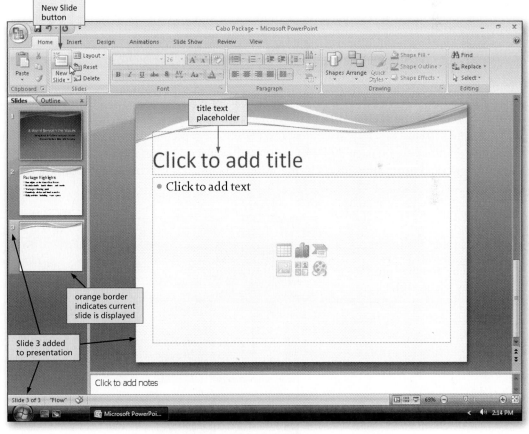

Figure 1–45

- Click the title text placeholder and then type Rates and Booking in this placeholder. Do not press the ENTER key (Figure 1–46).

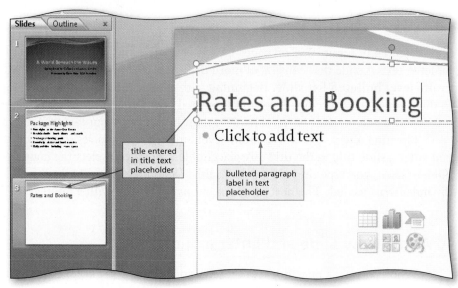

Figure 1–46

Other Ways
1. Press SHIFT+CTRL+M

To Type a Multi-Level Bulleted List

In a multi-level bulleted list, a lower-level paragraph is a subset of a higher-level paragraph. It usually contains information that supports the topic in the paragraph immediately above it.

The next step is to select the content text placeholder and then type the multi-level bulleted list, which consists of six entries (Figure 1–1c on page PPT 3). Creating a lower-level paragraph is called **demoting** text; creating a higher-level paragraph is called **promoting** text. The following steps create a list consisting of three levels.

- Click the bulleted paragraph text placeholder.

- Type Only $495 double occupancy and then press the ENTER key (Figure 1–47).

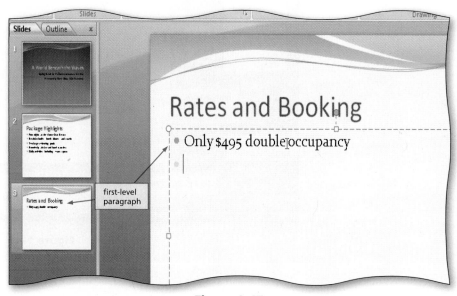

Figure 1–47

2

• Click the Increase List Level button in the Paragraph group to indent the second paragraph below the first and create a second-level paragraph (Figure 1–48).

Q&A Why does the bullet for this paragraph have a different size and color?

A different bullet is assigned to each paragraph level.

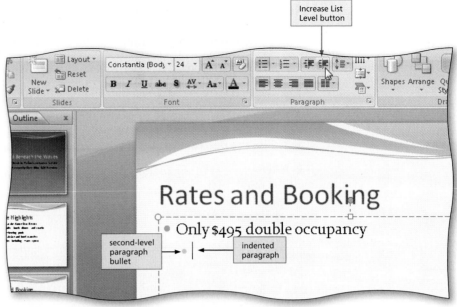

Figure 1–48

3

• Type Non-diver rate: $275 and then press the ENTER key to add a new paragraph at the same level as the previous paragraph.

• Type Single occupancy: add $150 and then press the ENTER key (Figure 1–49).

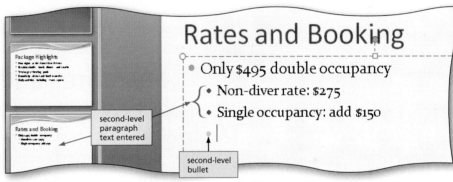

Figure 1–49

4

• Click the Decrease List Level button in the Paragraph group so that the second-level paragraph becomes a first-level paragraph (Figure 1–50).

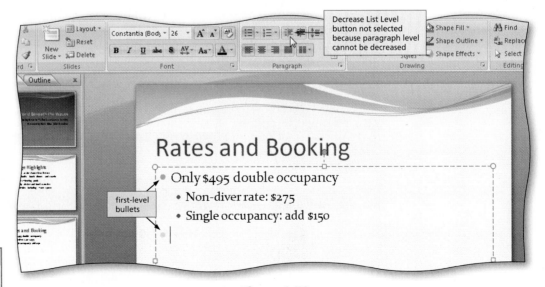

Figure 1–50

Other Ways

1. Press TAB to promote paragraph; press SHIFT+TAB to demote paragraph

To Type the Remaining Text for Slide 3

The following steps complete the text for Slide 3.

1 Type Nonrefundable $150 deposit required and then press the ENTER key.

2 Click the Increase List Level button in the Paragraph group to demote the paragraph.

3 Type Due by October 1 and then press the ENTER key.

4 Click the Decrease List Level button in the Paragraph group to promote the paragraph.

5 Type Travel insurance highly recommended but do not press the ENTER key (Figure 1–51).

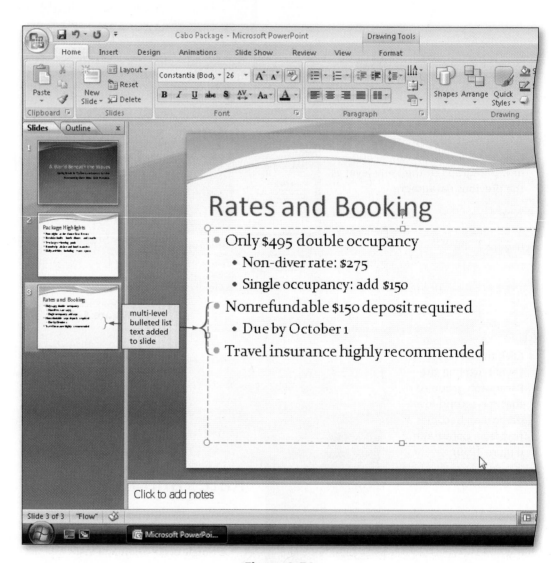

Figure 1–51

To Create Slide 4

Slide 4 is the final multi-level bulleted text slide in this presentation. It has three levels. The following steps create Slide 4.

1 Click the New Slide button in the Slides group.

2 Type `Snorkeling and Diving` in the title text placeholder.

3 Press CTRL+ENTER to move the insertion point to the text placeholder.

4 Type `Three days of two-tank boat dives` and then press the ENTER key.

5 Click the Increase List Level button. Type `Weights and tanks included` and then press the ENTER key (Figure 1–52).

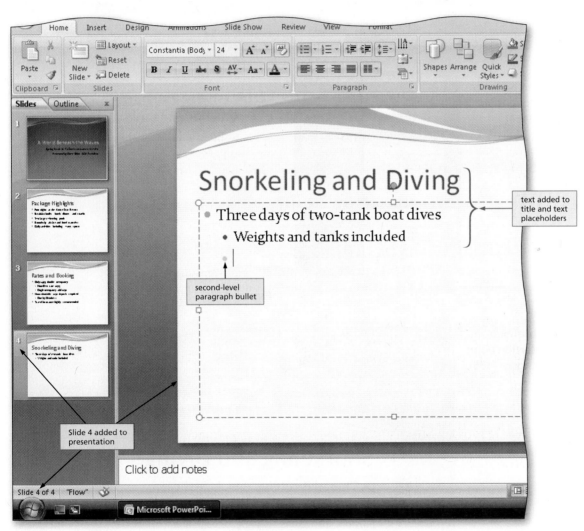

Figure 1–52

To Create a Third-Level Paragraph

Slide 4 contains detailed information about the particular dives. Each additional paragraph becomes more specific and supports the information in the paragraph above it.

The next line in Slide 4 is indented an additional level, to the third level. The following steps demote the text to a third-level paragraph.

1

- Click the Increase List Level button so that the second-level paragraph becomes a third-level paragraph (Figure 1–53).

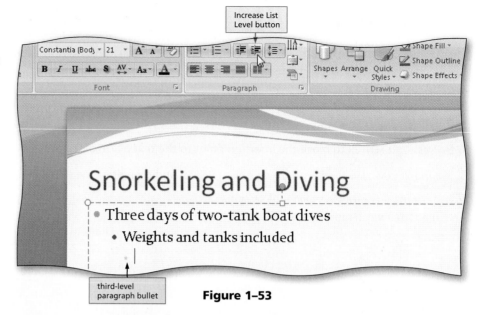

Figure 1–53

2

- Type Instructors available for beginners and then press the ENTER key to create a second third-level paragraph (Figure 1–54).

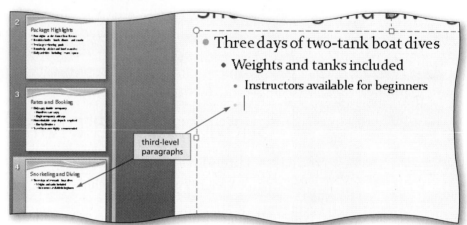

Figure 1–54

3

- Click the Decrease List Level button two times so that the insertion point appears at the first level (Figure 1–55).

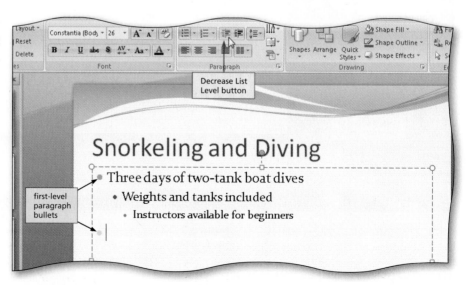

Figure 1–55

To Type the Remaining Text for Slide 4

The next three paragraphs concern what divers and snorkelers will view. The following steps type the remaining text for Slide 4.

1 Type `Various locations based on diving skills` and then press the ENTER key.

2 Press the TAB key to increase the indent to the second level.

3 Type `Spectacular underwater wildlife and landscapes` and then press the ENTER key.

4 Press the TAB key to increase the indent to the third level.

5 Type `See squids, sea turtles, snakes, barracudas, and stingrays` but do not press the ENTER key (Figure 1–56).

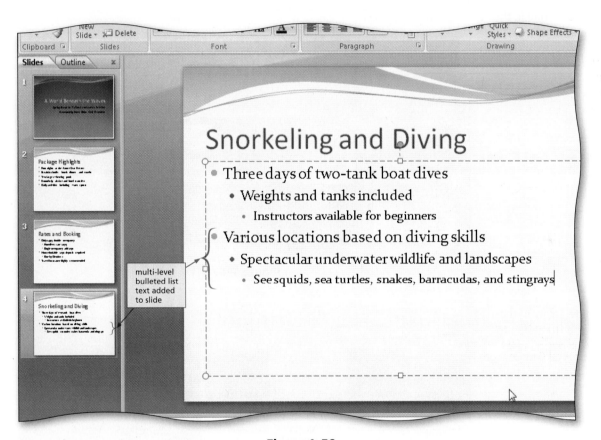

Figure 1–56

Choose the words for the slide.
After the last bulleted list slide in the slide show appears during a slide show, the default PowerPoint setting is to end the presentation with a **black slide**. This black slide appears only when the slide show is running and concludes the slide show, so your audience never sees the PowerPoint window. It is a good idea, however, to end the presentation with a final, closing slide to display at the end of the presentation. This slide ends the presentation gracefully and should be an exact copy, or a very similar copy, of your title slide. The audience will recognize that the presentation is drawing to a close when this slide appears. It can remain on the screen when the audience asks questions, approaches the speaker for further information, or exits the room.

Plan Ahead

Ending a Slide Show with a Closing Slide

All the text slides are created for the Cabo Package slide show. This presentation thus far consists of a title slide, one text slide with a single-level bulleted list, and two text slides with a multi-level bulleted list. A closing slide that resembles the title slide is the final slide to create.

To Duplicate a Slide

When two slides contain similar information and have the same format, duplicating one slide and then making minor modifications to the new slide saves time and increases consistency.

Slide 5 will have the same layout and design as Slide 1. The most expedient method of creating this slide is to copy Slide 1 and then make minor modifications to the new slide. The following steps duplicate the title slide.

1
- Click the Slide 1 thumbnail in the Slides tab to display Slide 1 (Figure 1–57).

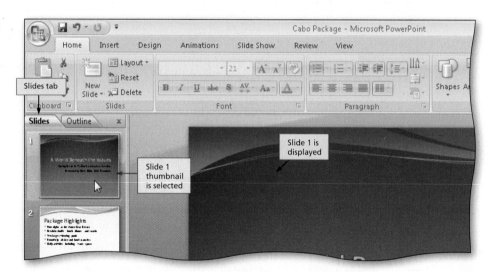

Figure 1–57

2
- Click the New Slide arrow in the Slides group on the Home tab to display the Flow layout gallery (Figure 1–58).

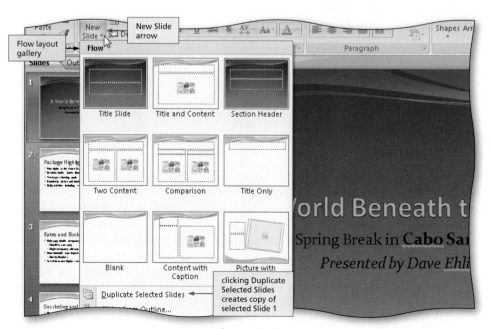

Figure 1–58

● Click Duplicate Selected Slides in the Flow layout gallery to create a new Slide 2, which is a duplicate of Slide 1 (Figure 1–59).

Figure 1–59

To Arrange a Slide

The new Slide 2 was inserted directly below Slide 1 because Slide 1 was the selected slide. This duplicate slide needs to display at the end of the presentation directly after the final title and content slide.

Changing slide order is an easy process and is best performed in the Tabs pane. When you click the slide thumbnail and begin to drag it to a new location, a line indicates the new location of the selected slide. When you release the mouse button, the slide drops into the desired location. Hence, this process of dragging and then dropping the thumbnail in a new location is called **drag and drop**. You can use the drag-and-drop method to move any selected item, including text and graphics. The following step moves the new Slide 2 to the end of the presentation so that it becomes a closing slide.

- With Slide 2 selected, drag the Slide 2 slide thumbnail in the Slides pane below the last slide thumbnail (Figure 1–60).

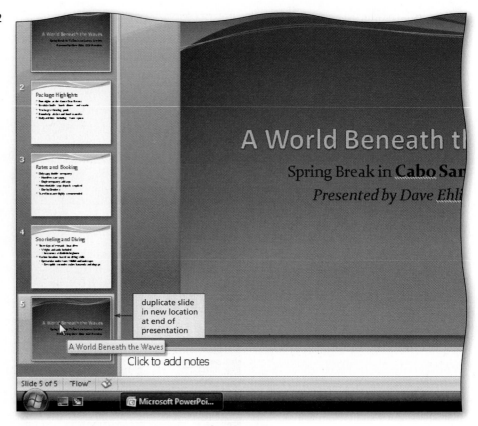

Figure 1–60

Other Ways

1. Click slide icon on Outline tab, drag icon to new location
2. In Slide Sorter view click slide thumbnail, drag thumbnail to new location

To Delete All Text in a Placeholder

To keep the ending slide clean and simple, you want only the slide show title, A World Beneath the Waves, to display on Slide 5. The following steps delete both paragraphs in the subtitle placeholder.

- With Slide 5 selected, click the subtitle text placeholder to select it (Figure 1–61).

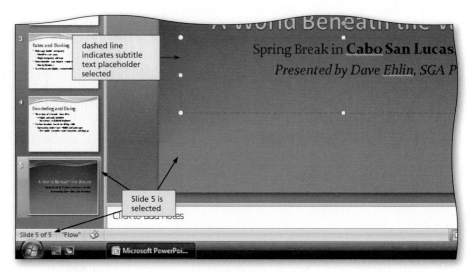

Figure 1–61

2

- Click the subtitle text placeholder border to change the border from a dashed line to a solid line (Figure 1–62).

Figure 1–62

3

- Click the Cut button in the Clipboard group on the Home tab to delete all the text in the subtitle text placeholder (Figure 1–63).

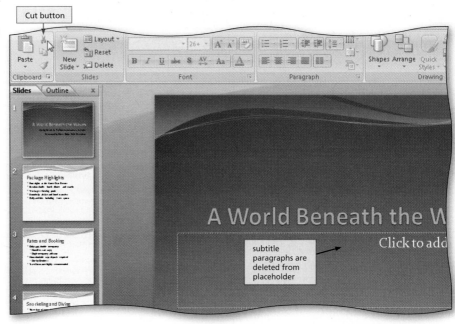

Figure 1–63

Other Ways

1. Right-click selected text, click Cut on shortcut menu
2. Select text, press DELETE key
3. Select text, press CTRL+X

Changing Document Properties and Saving Again

PowerPoint helps you organize and identify your files by using document properties, which are the details about a file. **Document properties**, also known as **metadata**, can include such information as the project author, title, or subject. **Keywords** are words or phrases that further describe the document. For example, a class name or document topic can describe the file's purpose or content.

Document properties are valuable for a variety of reasons:

- Users can save time locating a particular file because they can view a document's properties without opening the document.
- By creating consistent properties for files having similar content, users can better organize their documents.
- Some organizations require PowerPoint users to add document properties so that other employees can view details about these files.

Five different types of document properties exist, but the more common ones used in this book are standard and automatically updated properties. **Standard properties**

BTW

Converters for Earlier PowerPoint Versions
The Microsoft Web site has updates and converters if you are using earlier versions of PowerPoint. The Microsoft Office Compatibility Pack for Word, Excel and PowerPoint 2007 File Format will allow you to open, edit, and save Office 2007 documents that you receive without saving them in the earlier version's file format.

are associated with all Microsoft Office documents and include author, title, and subject. **Automatically updated properties** include file system properties, such as the date you create or change a file, and statistics, such as the file size.

To Change Document Properties

The **Document Information Panel** contains areas where you can view and enter document properties. You can view and change information in this panel at any time while you are creating a document. Before saving the presentation again, you want to add your name and class name as document properties. The following steps use the Document Information Panel to change document properties.

1

- Click the Office Button to display the Office Button menu.

- Point to Prepare on the Office Button menu to display the Prepare submenu (Figure 1–64).

Q&A What other types of actions besides changing properties can you take to set up a document for distribution?

The Prepare submenu provides commands related to sharing a document with others, such as allowing or restricting people to view and modify your document, checking to see if your presentation will run in earlier versions of PowerPoint, and searching for hidden personal information.

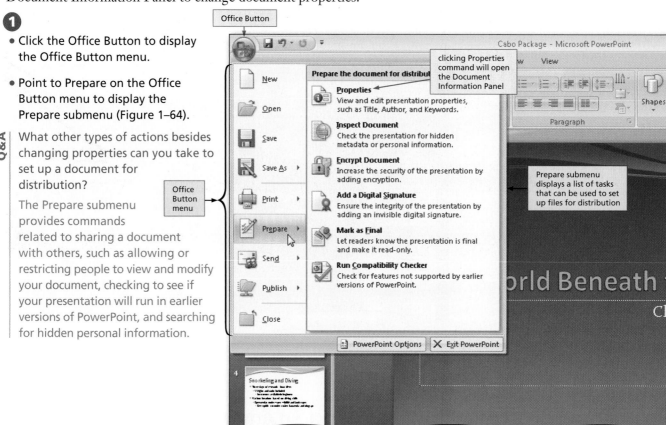

Figure 1–64

2

- Click Properties on the Prepare submenu to display the Document Information Panel (Figure 1–65).

Q&A Why are some of the document properties in my Document Information Panel already filled in?

The person who installed Microsoft Office 2007 on your computer or network may have set or customized the properties.

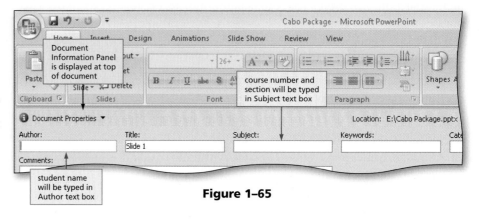

Figure 1–65

3

- Click the Author text box, if necessary, and then type your name as the Author property. If a name already is displayed in the Author text box, delete it before typing your name.

- Click the Subject text box, if necessary delete any existing text, and then type your course number and section as the Subject property (Figure 1–66).

Q&A

What types of document properties does PowerPoint collect automatically?

PowerPoint records such details as how long you worked at creating your project, how many times you revised the document, and what fonts and themes are used.

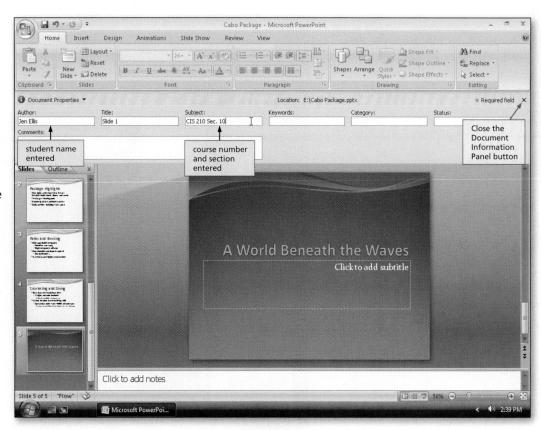

Figure 1–66

4

- Click the Close the Document Information Panel button so that the Document Information Panel no longer is displayed.

To Save an Existing Presentation with the Same File Name

Saving frequently cannot be overemphasized. You have made several modifications to the presentation since you saved it earlier in the chapter. When you first saved the document, you clicked the Save button on the Quick Access Toolbar, the Save As dialog box appeared, and you entered the file name, Cabo Package. If you want to use the same file name to save the changes made to the document, you again click the Save button on the Quick Access Toolbar. The following step saves the presentation again.

1

- Click the Save button on the Quick Access Toolbar to overwrite the previous Cabo Package file on the USB flash drive (Figure 1–67).

Q&A

Why did the Save As dialog box not appear?

PowerPoint overwrites the document using the settings specified the first time you saved the document. To save the file with a different file name or on different media, display the Save As dialog box by clicking the Office Button and then clicking Save As on the Office Button menu. Then, fill in the Save As dialog box as described in Steps 2 through 5 on pages PPT 27 through PPT 29.

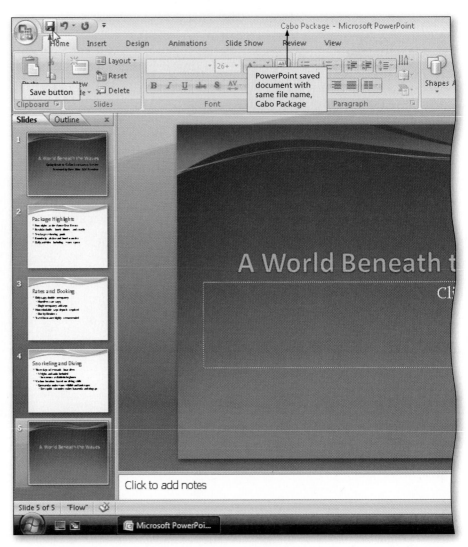

Figure 1–67

Other Ways

1. Press CTRL+S or press SHIFT+F12, press ENTER

Moving to Another Slide in Normal View

When creating or editing a presentation in Normal view, you often want to display a slide other than the current one. You can move to another slide using several methods.

- Drag the scroll box on the vertical scroll bar up or down to move through the slides in the presentation.
- Click the Next Slide or Previous Slide button on the vertical scroll bar. Clicking the Next Slide button advances to the next slide in the presentation. Clicking the Previous Slide button backs up to the slide preceding the current slide.
- On the Slides tab, click a particular slide to display that slide in the Slide pane.

To Use the Scroll Box on the Slide Pane to Move to Another Slide

Before continuing with developing this project, you want to display the title slide by dragging the scroll box on the vertical scroll bar. When you drag the scroll box, the **slide indicator** shows the number and title of the slide you are about to display. Releasing the mouse button shows the slide. The following steps move from Slide 5 to Slide 1 using the scroll box on the Slide pane.

1

- Position the mouse pointer on the scroll box.

- Press and hold down the mouse button so that Slide: 5 of 5 A World Beneath the Waves appears in the slide indicator (Figure 1–68).

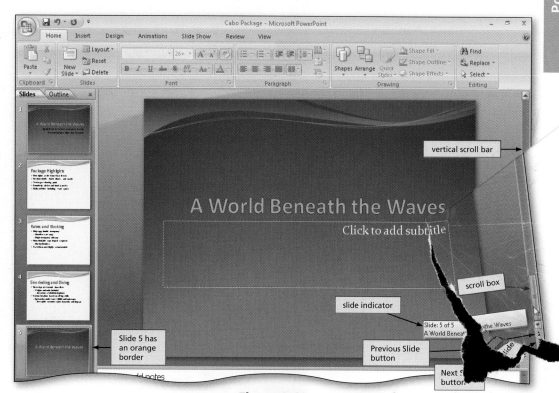

Figure 1–68

2

- Drag the scroll box up the vertical scroll bar until Slide: 1 of 5 A World Beneath the Waves appears in the slide indicator (Figure 1–69).

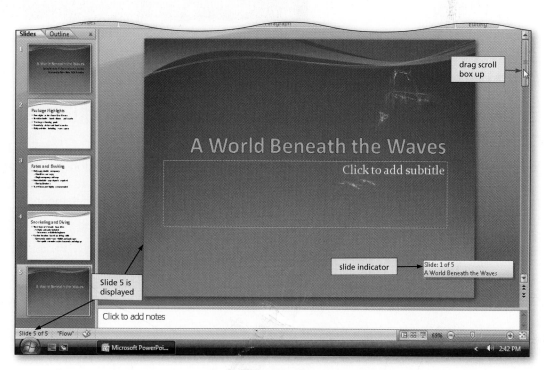

Figure 1–69

3

- Release the mouse button so that Slide 1 appears in the Slide pane and the Slide 1 thumbnail has an orange border in the Slides tab (Figure 1–70).

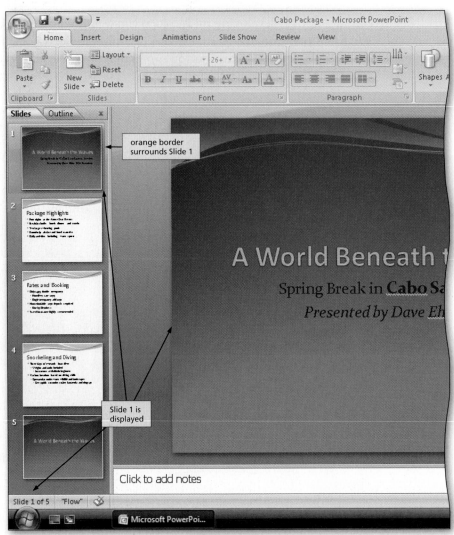

Figure 1–70

Viewing the Presentation in Slide Show View

The Slide Show button, located in the lower-right corner of the PowerPoint window above the status bar, allows you to show a presentation using a computer. The computer acts like a slide projector, displaying each slide on a full screen. The full-screen slide hides the toolbars, menus, and other PowerPoint window elements.

To Start Slide Show View

When making a presentation, you use **Slide Show view**. You can start Slide Show view from Normal view or Slide Sorter view. Slide Show view begins when you click the Slide Show button in the lower-right corner of the PowerPoint window on the status bar. PowerPoint then shows the current slide on the full screen without any of the PowerPoint window objects, such as the menu bar or toolbars. The following steps start Slide Show view.

1
- Point to the Slide Show button in the lower-right corner of the PowerPoint window on the status bar (Figure 1–71).

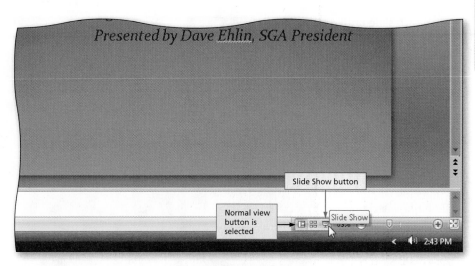

Figure 1–71

2
- Click the Slide Show button to display the title slide (Figure 1–72).

Q&A Where is the PowerPoint window?

When you run a slide show, the PowerPoint window is hidden. It will reappear once you end your slide show.

Figure 1–72

Other Ways

1. Click Slide Show tab, click From Beginning button in Start Slide Show group
2. Press F5

To Move Manually through Slides in a Slide Show

After you begin Slide Show view, you can move forward or backward through the slides. PowerPoint allows you to advance through the slides manually or automatically. During a slide show, each slide in the presentation shows on the screen, one slide at a time. Each time you click the mouse button, the next slide appears. The following steps move manually through the slides.

1

- Click each slide until Slide 5 (A World Beneath the Waves) is displayed (Figure 1–73).

I see a small toolbar in the lower-left corner of my slide. What is this toolbar?

The Slide Show toolbar appears when you begin running a slide show and then move the mouse pointer. The buttons on this toolbar allow you to navigate to the next slide, the previous slide, to mark up the current slide, or to change the current display.

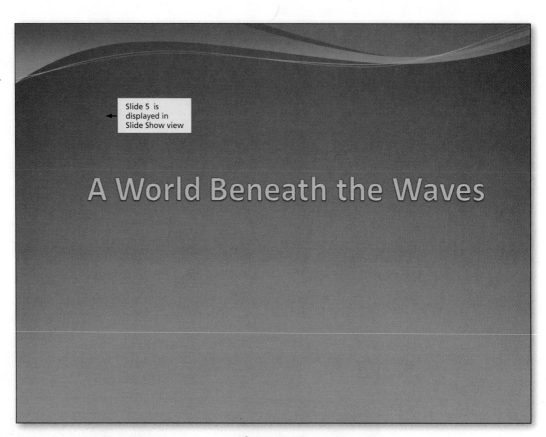

Slide 5 is displayed in Slide Show view

A World Beneath the Waves

Figure 1–73

2

- Click Slide 5 so that the black slide appears with a message announcing the end of the slide show (Figure 1–74).

How can I end the presentation at this point?

Click the black slide to return to Normal view in the PowerPoint window or press the ESC key.

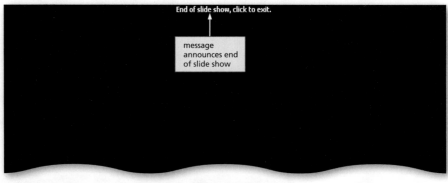

End of slide show, click to exit.

message announces end of slide show

Figure 1–74

Other Ways

1. Press PAGE DOWN to advance one slide at a time, or press PAGE UP to go back one slide at a time

2. Press RIGHT ARROW or DOWN ARROW to advance one slide at a time, or press LEFT ARROW or UP ARROW to go back one slide at a time

3. If Slide Show toolbar is displayed, click Next Slide or Previous Slide button on toolbar

To Display the Pop-Up Menu and Go to a Specific Slide

Slide Show view has a shortcut menu, called a **pop-up menu**, that appears when you right-click a slide in Slide Show view. This menu contains commands to assist you during a slide show.

When the pop-up menu appears, clicking the Next command moves to the next slide. Clicking the Previous command moves to the previous slide. Pointing to the Go to Slide command and then clicking the desired slide allows you to move to any slide in the presentation. The Go to Slide submenu contains a list of the slides in the presentation. You can go to the requested slide by clicking the name of that slide. Additional pop-up menu commands allow you to change the mouse pointer to a ballpoint or felt tip pen or highlighter that draws in various colors, make the screen black or white, create speaker notes, and end the slide show. The following steps go to the title slide (Slide 1) in the Cabo Package presentation.

- With the black slide displaying in Slide Show view, right-click the slide to display the pop-up menu.

- Point to Go to Slide on the pop-up menu, and then point to 2 Package Highlights in the Go to Slide submenu (Figure 1–75).

Q&A

Why does my pop-up menu appear in a different location on my screen?

The pop-up menu appears near the location of the mouse pointer at the time you right-click.

- Click 2 Package Highlights to display Slide 2.

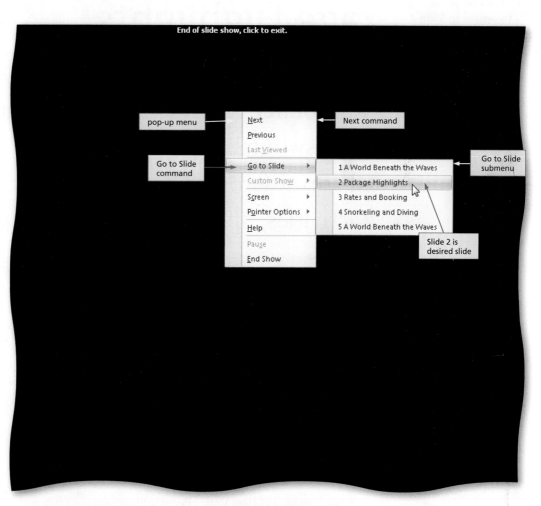

Figure 1–75

To Use the Pop-Up Menu to End a Slide Show

The End Show command on the pop-up menu ends Slide Show view and returns to the same view as when you clicked the Slide Show button. The following steps end Slide Show view and return to Normal view.

- Right-click Slide 2 and then point to End Show on the pop-up menu (Figure 1–76).

- Click End Show to return to Slide 2 in the Slide pane in Normal view.

- If the Microsoft Office PowerPoint dialog box appears, click the Yes button.

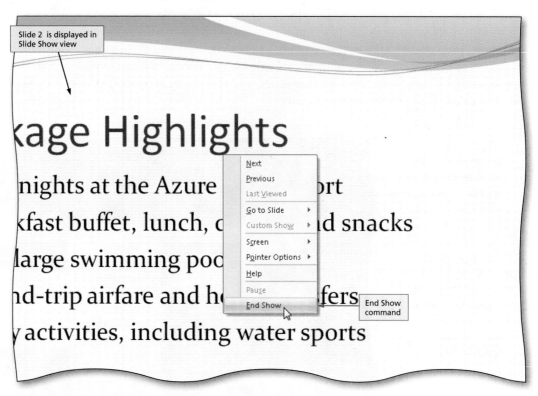

Figure 1–76

Other Ways

1. Press ESC (shows slide last viewed in Slide Show view)

Quitting PowerPoint

When you quit PowerPoint, if you have made changes to a presentation since the last time the file was saved, PowerPoint displays a dialog box asking if you want to save the changes you made to the file before it closes that window. The dialog box contains three buttons with these resulting actions:

- Yes button — Saves the changes and then quits PowerPoint
- No button — Quits PowerPoint without saving changes
- Cancel button — Closes the dialog box and redisplays the presentation without saving the changes

If no changes have been made to an open presentation since the last time the file was saved, PowerPoint will close the window without displaying a dialog box.

To Quit PowerPoint with One Document Open

You saved the presentation prior to running the slide show and did not make any changes to the project. The presentation now is complete, and you are ready to quit PowerPoint. When you have one document open, the following steps quit PowerPoint.

1

Point to the Close button on the right side of the PowerPoint title bar (Figure 1–77).

2

• Click the Close button to quit PowerPoint.

Q&A

What if I have more than one PowerPoint document open?

You would click the Close button for each open document. When you click the last open document's Close button, PowerPoint also quits. As an alternative, you could click the Office Button and then click the Exit PowerPoint button on the Office Button menu, which closes all open PowerPoint documents and then quits PowerPoint.

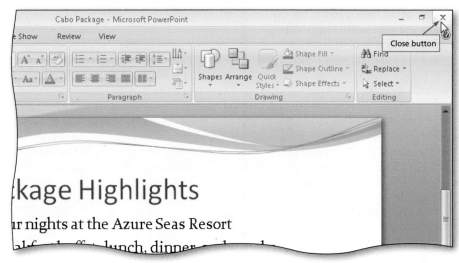

Figure 1–77

Other Ways

1. With one document open, double-click Office Button
2. Click Office Button, click Exit PowerPoint on Office Button menu
3. With one document open, right-click Microsoft

PowerPoint button on Windows Vista taskbar, click Close on shortcut menu
4. With one document open, press ALT+F4

Starting PowerPoint and Opening a Presentation

Once you have created and saved a presentation, you may need to retrieve it from your storage medium. For example, you might want to revise the document or print it. Opening a presentation requires that PowerPoint is running on your computer.

To Start PowerPoint

The following steps, which assume Windows Vista is running, start PowerPoint.

Note: If you are using Windows XP, see Appendix F for alternate steps.

1 Click the Start button on the Windows Vista taskbar to display the Start menu.

2 Click All Programs at the bottom of the left pane on the Start menu to display the All Programs list and then click Microsoft Office in the All Programs list to display the Microsoft Office list.

3 Click Microsoft Office PowerPoint 2007 on the Microsoft Office list to start PowerPoint and display a new blank presentation in the PowerPoint window.

4 If the PowerPoint window is not maximized, click the Maximize button on its title bar to maximize the window.

To Open a Presentation from PowerPoint

Earlier in this chapter you saved your project on a USB flash drive using the file name, Cabo Package. The following steps open the Cabo Package file from the USB flash drive.

1

- With your USB flash drive connected to one of the computer's USB ports, click the Office Button to display the Office Button menu (Figure 1–78).

Q&A

What files are shown in the Recent Documents list?

PowerPoint displays the most recently opened document file names in this list. If the name of the file you want to open appears in the Recent Documents list, you could click it to open the file.

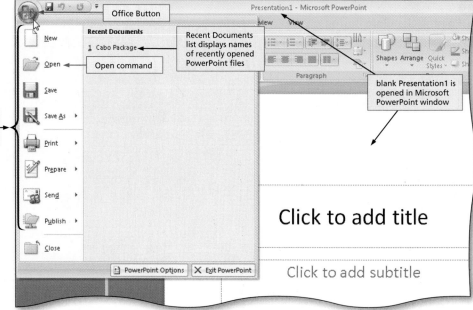

Figure 1–78

2

- Click Open on the Office Button menu to display the Open dialog box.

- If the Folders list is displayed below the Folders button, click the Folders button to remove the Folders list.

- If necessary, click Computer in the Favorite Links section and then scroll until UDISK 2.0 (E:) appears in the list of available drives.

- Double-click UDISK 2.0 (E:) to select the USB flash drive, Drive E in this case, as the new open location.

- Click Cabo Package to select the file name (Figure 1–79).

Q&A

How do I open the file if I am not using a USB flash drive?

Use the same process, but be certain to select your device in the Computer list.

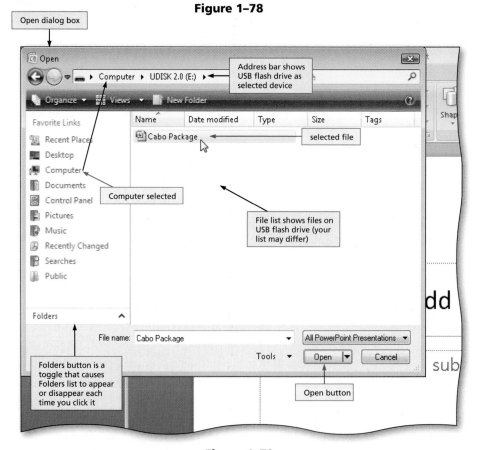

Figure 1–79

3

• Click the Open button to open the selected file and display Slide 1 in the PowerPoint window (Figure 1–80).

Q&A

Why are the PowerPoint icon and name on the Windows Vista taskbar?

When you open a PowerPoint file, a PowerPoint program button is displayed on the taskbar. The button contains an ellipsis because some of its contents do not fit in the allotted button space. If you point to a program button, its entire contents appear in a ScreenTip, which in this case would be the program name followed by the file name.

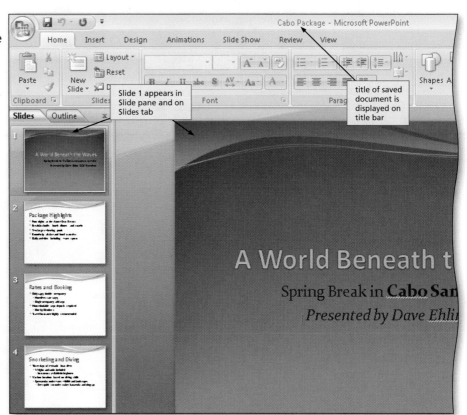

Figure 1–80

Other Ways

1. Click Office Button, double-click file name in Recent Documents list
2. Press CTRL+O, select file name, press ENTER

Checking a Presentation for Spelling Errors

After you create a presentation, you should check it visually for spelling errors and style consistency. In addition, you use PowerPoint's Spelling tool to identify possible misspellings. Do not rely on the spelling checker to catch all your mistakes. While PowerPoint's spelling checker is a valuable tool, it is not infallible. You should proofread your presentation carefully by pointing to each word and saying it aloud as you point to it. Be mindful of commonly misused words such as its and it's, through and though, and to and too.

PowerPoint checks the entire presentation for spelling mistakes using a standard dictionary contained in the Microsoft Office group. This dictionary is shared with the other Microsoft Office applications such as Word and Excel. A **custom dictionary** is available if you want to add special words such as proper names, cities, and acronyms. When checking a presentation for spelling errors, PowerPoint opens the standard dictionary and the custom dictionary file, if one exists. When a word appears in the Spelling dialog box, you can perform one of several actions.

Table 1–1 Spelling Dialog Box Buttons and Actions		
Button Name	**When To Use**	**Action**
Ignore	Word is spelled correctly but not found in dictionaries	Continues checking rest of the presentation but will flag that word again if it appears later in document
Ignore All	Word is spelled correctly but not found in dictionaries	Ignores all occurrences of the word and continues checking rest of presentation
Change	Word is misspelled	Click proper spelling of the word in Suggestions list. PowerPoint corrects word, continues checking rest of presentation, but will flag that word again if it appears later in document.
Change All	Word is misspelled	Click proper spelling of word in Suggestions list. PowerPoint changes all occurrences of misspelled word and continues checking rest of presentation.
Add	Add word to custom dictionary	PowerPoint opens custom dictionary, adds word, and continues checking rest of presentation.
Suggest	Correct spelling is uncertain	Lists alternative spellings. Click the correct word from the Suggestions box or type the proper spelling. Corrects the word and continues checking the rest of the presentation.
AutoCorrect	Add spelling error to AutoCorrect list	PowerPoint adds spelling error and its correction to AutoCorrect list. Any future misspelling of word is corrected automatically as you type.
Close	Stop spelling checker	PowerPoint closes spelling checker and returns to PowerPoint window.

To Check Spelling

The standard dictionary contains commonly used English words. It does not, however, contain many proper names, abbreviations, technical terms, poetic contractions, or antiquated terms. PowerPoint treats words not found in the dictionaries as misspellings. The following steps check the spelling on all slides in the Cabo Package presentation.

- Click Review on the Ribbon to display the Review tab (Figure 1–81).

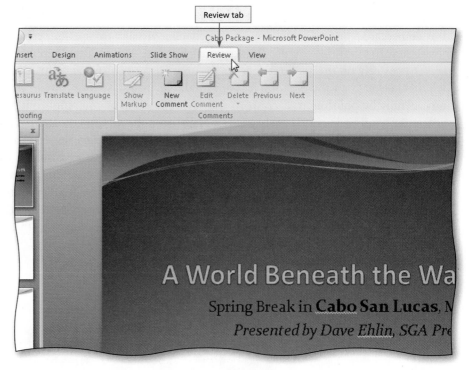

Figure 1–81

2

- Click the Spelling button in the Proofing group to start the spelling checker and display the Spelling dialog box (Figure 1–82).

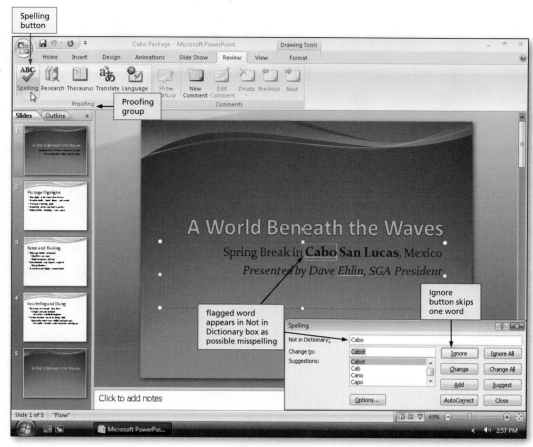

Figure 1–82

3

- Click the Ignore button to skip the word, Cabo (Figure 1–83).

Q&A

Cabo is not flagged as a possible misspelled word. Why not?

Your custom dictionary contains the word, so it is recognized as a correct word.

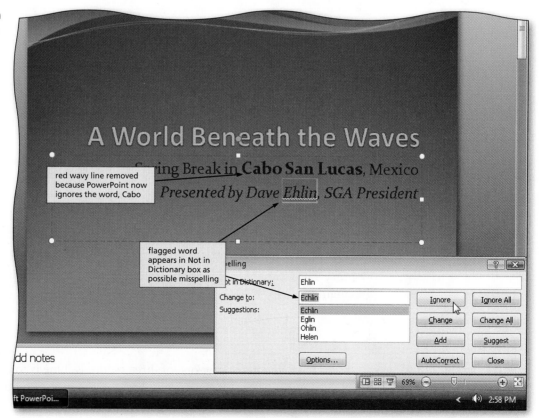

Figure 1–83

4
- Click the Ignore button to skip the word, Ehlin.

- When the Microsoft Office PowerPoint dialog box appears, click the OK button to close the spelling checker and return to the current slide, Slide 1, or to the slide where a possible misspelled word appeared.

- Click the slide to remove the box from the word, Ehlin (Figure 1–84).

Figure 1–84

Correcting Errors

After creating a presentation and running the spelling checker, you may find that you must make changes. Changes may be required because a slide contains an error, the scope of the presentation shifts, or the style is inconsistent. This section explains the types of errors that commonly occur when creating a presentation.

Types of Corrections Made to Presentations

You generally make three types of corrections to text in a presentation: additions, deletions, and replacements.

- Additions are necessary when you omit text from a slide and need to add it later. You may need to insert text in the form of a sentence, word, or single character. For example, you may want to add the presenter's middle name on the title slide.
- Deletions are required when text on a slide is incorrect or no longer is relevant to the presentation. For example, a slide may look cluttered. Therefore, you may want to remove one of the bulleted paragraphs to add more space.
- Replacements are needed when you want to revise the text in a presentation. For example, you may want to substitute the word, their, for the word, there.

Editing text in PowerPoint basically is the same as editing text in a word processing program. The following sections illustrate the most common changes made to text in a presentation.

Deleting Text

You can delete text using one of three methods. One is to use the BACKSPACE key to remove text just typed. The second is to position the insertion point to the left of the text you wish to delete and then press the DELETE key. The third method is to drag through the text you wish to delete and then press the DELETE key. Use the third method when deleting large sections of text.

Replacing Text in an Existing Slide

When you need to correct a word or phrase, you can replace the text by selecting the text to be replaced and then typing the new text. As soon as you press any key on the keyboard, the selected text is deleted and the new text is displayed.

PowerPoint inserts text to the left of the insertion point. The text to the right of the insertion point moves to the right (and shifts downward if necessary) to accommodate the added text.

Displaying a Presentation in Grayscale

Printing handouts of a presentation allows you to use them to make overhead transparencies. The Color/Grayscale button on the Color/Grayscale group on the View tab shows the presentation in black and white before you print. Pure Black and White alters the slides' appearance so that black lines display on a white background. Shadows and other graphical effects are hidden. Grayscale shows varying degrees of gray.

To Display a Presentation in Grayscale

The Color/Grayscale button on the Color/Grayscale group on the View tab changes from color bars to shades of black, called grayscale, and white. After you view the text objects in the presentation in grayscale, you can make any changes that will enhance printouts produced from a black and white printer or photocopier. The following steps display the presentation in grayscale.

1

• Click View on the Ribbon to display the View tab (Figure 1–85).

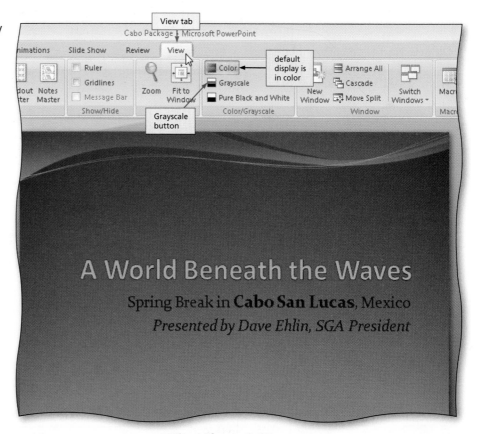

Figure 1–85

2

- Click Grayscale in the Color/Grayscale group to display Slide 1 in grayscale in the Slide pane (Figure 1–86).

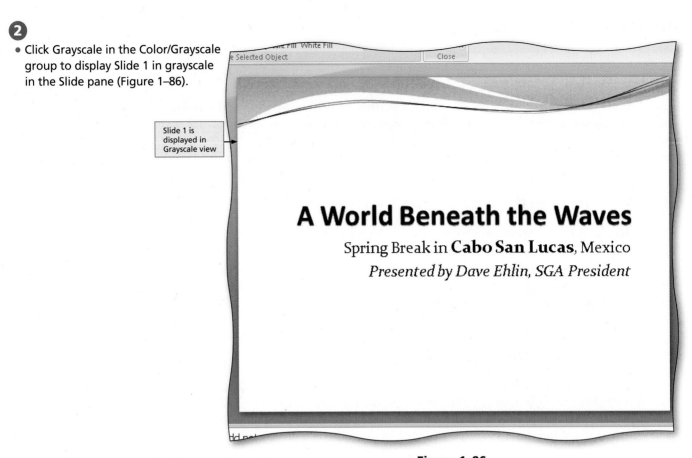

Slide 1 is displayed in Grayscale view

Figure 1–86

3

- Click the Next Slide button four times to view all slides in the presentation in grayscale (Figure 1–87).

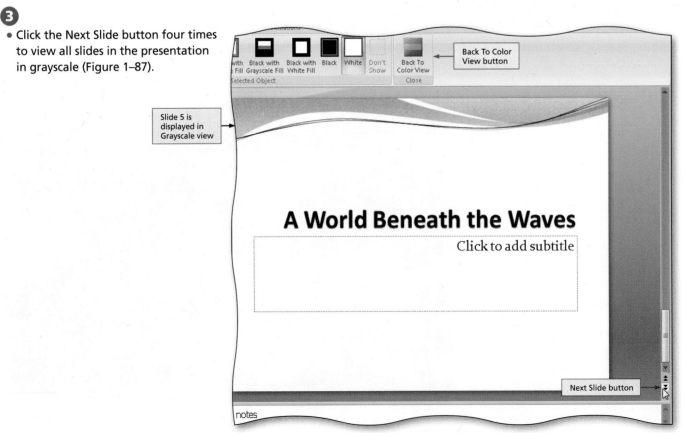

Back To Color View button

Slide 5 is displayed in Grayscale view

Next Slide button

Figure 1–87

4

- Click the Back To Color View button in the Close group to return to the previous tab and display Slide 5 with the default Flow color scheme (Figure 1–88).

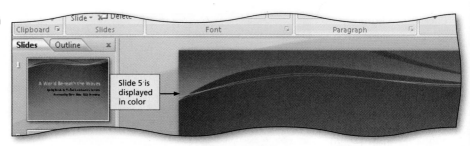

Figure 1–88

Printing a Presentation

After you create a presentation, you often want to print it. A printed version of the presentation is called a **hard copy** or **printout**.

Printed copies of your presentation can be useful for the following reasons:

- Many people prefer proofreading a hard copy of the presentation rather than viewing the slides on the screen to check for errors and readability.

- Someone without computer access or who could not attend your live presentation can view the slides' content.

- Copies can be distributed as handouts to people viewing your presentation.

- Hard copies can serve as reference material if your storage medium is lost or becomes corrupted and you need to re-create the presentation.

It is a good practice to save a presentation before printing it, in the event you experience difficulties with the printer.

To Print a Presentation

With the completed presentation saved, you may want to print it. The following steps print all five completed presentation slides in the saved Cabo Package project.

1

- Click the Office Button to display the Office Button menu.

- Point to Print on the Office Button menu to display the Print submenu (Figure 1–89).

Can I print my presentation in black and white to conserve ink or toner?

Yes. Click the Office Button, point to the arrow next to Print on the Office Button menu, and then click Print Preview on the Print submenu. Click the Options button on the Print Preview tab, point to Color/Grayscale on the Options button menu, and then click Pure Black and White on the Color/Grayscale submenu. Click the Print button on the Print submenu.

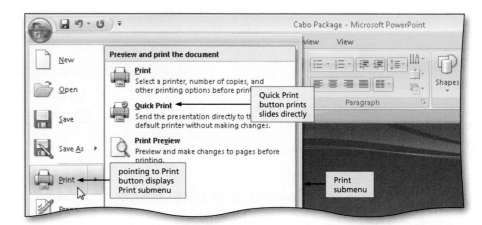

Figure 1–89

2

- Click Quick Print on the Print submenu to print the slides.
- When the printer stops, retrieve the hard copy of the five Cabo Package slides (Figures 1–90a through 1–90e).

(a) Slide 1

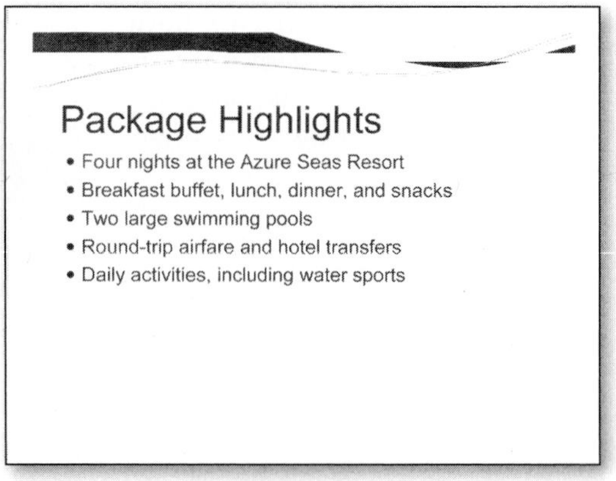

(b) Slide 2

(c) Slide 3

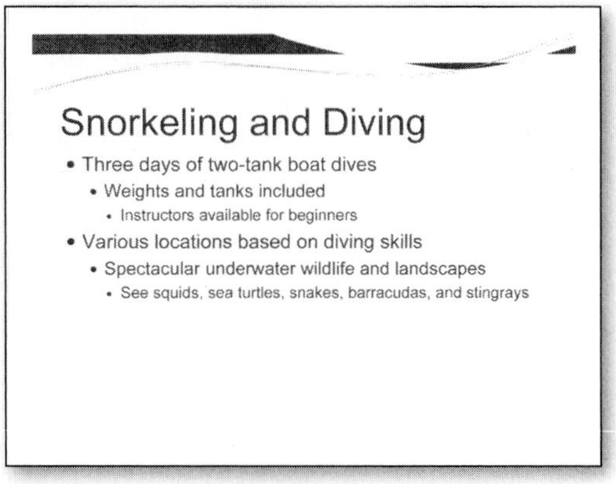

(d) Slide 4

(e) Slide 5

Figure 1–90

Q&A How can I print multiple copies of my document other than clicking the Print button twice?

Click the Office Button, point to Print on the Office Button menu, click Print on the Print submenu, increase the number in the Number of copies box, and then click the OK button.

Q&A Do I have to wait until my presentation is complete to print it?

No, you can follow these steps to print your slides at any time while you are creating your presentation.

Other Ways

1. Press CTRL+P

BTW **Quick Reference**

For a table that lists how to complete the tasks covered in this book using the mouse, Ribbon, shortcut menu, and keyboard, see the Quick Reference Summary at the back of this book, or visit the PowerPoint 2007 Quick Reference Web page (scsite.com/ppt2007/qr).

Making a Transparency

With the handouts printed, you now can make overhead transparencies using one of several devices. One device is a printer attached to your computer, such as an inkjet printer or a laser printer. Transparencies produced on a printer may be in black and white or color, depending on the printer. Another device is a photocopier. Because each of these devices requires a special transparency film, check the user's manual for the film requirement of your specific device, or ask your instructor.

PowerPoint Help

At any time while using PowerPoint, you can find answers to questions and display information about various topics through **PowerPoint Help**. Used properly, this form of assistance can increase your productivity and reduce your frustrations by minimizing the time you spend learning how to use PowerPoint.

This section introduces you to PowerPoint Help. Additional information about using PowerPoint Help is available in Appendix C.

BTW

PowerPoint Help
The best way to become familiar with PowerPoint Help is to use it. Appendix C includes detailed information about PowerPoint Help and exercises that will help you gain confidence in using it.

To Search for PowerPoint Help

Using PowerPoint Help, you can search for information based on phrases such as save a presentation or format a chart, or key terms such as copy, save, or format. PowerPoint Help responds with a list of search results displayed as links to a variety of resources. The following steps, which use PowerPoint Help to search for information about using document themes, assume you are connected to the Internet.

1

• Click the Microsoft Office PowerPoint Help button near the upper-right corner of the PowerPoint window to open the PowerPoint Help window.

• Type document theme in the Type words to search for text box at the top of the PowerPoint Help window (Figure 1–91).

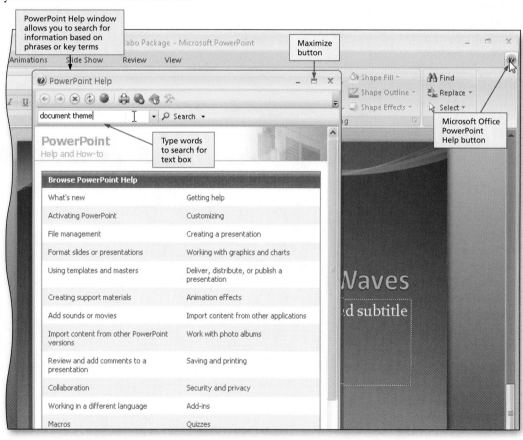

Figure 1–91

2

- Press the ENTER key to display the search results.

- Click the Maximize button on the PowerPoint Help window title bar to maximize the Help window (Figure 1–92).

Q&A Where is the PowerPoint window with Slide 1?

PowerPoint is open in the background, but the PowerPoint Help window is overlaid on top of the Microsoft PowerPoint window. When the PowerPoint Help window is closed, the slide will reappear.

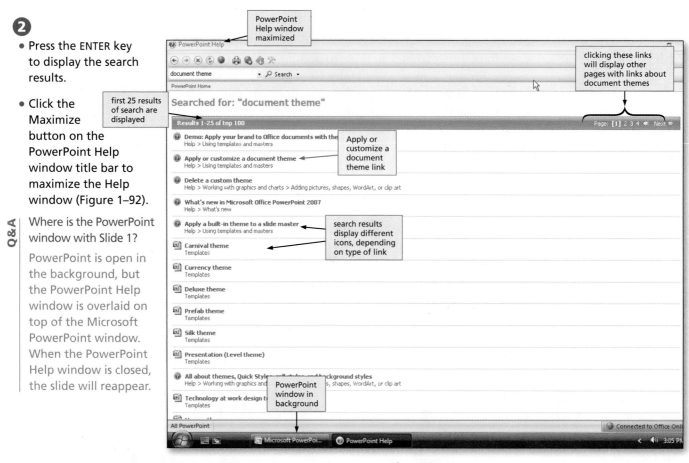

Figure 1–92

3

- Click the 'Apply or customize a document theme' link to display information regarding applying or customizing themes (Figure 1–93).

Q&A What is the purpose of the buttons at the top of the Power-Point Help window?

Use the buttons in the upper-left corner of the PowerPoint Help window to navigate through the Help system, change the display, show the PowerPoint Help table of contents, and print the contents of the window.

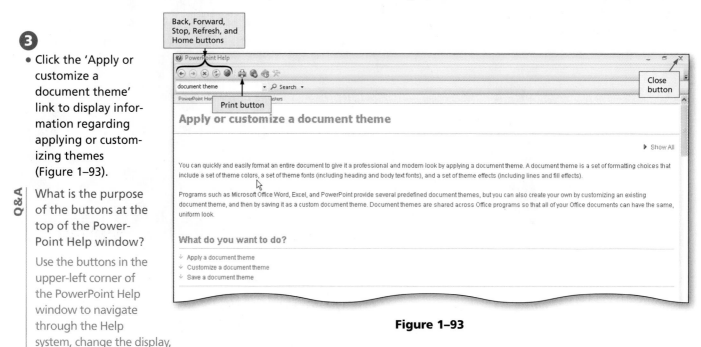

Figure 1–93

4

- Click the Close button on the PowerPoint Help window title bar to close the PowerPoint Help window and display Slide 5.

Other Ways

1. Press F1

To Quit PowerPoint

The following steps quit PowerPoint.

1 Click the Close button on the right side of the title bar to quit PowerPoint; or, if you have multiple PowerPoint documents open, click the Office Button and then click the Exit PowerPoint button on the Office Button menu to close all open documents and quit PowerPoint.

2 If necessary, click the No button in the Microsoft Office PowerPoint dialog box so that any changes you have made are not saved.

Chapter Summary

In this chapter you have learned how to apply a document theme, create a title slide and text slides with bulleted lists, format text, view the presentation in Slide Show view, and print slides as handouts. The items listed below include all the new PowerPoint skills you have learned in this chapter.

1. Start PowerPoint (PPT 5)
2. Choose a Document Theme (PPT 16)
3. Enter the Presentation Title (PPT 18)
4. Enter the Presentation Subtitle Paragraph (PPT 20)
5. Select a Paragraph (PPT 21)
6. Italicize Text (PPT 22)
7. Select Multiple Paragraphs (PPT 22)
8. Change the Text Color (PPT 23)
9. Select a Group of Words (PPT 24)
10. Increase Font Size (PPT 24)
11. Bold Text (PPT 25)
12. Decrease the Title Slide Title Text Font Size (PPT 25)
13. Save a Presentation (PPT 27)
14. Add a New Text Slide with a Bulleted List (PPT 29)
15. Enter a Slide Title (PPT 31)
16. Select a Text Placeholder (PPT 31)
17. Type a Single-Level Bulleted List (PPT 32)
18. Add a New Slide and Enter a Slide Title (PPT 33)
19. Type a Multi-Level Bulleted List (PPT 34)
20. Create a Third-Level Paragraph (PPT 37)
21. Duplicate a Slide (PPT 40)
22. Arrange a Slide (PPT 41)
23. Delete All Text in a Placeholder (PPT 42)
24. Change Document Properties (PPT 44)
25. Save an Existing Presentation with the Same File Name (PPT 45)
26. Use the Scroll Box on the Slide Pane to Move to Another Slide (PPT 47)
27. Start Slide Show View (PPT 49)
28. Move Manually through Slides in a Slide Show (PPT 50)
29. Display the Pop-Up Menu and Go to a Specific Slide (PPT 51)
30. Use the Pop-Up Menu to End a Slide Show (PPT 52)
31. Quit PowerPoint with One Document Open (PPT 53)
32. Open a Presentation from PowerPoint (PPT 54)
33. Check Spelling (PPT 55)
34. Display a Presentation in Grayscale (PPT 59)
35. Print a Presentation (PPT 61)
36. Search for PowerPoint Help (PPT 63)

 If you have a SAM user profile, you may have access to hands-on instruction, practice, and assessment. Log in to your SAM account (http://sam2007.course.com) to launch any assigned training activities or exams that relate to the skills covered in this chapter.

Learn It Online

Test your knowledge of chapter content and key terms.

Instructions: To complete the Learn It Online exercises, start your browser, click the Address bar, and then enter the Web address `scsite.com/ppt2007/learn`. When the Office 2007 Learn It Online page is displayed, click the link for the exercise you want to complete and then read the instructions.

Chapter Reinforcement TF, MC, and SA
A series of true/false, multiple choice, and short answer questions that test your knowledge of the chapter content.

Flash Cards
An interactive learning environment where you identify chapter key terms associated with displayed definitions.

Practice Test
A series of multiple choice questions that test your knowledge of chapter content and key terms.

Who Wants To Be a Computer Genius?
An interactive game that challenges your knowledge of chapter content in the style of a television quiz show.

Wheel of Terms
An interactive game that challenges your knowledge of chapter key terms in the style of the television show *Wheel of Fortune*.

Crossword Puzzle Challenge
A crossword puzzle that challenges your knowledge of key terms presented in the chapter.

Apply Your Knowledge

Reinforce the skills and apply the concepts you learned in this chapter.

Modifying Character Formats and Paragraph Levels

Instructions: Start PowerPoint. Open the presentation, Apply 1-1 Keep Your Cool, from the Data Files for Students. See the inside back cover of this book for instructions on downloading the Data Files for Students, or contact your instructor for more information about accessing the required files.

The two slides in the presentation stress the importance of drinking plenty of water on hot days. The document you open is an unformatted presentation. You are to modify the document theme and text, indent the paragraphs, and format the text so the slides look like Figure 1–94.

Perform the following tasks:

1. Change the document theme to Trek. Note that the Trek theme uses all capital letters for the title text. On the title slide, use your name in place of Student Name and bold and italicize your name. Increase the title text font size to 44 point.

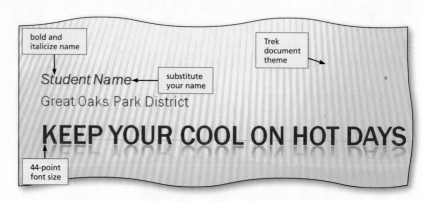

(a) Slide 1 (Title Slide)
Figure 1–94

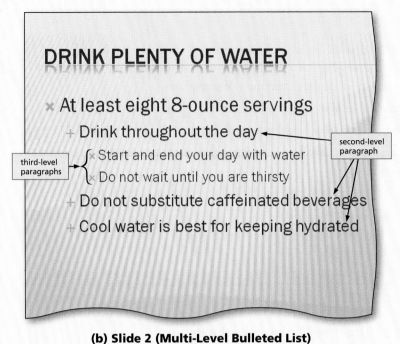

(b) Slide 2 (Multi-Level Bulleted List)
Figure 1–94 (continued)

2. On Slide 2, increase the indent of the second, fifth, and sixth paragraphs (Drink throughout the day; Do not substitute caffeinated beverages; Cool water is best for keeping hydrated) to second-level paragraphs. Then change paragraphs three and four (Start and end your day with water; Do not wait until you are thirsty) to third-level paragraphs.

3. Check the spelling, and then display the revised presentation in grayscale.

4. Change the document properties, as specified by your instructor. Save the presentation using the file name, Apply 1-1 Drink Water. Submit the revised document in the format specified by your instructor.

Extend Your Knowledge

Extend the skills you learned in this chapter and experiment with new skills. You may need to use Help to complete the assignment.

Changing Slide Theme and Text

Instructions: Start PowerPoint. Open the presentation, Extend 1-1 Nutrition, from the Data Files for Students. See the inside back cover of this book for instructions on downloading the Data Files for Students, or contact your instructor for more information about accessing the required files.

You will choose a theme (Figure 1–95), format slides, and create a closing slide.

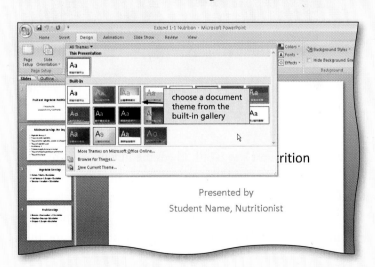

Figure 1–95

Perform the following tasks:

1. Apply an appropriate document theme.

2. On Slide 1, use your name in place of Student Name. Format the text using techniques you learned in this chapter, such as changing the font size and color and also bolding and italicizing words.

Continued >

Extend Your Knowledge *continued*

3. On Slide 2, adjust the paragraph levels so that the lines of text are arranged under vegetable and fruit categories. Edit the text so that the slide meets the 7 × 7 rule, which states that each line should have a maximum of seven words, and each slide should have a maximum of seven lines.

4. On Slides 3 and 4, create paragraphs and adjust the paragraph levels.

5. Create an appropriate closing slide using the title slide as a guide.

6. Change the document properties, as specified by your instructor. Save the presentation using the file name, Extend 1-1 Fruit and Vegetables.

7. Add the Print button to the Quick Access Toolbar and then click this button to print the slides.

8. Delete the Print button from the Quick Access Toolbar.

9. Submit the revised document in the format specified by your instructor.

Make It Right

Analyze a presentation and correct all errors and/or improve the design.

Correcting Formatting and List Levels

Instructions: Start PowerPoint. Open the presentation, Make It Right 1-1 Indulge, from the Data Files for Students. See the inside back cover of this book for instructions on downloading the Data Files for Students, or contact your instructor for more information about accessing the required files.

Correct the formatting problems and errors in the presentation while keeping in mind the guidelines presented in this chapter.

Perform the following tasks:

1. Change the document theme from Metro, shown in Figure 1–96, to Opulent.

2. On Slide 1, replace the words, Fall Semester, with your name. Format your name so that it displays prominently on the slide.

3. Move Slide 2 to the end of the presentation so that it becomes the new Slide 4.

4. Use the spell checker to correct the misspellings. Analyze the slides for other word usage errors that the spell checker did not find.

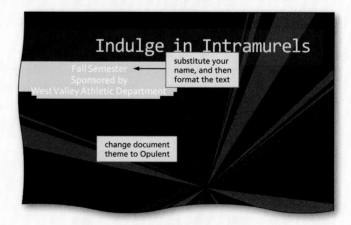

Figure 1–96

5. On Slide 2, increase the Slide 2 title (Athletic Events) font size to 40. Make the indent levels for paragraphs 2, 4, and 6 the same level.

6. On Slide 3, change the title text (Awards Ceremony) font size to 40. Make the indent levels for paragraphs 3 and 5 the same level.

7. Change the document properties, as specified by your instructor. Save the presentation using the file name, Make It Right 1-1 Intramurals.

8. Submit the revised document in the format specified by your instructor.

In the Lab

Design and/or create a presentation using the guidelines, concepts, and skills presented in this chapter. Labs 1, 2, and 3 are listed in order of increasing difficulty.

Lab 1: Creating a Presentation with Bulleted Lists

Problem: Many of the important steps you will take in your life are influenced by your credit report. Buying a car, renting an apartment, and even applying for a job often require a credit check. Your credit score can make or break your ability to obtain the goods you truly want and need. One of your assignments in your economics class is to give a speech about establishing credit. You develop the outline shown in Figure 1–97 and then prepare the PowerPoint presentation shown in Figures 1–98a through 1–98d.

Instructions: Perform the following tasks.

1. Create a new presentation using the Aspect document theme.

2. Using the typed notes illustrated in Figure 1–97, create the title slide shown in Figure 1–98a using your name in place of Marc Kantlon. Italicize your name. Decrease the font size of the title paragraph, Give Yourself Some Credit, to 40. Increase the font size of the first paragraph of the subtitle text, Understanding Your Credit Report, to 28.

3. Using the typed notes in Figure 1–97, create the three text slides with bulleted lists shown in Figures 1–98b through 1–98d.

Give Yourself Some Credit
  Understanding Your Credit Report
  Marc Kantlon
  Economics 101

Credit Report Fundamentals
  Generated by three companies
      Experian, Equifax, TransUnion
  Factors
      How much you owe to each company
      Payment history for each company
          Includes utilities, medical expenses, rent

How FICO Is Calculated
  Range - 760 (excellent) to 620 (poor)
      35% - Payment history
      30% - Amounts owed
      15% - Credit history length
      10% - New credit
      10% - Credit types

Improve Your FICO Score
  Pay bills on time
  Avoid opening many new accounts
      Open only if you intend to use
  Keep balances low
      Less than 25% of credit limit
  Review credit report yearly

Figure 1–97

Continued >

In the Lab *continued*

4. On Slide 3, change the font color of the number, 760, to green and the number, 620, to red.

5. Check the spelling and correct any errors.

6. Drag the scroll box to display Slide 1. Click the Slide Show button to start Slide Show view. Then click to display each slide.

7. Change the document properties, as specified by your instructor. Save the presentation using the file name, Lab 1-1 Credit.

8. Submit the document in the format specified by your instructor.

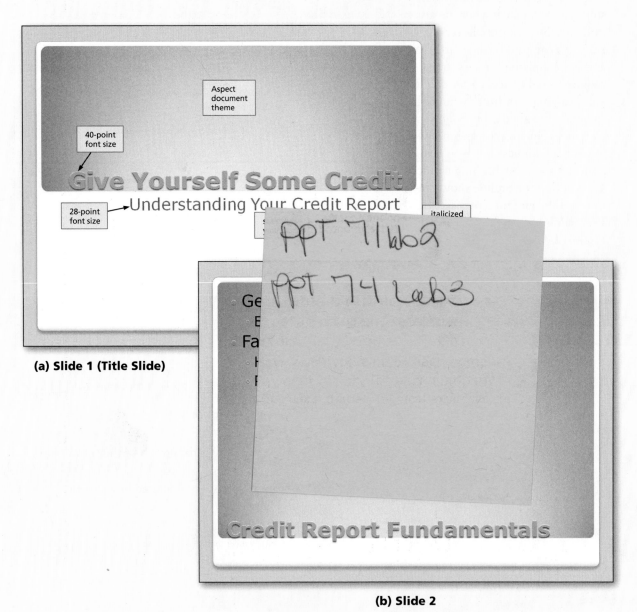

(a) Slide 1 (Title Slide)

(b) Slide 2

Figure 1–98

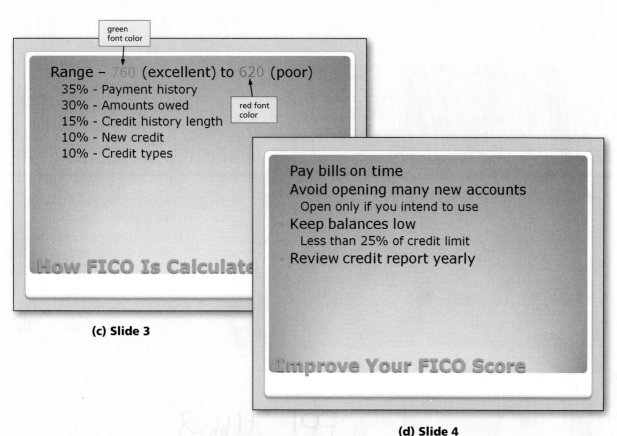

(c) Slide 3

(d) Slide 4

Figure 1–98 (continued)

In the Lab

Lab 2: Creating a Presentation with Bulleted Lists and a Closing Slide

Problem: Hybrid vehicles have received much attention in recent years. Everyone from environmentalists to movie stars are driving them, and potential buyers wait for months until the vehicles arrive in dealers' showrooms. You work part-time at Midwest State Bank, and the loan department manager, Jen Westbrook, has asked you to develop a PowerPoint presentation to accompany her upcoming speech. She hands you the outline shown in Figure 1–99 and asks you to create the presentation shown in Figures 1–100a through 1–100e.

Is a Hybrid Car Right for You?
  Jen Westbrook, Midwest State Bank Loan Department Manager

Are They a Good Value?
    Depends upon your driving habits
    Government offers tax credits
    Excellent resale value
    Efficient gas consumption

What Is Their Gas Mileage?
    Depends upon make and size
        City: Ranges from 18 to 60 mpg
        Highway: Ranges from 21 to 66 mpg
    Actual mileage affected by driving patterns

What Makes Them Work?
    Use two motors
        Gas
            Smaller, more efficient than traditional vehicle
        Electric
            Gives gas engine extra power boost
            May power car entirely

See me for your next car purchase
  Jen Westbrook, Midwest State Bank Loan Department Manager

Figure 1–99

Continued >

In the Lab *continued*

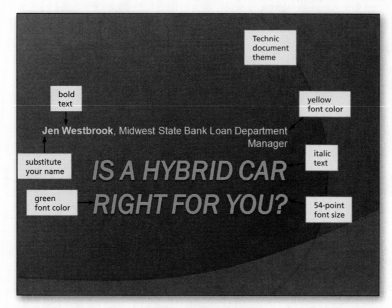

(a) Slide 1 (Title Slide)

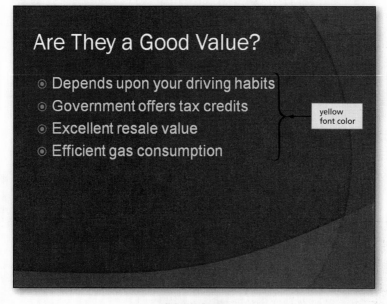

(b) Slide 2

Figure 1–100

Instructions: Perform the following tasks.

1. Create a new presentation using the Technic document theme.

2. Using the typed notes illustrated in Figure 1–99, create the title slide shown in Figure 1–100a using your name in place of Jan Westbrook. Bold your name. Italicize the title, Is a Hybrid Car Right for You?, and increase the font size to 54. Change the font color of the title text to green and the subtitle text to yellow.

3. Using the typed notes in Figure 1–99, create the three text slides with bulleted lists shown in Figures 1–100b through 1–100d. Change the color of all the bulleted list paragraph text to yellow.

4. Duplicate the title slide and then move the new closing slide to the end of the presentation. Change the Slide 5 title text, increase the font size to 66, and remove the italics.

5. Check the spelling and correct any errors.

6. Drag the scroll box to display Slide 1. Click the Slide Show button to start Slide Show view. Then click to display each slide.

7. Change the document properties, as specified by your instructor. Save the presentation using the file name, Lab 1-2 Hybrids.

8. Submit the revised document in the format specified by your instructor.

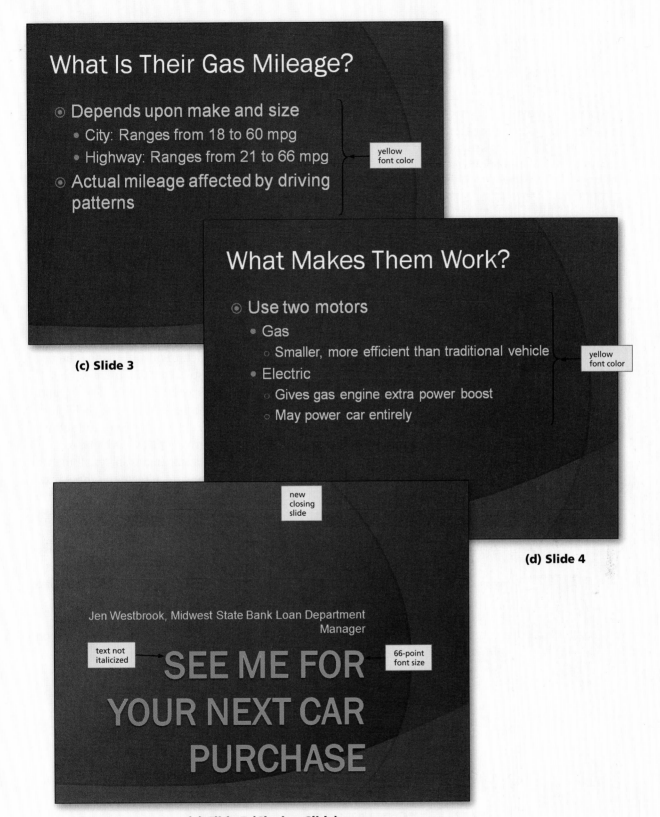

(c) Slide 3

(d) Slide 4

(e) Slide 5 (Closing Slide)

Figure 1–100 (continued)

In the Lab

Lab 3: Creating and Updating Presentations

Problem: Bobbie Willis, the public relations director for the South Haven Park District, plans activities every season for community residents and promotes the offerings using a PowerPoint presentation. The new seminars for senior citizens this spring are quilting and t'ai chi. Adults can register for gourmet cooking lessons and kickball. Teens can enroll in sailing and fencing lessons.

Instructions Part 1: Using the outline in Figure 1–101, create the presentation shown in Figure 1–102. Use the Oriel document theme. On the title slide shown in Figure 1–102a, type your name in place of Bobbie Willis, increase the font size of the title paragraph, South Haven Park District, to 60 and change the text font style to italic. Increase the font size of the subtitle paragraph, New Spring Seminars, to 32, and change the font size of the subtitle paragraph with your name to 37 or to a size that displays all the text on one line. Create the three text slides with multi-level bulleted lists shown in Figures 1–102b through 1–102d.

Correct any spelling mistakes. Change the document properties, as specified by your instructor. Save the presentation using the file name, Lab 1-3 Part One Spring Seminars. Display the presentation in grayscale.

South Haven Park District
New Spring Seminars
Bobbie Willis, Director

Seniors' Seminars
    Quilting
        Quilts made from donated fabrics
        Sewing machines provided
    T'ai Chi
        Gentle warm-ups
        12 slow, continuous movements
        Easy cool-down exercises

Adults' Seminars
    Almost Gourmet
        Learn techniques from a professional chef
            Everyone prepares and enjoys the dinners
                Come hungry!
    Kickball
        Learn techniques and rules

Teens' Seminars
    Sailing
        Sail a 30-foot sailboat at your first class
    Fencing
        Three levels
            Level 1 – Beginning Foil
           Level 2 – Foil, Epee, and Saber
           Level 3 – Open Strip Fencing

Figure 1–101

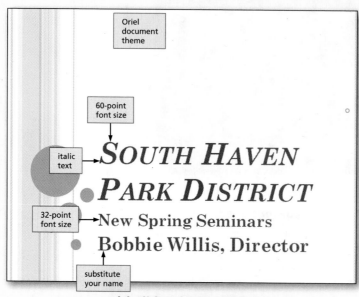

(a) Slide 1 (Title Slide)
Figure 1–102

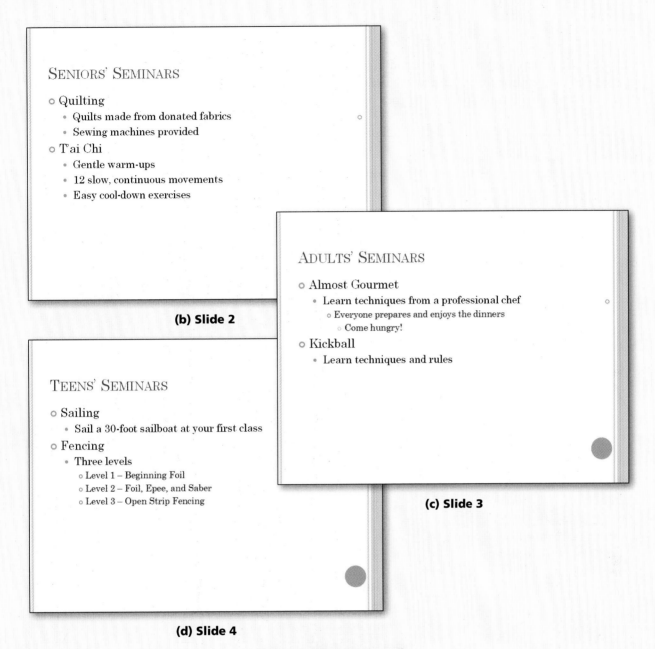

(b) Slide 2

(c) Slide 3

(d) Slide 4

Figure 1–102 (continued)

Instructions Part 2: The South Haven Park District staff members want to update this presentation to promote the new Fall seminars. Modify the presentation created in Part 1 to create the presentation shown in Figure 1–103. To begin, save the current presentation with the new file name, Lab 1-3 Part Two Fall Seminars. Change the document theme to Civic. On the title slide, remove the italics from the title paragraph, South Haven Park District, decrease the font size to 44, and bold the text. Change the first subtitle paragraph to New Fall Seminars. Then change your title in the second subtitle paragraph to Executive Director and change the font size of the entire paragraph to 28.

On Slide 2, change the first first-level paragraph, Quilting, to Quilting for the Holidays. Change the first second-level paragraph, Quilts made from donated fabrics, to Quilts will be raffled at Annual Bazaar. Change the title of the second seminar to Intermediate T'ai Chi.

On Slide 3, change the first second-level paragraph under Almost Gourmet to Holiday feasts and parties. Then change the second-level paragraph under Kickball to Seminar concludes with single elimination tournament.

On Slide 4, change the first class from Sailing to Climbing and then change the course description second-level paragraph to Covers verbal signals, rope, knots, harnesses, belaying.

Continued >

In the Lab *continued*

Correct any spelling mistakes, and then view the slide show. Change the document properties, as specified by your instructor. Display the presentation in grayscale. Submit both Part One and Part Two documents in the format specified by your instructor.

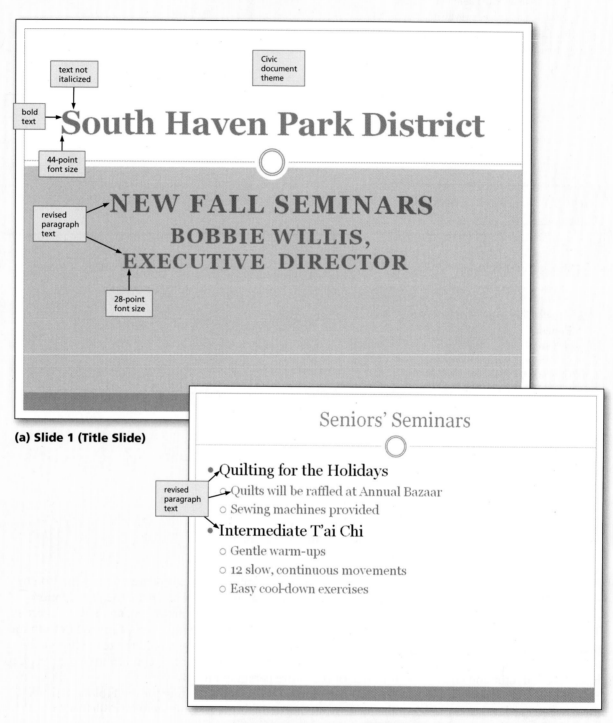

(a) Slide 1 (Title Slide)

(b) Slide 2

Figure 1–103

(c) Slide 3

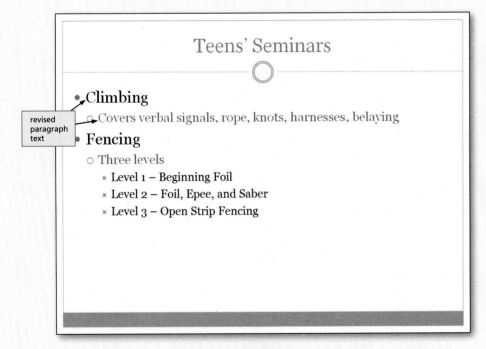

(d) Slide 4

Figure 1–103 (continued)

Cases and Places

Apply your creative thinking and problem solving skills to design and implement a solution.

• EASIER   •• MORE DIFFICULT

Note: Remember to use the 7 × 7 rule as you design the presentations: a maximum of seven words on a line and a maximum of seven lines on one slide.

• 1: Design and Create an Ocean and Seas Presentation

Salt water covers more than two-thirds of the Earth's surface. This water flows freely between the Earth's five oceans and seas, which all are connected. In preparation for your next snorkeling and diving adventure, you have been reading about the oceans and seas. You decide to prepare a PowerPoint presentation to accompany a speech that is required in your Earth Science class. You create the outline shown in Figure 1–104 about these waters. Use this outline along with the concepts and techniques presented in this chapter to develop and format a slide show with a title slide and three text slides with bulleted lists. Be sure to check spelling.

Water, Water, Everywhere
The Earth's Oceans and Seas
Jamel Thomas
Earth Science 203

Major Bodies of Water
Four oceans: Pacific, Atlantic, Indian, and Arctic
Pacific is largest and deepest
64,186,300 square miles
12,925 feet average depth
Fifth ocean delimited in 2000
Southern Ocean north of Antarctica

Coral Reefs
Form in shallow, warm seas
Made of coral polyps' skeletons
Grow on top of old skeletons
Spend adult lives fixed to same spot
Coral diseases increasing dramatically past 10 years
Responding to onset of bacteria, fungi, viruses

Ocean Zones
Sunlit (down to 650 feet)
Sea plants and many animals
Twilight (down to 3,300 feet)
Many different fish
Sunless (down to 13,100 feet)
Animals feed on dead food from above

Figure 1–104

• 2: Design and Create an Industrial Revolution Presentation

The Industrial Revolution changed the way people worked and lived in many parts of the world. With its roots in Britain in the 18th century, the Industrial Revolution introduced new machines, steam power, and trains. As part of your World History homework assignments, you develop the outline shown in Figure 1–105 about the Industrial Revolution and then create an accompanying PowerPoint presentation. Use the concepts and techniques presented in this chapter to develop and format this slide show with a title slide, three text slides with bulleted lists, and a closing slide. Be sure to check spelling.

The Industrial Revolution
1700 - 1850
Sonia Banks
World History 108

British Inventors
   First machines spun and wove cloth quickly
      Wealthy businessmen built factories
        Spinning Jenny machine spun 16 threads simultaneously
   Angered people who made cloth at home
      Luddites protested by smashing machines
        Led by Ned Ludd

Steam Power
   James Watt invented first steam engine in 1782
      Hundreds of his engines used throughout Britain
   George Stephenson designed steam train, The Rocket
      Peak speed: 30 mph
      Used to transport goods in 1829

Coal Mining
   Coal needed to boil water to create steam
   Mining towns boomed
      Deep mines dug
      Men, women, and children worked long hours
        Many people killed and injured

Figure 1–105

Continued >

Cases and Places *continued*

•• 3: Design and Create a Recycling Presentation

Many communities require recycling of household waste. Residents are required to separate paper, plastics, and glass and put each material in special bins or bags. Electronic equipment also can be recycled. Your community has developed a special program for broken or obsolete computers and peripherals, office equipment and products, small home appliances, and entertainment equipment. These items include personal computers, printers, cellular telephones, toasters, televisions, DVD players, and video game consoles. Community officials will be collecting these items during the next two Fridays at your local police station and a nearby shopping center. They will not accept air conditioners, humidifiers, and hazardous wastes. Using the concepts and techniques presented in this chapter, develop a short PowerPoint presentation to show at various businesses and offices in your community. Emphasize that recycling is important because electronic products have very short useful lives. They produce waste and may contain hazardous materials, but many components can be salvaged. Include one slide with acceptable products and another with unacceptable products.

•• 4 Design and Create Your Favorite or Dream Car Presentation

Make It Personal

Ever since Henry Ford rolled the first Model T off his assembly line in 1908, people have been obsessed with cars. From the sporty Corvette to the environmentally friendly Prius, everyone has a favorite car or dream car. Use the concepts and techniques presented in this chapter to create a slide show promoting a particular vehicle. Include a title slide, at least three text slides with bulleted lists, and a closing slide. Format the text using colors, bolding, and italics where needed for emphasis. Be sure to check spelling.

•• 5: Design and Create a Financial Institutions Presentation

Working Together

Financial institutions such as banks, savings and loans, and credit unions offer a variety of products. Have each member of your team visit, telephone, or view Web sites of three local financial institutions. Gather data about:

1) Savings accounts

2) Checking accounts

3) Mortgages

4) Certificates of deposit

After coordinating the data, create a presentation with at least one slide showcasing each financial institution. As a group, critique each slide. Submit your assignment in the format specified by your instructor.

Appendix A
Project Planning
Guidelines

Using Project Planning Guidelines

The process of communicating specific information to others is a learned, rational skill. Computers and software, especially Microsoft Office 2007, can help you develop ideas and present detailed information to a particular audience.

Using Microsoft Office 2007, you can create projects such as Word documents, Excel spreadsheets, Access databases, and PowerPoint presentations. Computer hardware and productivity software such as Microsoft Office 2007 minimizes much of the laborious work of drafting and revising projects. Some communicators handwrite ideas in notebooks, others compose directly on the computer, and others have developed unique strategies that work for their own particular thinking and writing styles.

No matter what method you use to plan a project, follow specific guidelines to arrive at a final product that presents information correctly and effectively (Figure A–1). Use some aspects of these guidelines every time you undertake a project, and others as needed in specific instances. For example, in determining content for a project, you may decide that a bar chart communicates trends more effectively than a paragraph of text. If so, you would create this graphical element and insert it in an Excel spreadsheet, a Word document, or a PowerPoint slide.

Determine the Project's Purpose

Begin by clearly defining why you are undertaking this assignment. For example, you may want to track monetary donations collected for your club's fundraising drive. Alternatively, you may be urging students to vote for a particular candidate in the next election. Once you clearly understand the purpose of your task, begin to draft ideas of how best to communicate this information.

Analyze Your Audience

Learn about the people who will read, analyze, or view your work. Where are they employed? What are their educational backgrounds? What are their expectations? What questions do they have?

PROJECT PLANNING GUIDELINES

1. DETERMINE THE PROJECT'S PURPOSE
Why are you undertaking the project?

2. ANALYZE YOUR AUDIENCE
Who are the people who will use your work?

3. GATHER POSSIBLE CONTENT
What information exists, and in what forms?

4. DETERMINE WHAT CONTENT TO PRESENT TO YOUR AUDIENCE
What information will best communicate the project's purpose to your audience?

Figure A–1

Design experts suggest drawing a mental picture of these people or finding photographs of people who fit this profile so that you can develop a project with the audience in mind.

By knowing your audience members, you can tailor a project to meet their interests and needs. You will not present them with information they already possess, and you will not omit the information they need to know.

Example: Your assignment is to raise the profile of your college's nursing program in the community. How much do they know about your college and the nursing curriculum? What are the admission requirements? How many of the applicants admitted complete the program? What percent pass the state Boards?

Gather Possible Content

Rarely are you in a position to develop all the material for a project. Typically, you would begin by gathering existing information that may reside in spreadsheets or databases. Web sites, pamphlets, magazine and newspaper articles, and books could provide insights of how others have approached your topic. Personal interviews often provide perspectives not available by any other means. Consider video and audio clips as potential sources for material that might complement or support the factual data you uncover.

Determine What Content to Present to Your Audience

Experienced designers recommend writing three or four major ideas you want an audience member to remember after reading or viewing your project. It also is helpful to envision your project's endpoint, the key fact you wish to emphasize. All project elements should lead to this ending point.

As you make content decisions, you also need to think about other factors. Presentation of the project content is an important consideration. For example, will your brochure be printed on thick, colored paper or transparencies? Will your PowerPoint presentation be viewed in a classroom with excellent lighting and a bright projector, or will it be viewed on a notebook computer monitor? Determine relevant time factors, such as the length of time to develop the project, how long readers will spend reviewing your project, or the amount of time allocated for your speaking engagement. Your project will need to accommodate all of these constraints.

Decide whether a graph, photograph, or artistic element can express or emphasize a particular concept. The right hemisphere of the brain processes images by attaching an emotion to them, so audience members are more apt to recall these graphics long term rather than just reading text.

As you select content, be mindful of the order in which you plan to present information. Readers and audience members generally remember the first and last pieces of information they see and hear, so you should put the most important information at the top or bottom of the page.

Summary

When creating a project, it is beneficial to follow some basic guidelines from the outset. By taking some time at the beginning of the process to determine the project's purpose, analyze the audience, gather possible content, and determine what content to present to the audience, you can produce a project that is informative, relevant, and effective.

Appendix B

Introduction to Microsoft Office 2007

What Is Microsoft Office 2007?

Microsoft Office 2007 is a collection of the more popular Microsoft application software. It is available in Basic, Home and Student, Standard, Small Business, Professional, Ultimate, Professional Plus, and Enterprise editions. Each edition consists of a group of programs, collectively called a suite. Table B-1 lists the suites and their components. **Microsoft Office Professional Edition 2007** includes these six programs: Microsoft Office Word 2007, Microsoft Office Excel 2007, Microsoft Office Access 2007, Microsoft Office PowerPoint 2007, Microsoft Office Publisher 2007, and Microsoft Office Outlook 2007. The programs in the Office suite allow you to work efficiently, communicate effectively, and improve the appearance of the projects you create.

Table B–1

	Microsoft Office Basic 2007	Microsoft Office Home & Student 2007	Microsoft Office Standard 2007	Microsoft Office Small Business 2007	Microsoft Office Professional 2007	Microsoft Office Ultimate 2007	Microsoft Office Professional Plus 2007	Microsoft Office Enterprise 2007
Microsoft Office Word 2007	✓	✓	✓	✓	✓	✓	✓	✓
Microsoft Office Excel 2007	✓	✓	✓	✓	✓	✓	✓	✓
Microsoft Office Access 2007					✓	✓	✓	✓
Microsoft Office PowerPoint 2007		✓	✓	✓	✓	✓	✓	✓
Microsoft Office Publisher 2007				✓	✓	✓	✓	✓
Microsoft Office Outlook 2007	✓		✓				✓	✓
Microsoft Office OneNote 2007		✓				✓		
Microsoft Office Outlook 2007 with Business Contact Manager				✓	✓	✓		
Microsoft Office InfoPath 2007						✓	✓	✓
Integrated Enterprise Content Management						✓	✓	✓
Electronic Forms						✓	✓	✓
Advanced Information Rights Management and Policy Capabilities						✓	✓	✓
Microsoft Office Communicator 2007							✓	✓
Microsoft Office Groove 2007						✓		✓

Microsoft has bundled additional programs in some versions of Office 2007, in addition to the main group of Office programs. Table B–1 on the previous page lists the components of the various Office suites.

In addition to the Office 2007 programs noted previously, Office 2007 suites can contain other programs. Microsoft Office OneNote 2007 is a digital notebook program that allows you to gather and share various types of media, such as text, graphics, video, audio, and digital handwriting. Microsoft Office InfoPath 2007 is a program that allows you to create and use electronic forms to gather information. Microsoft Office Groove 2007 provides collaborative workspaces in real time. Additional services that are oriented toward the enterprise solution also are available.

Office 2007 and the Internet, World Wide Web, and Intranets

Office 2007 allows you to take advantage of the Internet, the World Wide Web, and intranets. The Microsoft Windows operating system includes a **browser**, which is a program that allows you to locate and view a Web page. The Windows browser is called Internet Explorer.

One method of viewing a Web page is to use the browser to enter the Web address for the Web page. Another method of viewing a Web page is clicking a hyperlink. A **hyperlink** is colored or underlined text or a graphic that, when clicked, connects to another Web page. Hyperlinks placed in Office 2007 documents allow for direct access to a Web site of interest.

An **intranet** is a private network, such as a network used within a company or organization for internal communication. Like the Internet, hyperlinks are used within an intranet to access documents, pages, and other destinations on the intranet. Unlike the Internet, the materials on the network are available only for those who are part of the private network.

Online Collaboration Using Office

Organizations that, in the past, were able to make important information available only to a select few, now can make their information accessible to a wider range of individuals who use programs such as Office 2007 and Internet Explorer. Office 2007 allows colleagues to use the Internet or an intranet as a central location to view documents, manage files, and work together.

Each of the Office 2007 programs makes publishing documents on a Web server as simple as saving a file on a hard disk. Once placed on the Web server, users can view and edit the documents and conduct Web discussions and live online meetings.

Using Microsoft Office 2007

The various Microsoft Office 2007 programs each specialize in a particular task. This section describes the general functions of the more widely used Office 2007 programs, along with how they are used to access the Internet or an intranet.

Microsoft Office Word 2007

Microsoft Office Word 2007 is a full-featured word processing program that allows you to create many types of personal and business documents, including flyers, letters, resumes, business documents, and academic reports.

Word's AutoCorrect, spelling, and grammar features help you proofread documents for errors in spelling and grammar by identifying the errors and offering suggestions for corrections as you type. The live word count feature provides you with a constantly updating word count as you enter and edit text. To assist with creating specific documents, such as a business letter or resume, Word provides templates, which provide a formatted document before you type the text of the document. Quick Styles provide a live preview of styles from the Style gallery, allowing you to preview styles in the document before actually applying them.

Word automates many often-used tasks and provides you with powerful desktop publishing tools to use as you create professional looking brochures, advertisements, and newsletters. SmartArt allows you to insert interpretive graphics based on document content.

Word makes it easier for you to share documents for collaboration. The Send feature opens an e-mail window with the active document attached. The Compare Documents feature allows you easily to identify changes when comparing different document versions.

Word 2007 and the Internet   Word makes it possible to design and publish Web pages on the Internet or an intranet, insert a hyperlink to a Web page in a word processing document, as well as access and search the content of other Web pages.

Microsoft Office Excel 2007

Microsoft Office Excel 2007 is a spreadsheet program that allows you to organize data, complete calculations, graph data, develop professional looking reports, publish organized data to the Web, and access real-time data from Web sites.

In addition to its mathematical functionality, Excel 2007 provides tools for visually comparing data. For instance, when comparing a group of values in cells, you can set cell backgrounds with bars proportional to the value of the data in the cell. You can also set cell backgrounds with full-color backgrounds, or use a color scale to facilitate interpretation of data values.

Excel 2007 provides strong formatting support for tables with the new Style Preview gallery.

Excel 2007 and the Internet   Using Excel 2007, you can create hyperlinks within a worksheet to access other Office documents on the network or on the Internet. Worksheets saved as static, or unchanging Web pages can be viewed using a browser. The person viewing static Web pages cannot change them.

In addition, you can create and run queries that retrieve information from a Web page and insert the information directly into a worksheet.

Microsoft Office Access 2007

Microsoft Office Access 2007 is a comprehensive database management system (DBMS). A **database** is a collection of data organized in a manner that allows access, retrieval, and use of that data. Access 2007 allows you to create a database; add, change, and delete data in the database; sort data in the database; retrieve data from the database; and create forms and reports using the data in the database.

Access 2007 and the Internet   Access 2007 lets you generate reports, which are summaries that show only certain data from the database, based on user requirements.

Microsoft Office PowerPoint 2007

Microsoft Office PowerPoint 2007 is a complete presentation graphics program that allows you to produce professional looking presentations. With PowerPoint 2007, you can create informal presentations using overhead transparencies, electronic presentations using a projection device attached to a personal computer, formal presentations using 35mm slides or a CD, or you can run virtual presentations on the Internet.

PowerPoint 2007 and the Internet   PowerPoint 2007 allows you to publish presentations on the Internet or other networks.

Microsoft Office Publisher 2007

Microsoft Office Publisher 2007 is a desktop publishing program (DTP) that allows you to design and produce professional quality documents (newsletters, flyers, brochures, business cards, Web sites, and so on) that combine text, graphics, and photographs. Desktop publishing software provides a variety of tools, including design templates, graphic manipulation tools, color schemes or libraries, and various page wizards and templates. For large jobs, businesses use desktop publishing software to design publications that are **camera ready**, which means the files are suitable for production by outside commercial printers. Publisher 2007 also allows you to locate commercial printers, service bureaus, and copy shops willing to accept customer files created in Publisher.

Publisher 2007 allows you to design a unique image, or logo, using one of more than 45 master design sets. This, in turn, permits you to use the same design for all your printed documents (letters, business cards, brochures, and advertisements) and Web pages. Publisher includes 70 coordinated color schemes; 30 font schemes; more than 10,000 high-quality clip art images; 1,500 photographs; 1,000 Web-art graphics; 340 animated graphics; and hundreds of unique Design Gallery elements (quotations, sidebars, and so on). If you wish, you also can download additional images from the Microsoft Office Online Web page on the Microsoft Web site.

Publisher 2007 and the Internet   Publisher 2007 allows you easily to create a multipage Web site with custom color schemes, photographic images, animated images, and sounds.

Microsoft Office Outlook 2007

Microsoft Office Outlook 2007 is a powerful communications and scheduling program that helps you communicate with others, keep track of your contacts, and organize your schedule. Outlook 2007 allows you to view a To-Do bar containing tasks and appointments from your Outlook calendar. Outlook 2007 allows you to send and receive electronic mail (e-mail) and permits you to engage in real-time communication with family, friends, or coworkers using instant messaging. Outlook 2007 also provides you with the means to organize your contacts, and you can track e-mail messages, meetings, and notes with a particular contact. Outlook's Calendar, Contacts, Tasks, and Notes components aid in this organization. Contact information is available from the Outlook Calendar, Mail, Contacts, and Task components by accessing the Find a Contact feature. **Personal information management (PIM)** programs such as Outlook provide a way for individuals and workgroups to organize, find, view, and share information easily.

Microsoft Office 2007 Help

At any time while you are using one of the Office programs, you can interact with **Microsoft Office 2007 Help** for that program and display information about any topic associated with the program. Several categories of help are available. In all programs, you can access Help by pressing the F1 key on the keyboard. In Publisher 2007 and Outlook 2007, the Help window can be opened by clicking the Help menu and then selecting Microsoft Office Publisher or Outlook Help command, or by entering search text in the 'Type a question for help' text box in the upper-right corner of the program window. In the other Office programs, clicking the Microsoft Office Help button near the upper-right corner of the program window opens the program Help window.

The Help window in all programs provides several methods for accessing help about a particular topic, and has tools for navigating around Help. Appendix C contains detailed instructions for using Help.

Collaboration and SharePoint

While not part of the Microsoft Office 2007 suites, SharePoint is a Microsoft tool that allows Office 2007 users to share data using collaborative tools that are integrated into the main Office programs. SharePoint consists of Windows SharePoint Services, Office SharePoint Server 2007, and, optionally, Office SharePoint Designer 2007.

Windows SharePoint Services provides the platform for collaboration programs and services. Office SharePoint Server 2007 is built on top of Windows SharePoint Services. The result of these two products is the ability to create SharePoint sites. A SharePoint site is a Web site that provides users with a virtual place for collaborating and communicating with their colleagues while working together on projects, documents, ideas, and information. Each member of a group with access to the SharePoint site has the ability to contribute to the material stored there. The basic building blocks of SharePoint sites are lists and libraries. Lists contain collections of information, such as calendar items, discussion points, contacts, and links. Lists can be edited to add or delete information. Libraries are similar to lists, but include both files and information about files. Types of libraries include document, picture, and forms libraries.

The most basic type of SharePoint site is called a Workspace, which is used primarily for collaboration. Different types of Workspaces can be created using SharePoint to suit different needs. SharePoint provides templates, or outlines of these Workspaces, that can be filled in to create the Workspace. Each of the different types of Workspace templates contain a different collection of lists and libraries, reflecting the purpose of the Workspace. You can create a Document Workspace to facilitate collaboration on documents. A Document Workspace contains a document library for documents and supporting files, a Links list that allows you to maintain relevant resource links for the document, a Tasks list for listing and assigning To-Do items to team members, and other links as needed. Meeting Workspaces allow users to plan and organize a meeting, with components such as Attendees, Agenda, and a Document Library. Social Meeting Workspaces provide a place to plan social events, with lists and libraries such as Attendees, Directions, Image/Logo, Things To Bring, Discussions, and Picture Library. A Decision Meeting Workspace is a Meeting Workspace with a focus on review and decision-making, with lists and libraries such as Objectives, Attendees, Agenda, Document Library, Tasks, and Decisions.

Users also can create a SharePoint site called a WebParts page, which is built from modules called WebParts. WebParts are modular units of information that contain a title bar and content that reflects the type of WebPart. For instance, an image WebPart would contain a title bar and an image. WebParts allow you quickly to create and modify a SharePoint site, and allow for the creation of a unique site that can allow users to access and make changes to information stored on the site.

Large SharePoint sites that include multiple pages can be created using templates as well. Groups needing more refined and targeted sharing options than those available with SharePoint Server 2007 and Windows SharePoint Services can add SharePoint Designer 2007 to create a site that meets their specific needs.

Depending on which components have been selected for inclusion on the site, users can view a team calendar, view links, read announcements, and view and edit group documents and projects. SharePoint sites can be set up so that documents are checked in and out, much like a library, to prevent multiple users from making changes simultaneously. Once a SharePoint site is set up, Office programs are used to perform maintenance of the site. For example, changes in the team calendar are updated using Outlook 2007, and changes that users make in Outlook 2007 are reflected on the SharePoint site. Office 2007 programs include a Publish feature that allows users easily to save file updates to a SharePoint site. Team members can be notified about changes made to material on the site either by e-mail or by a news feed, meaning that users do not have to go to the site to check to see if anything has been updated since they last viewed or worked on it. The search feature in SharePoint allows users quickly to find information on a large site.

Appendix C
Microsoft Office 2007 Help

Using Microsoft Office Help

This appendix shows how to use Microsoft Office Help. At any time while you are using one of the Microsoft Office 2007 programs, you can use Office Help to display information about all topics associated with the program. To illustrate the use of Office Help, this appendix uses Microsoft Office Word 2007. Help in other Office 2007 programs responds in a similar fashion.

In Office 2007, Help is presented in a window that has Web browser-style navigation buttons. Each Office 2007 program has its own Help home page, which is the starting Help page that is displayed in the Help window. If your computer is connected to the Internet, the contents of the Help page reflect both the local help files installed on the computer and material from Microsoft's Web site. As shown in Figure C–1, two methods for accessing Word's Help are available:

1. Microsoft Office Word Help button near the upper-right corner of the Word window
2. Function key F1 on the keyboard

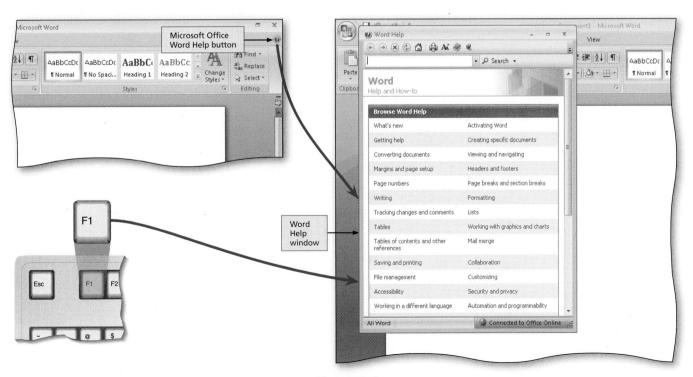

Figure C–1

To Open the Word Help Window

The following steps open the Word Help window and maximize the window.

- Start Microsoft Word, if necessary. Click the Microsoft Office Word Help button near the upper-right corner of the Word window to open the Word Help window (Figure C–2).

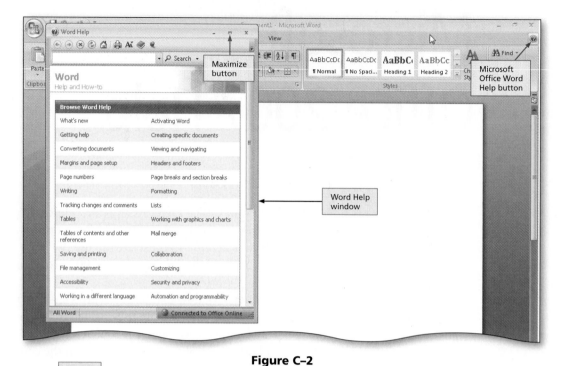

Figure C–2

- Click the Maximize button on the Help title bar to maximize the Help window (Figure C–3).

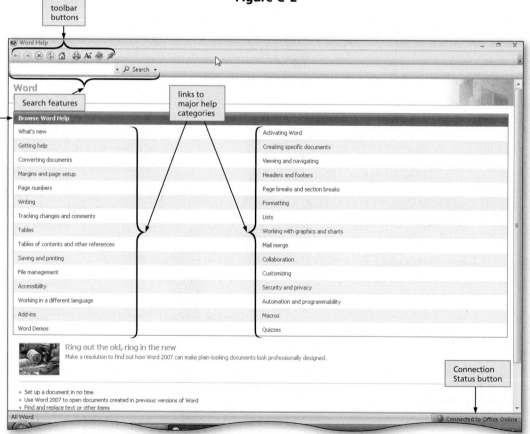

Figure C–3

The Word Help Window

The Word Help window provides several methods for accessing help about a particular topic, and also has tools for navigating around Help. Methods for accessing Help include searching the help content installed with Word, or searching the online Office content maintained by Microsoft.

Figure C–3 shows the main Word Help window. To navigate Help, the Word Help window includes search features that allow you to search on a word or phrase about which you want help; the Connection Status button, which allows you to control where Word Help searches for content; toolbar buttons; and links to major Help categories.

Search Features

You can perform Help searches on words or phrases to find information about any Word feature using the 'Type words to search for' text box and the Search button (Figure C–4a). Click the 'Type words to search for' text box and then click the Search button or press the ENTER key to initiate a search of Word Help.

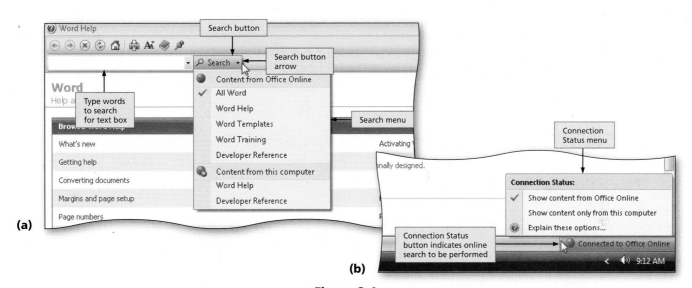

Figure C–4

Word Help offers the user the option of searching the online Help Web pages maintained by Microsoft or the offline Help files placed on your computer when you install Word. You can specify whether Word Help should search online or offline from two places: the Connection Status button on the status bar of the Word Help window, or the Search button arrow on the toolbar. The Connection Status button indicates whether Help currently is set up to work with online or offline information sources. Clicking the Connection Status button provides a menu with commands for selecting online or offline searches (Figure C–4b). The Connection Status menu allows the user to select whether Help searches will return content only from the computer (offline), or content from the computer and from Office Online (online).

Clicking the Search button arrow also provides a menu with commands for an online or offline search (Figure C–4a). These commands determine the source of information that Help searches for during the current Help session only. For example, assume that your preferred search is an offline search because you often do not have Internet access. You would set Connection Status to 'Show content only from this computer'. When you have Internet access, you can select an online search from the Search menu to search Office Online for information for your current search session only. Your search will use the Office Online resources until you quit Help. The next time you start Help, the Connection Status once again will be offline. In addition to setting the source of information that Help searches for during the current Help session, you can use the Search menu to further target the current search to one of four subcategories of online Help: Word Help, Word Templates, Word Training, and Developer Reference. The local search further can target one subcategory, Developer Reference.

In addition to searching for a word or string of text, you can use the links provided on the Browse Word Help area (Figure C–3 on page APP 10) to search for help on a topic. These links direct you to major help categories. From each major category, subcategories are available to further refine your search.

Finally, you can use the Table of Contents for Word Help to search for a topic the same way you would in a hard copy book. The Table of Contents is accessed via a toolbar button.

Toolbar Buttons

You can use toolbar buttons to navigate through the results of your search. The toolbar buttons are located on the toolbar near the top of the Help Window (Figure C–5). The toolbar buttons contain navigation buttons as well as buttons that perform other useful and common tasks in Word Help, such as printing.

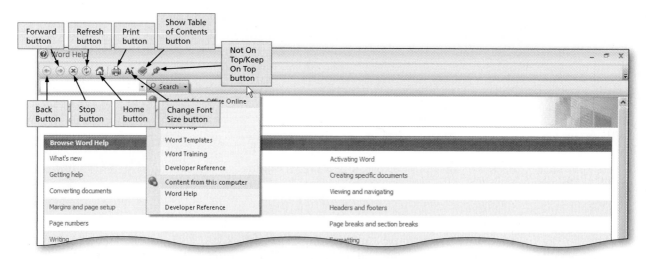

Figure C–5

The Word Help navigation buttons are the Back, Forward, Stop, Refresh, and Home buttons. These five buttons behave like the navigation buttons in a Web browser window. You can use the Back button to go back one window, the Forward button to go forward one window, the Stop button to stop loading the current page, and the Home button to redisplay the Help home page in the Help window. Use the Refresh button to reload the information requested into the Help window from its original source. When getting Help information online, this button provides the most current information from the Microsoft Help Web site.

The buttons located to the right of the navigation buttons — Print, Change Font Size, Show Table of Contents, and Not on Top — provide you with access to useful and common commands. The Print button prints the contents of the open Help window. The Change Font Size button customizes the Help window by increasing or decreasing the size of its text. The Show Table of Contents button opens a pane on the left side of the Help window that shows the Table of Contents for Word Help. You can use the Table of Contents for Word Help to navigate through the contents of Word Help much as you would use the Table of Contents in a book to search for a topic. The Not On Top button is an example of a toggle button, which is a button that can be switched back and forth between two states. It determines how the Word Help window behaves relative to other windows. When clicked, the Not On Top button changes to Keep On Top. In this state, it does not allow other windows from Word or other programs to cover the Word Help window when those windows are the active windows. When in the Not On Top state, the button allows other windows to be opened or moved on top of the Word Help window.

You can customize the size and placement of the Help window. Resize the window using the Maximize and Restore buttons, or by dragging the window to a desired size. Relocate the Help window by dragging the title bar to a new location on the screen.

Searching Word Help

Once the Word Help window is open, several methods exist for navigating Word Help. You can search for help by using any of the three following methods from the Help window:

1. Enter search text in the 'Type words to search for' text box
2. Click the links in the Help window
3. Use the Table of Contents

To Obtain Help Using the Type words to search for Text Box

Assume for the following example that you want to know more about watermarks. The following steps use the 'Type words to search for' text box to obtain useful information about watermarks by entering the word, watermark, as search text. The steps also navigate in the Word Help window.

- Type watermark in the 'Type words to search for' text box at the top of the Word Help window.

- Click the Search button arrow to display the Search menu (Figure C–6).

- If it is not selected already, click All Word on the Search menu to select the command. If All Word is already selected, click the Search button arrow again to close the Search menu.

Q&A

Why select All Word on the Search menu?

Selecting All Word on the Search menu ensures that Word Help will search all possible sources for information on your search term. It will produce the most complete search results.

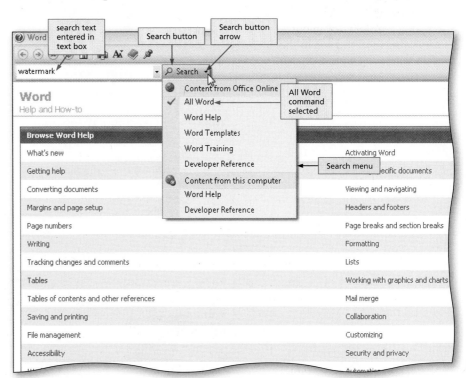

Figure C–6

2

- Click the Search button to display the search results (Figure C–7).

Q&A

Why do my results differ?

If you do not have an Internet connection, your results will reflect only the content of the Help files on your computer. When searching for help online, results also can change as material is added, deleted, and updated on the online Help Web pages maintained by Microsoft.

Q&A

Why were my search results not very helpful?

When initiating a search, keep in mind to check the spelling of the search text; and to keep your search very specific, with fewer than seven words, to return the most accurate results.

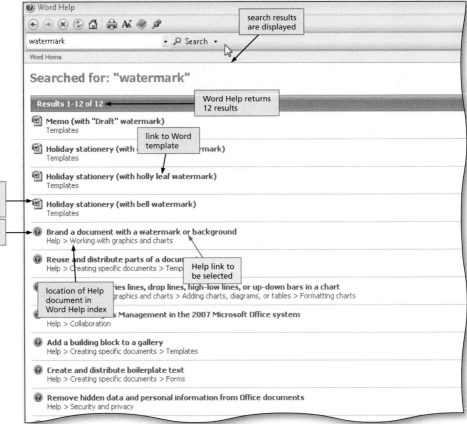

Figure C–7

3

- Click the 'Brand a document with a watermark or background' link to open the Help document associated with the link in the Help window (Figure C–8).

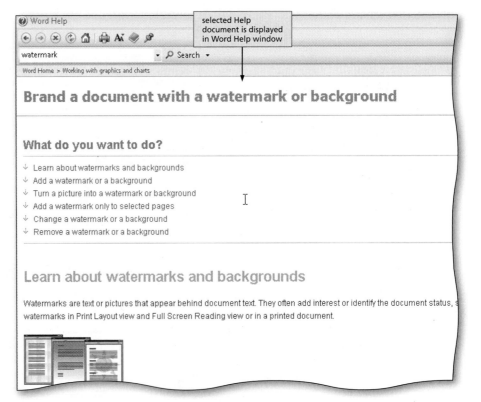

Figure C–8

4

- Click the Home button on the task-bar to clear the search results and redisplay the Word Help home page (Figure C–9).

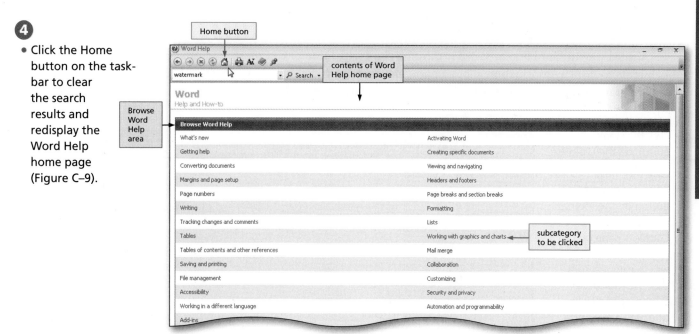

Figure C–9

To Obtain Help Using the Help Links

If your topic of interest is listed in the Browse Word Help area, you can click the link to begin browsing Word Help categories instead of entering search text. You browse Word Help just like you would browse a Web site. If you know in which category to find your Help information, you may wish to use these links. The following steps find the watermark Help information using the category links from the Word Help home page.

1

- Click the 'Working with graphics and charts' link to open the 'Working with graphics and charts' page.

- Click the 'Brand a document with a watermark or background' link to open the Help document associated with the link (Figure C–10).

Q&A

What does the Show All link do?

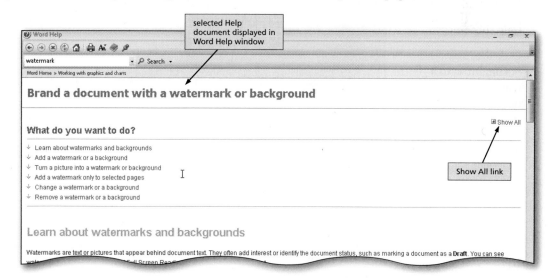

Figure C–10

In many Help documents, additional information about terms and features is available by clicking a link in the document to display additional information in the Help document. Clicking the Show All link opens all the links in the Help document that expand to additional text.

To Obtain Help Using the Help Table of Contents

A third way to find Help in Word is through the Help Table of Contents. You can browse through the Table of Contents to display information about a particular topic or to familiarize yourself with Word. The following steps access the watermark Help information by browsing through the Table of Contents.

1

- Click the Home button on the toolbar.

- Click the Show Table of Contents button on the toolbar to open the Table of Contents pane on the left side of the Help window. If necessary, click the Maximize button on the Help title bar to maximize the window (Figure C–11).

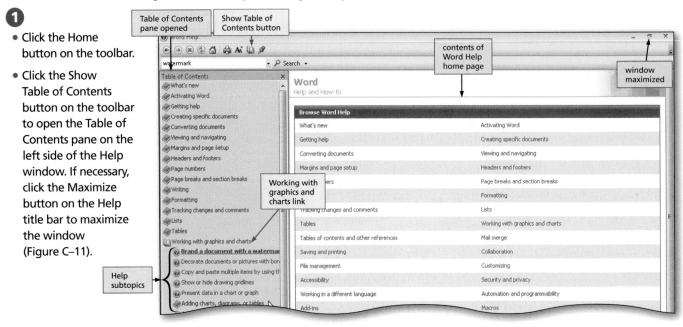

Figure C–11

2

- Click the 'Working with graphics and charts' link in the Table of Contents pane to view a list of Help subtopics.

- Click the 'Brand a document with a watermark or background' link in the Table of Contents pane to view the selected Help document in the right pane (Figure C–12).

 How do I remove the Table of Contents pane when I am finished with it?

The Show Table of Contents button acts as a toggle switch. When the Table of Contents pane is visible, the button changes to Hide Table of Contents. Clicking it hides the Table of Contents pane and changes the button to Show Table of Contents.

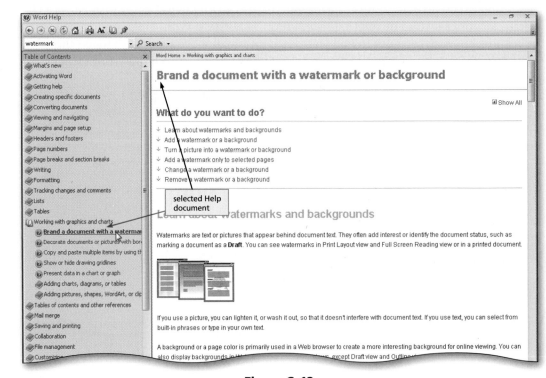

Figure C–12

Obtaining Help while Working in Word

Often you may need help while working on a document without already having the Help window open. For example, you may be unsure about how a particular command works, or you may be presented with a dialog box that you are not sure how to use. Rather than opening the Help window and initiating a search, Word Help provides you with the ability to search directly for help.

Figure C–13 shows one option for obtaining help while working in Word. If you want to learn more about a command, point to the command button and wait for the Enhanced ScreenTip to appear. If the Help icon appears in the Enhanced ScreenTip, press the F1 key while pointing to the command to open the Help window associated with that command.

Figure C–13

Figure C–14 shows a dialog box with a Get help button in it. Pressing the F1 key while the dialog box is displayed opens a Help window. The Help window contains help about that dialog box, if available. If no help file is available for that particular dialog box, then the main Help window opens.

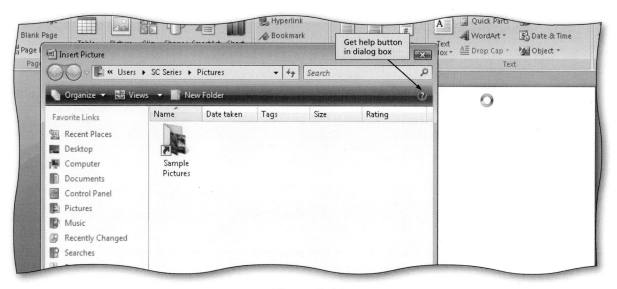

Figure C–14

Use Help

1 Obtaining Help Using Search Text

Instructions: Perform the following tasks using Word Help.

1. Use the 'Type words to search for' text box to obtain help about landscape printing. Use the Connection Status menu to search online help if you have an Internet connection.

2. Click Select page orientation in the list of links in the search results. Double-click the Microsoft Office Word Help window title bar to maximize it. Read and print the information. At the top of the printout, write down the number of links Word Help found.

3. Use the Search menu to search for help offline. Repeat the search from Step 1. At the top of the printout, write down the number of links that Word Help found searching offline. Submit the printouts as specified by your instructor.

4. Use the 'Type words to search for' text box to search for information online about adjusting line spacing. Click the 'Adjust the spacing between a list bullet or number and the text' link in the search results. If necessary, maximize the Microsoft Office 2007 Word Help window. Read and print the contents of the window. Close the Microsoft Office Word Help window. Submit the printouts as specified by your instructor.

5. For each of the following words and phrases, click one link in the search results, click the Show All link, and then print the page: page zoom; date; print preview; Ribbon; word count; and citation. Submit the printouts as specified by your instructor.

2 Expanding on Word Help Basics

Instructions: Use Word Help to better understand its features and answer the questions listed below. Answer the questions on your own paper, or submit the printed Help information as specified by your instructor.

1. Use Help to find out how to customize the Help window. Change the font size to the smallest option and then print the contents of the Microsoft Office Word Help window. Change the font size back to its original setting. Close the window.

2. Press the F1 key. Search for information about tables, restricting the search results to Word Templates. Print the first page of the Search results.

3. Search for information about tables, restricting the search results to Word Help files. Print the first page of the Search results.

4. Use Word Help to find out what happened to the Office Assistant, a feature in the previous version of Word. Print out the Help document that contains the answer.

Appendix D
Publishing Office 2007 Web Pages to a Web Server

With the Office 2007 programs, you use the Save As command on the Office Button menu to save a Web page to a Web server using one of two techniques: Web folders or File Transfer Protocol. A **Web folder** is an Office shortcut to a Web server. **File Transfer Protocol (FTP)** is an Internet standard that allows computers to exchange files with other computers on the Internet.

You should contact your network system administrator or technical support staff at your Internet access provider to determine if their Web server supports Web folders, FTP, or both, and to obtain necessary permissions to access the Web server. If you decide to publish Web pages using a Web folder, you must have the Office Server Extensions (OSE) installed on your computer.

Using Web Folders to Publish Office 2007 Web Pages

When publishing to a Web folder, someone first must create the Web folder before you can save to it. If you are granted permission to create a Web folder, you must obtain the Web address of the Web server, a user name, and possibly a password that allows you to access the Web server. You also must decide on a name for the Web folder. Table D–1 explains how to create a Web folder.

Office 2007 adds the name of the Web folder to the list of current Web folders. You can save to this folder, open files in the folder, rename the folder, or perform any operations you would to a folder on your hard disk. You can use your Office 2007 program or Windows Explorer to access this folder. Table D–2 explains how to save to a Web folder.

Table D–1 Creating a Web Folder
1. Click the Office Button and then click Save As or Open.
2. When the Save As dialog box (or Open dialog box) appears, click the Tools button arrow, and then click Map Network Drive... When the Map Network Drive dialog box is displayed, click the 'Connect to a Web site that you can use to store your documents and pictures' link.
3. When the Add Network Location Wizard dialog box appears, click the Next button. If necessary, click Choose a custom network location. Click the Next button. Click the View examples link, type the Internet or network address, and then click the Next button. Click 'Log on anonymously' to deselect the check box, type your user name in the User name text box, and then click the Next button. Enter the name you want to call this network place and then click the Next button. Click to deselect the 'Open this network location when I click Finish' check box, and then click the Finish button.

Table D–2 Saving to a Web Folder
1. Click the Office Button, click Save As.
2. When the Save As dialog box is displayed, type the Web page file name in the File name text box. Do not press the ENTER key.
3. Click the Save as type box arrow and then click Web Page to select the Web Page format.
4. Click Computer in the Navigation pane.
5. Double-click the Web folder name in the Network Location list.
6. If the Enter Network Password dialog box appears, type the user name and password in the respective text boxes and then click the OK button.
7. Click the Save button in the Save As dialog box.

Using FTP to Publish Office 2007 Web Pages

When publishing a Web page using FTP, you first must add the FTP location to your computer before you can save to it. An FTP location, also called an **FTP site**, is a collection of files that reside on an FTP server. In this case, the FTP server is the Web server.

To add an FTP location, you must obtain the name of the FTP site, which usually is the address (URL) of the FTP server, and a user name and a password that allows you to access the FTP server. You save and open the Web pages on the FTP server using the name of the FTP site. Table D–3 explains how to add an FTP site.

Office 2007 adds the name of the FTP site to the FTP locations list in the Save As and Open dialog boxes. You can open and save files using this list. Table D–4 explains how to save to an FTP location.

Table D–3 Adding an FTP Location
1. Click the Office Button and then click Save As or Open.
2. When the Save As dialog box (or Open dialog box) appears, click the Tools button arrow, and then click Map Network Drive... When the Map Network Drive dialog box is displayed, click the 'Connect to a Web site that you can use to store your documents and pictures' link.
3. When the Add Network Location Wizard dialog box appears, click the Next button. If necessary, click Choose a custom network location. Click the Next button. Click the View examples link, type the Internet or network address, and then click the Next button. If you have a user name for the site, click to deselect 'Log on anonymously' and type your user name in the User name text box, and then click Next. If the site allows anonymous logon, click Next. Type a name for the location, click Next, click to deselect the 'Open this network location when I click Finish' check box, and click Finish. Click the OK button.
4. Close the Save As or the Open dialog box.

Table D–4 Saving to an FTP Location
1. Click the Office Button and then click Save As.
2. When the Save As dialog box is displayed, type the Web page file name in the File name text box. Do not press the ENTER key.
3. Click the Save as type box arrow and then click Web Page to select the Web Page format.
4. Click Computer in the Navigation pane.
5. Double-click the name of the FTP site in the Network Location list.
6. When the FTP Log On dialog box appears, enter your user name and password and then click the OK button.
7. Click the Save button in the Save As dialog box.

Appendix E

Customizing Microsoft Office 2007

This appendix explains how to change the screen resolution in Windows Vista to the resolution used in this book. It also describes how to customize the Word window by changing the Ribbon, Quick Access Toolbar, and the color scheme.

Changing Screen Resolution

Screen resolution indicates the number of pixels (dots) that the computer uses to display the letters, numbers, graphics, and background you see on the screen. When you increase the screen resolution, Windows displays more information on the screen, but the information decreases in size. The reverse also is true: as you decrease the screen resolution, Windows displays less information on the screen, but the information increases in size.

The screen resolution usually is stated as the product of two numbers, such as 1024×768 (pronounced "ten twenty-four by seven sixty-eight"). A 1024×768 screen resolution results in a display of 1,024 distinct pixels on each of 768 lines, or about 786,432 pixels. The figures in this book were created using a screen resolution of 1024×768.

The screen resolutions most commonly used today are 800×600 and 1024×768, although some Office specialists set their computers at a much higher screen resolution, such as 2048×1536.

To Change the Screen Resolution

The following steps change the screen resolution from 1280×1024 to 1024×768. Your computer already may be set to 1024×768 or some other resolution.

- If necessary, minimize all programs so that the Windows Vista desktop appears.

- Right-click the Windows Vista desktop to display the Windows Vista desktop shortcut menu (Figure E–1).

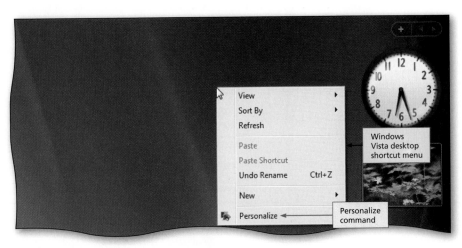

Figure E–1

● Click Personalize on the shortcut menu to open the Personalization window.

● Click Display Settings in the Personalization window to display the Display Settings dialog box (Figure E–2).

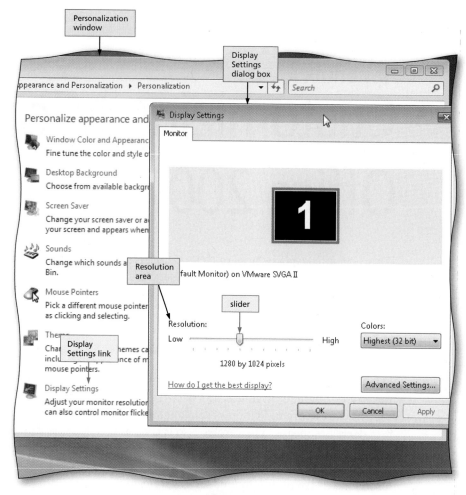

Figure E–2

● Drag the slider in the Resolution area so that the screen resolution changes to 1024 × 768 (Figure E–3).

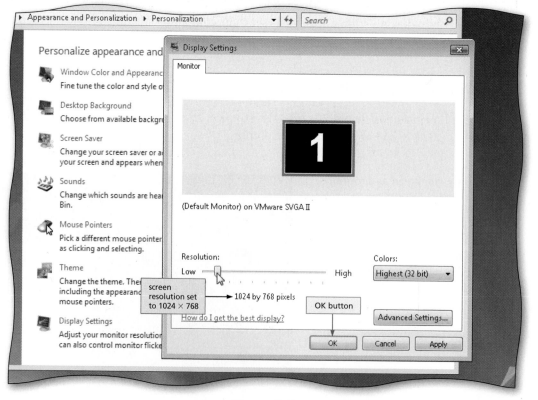

Figure E–3

4

- Click the OK button to change the screen resolution from 1280 × 1024 to 1024 × 768 (Figure E–4).

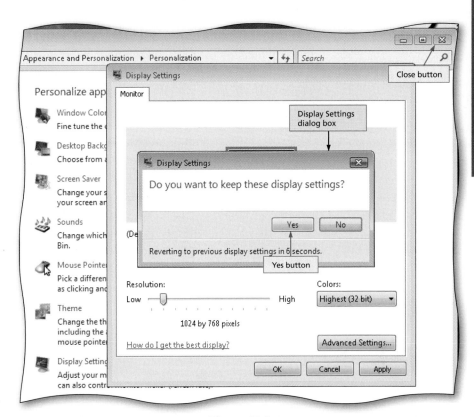

Figure E–4

5

- Click the Yes button in the Display Settings dialog box to accept the new screen resolution (Figure E–5).

 Q&A

What if I do not want to change the screen resolution after seeing it applied after I click the OK button?

You either can click the No button in the inner Display Settings dialog box, or wait for the timer to run out, at which point Windows Vista will revert to the original screen resolution.

- Click the Close button to close the Personalization Window.

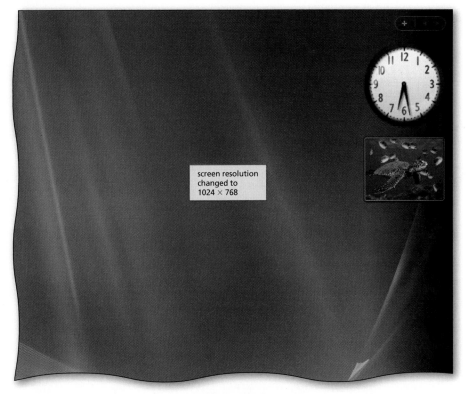

Figure E–5

Screen Resolution and the Appearance of the Ribbon in Office 2007 Programs

Changing the screen resolution affects how the Ribbon appears in Office 2007 programs. Figure E–6 shows the Word Ribbon at the screen resolutions of 800 × 600, 1024 × 768, and 1280 × 1024. All of the same commands are available regardless of screen resolution. Word, however, makes changes to the groups and the buttons within the groups to accommodate the various screen resolutions. The result is that certain commands may need to be accessed differently depending on the resolution chosen. A command that is visible on the Ribbon and available by clicking a button at one resolution may not be visible and may need to be accessed using its group button at a different resolution.

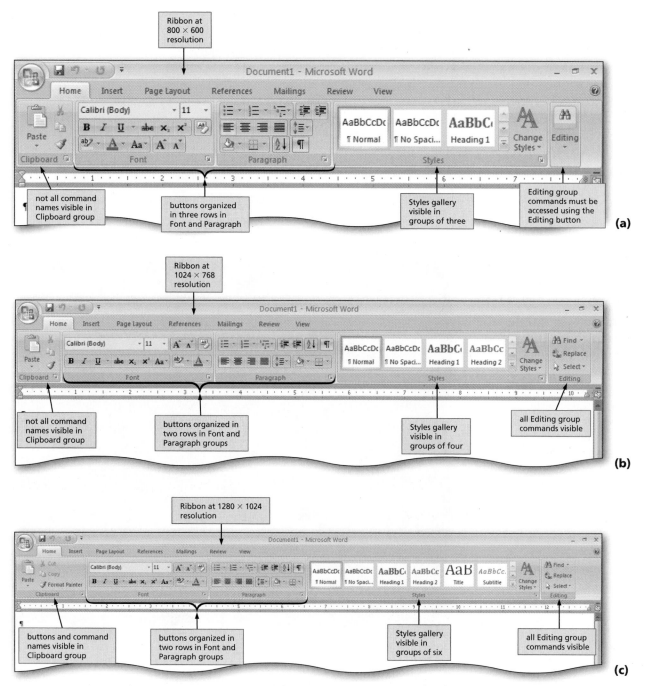

Figure E–6

Comparing the three Ribbons, notice changes in content and layout of the groups and galleries. In some cases, the content of a group is the same in each resolution, but the layout of the group differs. For example, the same buttons appear in the Font and Paragraph groups in the three resolutions, but the layouts differ. The buttons are displayed in three rows at the 800×600 resolution, and in two rows in the 1024×768 and 1280×1024 resolutions. In other cases, the content and layout are the same across the resolution, but the level of detail differs with the resolution. In the Clipboard group, when the resolution increases to 1280×1024, the names of all the buttons in the group appear in addition to the buttons themselves. At the lower resolution, only the buttons appear.

Changing resolutions also can result in fewer commands being visible in a group. Comparing the Editing groups, notice that the group at the 800×600 resolution consists of an Editing button, while at the higher resolutions, the group has three buttons visible. The commands that are available on the Ribbon at the higher resolutions must be accessed using the Editing button at the 800×600 resolution.

Changing resolutions results in different amounts of detail being available at one time in the galleries on the Ribbon. The Styles gallery in the three resolutions presented show different numbers of styles. At 800×600, you can scroll through the gallery three styles at a time, at 1024×768, you can scroll through the gallery four styles at a time, and at 1280×1024, you can scroll through the gallery six styles at a time.

Customizing the Word Window

When working in Word, you may want to make your working area as large as possible. One option is to minimize the Ribbon. You also can modify the characteristics of the Quick Access Toolbar, customizing the toolbar's commands and location to better suit your needs.

To Minimize the Ribbon in Word

The following steps minimize the Ribbon.

- Start Word.

- Maximize the Word window, if necessary.

- Click the Customize Quick Access Toolbar button on the Quick Access Toolbar to display the Customize Quick Access Toolbar menu (Figure E–7).

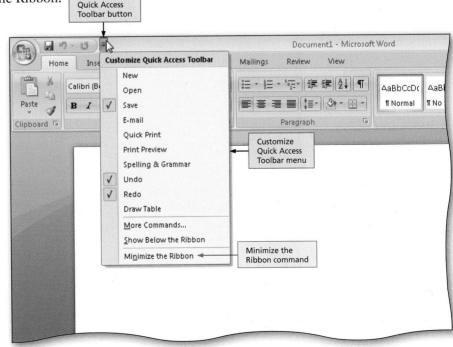

Figure E–7

2

- Click Minimize the Ribbon on the Quick Access Toolbar to reduce the Ribbon display to just the tabs (Figure E–8).

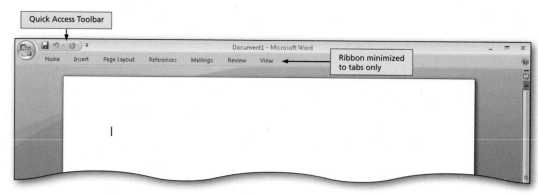

Figure E–8

Other Ways

1. Double-click the active Ribbon tab
2. Press CTRL+F1

Customizing and Resetting the Quick Access Toolbar

The Quick Access Toolbar, located to the right of the Microsoft Office Button by default, provides easy access to some of the more frequently used commands in Word (Figure E–7). By default, the Quick Access Toolbar contains buttons for the Save, Undo, and Redo commands. Customize the Quick Access Toolbar by changing its location in the window and by adding additional buttons to reflect which commands you would like to be able to access easily.

To Change the Location of the Quick Access Toolbar

The following steps move the Quick Access Toolbar to below the Ribbon.

1

- Double-click the Home tab to redisplay the Ribbon.

- Click the Customize Quick Access Toolbar button on the Quick Access Toolbar menu to display the Customize Quick Access Toolbar menu (Figure E–9).

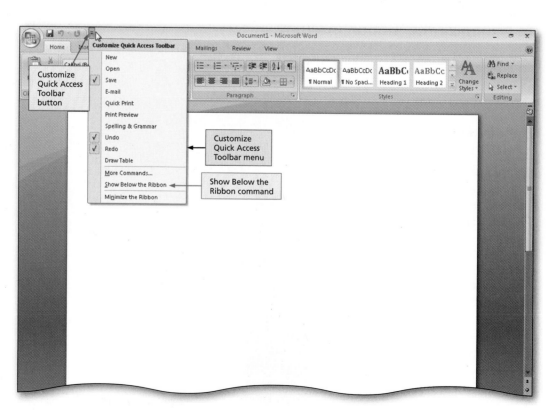

Figure E–9

- Click Show Below the Ribbon on the Quick Access Toolbar menu to move the Quick Access Toolbar below the Ribbon (Figure E–10).

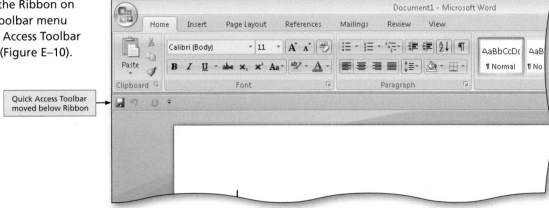

Quick Access Toolbar moved below Ribbon

Figure E–10

To Add Commands to the Quick Access Toolbar Using the Customize Quick Access Toolbar Menu

Some of the more commonly added commands are available for selection from the Customize Quick Access Toolbar menu. The following steps add the Quick Print button to the Quick Access Toolbar.

- Click the Customize Quick Access Toolbar button to display the Customize Quick Access Toolbar menu (Figure E–11).

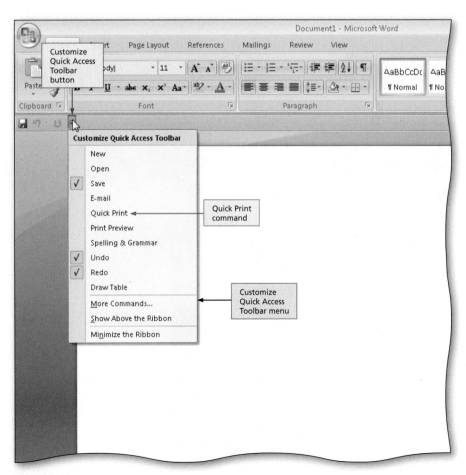

Figure E–11

- Click Quick Print on the Quick Access Toolbar menu to add the Quick Print button to the Quick Access Toolbar (Figure E–12).

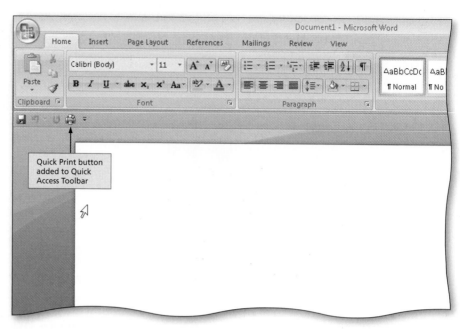

Figure E–12

To Add Commands to the Quick Access Toolbar Using the Shortcut Menu

Commands also can be added to the Quick Access Toolbar from the Ribbon. Adding an existing Ribbon command that you use often to the Quick Access Toolbar makes the command immediately available, regardless of which tab is active.

- Click the Review tab on the Ribbon to make it the active tab.

- Right-click the Spelling & Grammar button on the Review tab to display a shortcut menu (Figure E–13).

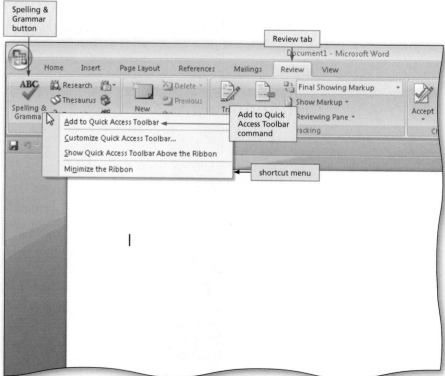

Figure E–13

2

- Click Add to Quick Access Toolbar on the shortcut menu to add the Spelling & Grammar button to the Quick Access Toolbar (Figure E–14).

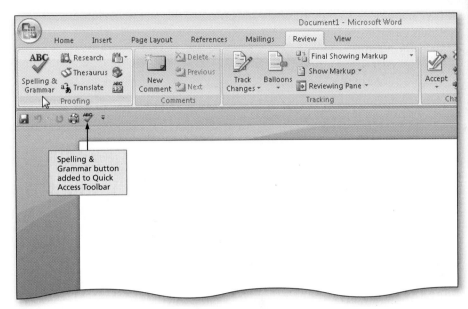

Figure E–14

To Add Commands to the Quick Access Toolbar Using Word Options

Some commands do not appear on the Ribbon. They can be added to the Quick Access Toolbar using the Word Options dialog box.

1

- Click the Office Button to display the Office Button menu (Figure E–15).

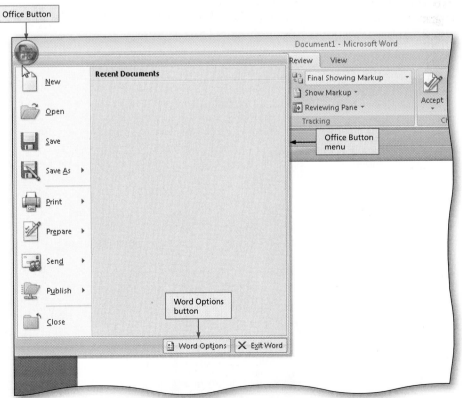

Figure E–15

- Click the Word Options button on the Office Button menu to display the Word Options dialog box (Figure E–16).

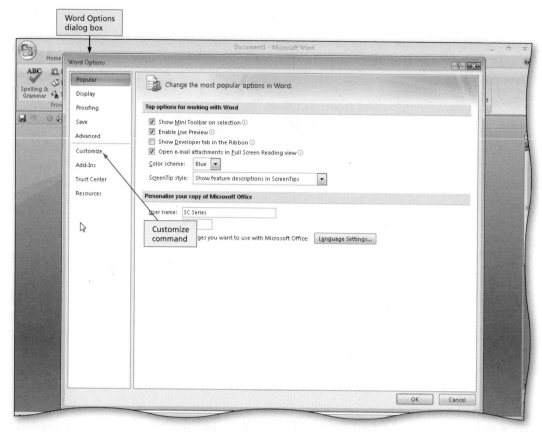

Figure E–16

- Click Customize in the left pane.

- Click 'Choose commands from' box arrow to display the 'Choose commands from' list.

- Click Commands Not in the Ribbon in the 'Choose commands from' list.

- Scroll to display the Web Page Preview command.

- Click Web Page Preview to select it (Figure E–17).

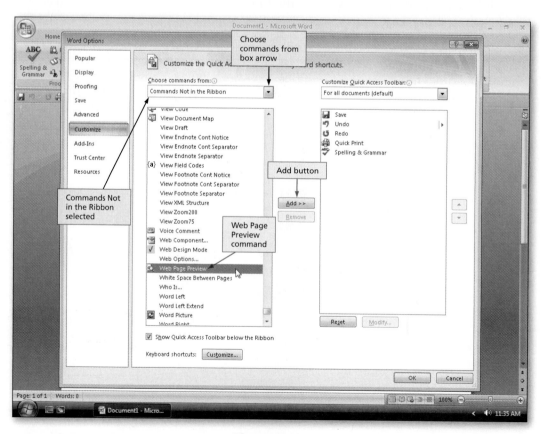

Figure E–17

- Click the Add button
to add the Web Page
Preview button to
the list of buttons
on the Quick Access
Toolbar (Figure E–18).

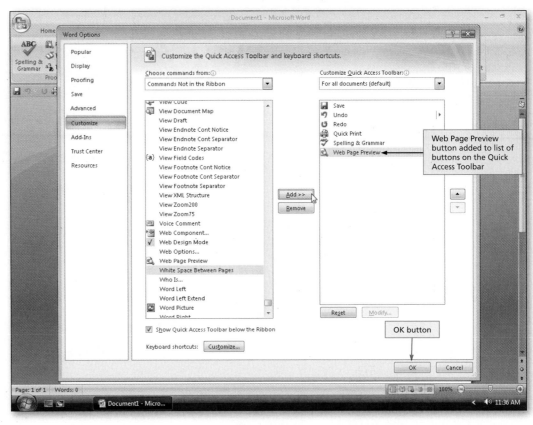

Figure E–18

- Click the OK button to add
the Web Page Preview button
to the Quick Access Toolbar
(Figure E–19).

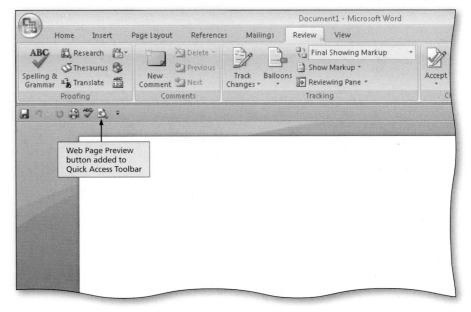

Figure E–19

Other Ways

1. Click Customize Quick
   Access Toolbar button,
   click More Commands,
   select commands to
   add, click Add button,
   click OK button

To Remove a Command from the Quick Access Toolbar

1

● Right-click the Web Page Preview button on the Quick Access Toolbar to display a shortcut menu (Figure E–20).

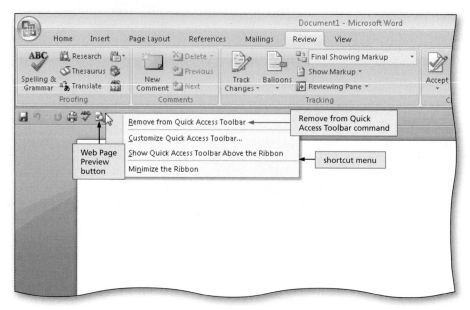

Figure E–20

2

● Click Remove from Quick Access Toolbar on the shortcut menu to remove the button from the Quick Access Toolbar (Figure E–21).

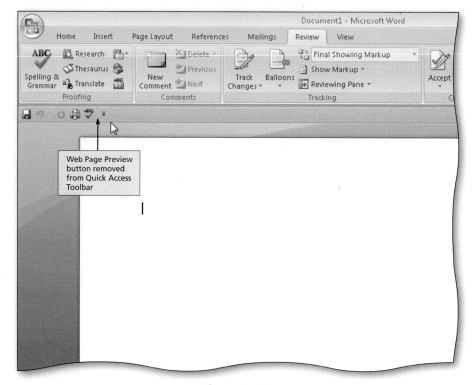

Figure E–21

Other Ways

1. Click Customize Quick Access Toolbar button, click More Commands, click the command you wish to remove in the Customize Quick Access Toolbar list, click Remove button, click OK button

2. If the command appears on the Customize Quick Access Toolbar menu, click the Customize Quick Access Toolbar button, click the command you wish to remove

To Reset the Quick Access Toolbar

1

- Click the Customize Quick Access Toolbar button on the Quick Access Toolbar.

- Click More Commands on the Quick Access Toolbar menu to display the Word Options Dialog box.

- Click the Show Quick Access Toolbar below the Ribbon check box to deselect it (Figure E–22).

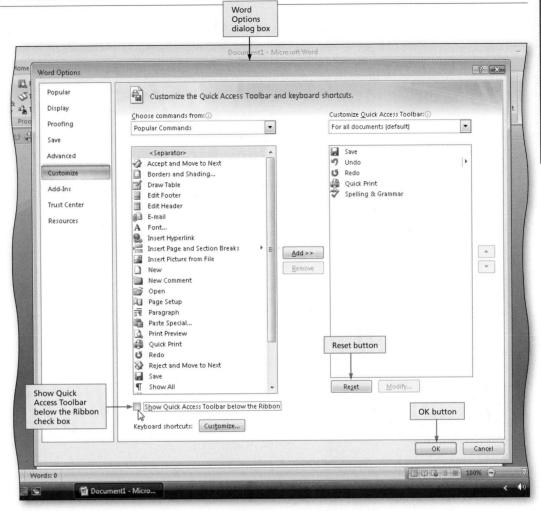

Figure E–22

- Click the Reset button, click the Yes button in the dialog box that appears, and then click the OK button in the Word Options dialog box, to reset the Quick Access Toolbar to its original position to the right of the Office Button, with the original three buttons (Figure E–23).

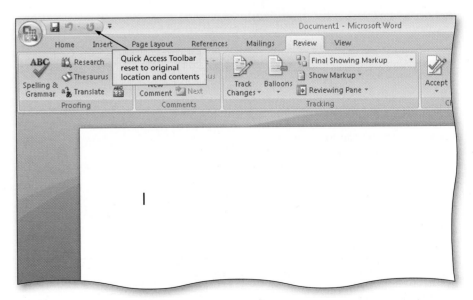

Figure E–23

Changing the Word Color Scheme

The Microsoft Word window can be customized by selecting a color scheme other than the default blue one. Three color schemes are available in Word.

To Change the Word Color Scheme

The following steps change the color scheme.

1

- Click the Office Button to display the Office Button menu.

- Click the Word Options button on the Office Button menu to display the Word Options dialog box.

- If necessary, click Popular in the left pane. Click the Color scheme box arrow to display a list of color schemes (Figure E–24).

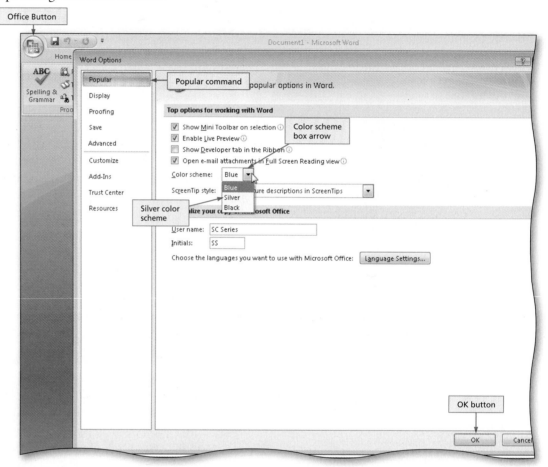

Figure E–24

2

- Click Silver in the list.

- Click the OK button to change the color scheme to silver (Figure E–25).

How do I switch back to the default color scheme?

Follow the steps for changing the Word color scheme, and select Blue from the list of color schemes.

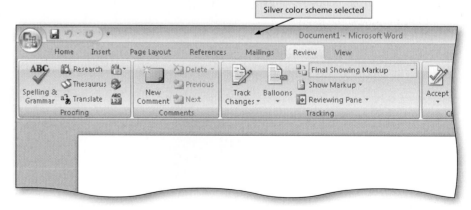

Figure E–25

Appendix F
Steps for the Windows XP User

For the XP User of this Book

For most tasks, no differences exist between using Office 2007 under the Windows Vista operating system and using an Office 2007 program under the Windows XP operating system. With some tasks, however, you will see some differences, or need to complete the tasks using different steps. This appendix shows how to Start an Application, Save a Document, Open a Document, Insert a Picture, and Insert Text from a File while using Microsoft Office under Windows XP. To illustrate these tasks, this appendix uses Microsoft Word. The tasks can be accomplished in other Office programs in a similar fashion.

To Start Word

The following steps, which assume Windows is running, start Word based on a typical installation. You may need to ask your instructor how to start Word for your computer.

1

- Click the Start button on the Windows taskbar to display the Start menu.

- Point to All Programs on the Start menu to display the All Programs submenu.

- Point to Microsoft Office on the All Programs submenu to display the Microsoft Office submenu (Figure F–1).

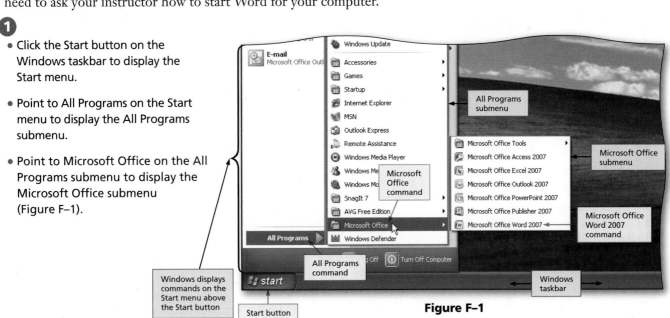

Figure F–1

- Click Microsoft Office Word 2007 to start Word and display a new blank document in the Word window (Figure F–2).

- If the Word window is not maximized, click the Maximize button next to the Close button on its title bar to maximize the window.

- If the Print Layout button is not selected, click it so that your screen layout matches Figure F–2.

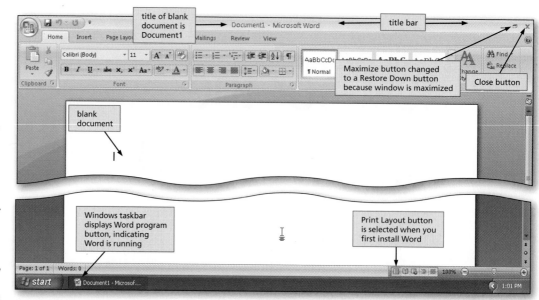

Figure F–2

Other Ways

1. Double-click Word icon on desktop, if one is present
2. Click Microsoft Office Word 2007 on Start menu

To Save a Document

After editing, you should save the document. The following steps save a document on a USB flash drive using the file name, Horseback Riding Lessons Flyer.

- With a USB flash drive connected to one of the computer's USB ports, click the Save button on the Quick Access Toolbar to display the Save As dialog box (Figure F–3).

Q&A

Do I have to save to a USB flash drive?

No. You can save to any device or folder. A **folder** is a specific location on a storage medium. You can save to the default folder or a different folder. You also can create your own folders, which is explained later in this book.

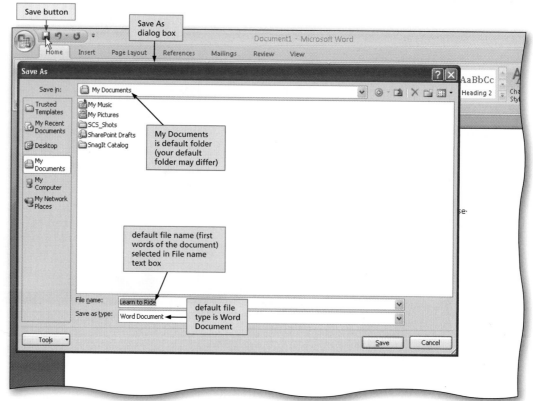

Figure F–3

②

- Type the name of your file (Horseback Riding Lessons Flyer in this example) in the File name text box to change the file name. Do not press the ENTER key after typing the file name (Figure F–4).

 Q&A What characters can I use in a file name?

A file name can have a maximum of 255 characters, including spaces. The only invalid characters are the backslash (\), slash (/), colon (:), asterisk (*), question mark (?), quotation mark ("), less than symbol (<), greater than symbol (>), and vertical bar (|).

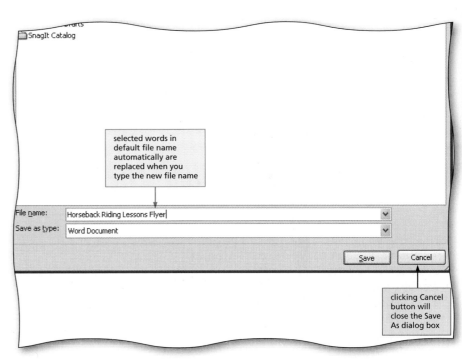

Figure F–4

③

- Click the Save in box arrow to display a list of available drives and folders (Figure F–5).

Q&A Why is my list of files, folders, and drives arranged and named differently from those shown in the figure?

Your computer's configuration determines how the list of files and folders is displayed and how drives are named. You can change the save location by clicking shortcuts on the **My Places bar**.

Q&A How do I save the file if I am not using a USB flash drive?

Use the same process, but be certain to select your device in the Save in list.

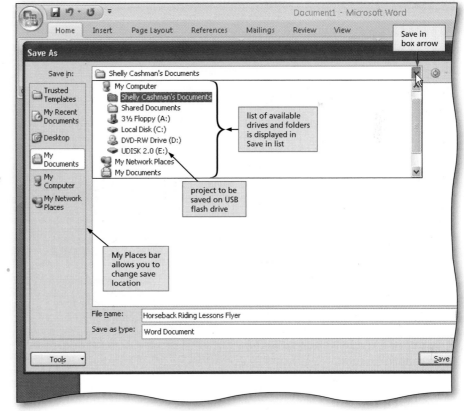

Figure F–5

- Click UDISK 2.0 (E:) in the Save in list to select the USB flash drive, Drive E in this case, as the new save location (Figure F–6).

- Click the Save button to save the document.

Q&A What if my USB flash drive has a different name or letter?

It is very likely that your USB flash drive will have a different name and drive letter and be connected to a different port. Verify the device in your Save in list is correct.

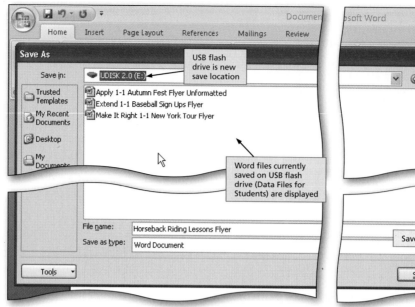
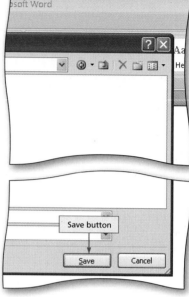

Figure F–6

Other Ways

1. Click Office Button, click Save, type file name, select drive or folder, click Save button

2. Press CTRL+S or press SHIFT+F12, type file name, select drive or folder, click Save button

To Open a Document

The following steps open the Horseback Riding Lessons Flyer file from the USB flash drive.

1

- With your USB flash drive connected to one of the computer's USB ports, click the Office Button to display the Office Button menu.

- Click Open on the Office Button menu to display the Open dialog box.

- If necessary, click the Look in box arrow and then click UDISK 2.0 (E:) to select the USB flash drive, Drive E in this case, in the Look in list as the new open location.

- Click Horseback Riding Lessons Flyer to select the file name (Figure F–7).

- Click the Open button to open the document.

Q&A How do I open the file if I am not using a USB flash drive?

Use the same process, but be certain to select your device in the Look in list.

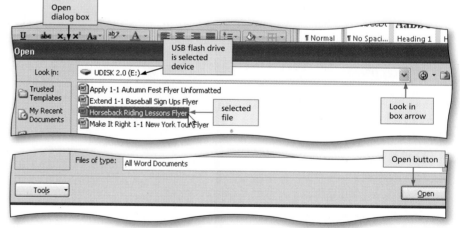

Figure F–7

Other Ways

1. Click Office Button, double-click file name in Recent Documents list

2. Press CTRL+O, select file name, press ENTER

To Insert a Picture

The following steps insert a centered picture, which, in this example, is located on a USB flash drive.

1 Position the insertion point where you want the picture to be located. Click Insert on the Ribbon to display the Insert tab. Click the Insert Picture from File button on the Insert tab to display the Insert Picture dialog box.

2 With your USB flash drive connected to one of the computer's USB ports, if necessary, click the Look in box arrow and then click UDISK 2.0 (E:) to select the USB flash drive, Drive E in this case, in the Look in list as the device that contains the picture. Select the file name of the picture file.

3 Click the Insert button in the dialog box to insert the picture at the location of the insertion point in the document.

To Insert Text from a File

The following steps insert text from a file located on the USB flash drive.

1 Click where you want to insert the text. Click Insert on the Ribbon to display the Insert tab. Click the Object button arrow in the Text group to display the Object menu. Click Text from File to display the Insert File dialog box.

2 With your USB flash drive connected to one of the computer's USB ports, if necessary, click the Look in box arrow and then click UDISK 2.0 (E:) to select the USB flash drive, Drive E in this case, in the Look in list as the device that contains the file. Click to select the file name.

3 Click the Insert button in the dialog box to insert the file at the location of the insertion point in the document.

To Create a New Database

The following steps create a database on a USB flash drive.

1 With a USB flash drive connected to one of the computer's USB ports, click Blank Database in the Getting Started with Microsoft Office Access screen to create a new blank database.

2 Type the name of your database in the File Name text box and then click the 'Browse for a location to put your database' button to display the File New Database dialog box.

3 Click the Save in box arrow to display a list of available drives and folders and then click UDISK 2.0 (E:) (your letter may be different) in the Save in list to select the USB flash drive as the new save location.

4 Click the OK button to select the USB flash drive as the location for the database and to return to the Getting Started with Microsoft Office Access screen.

5 Click the Create button to create the database on the USB flash drive with the file name you selected.

To Open a Database

The following steps use the More button to open a database from the USB flash drive.

1 With your USB flash drive connected to one of the computer's USB ports, click the More button to display the Open dialog box.

2 If necessary, click the Look in box arrow and then click UDISK 2.0 (E:) to select the USB flash drive in the Look in list as the new open location. (Your drive letter might be different.)

3 Select the file name. Click the Open button to open the database.

4 If a Security Warning appears, click the Options button to display the Microsoft Office Security Options dialog box. With the option button to enable this content selected, click the OK button to enable the content.

Appendix G
Microsoft Business Certification Program

What Is the Microsoft Business Certification Program?

The Microsoft Business Certification Program enables candidates to show that they have something exceptional to offer – proved expertise in Microsoft Office 2007 programs. The two certification tracks allow candidates to choose how they want to exhibit their skills, either through validating skills within a specific Microsoft product or taking their knowledge to the next level and combining Microsoft programs to show that they can apply multiple skill sets to complete more complex office tasks. Recognized by businesses and schools around the world, more than 3 million certifications have been obtained in more than 100 different countries. The Microsoft Business Certification Program is the only Microsoft-approved certification program of its kind.

What Is the Microsoft Certified Application Specialist Certification?

The Microsoft Certified Application Specialist certification exams focus on validating specific skill sets within each of the Microsoft Office system programs. Candidates can choose which exam(s) they want to take according to which skills they want to validate. The available Application Specialist exams include:

- Using Windows Vista™
- Using Microsoft® Office Word 2007
- Using Microsoft® Office Excel® 2007
- Using Microsoft® Office PowerPoint® 2007
- Using Microsoft® Office Access™ 2007
- Using Microsoft® Office Outlook® 2007

> For more information and details on how Shelly Cashman Series textbooks map to Microsoft Certified Application Specialist certification, visit scsite.com/off2007/cert.

What Is the Microsoft Certified Application Professional Certification?

The Microsoft Certified Application Professional certification exams focus on a candidate's ability to use the 2007 Microsoft® Office system to accomplish industry-agnostic functions, for example Budget Analysis and Forecasting, or Content Management and Collaboration. The available Application Professional exams currently include:

- Organizational Support
- Creating and Managing Presentations
- Content Management and Collaboration
- Budget Analysis and Forecasting

Index

Quick Reference Summary

In the Microsoft Office 2007 programs, you can accomplish a task in a number of ways. The following four tables (one each for Microsoft Office Word 2007, Microsoft Office Excel 2007, Microsoft Office Access 2007 and Microsoft Office PowerPoint 2007) provide a quick reference to each task presented in this textbook. The first column identifies the task. The second column indicates the page number on which the task is discussed in the book. The subsequent four columns list the different ways the task in column one can be carried out.

Table 1 Microsoft Office Word 2007 Quick Reference Summary

Task	Page Number	Mouse	Ribbon	Shortcut Menu	Keyboard Shortcut
Bold	WD 34	Bold button on Mini toolbar	Bold button on Home tab	Font | Font tab | Bold in Font style list	CTRL+B
Bullets, Apply	WD 32	Bullets button on Mini toolbar	Bullets button on Home tab	Bullets	ASTERISK KEY | SPACEBAR
Center	WD 26	Center button on Mini toolbar	Center button on Home tab	Paragraph | Indents and Spacing tab	CTRL+E
Close Document	WD 60	Office Button | Close			
Delete Text	WD 59				DELETE
Document Properties, Set or View	WD 51	Office Button | Prepare | Properties			
Double-Underline	WD 35		Font Dialog Box Launcher on Home tab	Font | Font tab	CTRL+SHIFT+D
Font Size, Change	WD 28	Font Size box arrow on Mini toolbar	Font Size box arrow on Home tab	Font | Font tab	CTRL+SHIFT+P
Font, Change	WD 29	Font box arrow on Mini toolbar	Font box arrow on Home tab	Font | Font tab	CTRL+SHIFT+F
Formatting Marks	WD 14		Show/Hide ¶ button on Home tab		CTRL+SHIFT+*
Graphic, Resize	WD 46	Drag sizing handle	Format tab in Picture Tools tab or Size Dialog Box Launcher on Format tab	Size | Size tab	
Help	WD 60		Office Word Help button		F1
Insertion Point, Move to Beginning of Document	WD 24	Scroll to top of document, click			CTRL+HOME

Table 1 Microsoft Office Word 2007 Quick Reference Summary *(continued)*

Task	Page Number	Mouse	Ribbon	Shortcut Menu	Keyboard Shortcut
Insertion Point, Move to End of Document	WD 25	Scroll to bottom of document, click			CTRL+END
Italicize	WD 36	Italic button on Mini toolbar	Italic button on Home tab	Font	Font tab	CTRL+I
Open Document	WD 56	Office Button	Open			CTRL+O
Page Border, Add	WD 48		Page Borders button on Page Layout tab		
Paragraphs, Change Spacing Above and Below	WD 50		Spacing Before box arrow on Page Layout tab	Paragraph	Indents and Spacing tab	
Picture Border, Change	WD 45		Picture Border button on Format tab		
Picture Style, Apply	WD 44		Picture Tools and Format tabs	More button in Picture Styles gallery		
Picture, Insert	WD 41		Picture button on Insert tab		
Print Document	WD 54	Office Button	Print	Print			CTRL+P
Quit Word	WD 55	Close button on right side of Word title bar			ALT+F4
Save Document, Same Name	WD 53	Save button on Quick Access Toolbar			CTRL+S
Save New Document	WD 19	Save button on Quick Access Toolbar			CTRL+S
Select Block of Text	WD 33	Click at beginning of text, hold down SHIFT key and click at end of text to select; or drag through text			CTRL+SHIFT+RIGHT ARROW and/or DOWN ARROW
Select Graphic	WD 46	Click graphic			
Select Line	WD 27	Point to left of line and click			SHIFT+DOWN ARROW
Select Lines	WD 30	Point to left of first line and drag up or down			CTRL+SHIFT+DOWN ARROW
Select Paragraphs	WD 30	Point to left of first paragraph, double-click, and drag up or down			
Select Word	WD 59	Double-click word			CTRL+SHIFT+RIGHT ARROW
Select Words	WD 33	Drag through words			CTRL+SHIFT+RIGHT ARROW
Spelling and Grammar Check as You Type	WD 16	Spelling and Grammar Check icon on status bar		Correct word on shortcut menu	
Style Set, Change	WD 37		Change Styles button on Home tab	Style Set on Change Styles menu		
Styles Task Pane, Open	WD 25		Styles Dialog Box Launcher		ATL+CTRL+SHIFT+S

Table 1 Microsoft Office Word 2007 Quick Reference Summary *(continued)*

Task	Page Number	Mouse	Ribbon	Shortcut Menu	Keyboard Shortcut
Styles, Apply	WD 24		Styles gallery		
Theme Colors, Change	WD 39		Change Styles button on Home tab	Colors on Change Styles menu		
Theme Fonts, Change	WD 40		Change Styles button on Home tab	Fonts on Change Styles menu		
Underline	WD 35		Underline button on Home tab	Font	Font tab	CTRL+U
Zoom	WD 46	Zoom Out and Zoom In buttons on status bar	Zoom button on View tab		

Table 2 Microsoft Office Excel 2007 Quick Reference Summary

Task	Page Number	Mouse	Ribbon	Shortcut Menu	Keyboard Shortcut
AutoCalculate	EX 62	Select range	right-click AutoCalculate area	click calculation			
Bold	EX 38	Bold button on Mini toolbar	Bold button on Home tab or Font Dialog Box Launcher on Home tab	Font tab	Format Cells	Font tab	Bold in Font style list	CTRL+B
Cell Style, change	EX 35		Cell Styles button on Home tab		
Center Across Columns	EX 40	Right-click selection	Merge & Center button on Mini toolbar	Merge & Center button on Home tab or Alignment Dialog Box Launcher on Home tab	Format Cells	Alignment tab	CTRL+1	A
Chart, Add	EX 50		Dialog Box Launcher in Charts group on Insert tab		F11
Clear Cell	EX 66	Drag fill handle back	Clear button on Home tab	Clear Contents	DELETE
Clear Worksheet	EX 66		Select All button on worksheet	Clear button on Home tab		
Close Workbook	EX 59		Close button on Ribbon or Office Button	Close		CTRL+W
Column Width	EX 46	Drag column heading boundary	Home tab	Format button	Column Width	Column Width	ALT+O	C	W
Comma Style Format	EX 44		Comma Style button on Home tab or Number Dialog Box Launcher on Home tab	Accounting	Format Cells	Number tab	Accounting	CTRL+1	N

Table 2 Microsoft Office Excel 2007 Quick Reference Summary *(continued)*

Task	Page Number	Mouse	Ribbon	Shortcut Menu	Keyboard Shortcut
Copy to adjacent cells	EX 27	Select source area | drag fill handle through destination cells	Select source area | click Copy button on Home tab | select destination area | click Paste button on Home tab	Right-click source area | click Copy | right-click destination area | click Paste	
Cut	EX 64		Cut button on Home tab	Cut	CTRL+X
Document Properties, Set or View	EX 55	Office Button | Prepare | Properties			ALT+F | E | P
Embedded Chart, Delete	EX 67				Select chart, press DELETE
Font Color	EX 39	Font Color box arrow on Mini toolbar	Font Color button arrow on Home tab or Font Dialog Box Launcher on Home tab	Format Cells | Font tab	CTRL+1 | F
Font Size, Change	EX 38	Font Size box arrow on Mini toolbar	Font Size box arrow on Home tab or Font Dialog Box Launcher on Home tab	Format Cells | Font tab	CTRL+1 | F
Font Size, Increase	EX 39	Increase Font Size button on Mini toolbar	Increase Font Size button on Home tab		
Font Type	EX 36	Font box arrow on Mini toolbar	Font box arrow on Home tab or Font Dialog Box Launcher in Font group on Home tab	Format Cells | Font tab	CTRL+1 | F
Full Screen	EX 9		Full Screen button on View tab		ALT+V | U
Go To	EX 48	Click cell	Find & Select button on Home tab		F5
Help	EX 67 and Appendix C		Microsoft Office Excel Help button on Ribbon		F1
In-Cell Editing	EX 63	Double-click cell			F2
Merge Cells	EX 41		Merge & Center button on Home tab or Alignment Dialog Box Launcher on Home tab	Format Cells | Alignment tab	ALT+O | E | A
New Workbook	EX 67	Office Button | New			CTRL+N
Open Workbook	EX 61	Office Button | Open			CTRL+O
Quit Excel	EX 59	Close button on title bar Office Button | Exit Excel			ALT+F4
Redo	EX 65	Redo button on Quick Access Toolbar			ALT+3 or CTRL+Y
Save Workbook, New Name	EX 57		Office Button | Save As		ALT+F | A
Save Workbook, Same Name	EX 57	Save button on Quick Access Toolbar	Office Button | Save		CTRL+S
Select All of Worksheet	EX 67	Select All button on worksheet			CTRL+A

Table 2 Microsoft Office Excel 2007 Quick Reference Summary *(continued)*

Task	Page Number	Mouse	Ribbon	Shortcut Menu	Keyboard Shortcut
Select Cell	EX 15	Click cell or click Name box, type cell reference, press ENTER			Use arrow keys
Shortcut Menu	EX 12	Right-click object			SHIFT+F10
Split Cell	EX 41		Merge & Center button on Home tab or Alignment Dialog Box Launcher on Home tab | click Merge cells to deselect	Format Cells | Alignment tab | click Merge cells to deselect	ALT+O | E | A
Sum	EX 25	Function Wizard button in formula bar | SUM	Sum button on Home tab	Insert Function button on Formulas tab	ALT+=
Undo	EX 65	Undo button on Quick Access Toolbar			ALT+2, CTRL+Z

Table 3 Microsoft Office Access 2007 Quick Reference Summary

Task	Page Number	Mouse	Ribbon	Shortcut Menu	Keyboard Shortcut
Add New Field	AC 24	Right-click Add New Field in Datasheet	Insert Rows button on Design Tab	Design View | INSERT	
Add Record	AC 30, 38	New (blank) record button	New button on Home tab	Open | Click in field	CTRL+PLUS SIGN (+)
Change Database Properties	AC 60	Office button | Manage | Database Properties			
Change Primary Key	AC 28	Delete field | Primary Key button	Design View button on Design tab | select field | Primary Key button		
Close Object	AC 35	Close button for object		Right-click item | Close	
Create Database	AC 14	Blank Database button or Office Button | Save			CTRL+S or SHIFT+F12 or ALT+I
Create Report	AC 51		Report Wizard button on Create tab		
Create Table	AC 23	Office Button | Save button	Table button on Create tab		CTRL+S or SHIFT+F12
Define Fields in a Table	AC 24		Right-click Add New Field on Datasheet tab | Rename Column	Right-click Add New Field | Rename Column	
Field Size	AC 46		Design View button on Design tab | select field | Field Size box		
Move to First Record	AC 39	First Record button			
Move to Last Record	AC 39	Last Record button			
Move to Next Record	AC 39	Next Record button			
Move to Previous Record	AC 39	Previous Record button			
New Item	various	Office button | Open			

Table 3 Microsoft Office Access 2007 Quick Reference Summary *(continued)*

Task	Page Number	Mouse	Ribbon	Shortcut Menu	Keyboard Shortcut
Open Database	AC 37	More button | Open button or Office button | double-click file name			CTRL+O
Open Table	AC 26	Open button		Open	
Preview Table	AC 41	Office button | Print | Print Preview			ALT+F, W, V
Print Object	AC 41, 56	Office button | Print | Quick Print or Print			CTRL+P
Quit Access	AC 36	Close button			
Save Form	AC 58	Office button | Save			CTRL+S
Save Table	AC 27	Save button	Office button | Save	Save	CTRL+S
Search for Access Help	AC 62	Microsoft Office Access Help button			F1
Select Fields for Report	AC 51		Report Wizard button on Create tab | Add Field button		
Split Form	AC 57		Split Form button on Create tab		
Start Access	AC 12	Start button | All Programs | Microsoft Office | Microsoft Office Access 2007			
Switch Between Form and Datasheet Views	AC 57	Form View or Datasheet View button			

Table 4 Microsoft Office PowerPoint 2007 Quick Reference Summary

Task	Page Number	Mouse	Ribbon	Shortcut Menu	Keyboard Shortcut
Add Shapes	PPT 119		Shapes button on Home tab | select shape		
Demote a Paragraph	PPT 34	Increase List Level button on Mini toolbar	Increase List Level button on Home tab		TAB or ALT+SHIFT+ RIGHT ARROW
Display a Presentation in Grayscale	PPT 59		Grayscale button on View tab		ALT+V | C | U
Document Properties	PPT 44	Office Button | Prepare | Properties			
Document Theme, Choose	PPT 16		More button on Design tab | theme		
End Slide Show	PPT 54			End Show	ESC or HYPHEN
Font Color	PPT 23	Font Color button or Font Color arrow on Mini toolbar	Font Color button on Home tab or Font Color arrow on Home tab | select color or Font Dialog Box Launcher on Home tab | Font color button on Font tab | select color	Font | Font color button on Font tab | select color	CTRL+SHIFT+F | Font tab | Font color button | select color

Table 4 Microsoft Office PowerPoint 2007 Quick Reference Summary *(continued)*

Task	Page Number	Mouse	Ribbon	Shortcut Menu	Keyboard Shortcut
Font Size, Decrease	PPT 25	Decrease Font Size button or Font Size arrow on Mini toolbar	Decrease Font Size button on Home tab or Font Size arrow on Home tab | size	Font Size arrow | Size	CTRL+SHIFT+LEFT CARET (<)
Font Size, Increase	PPT 24	Increase Font Size button or Font Size arrow on Mini toolbar	Increase Font Size button on Home tab or Font Size arrow on Home tab | size	Font size arrow | Size	CTRL+SHIFT+RIGHT CARET (>)
Help	PPT 63 and Appendix A	Office PowerPoint Help button			F1
Next Slide	PPT 47	Next Slide button on vertical scroll bar			PAGE DOWN
Open Presentation	PPT 54	Office Button | Open | select file			CTRL+O
Previous Slide	PPT 50, 51	Previous Slide button on vertical scroll bar			PAGE UP
Print a Presentation	PPT 61	Office Button | Print			CTRL+P
Promote a Paragraph	PPT 34	Decrease List Level button on Mini toolbar	Decrease List Level button on Home tab		SHIFT+TAB or ALT+SHIFT+ LEFT ARROW
Quit PowerPoint	PPT 53	Double-click Office Button or Close button on title bar or Office Button | Exit PowerPoint		Right-click Microsoft PowerPoint button on taskbar | Close	ALT+F4 or CTRL+Q
Save a Presentation	PPT 27	Save button on Quick Access toolbar or Office Button | Save			CTRL+S or SHIFT+F12
Slide, Add	PPT 29		New Slide button on Home tab or New Slide arrow on Home tab | choose slide type		CTRL+M
Slide, Arrange	PPT 41	Drag slide in Slides tab to new position or in Slide Sorter View drag slide to new position			
Slide, Duplicate	PPT 40		New Slide arrow on Home tab | Duplicate Selected Slides		
Slide Show View	PPT 49	Slide Show button at lower-right PowerPoint window	Slide Show button on View tab or From Beginning button on Slide Show tab		F5 or ALT+V | W
Spelling Check	PPT 55		Spelling button on Review tab		F7
Text, Bold	PPT 25	Bold button on Mini toolbar	Bold button on Home tab		CTRL+B
Text, Change Color	PPT 23	Font Color button or Font Color arrow on Mini toolbar	Font color arrow on Home tab | choose color	Font | Font color button | choose color	
Text, Delete	PPT 42		Cut button on Home tab	Cut	DELETE or CTRL+X or BACKSPACE

Table 4 Microsoft Office PowerPoint 2007 Quick Reference Summary *(continued)*

Task	Page Number	Mouse	Ribbon	Shortcut Menu	Keyboard Shortcut
Text, Italicize	PPT 22	Italic button on Mini toolbar	Italic button on Home tab	Font | Font style arrow | Italics	CTRL+I
Text, Select	PPT 21	Drag to select | double-click to select word | triple-click to select paragraph			SHIFT+DOWN ARROW or SHIFT+RIGHT ARROW

(continued)

3. **Format specific elements of the text.** Examples of how you can modify the appearance, or **format**, of text include changing its shape, size, color, and position on the slide.

4. **Determine where to save the presentation.** You can store a document permanently, or **save** it, on a variety of storage media including a hard disk, USB flash drive, or CD. You also can indicate a specific location on the storage media for saving the document.

When necessary, more specific details concerning the above guidelines are presented at appropriate points in the chapter. The chapter also will identify the actions performed and decisions made regarding these guidelines during the creation of the slides shown in Figure 1–1.

Plan Ahead

Starting PowerPoint

If you are using a computer to step through the project in this chapter and you want your screen to match the figures in this book, you should change your screen's resolution to 1024 × 768. For information about how to change a computer's resolution, read Appendix E.

Note: If you are using Windows XP, see Appendix F for alternate steps.

BTW

Decreasing Resolution
You may need to decrease your computer's resolution if you know you are going to run your presentation on another computer that uses a lower resolution, such as 800 × 600 or 640 × 480. This lower resolution, however, may affect the appearance of your slides.

To Start PowerPoint

The following steps, which assume Windows Vista is running, start PowerPoint based on a typical installation. You may need to ask your instructor how to start PowerPoint for your computer.

1
- Click the Start button on the Windows Vista taskbar to display the Start menu.

- Click All Programs at the bottom of the left pane on the Start menu to display the All Programs list.

- Click Microsoft Office in the All Programs list to display the Microsoft Office (Figure 1–2).

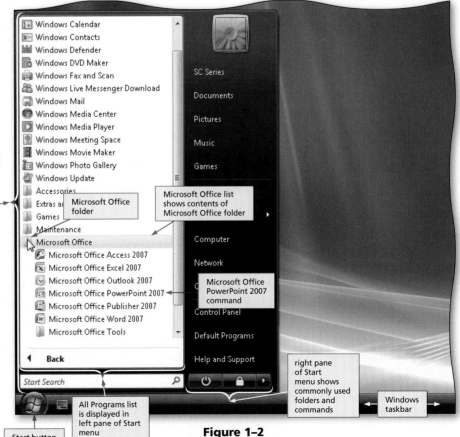

Figure 1–2

2

- Click Microsoft Office PowerPoint 2007 to start PowerPoint and display a new blank document in the PowerPoint window (Figure 1–3).

- If the PowerPoint window is not maximized, click the Maximize button next to the Close button on its title bar to maximize the window.

Q&A

What is a maximized window?

A maximized window fills the entire screen. When you maximize a window, the Maximize button changes to a Restore Down button. When you restore a maximized window, the Restore Down button changes to a Maximize button.

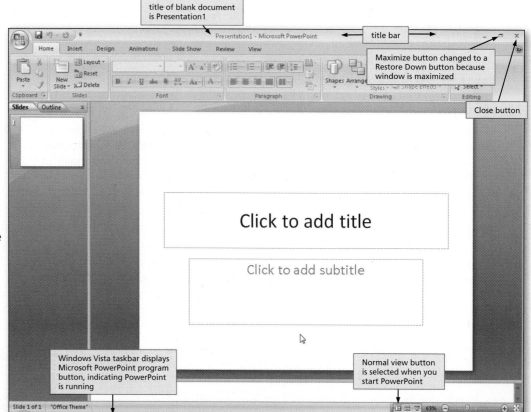

Figure 1–3

Other Ways

1. Double-click PowerPoint icon on desktop, if one is present
2. Click Microsoft Office PowerPoint 2007 on Start menu

BTW

Portrait Page Orientation

If your slide content is dominantly vertical, such as a skyscraper or a person, consider changing the slide layout to a portrait page orientation. To change the orientation, click the Slide Orientation button in the Page Setup group in the Design tab and then click the desired orientation. You can use both slide and portrait orientation in the same slide show.

The PowerPoint Window

The PowerPoint window consists of a variety of components to make your work more efficient and documents more professional. These include the document window, Ribbon, Mini toolbar and shortcut menus, Quick Access Toolbar, and Office Button. Some of these components are common to other Microsoft Office 2007 programs; others are unique to PowerPoint.

PowerPoint Window

The basic unit of a PowerPoint presentation is a **slide**. A slide may contain text and objects, such as graphics, tables, charts, and drawings. **Layouts** are used to position this content on the slide. When you open a new presentation, the default **Title Slide** layout appears (Figure 1–4). The purpose of this layout is to introduce the presentation to the audience. PowerPoint includes eight other built-in standard layouts.

The default (preset) slide layouts are set up in **landscape orientation**, where the slide width is greater than its height. In landscape orientation, the slide size is preset to 10 inches wide and 7.5 inches high when printed on a standard sheet of paper measuring 11 inches wide and 8.5 inches high.

The PowerPoint window in Figure 1–4 contains placeholders, a mouse pointer, and a status bar. Other elements that may appear in the window are discussed later in this and subsequent chapters.

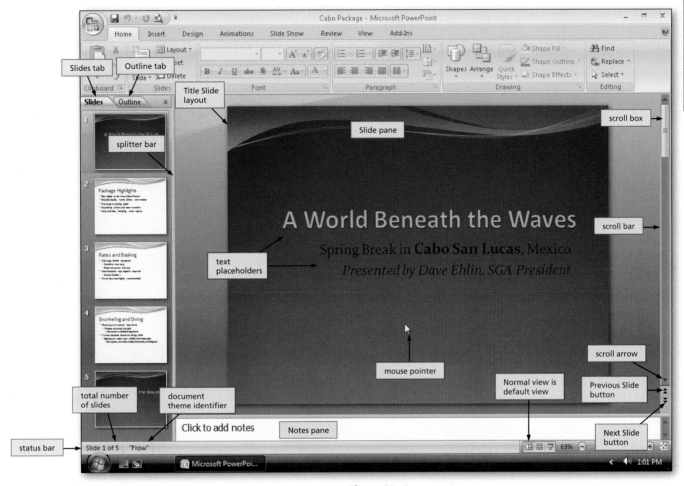

Figure 1–4

PLACEHOLDERS   **Placeholders** are boxes with dotted or hatch-marked borders that are displayed when you create a new slide. All layouts except the Blank slide layout contain placeholders. Depending on the particular slide layout selected, title and subtitle placeholders are displayed for the slide title and subtitle; a content text placeholder is displayed for text, art, or a table, chart, picture, graphic, or movie. The title slide in Figure 1–4 has two text placeholders where you will type the main heading, or title, of a new slide and the subtitle.

MOUSE POINTER   The **mouse pointer** becomes different shapes depending on the task you are performing in PowerPoint and the pointer's location on the screen. The mouse pointer in Figure 1–4 is the shape of a block arrow.

SCROLL BAR   You use the **vertical scroll bar** to display different slides in the document window. When you add a second slide to a presentation, this vertical scroll bar appears on the right side of the Slide pane. On the scroll bar, the position of the **scroll box** reflects the location of the slide in the presentation that is displayed in the document window. A **scroll arrow** is located at each end of a scroll bar. To scroll through, or display different portions of the document in the document window, you can click a scroll arrow or drag the scroll box to move forward or backward through the presentation.

The Previous Slide button and the Next Slide button appear at the bottom of the vertical scroll bar. Click one of these buttons to advance through the slides backwards or forwards.

The **horizontal scroll bar** also may appear. It is located on the bottom of the Slide pane and allows you to display a portion of the slide when the entire slide does not fit on the screen.

STATUS BAR The **status bar**, located at the bottom of the document window above the Windows Vista taskbar, presents information about the document, the progress of current tasks, and the status of certain commands and keys; it also provides controls for viewing the document. As you type text or perform certain commands, various indicators may appear on the status bar.

The left edge of the status bar in Figure 1–4 shows the current slide number followed by the total number of slides in the document and a document theme identifier. A **document theme** provides consistency in design and color throughout the entire presentation by setting the color scheme, font and font size, and layout of a presentation. Toward the right edge are buttons and controls you can use to change the view of a slide and adjust the size of the displayed document.

BTW

Using the Notes Pane
As you create your presentation, type comments to yourself in the Notes pane. This material can be used as part of the spoken information you will share with your audience as you give your presentation. You can print these notes for yourself or to distribute to your audience.

PowerPoint Views

The PowerPoint window display varies depending on the view. A **view** is the mode in which the presentation appears on the screen. PowerPoint has three main views: Normal, Slide Sorter, and Slide Show, and also Notes Page. The default view is **Normal view**, which is composed of three working areas that allow you to work on various aspects of a presentation simultaneously. The left side of the screen has a Tabs pane that consists of a **Slides tab** and an **Outline tab** that alternate between views of the presentation in a thumbnail, or miniature, view of the slides and an outline of the slide text. You can type the text of the presentation on the Outline tab and easily rearrange bulleted lists, paragraphs, and individual slides. As you type, you can view this text in the **Slide pane**, which shows a large view of the current slide on the right side of the window. You also can enter text, graphics, animations, and hyperlinks directly in the Slide pane. The **Notes pane** at the bottom of the window is an area where you can type notes and additional information. This text can consist of notes to yourself or remarks to share with your audience. If you want to work with your notes in full page format, you can display them in **Notes Page view**.

In Normal view, you can adjust the width of the Slide pane by dragging the **splitter bar** and the height of the Notes pane by dragging the pane borders. After you have created at least two slides, **scroll bars**, **scroll arrows**, and **scroll boxes** will appear on the right edge of the window.

Ribbon

The **Ribbon**, located near the top of the PowerPoint window, is the control center in PowerPoint (Figure 1–5a). The Ribbon provides easy, central access to the tasks you perform while creating a slide show. The Ribbon consists of tabs, groups, and commands. Each **tab** surrounds a collection of groups, and each group contains related commands.

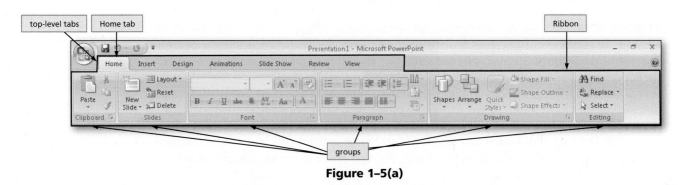

Figure 1–5(a)